NINE GATES
TO THE
CHASSIDIC
MYSTERIES

JIRI LANGER

NINE GATES TO THE CHASSIDIC MYSTERIES

Translated by Stephen Jolly

Published by
BEHRMAN HOUSE, INC., NEW YORK

A Jewish Legacy Book
Series Editor: Seymour Rossel

Published by arrangement with David McKay Company, Inc., New York

Library of Congress Cataloging in Publication Data

Langer, Mordecai Georgo, 1894-1943.
    Nine gates to the Chassidic mysteries.

    (A Jewish legacy book)
    Translation of Devět bran.
    1. Tales, Hasidic.   I. Title.
[BM532.L313   1976]   296.8'33   76-5859
ISBN 0-87441-241-2

Manufactured in the United States of America.

10 9 8 7 6 5 4 3 2   82 81 80 79 78 77

Written with the help of God in the town of Prague which between two castles lies at the confluence of the waters of the Veltava and Botitch in the country called Bohemia: In the six hundred and ninety-seventh year of the sixth millenium since the creation of the world: Enter his gates with song and his courts with praise as is written by the hand of King David, Amen.

A WORD BEFORE THE FOREWORD

I t is several hours after midnight when, say the teachers of our mysteries, the hidden may become clear, and I've just finished another reading of *Nine Gates to the Chassidic Mysteries*. Why, I ask myself, does the prospect of seeing this book reprinted give me a sense of urgent need fulfilled—a need not only personal but what kabbalists call *Tzorech G'voah*—a "Higher Need."

Surface reasons come easily. This book belongs to that intriguing category of reportage which can be reproduced only by an inside-outsider—a person who, while deeply and personally involved with the milieu he is describing, is still able to look at it from the outside with a smile, maybe even with a smidgen of skepticism. Such a position is costly. He who occupies it may begin to look like those Picasso faces which have one eye staring forward and another eye looking sideways. His inner being may take on the characteristics of what the Kabbalah calls a *neshama Artla'it*—a naked soul which flies from world to world seeking its clothing, seeking in vain. Such people don't usually have it "together." Harmony, fulfillment, happiness is not likely to be a major mood of their lives; it doesn't seem to have been Jiri Langer's life portion, as his brother's intelligent introduction makes clear. But it is precisely problems and ambivalences which can—when combined with genuine writing talent, a delicious sense of humor, non-ponderous scholarship and a *heiche neshama*—a "high soul"—produce a very good book.

And this is an excellent book. For this judgment I cite no less an authority than Gershom Scholem, Professor Emeritus of Jewish Mysticism at the Hebrew University in Jerusalem. My own opinion, offered not without a bit of envy, since I've written in the same field, is that Langer's "Nine Gates" offers just about the most authentic and delightful entry into the world of chassidic mysteries available in our day to a serious seeker.

As for the deeper reasons which move me—well, Chassidism divides everything into *pnimiut*—"innerness," and *chitzoniut*—"outerness." Sometimes it calls the outer coverings *klipot* or "shells." That's not necessarily a pejorative term for there can be no inside without an outside, no soul without a body, no content without shells. *(Klipot* become negative when they become too thick, too obscuring of the inner light.) But it seems to me that much contemporary writing about mysticism, though it may use terms like soul, light and love, is really *klipot* literature—concerned with external matters: scholarly information, techniques for breathing, sitting, thinking or not thinking. It hardly affects the soul of the reader. Or, to become a bit more technical, it impinges on the lower levels of the soul for the Kabbalah sees the soul as an entity with potential for several levels of existence. Its higher levels, being close to the source, can involve a phenomenon which Judaism calls *Tshuvah*—meaning "return" or "turning." A person meeting this level of soul may feel a call to change his own life. There is an urgent need, a "Higher Need" in our day for this "inner" word, especially in the Jewish world.

I believe that Langer's book, though offering simple delight and entertainment, fits this category of mystical literature. And it may be especially effective precisely because it is so light of touch. In any case, I urge the reader to savor it in small sips, with long pauses for inner-directed reflection. Its bouquet improves with age.

I want to add a final word about the exotic aspects of the world to which Jiri Langer introduces us. Certainly it is a strange, foreign, almost paranoically, Jewish scene. Most seekers in our day are attracted by the non-parochial, the universal, but somehow eastern robes, mantras, and rituals do not put off seekers for universal truths. Yiddish, chassidic garb, and rebbes are a different matter. Well the fact is that Judaism does try to set itself apart and Chassidism is an extreme expression of Judaism. But in the world of religion as in the world of physics, the deeper our exploration of the concrete, the more we encounter universal laws and truths. Depth calleth to depth and the exotic and exceedingly particularistic world of Chassidism, as many non-Jews have discovered, can offer universal soul food.

But it's nearly dawn and I must take myself out of the way so that you can enter the gates—so unsophisticated, even primitive when compared to the gates offered by other worlds. But, reader, enter them with respect. The ground upon which you are about to tread is holy.

HERBERT WEINER
South Orange, New Jersey
December 18, 1975
14 Tevet 5736

FOREWORD BY FRANTISEK LANGER

My Brother Jiří

To write this book my brother Jiří Langer had to transport himself from the living reality of the twentieth century into the mystical and ecstatic atmosphere of the Middle Ages. Nor could this be effected merely in a metaphorical way, on the wings of fantasy. It had to begin with the reality of purchasing a railway ticket at a station in Prague to a little place in Eastern Galicia. This was very easy to do, for at the beginning of this century the Austrian Monarchy was still in existence, linking together a variety of distances and nations. Thus it was that after twenty-four hours of travel, or a little longer, in a dirty train, Jiří found himself five hundred kilometres away to the east, and simultaneously two, or even five centuries back in time. A lad from the beautiful city of Prague, a lad from a Jewish family accustomed to a twentieth century environment with all the advantages of modern town life, had taken up his abode among fellow-believers living as a little nation entirely on their own, beyond some inner frontier, and hence all the more inaccessible to time and space. They were a people who had their own religion and languages, their own traditions and history, their own education, a people who had retained ancient customs, disputes and quarrels, who cherished superstitions and backward ideas, some of which belonged to earliest times, often as far back as four thousand years ago. They were a people who had rejected everything spiritual and material which the contemporary present or their surroundings, whether near or distant, could give them—all those practical advantages which the new age had brought. The inventions of this new age, as far as they were concerned, ended presumably with the printing of books and the pleasures of tobacco. The most devout communities in these Chassidic colonies lived their lives in an un-

vii

broken mystical trance, a state of unending ecstasy entirely beyond time, space and matter. A traveller who wished to visit these strange people would not find the journey in any way difficult, but should he desire to meet them face to face, to lose himself amongst them, to live their life and acquire within himself the spirit of the most uplifted of them—an essential prerequisite for the writing of so truthful a book as the present one —his task was indeed both hard and long.

At the turn of the twentieth century Jewish families in Central Europe were for the most part lukewarm in the practice of their religion. In fact the way of life in which religion played an important role had ended with our grandfathers. My grandfather on my father's side lived in a mountain village called Ransko which had been established a long time ago in the vicinity of an ironworks; the latter was already a mere ruin when I was a child. This ironworks had been built by Cardinal Dietrichstein in the middle of the seventeenth century. From Holland the Cardinal had brought with him his "Hofjude" who came to live at the village. The Hofjude was our most notable forbear. For more than two hundred and fifty years our family lived in the same cottage in this village. I can recall my grandfather vividly, since I often went to visit him and once spent the entire school holidays with him. He was tall and thin, and like all the villagers he was clean-shaven on his cheeks and chin. His shaving however was not performed with a razor, which no honest Jew should allow to touch the skin of his face, but with a lime preparation which enabled the beard to be removed by a simple rubbing action. Besides a modest piece of land he possessed a small shop to which he brought goods on a wheelbarrow from the nearest station; subsequently he acquired some horses and used occasionally to go out trading in a basket-covered cart. I used to see him in the morning tying on his phylacteries; as might be expected, he was perfectly familiar with all the Hebrew prayers which are recited as the phylacteries are put in place; he was even able to write Hebrew. He spoke German reasonably well and his Czech showed the same mountain accent as that of the rest of the villagers. For the services on Fridays, Saturdays and festivals he would assemble with the Jews from the surrounding neighbourhood in the little township. Grandmother, of course, used to cook strictly kosher food, having retained all the practices prescribed by ritual. Grandfather was as poor as all his neighbours, and apart from his deviations, to which the village had become accustomed, he used to live as they did and in good friendship with them. When he died, the entire population of the village and many of his friends from the countryside accompanied him to the Jewish cemetery in scores of carts—a journey which took the slow funeral procession four hours.

This was the normal pattern of life for Jews in Czech villages towards the end of the last century. Our fathers moved to the towns, taking with them their store of religious customs and their awareness of being Jewish, which they had known at home. The new environment, the new way of life, the daily bustle, and all the secular cares and ideas which pressed in upon them provided no stimulus to their religious feeling and made it difficult for them to keep up some of the old customs. Moreover the townspeople of that time boasted a religious liberalism, which rapidly attracted the Jews who had newly joined this society. This in its turn further weakened their adherence to the faith of their fathers. I remember how, while I was still a child, I used to watch Father every morning bind his phylacteries round his stout arm, but later this ceased to be a regular habit and eventually became a rare one. I do not know whether or not he kept it up after I had left home. As he put on the phylacteries he would read aloud the Hebrew prayers, but he did not understand the words. Fortunately they were accompanied by a good translation. For many years we kept to kosher food, but this was mainly due to Julia, a devout Christian, who during her youth had worked for our aunt, a strict Jewess, and who saw to it that we observed not only the proper regulations regarding food but also other precepts of the Jewish religion. Outwardly Father's attachment to his faith was to be seen in his regular attendance at the luxuriously appointed synagogue in our suburb of Prague, Královské Vinohrady, in his membership of various Jewish charitable organizations and in the way in which his heart and hand were open to needy fellow-believers. In order to hold his own against competition in business he was obliged to serve behind the counter on Saturdays, but to offset this—it is said that he gave his grandfather a promise to this effect—he refrained from smoking from Friday evening to Saturday evening, in spite of being a heavy smoker. In consequence he was always on edge of a Saturday and quite impossible to deal with.

Father's family were practical people. Mother's family hailed from the same part of the countryside but were more refined and cultured. Among her forbears had been a revered rabbi. One of our uncles was a wood engraver and among our numerous cousins were several doctors, a mathematician and a poet. We three brothers took after her. Mother herself, poor thing, was deaf, shut up within herself, quiet and gentle, and played a passive, almost invisible role in the life of the family.

On Sunday afternoons Father used to take the whole family out of town. It goes without saying that he sent us children to Czech schools and saw to it that we had Czech books to read from babyhood. He belonged to about ten societies, not excepting the patriotic Sokol movement. Now and again he went to cafés to play cards. In short he lived like all the small shopkeepers in the particular street where we lived in our suburb of Prague. This adaptation to environment was even more characteristic of the younger generation to which we belonged. At school, in our religious education lessons, we barely succeeded in learning to read the Hebrew letters, but with such lack of thoroughness that in later years I have had to be content to admire these magnificent ancient characters without understanding their import. We learnt no more of Jewish history than, for instance, of Roman history, and we imbibed little of the essence and ethics of the Jewish religion. From our homes, too, we acquired little in this respect, and in our particular case almost nothing. My last religious act was reading aloud from the Torah when I became *bar-mitzvah*.

We were surrounded exclusively by rationalistic thought, and the outlook of our entire generation, both Jewish and non-Jewish, was far removed from any feeling for metaphysics. As we were better fed and more hygienically brought up than our fathers, we grew up to be at least a head taller than they and consequently were popular members of a football side or sports team. So long as anti-Semitism did not rear its head too close to us or too noisily, our generation looked upon the register of births as its only link with Jewry. Otherwise it interested itself in all the various questions which stirred the world at that time, or the nation in which it lived, in whose culture it had been brought up and in which it aspired to play a full part. Perhaps our origin helped to endow us with our keen social sense. It was this social sense that made us aware of the suffering of the Jews, wherever it might be throughout the world, just as we were aware of the suffering of all social pariahs.

The Zionists, who at that time were only to be found in small numbers, were radically different from our generation. In their dreams they saw Palestine as a Jewish country, the Jews as a nation and their religion as a sign of their nationality, just as in due course they expected Hebrew to be. It goes without saying that in Prague, as in the rest of Central Europe, there were Jewish families which felt themselves to be in varying degrees more religious than our family and those like it. But on the other hand there were others who felt themselves to be less religious; such people went so far as to break with the Jewish community and had no qualms about mixed marriages—which horrified even those who set but little store by their religion. Similarly in Prague, apart from the twenty or thirty thousand who were lukewarm in the faith, there still existed circles of believers who were uncompromising in their orthodoxy and who formed in fact a kind of Jewish religious aristocracy. This was quite inevitable in the city which the old Jewish poets had called the "Pearl of Cities" and "Crown of the World", the city which had been made famous by the Jewish synagogue of the thirteenth century, by the beautiful, poetic, old Jewish cemetery, and which from time immemorial had been a place where countless outstanding Jewish savants had worked. It was in these circles of religious Jews and cultured Judaists that my brother Jiří found a teacher of Hebrew and religious traditions, and an adviser and support in his subsequent study. For this he had to go far away from his family.

Jiří was the youngest of us three brothers. He was born in Prague on the 7th of April 1894. He was six years younger than I, and four years younger than my second brother Josef. Although somewhat of a lonely child in his youth, he was the most robust and healthy of all three of us. He was not a hard worker either at his primary school or at his secondary school. He loved music, at least as a listener, and while still a young student used to go to concerts of serious music. In Prague he had plenty of opportunity for this. He was an omnivorous reader and appreciated a good book. I had just published my first literary work at the time and Jiří looked upon me as an authority who could recommend him what to read. Once—he must have been fifteen at the time—he surprised me by asking which of the Czech poets were mystics. I advised him to read Otokar Březina, one of the greatest of our poets, if somewhat difficult to understand. My brother read all his works and was profoundly taken with them. This could have been my first opportunity of recognizing in which direction his interests were taking him. But it was not until a year or two later, when my brother began to be passionately interested in religious questions, that I was to recognize this to the full. By then, however, it was no longer a matter merely of interest and asking questions; for he was already totally immersed in religion, in the full range of that mystical, abstract, spiritual universe which is called religion.

It was natural enough that it should be the Jewish religion, but it did not have to be. As we saw it, the fact of his becoming caught up in this ecstasy of mysticism was mainly due to the influence of a friend of his, Alfred Fuchs, who like Jiří came of a Jewish family where there was no great enthusiasm for religion. Fuchs was a slim, good-looking fellow, always somewhat of a dreamer but brilliant at his school work. It would seem that it was he who was the first to be attracted to religious mysticism. My brother became infected with his enthusiasm and the two of them turned first to Jewish literature. To this end they learnt Hebrew and it was at this time that I first saw Jiří poring over borrowed Hebrew folios. Subsequently Fuchs came to the conclusion that the Catholic religion had more to offer in the sphere of mysticism, being richer, more varied in form, more inspiring and exhilarating. He set about exploring it with the same ecstatic fervour as he had brought to the Jewish faith. For the most part he studied the old Latin Christian texts. This caused the two young men to part company, a separation which was further emphasized when Fuchs, who was not a man to be content with half measures, accepted baptism. A passionate convert, he became a profound religious thinker and courageous Catholic philosopher. During the German occupation he was arrested by the Gestapo when he was at a monastery. He was cruelly tortured, both on account of his Jewish origin and because of the saintly devotion which he showed to the faith he had embraced. In the years immediately after the war there was even talk of his being canonized.

After some initial uncertainty my brother continued to feel himself drawn towards the Jewish religion. It was not long before he was concentrating all his powers on the study of Jewish teaching, traditional commandments and customs, delving into all manner of ancient rites and preoccupying himself with details that bordered on superstition. It would seem to me that in this earlier stage of his development religious ritual held a greater attraction for him than did the actual content of the religious idea. He only came to understand the latter in the course of his study of the vast folios of the Talmud, which he would sit over night after night, his hat on his head, reading aloud in a low voice. He made a point of observing all religious practices in a very ostentatious way and devoted himself to his new study so completely that he entirely ceased to go to school. He would escape from the family atmosphere around him by shutting himself up in the wrapped silence of the hermit, as though he found worldly things unworthy of his attention. He renounced all the normal pleasures of a young man—friends, sport, and even the Czech Philharmonic concerts. As for me, I was able to consider his behaviour from two different points of view. As a medical student in my final years of study, I could

only suppose that his was a case of belated adolescent psycho-
pathy, which I hoped was a mere passing phenomenon. As a
writer I had come to think of him as the Dreamer of the Ghetto.
Father would give him a paternal homily every day, entreating
him to think of the practical side of life, of his future, and urging
him to be wise and return to school. Jiří would listen without
making the least murmur of protest, almost craven in his silence.
Father became slightly reconciled to the eccentric behaviour of
his son when on one occasion the latter was greeted with respect
by a wealthy Jew of some distinction, who had been decorated
with all manner of official titles and was moreover the head of
the fraternity of undertakers. This gentleman congratulated him
on his son and declared that the day would surely come when
he would be an eminent Jewish scholar and the pride of Prague's
Jewry. After this Jiří was more free to live his modest, solitary
existence at home.

In 1913, my brother packed a small suitcase with a few essential clothes, some books and his phylacteries, and set out on a
journey. He told no one save Julia to whom he confided that he
was going to Galicia and would be writing home about his
journey. He had always been close to her and she to him, perhaps
because each, albeit in different ways, was a sincere believer. It
was only after a few weeks had gone by that a postcard arrived.
It came from Eastern Galicia, from the town of Belz, and asked
us not to worry for he was quite well and would be there for
some time. This, then, was his first journey to the Chassidim, his
first sojourn among them, as he himself describes it in his
introduction to *Nine Gates*.

In this introduction he also outlines the reasons why he
was at first unable to endure life at Belz, why he returned and
what it was that drove him home: the isolation from the world,
the ignorance, backwardness and dirt which he found there, and
perhaps too the sad, marshy countryside. In other words it might
have been expected that his return to Prague, with its civilization
and other advantages, would be an occasion of great rejoicing
for him. With what abandon he would embrace his parents!
Perhaps on the very first day he would want to go to gaze on

the Vltava and the magnificent panorama of the Hradčany.
Perhaps he would travel to the mountains and the forests, fra-
grant with the scent of resin, so different from the plains of
Galicia with their swamps and stench of stagnant water. On
Friday evening he would visit the glorious synagogue at Vinohrady, with its thousand lights shining on the ornaments which
his own uncle had gilded and its five hundred silken top hats on
the heads of worthy, well-to-do believers, with the organ playing in the choir and the solo sung in Hebrew by a Christian
singer from the German theatre.

His return, however, was not on this wise. Father told me with
a note of horror in his voice that Jiří had returned. I understood
what had filled him with dread as soon as I saw my brother. He
stood before me in a frayed, black overcoat, clipped like a caftan,
reaching from his chin to the ground. On his head he wore a
broad round hat of black velvet, thrust back towards his
neck. He stood there in a stooping posture; his whole face and
chin were covered with a red beard, and side whiskers in front
of his ears hung in ringlets down to his shoulders. All that remained to be seen of his face was some white, unhealthy skin
and eyes which at moments appeared tired and at others feverish.
My brother had not come back from Belz, to home and civilization; he had brought Belz with him.

Now he added a sharper edge to the customs which he had been
in the habit of observing before he went to the East. To some of
these he gave a different significance, and there were other new
ones which he had brought back with him. He no longer washed
his hands before every meal, as any god-fearing and hygienically-
minded person would do. Instead he made this a mere symbolical
act, pouring water alternately on to his two palms from a cup. He
would not shake hands with women—I do not know if he made
an exception to this rule when he was welcomed by Mother—
and whenever he spoke to a woman, even our old Julia, he
would turn his back on her. He said his prayers aloud, in a sing-
song voice, running round the room in a sort of trance. Now
even the kosher food provided at Prague's restaurants was
suspect, as far as he was concerned. He used to cook various

mashes at home on a spirit stove, but his staple diet was bread and onions which could be smelt all over the flat.

It was both possible and necessary to adopt a tolerant attitude towards what happened within the four walls of our flat. But the situation was more difficult when he left the house, for his attire, his way of doing his hair, and his gait, which resembled a vigorous double, drew people's attention to him and made him the laughing-stock of the street, the effects of which were felt by our entire family. For the last three generations, when the Jews had been allowed to live outside the confines of the ghetto, those in our part of the world had not looked in any way different in their outward appearance from other citizens. On the other hand the Jews who lived in the eastern part of the Austro-Hungarian Empire, in territory occupied by the Poles and White Russians, used still to wear the gloomy caftan, hat and other items peculiar to their folk costume. In Prague one only occasionally saw a Galician Jew wearing this outfit—usually in a very shabby state—when he was on his way through the city or had come to beg. On the other hand it was far from being a rare sight in the luxury Bohemian spas of Karlovy Vary and Mariánské Lázně where in the high season they were to be seen in large numbers. These however were rich Jews, their black caftans were of silk and flowed like robes, their side-whiskers were decoratively curled down their cheeks, and their beards, which varied from reddish and black to ermine white, were beautifully combed and wavy, like those of the biblical patriarchs in the churches. These people went to receive treatment for livers upset by heavy kosher food, with its goose delicacies. At the Czech spas they were welcomed as good-paying, exotic guests, albeit not so rare and substantial as the Maharajahs from the Orient. But the appearance of a solitary Polish Jew on the streets of Vinohrady in 1913, belonging to a well-known Vinohrady family, positively cried out to be noticed.

Needless to say, such exhibitionism, whether religious or otherwise, was exceedingly embarrassing to all of us at home. Like the rest of the Jewish community, our family had completely assimilated itself to all the outward signs and customs of our neighbourhood. Would not Jiří's appearance now make us all seem guilty of pretence and hypocrisy? I do not know what interpretation our neighbours put on his behaviour but I rather presume that they tapped their foreheads knowingly. It seems to me that my brother's get-up scared my father and his strata of society in yet another way. It disturbed his feeling for security and permanence; maybe it aroused in him memories of stories, long since forgotten, about the misery and congestion of the ghetto, of a life without rights and freedom, of an existence full of humiliation and injustice. This was no mere concern about the conventions or business interests. It was a spectre from the past that had come among us; somebody risen from the dead had come to warn us. I can well imagine all these feelings which his presence aroused. A quarter of a century later millions of Jews were to experience this when they had to wear on their coats the yellow badge prescribed by Hitler.

The attitude of our family to Jiří seemed to us at the time to resemble the situation in Kafka's novel, *Die Verwandlung*, in which an entire family finds its way of life completely upset when the son of the house is suddenly changed into an enormous cockroach, and consequently has to be hidden from the rest of the world, while the family strive in vain to find some place for him in their affections. At least Father tried to find a practical solution. He requested a rabbi in Vinohrady, a sensitive, erudite doctor of philosophy, to talk to Jiří, hoping that a religious authority of such consequence would lead my brother to modify his ways. But Jiří refused even to speak to this man; he looked upon him as an atheist who read the daily newspapers and other matter not printed in the Hebrew alphabet. However, after some time, he did make some modifications in his behaviour to suit the requirements of Prague. He had his coat cut somewhat shorter, so that it was not very different from an overcoat, he started wearing an ordinary black hat which he no longer placed far back on his head, he plaited his side-whiskers and smoothed them behind his ears. It is probable that he was advised to do this by his Jewish friends in Prague, whom he once again sought out and who supplied him with the cabbalistic literature which he had come to know among the Chassidim. But he made no change in his habits at home and hardly even came into contact with the rest of us. He would answer when we spoke to him, but he would not start a conversation himself. Perhaps his isolation was our own fault in that we did not know how to cope with it. Sometimes we would express sympathy in what we said to him, sometimes we would make appeal to reason, often impatiently and forcefully, whereas Jiří would probably have wanted us to behave as though his behaviour was quite natural. No doubt our behaviour in his eyes was below the level of naturalness. Under such circumstances, of course, it was difficult for us to find a common meeting ground. Not even many years later would he explain to me what he felt and thought at that time. He would not admit that being a mystic and visionary, who had renounced all that this world has to offer and had soared aloft into higher spheres, he felt the pride of one who is merely waiting for the call to sainthood, and had a fundamental contempt for us ignorant, coarse individuals who were tied to material things. Years afterwards he would merely wave his hands with a smile as if he did not wish to disturb a dream of the past.

He stayed on at home for a short time and then prepared his suitcase for a second journey to his Chassidim. This time his exultation was so intense that it communicated itself to those around him. He bade a very warm farewell to us all. He was overcome with joy—but I was not to learn this until I read his book—for the rabbi of Belz had appeared to him in our kitchen and had invited him to come to him.

He had only been a few months at Belz when the first world war broke out in 1914. The rabbi of Belz and his entire court found themselves in the midst of a battlefield, but fortunately were able to escape to Hungary. Here Jiří received his call-up papers. Subsequently he had to go to Prague to join up in the Army. At that time I was on the Eastern Front as a doctor. In 1915 I happened to have my first leave. I came home and found that Jiří had but recently been sent to the Army prison. He had made life in the Army very difficult for himself. In the barracks he used to get up an hour before reveille, while it was still night, so as to be able to say his prayers properly and eat his bread and onions, since he would not allow anything from the Army kitchen to pass his lips. All this the Army would have allowed him to do. But since a strict Jew is not permitted to carry anything on a Saturday, he refused to handle his rifle on that day or do any work at all. Naturally the court martial took a very serious view of this and my brother made things all the worse for himself by declining to answer their questions, or indeed to speak at all. I arrived just in time and was able to furnish the doctors responsible for examining the state of his mind with first-hand information and evidence as to his previous behaviour, with the result that they sent him home as a mental case. But Jiří was convinced that the rabbi of Belz had performed a miracle and delivered him from military service. When I told him of my part in his deliverance he declared that the miracle might have consisted in the fact of my having succeeded in getting leave from the front—which could of course have been true.

After this the war kept us apart from each other for five years. I spent the first part of this period in those regions where Jiří had previously lived. The war swept through the Galician villages, churning them into mud or sending them up in flames. I saw the Jewish, Chassidic settlements, and the infinite misery, agony and despair of their inhabitants who had no idea why all this destruction and murder was going on and why, in particular, it should have fallen on their heads. They fled in desperation, on foot, with bundles on their backs, or pushed before them, on wheelbarrows, a few bed-clothes and cooking utensils. A few of them made better pace on carts pulled by emaciated horses, loaded up with children and some miserable personal possessions. Years later it was difficult for me to compare these heart-searing pictures of frenzied horror with that naïve, carefree, almost childish state of bliss in which they had lived before this catastrophe and which was the underlying feature of the entire life of the Chassidim, as my brother has shown in his book.

After his discharge from the Army, Jiří returned to the rabbi of Belz and spent the rest of the war with him, far removed from the front. In the autumn of 1918, when the Austrian Monarchy fell, my brother's friends at Belz became subjects of the new Polish Republic and my brother of the new Czechoslovak Republic. Each returned to his home, henceforth separated from each other by new State boundaries. I did not meet Jiří until 1920, when I returned from the Army. To my surprise his outward appearance was, one might say, entirely European. His attitude to his family had also become more or less normal. He asked with great interest about my adventures during the war and told me of his experiences. But he had in no wise given up his feeling for religion, nor had he relinquished any of his former religious practices or those which he had taken over from the Chassidim. When speaking to a woman, for instance, he always faced sideways and would on no account shake hands with her. But he no longer wore a hat all the time; at home he wore the velvet rabbi's cap instead, and there was no longer any sign of side-whiskers. For food he went to a Chassidic restaurant in Prague—some groups of the Chassidim had succeeded in reestablishing themselves—and at home, as before, he cooked himself mash on a stove. He was no longer so obstinate as before the war. He would often call me to come and see how tasty his food was.

I received my greatest surprise, however, when I saw what was now occupying his attention. The books he was studying were not printed in Hebrew, but in Czech and German, and he was studying something other than the Talmud. This time it was the writings of Sigmund Freud and his disciples. He had collected all their works so far published and everything that had appeared in *Imago*, the official psycho-analytical journal. We now had in Freud plenty of material to discuss together, except that I was at the time more interested in Freud from the literary point of view. For me his teaching was in the nature of an utterly fantastic hypothesis, whereas my brother accepted Freud's discoveries as axioms with scientific validity. He began to use Freudian methods in analysing the essential meaning of the practices observed in Jewish ritual and in Jewish cults, applying them to his search for the subconscious sources of Jewish mysticism and the actual origin of the religious idea. It was a most remarkable spectacle to see him studying, a scientific work of the great psycho-analyst open in one hand and at his other hand an open folio of the Talmud, or more often some mystical work such as the *Zohar*.

He published the results of his new interest in 1923, in a book called *Die Erotik der Kabbala*, and subsequently in various articles printed in *Imago*. These appeared in German. Up to that time little had been known about Freud in Bohemia. Still less had any one concerned himself with any special connection that might be traced between psycho-analysis and Jewish religious teaching. It surprised me that in his writings Jiří did not hesitate to link the Jewish religion, and its origin, with the archaic phenomena of fetishes, totems and taboos in which Freud had traced the prehistoric consciousness of human social relations and laws. He did not hesitate to mention quasi-sacred Jewish symbols, such as the phylacteries or *mezuzehs* (doorpost signs), in connection with the most primitive idols in the form of sexual symbols which had figured in the cults of prehistoric man. Like Freud he even went so far as to ascribe an erotic derivation to the most spiritual laws and the supreme ethos of the Jewish faith. It seemed to me as a layman that any orthodox Jew would find much that was heretical and blasphemous in these inferences. And yet I saw that Jiří came to these conclusions in total innocence, that he received as much pleasure as the old commentators from each discovery he made in his study of the Talmud. I do not doubt that it was his unrealizable ideal that he should be permitted to write down these notions, that is, to print them in small letters at the side of the Talmud text and win thereby honour and glory as his predecessors had done.

I do not remember how his book was reviewed or whether in fact it attracted any attention at all in Prague. At all events his work did not cause him any difficulties, and his piety and reputation for learning led to his being appointed as a teacher at the Jewish College in Prague. Father above all was delighted that his son should at last have obtained permanent employment.

With his pupils, I am told, he was a great favourite since he was easy-going and always full of humour. He was less liked, however, by the school's Board of Governors since he was very off-hand and unpunctual. His lessons never started on time, and if his attention was taken up with something that he was working on privately, he might even fail to put in an appearance for several days on end. In consequence he frequently had differences with the school authorities and on several occasions was given notice; however the authorities invariably had pity on him and took him back. On one of his enforced holidays he made a journey to Palestine. He went more as a historian than a pilgrim or would-be settler. He returned deeply affected by the beauties of the country and the efforts being made by the pioneers of a Jewish homeland, but it was clear that the roots he had put down in Prague would hold him fast. He made another journey to Paris where he stayed for several weeks. It is to be presumed that he spent most of his time in museums since he said nothing of the other delights of the city. Finally he gave up teaching altogether. This involved him in no hardship for he could live with his parents. Moreover I had a decent income from my plays and my brother Josef was well enough off; consequently we were able to provide for his needs reasonably generously. He also earned some money himself on his articles and translations. He had great talent as a linguist. Besides his mother tongue he was completely at home in Hebrew and Yiddish. He had an excellent knowledge of Aramaic, Arabic, German, French and English and was able to read a number of other languages without the aid of a dictionary. On one occasion I remember seeing him leaning over some large photographs of stone slabs covered with cuneiform writing which he was in the process of deciphering. He wrote Hebrew and published a book of his verses in Prague under the title *Pijjutim ve-Shire Jedidut* (Poems and Songs of Friendship) and I understand that he was able to speak in the classical language of the Bible. It is interesting that this was the first book of Hebrew verses to be printed at the Jewish printing-works in Old Prague for a whole century.

All this time he remained as deeply religious as before and there is no reason to suppose that he infringed any commandments of his faith. Such practices as he allowed himself to give up were those which savoured of bigotry or were of minor importance. Thus, for instance, after many years, he ceased to look upon a bath merely as a ritualistic rite and saw it as a hygienic necessity. He not only shook hands with women but acquired a reputation for being very courteous, especially to old ladies. He even took great pains with his clothing. However when he came to visit me he would only drink coffee and never stay to supper. He continued to eat at the kosher restaurants in Prague, some of which were excellent. He read a great deal and was familiar with all the latest works of any consequence in world literature. He went to the theatre and never failed to come to my first nights. It goes without saying that he often went to concerts. He even started playing the violin; he had a teacher to instruct him in the basic principles and then went on to teach himself. He must have had remarkable talent. I never remember him playing from music. Above all he liked to walk about his room and improvise highly inventive variations on themes from the classical composers, from Jewish and Negro hymns, Czech music and Slovak songs. He played with a pure tone, with ease and passion, showing a marked fondness for stormy rhythms which he picked out with his bow like a gypsy. In summer he liked to go for a swim in the river, and in winter he would go skating. The latter was a sport in which he excelled and I often used to go with the children to the frozen Vltava to watch their uncle skating, dancing on the ice and showing off his skill. I understand that he even wrote an instruction book on figure-skating. He said nothing to me about this and I have not been able to find a copy since, which leads me to suppose that it was written under a pseudonym. By this time he no longer lived a hermit existence. He had a number of friends, whom I did not meet, and sometimes he would come home in high spirits in the early hours of the morning. During the war he had made friends with Franz Kafka, and the two men used to go for walks together in Prague. Kafka evidently found Jiří a kindred spirit; his diary contains several Chassidic myths and legends which he had

heard from Jiří. He retained his former equable and patient
nature side by side with the carefree attitude towards material
things which he had taken over from the Chassidim. He
seasoned all these good qualities with humour and accepted his
lack of success as a teacher and frequent unemployment with
equanimity.

After 1930 he began publishing some of his Chassidic stories
and legends. They came out in the Jewish Calendar, one each
year. Written in Czech, they were very different from the
learned cabbalistic literature, destined for a handful of experts,
such as he found at home. These stories were written for the
ordinary reader, especially the Czech reader. Their purpose was
to tell him something different about the Jews from that which
Nazi anti-Semitism was endeavouring to smuggle across the
Czechoslovak frontiers. Finally they were a work of the heart
and not of the brain; they had their roots in personal experience,
relationships and love. They required the full poetic resources of
the language and it was therefore natural that my brother should
tell them in the language which came most easy to him, his
mother tongue.

It was not until the year 1935 that Jiří brought me the bulky
sheaf of pages which first bore the title 'Nine Gates'. His
sketches had grown into a complete book, he told me, but he
was afraid that his style was far from perfect. As an experienced
writer I should be able to put right what was clumsy in his
work.

No sooner had I started reading than I forgot all about any
idea of improving the style. I was caught up by all the different
events and happenings described in the narrative and was completely carried away by the exotic fantasy and originality they
revealed. I read on and on. There was nothing misty or difficult
to fathom in the mysticism of the book, and far from the
various miracles and wonders, which were knitted into the
story, being overcharged with pathos and unduly removed
from reality, they were, so to speak, tailored to human propor-
tions; they made an endearing appeal. The legends told of saints,
wonder-working rabbis, capable of performing such miracles

but at the same time living in an almost intimate relationship with the Lord, so much so that they could even afford to be insolent to Him. In this setting any miracles that God might perform seemed to be nothing more than a little neighbourly assistance. The stories told of the little Chassidim, the special children of God, who by virtue of their infinite piety had the rare privilege of being allowed, through their saints, to ask for anything they needed for life from a favourable heaven. But at the same time their lives were so humble and their requests were in the same character; in consequence the little things they asked could be granted to them without any miracle; it was all beautifully human and earthly.

It was only when I had had my fill of the content that I began to give some thought to the style, as my brother had requested. Could it be that he had any doubts on this score? It seemed to me in every line that the magic effect of his legends lay precisely in the fact that they were told in such a bewitching way. The least change in tone or cadence, in the light touch and artless simplicity of the book, in the choice and arrangement of the words, would have taken away something of the appeal. The author had combined deft naïvety, which is the basis of all Jewish anecdotes, with that refined simplicity which is a characteristic gift of the greatest Jewish artists, such as Heine or Chagall. Jiří had laced his narrative throughout with two threads. One was the smiling scepticism of a very adult human being narrating to children the unbelievable miracles performed by fairy-tale rabbis. The other, contemporary thread was that of the trusting listener who with the gullibility of a child believes absolutely in every word he hears. The stories were told naturally, vividly, personally; you could almost see the author's mimicking, gesticulations and smiles, and the roguish wink in his eye, as he spoke direct from mouth to ear, with all the pauses, cadences, pianissimos and fortissimos; it was as though the story-teller were sitting immediately in front of his listeners in some oriental bazaar. Moreover the manner in which the book was put together corresponded to its content; naïve verses with assonances stood at the head of each set of stories and served as a sort of musical intermezzo. The book formed a complete whole and had all the atmosphere of a Chassidic *Thousand and One Nights*.

In other words, no need for corrections. What was necessary was a suitable publisher. It was some time before we could find one, so that the book did not appear until 1937, in the midst of the disturbances which had already begun to shake Europe. It aroused great interest among Czech readers. At a different period its original theme and superb narrative skill would have ensured its running into further editions and it would certainly have been translated into other languages. As it was, the impending events, which shortly became actual events, caused it to be limited to the original edition. Eighteen months after publication, during the Nazi occupation, the book was classified among the monstrosities of art, and the edition was destroyed. Only a few copies survived, hidden away by their devoted readers from the house-to-house inspections. Today each copy of *Devět Bran* (*Nine Gates*) is a much prized rarity.

Another way in which Jiří met the need to tell his compatriots, at such a crucial period of history, something truthful about the Jews, as he had done in *Nine Gates*, was by writing a popular book about the Talmud and its origin. He selected and translated into Czech a hundred examples of old Jewish wisdom from the Talmud, the humanism of whose commandments was so directly opposed to the brutalities of Nazi racialism. To acquaint the Czech reader with the great literature of the Jews he translated into Czech a selection from the Hebrew poets of the eleventh to the eighteenth centuries. All verse is extremely difficult to translate, and these ancient Jewish poets with their numerous archaisms and many departures from classical forms presented exceptional problems. Nevertheless it seems to me that Jiří, who was intimately acquainted with the subtleties of both Czech and Hebrew and who wrote poetry in both languages, has succeeded in preserving in his translation the beauty of the old poetry and has also retained that specific Jewish quality which differentiates the Hebrew lyric poets and minnesingers from their Christian contemporaries. This book of poems, called *Songs of the Rejected*, first appeared in 1937 and was republished in February 1939. The selection includes a translation of the mournful elegy written by Avigdor Karo, a Prague doctor who was one of the few Jews to survive the bloodshed in the Prague ghetto in 1389. This elegy is recited to this day at the oldest of Prague's synagogues on the Day of Atonement. The tragic title which my brother gave to his songs was no random choice, and after nearly six hundred years Reb Avigdor Karo's elegy has a prophetic ring about it.

The prophecy was fulfilled in the early spring of 1939 when the German Army occupied the Czechoslovak Republic. For the nation it meant the end of all freedom and rights; for the Jews it meant in addition the Nuremburg Laws, the first step towards the subsequent slaughter at Terezín and Auschwitz. At the beginning of July, I fled across the Polish frontier to France. My brother Josef chose suicide in preference to a slow death in the concentration camps. My parents had died while the times were still peaceful, in an age when it seemed that the world would enjoy peace, if not for all time, at least for long, long years.

In the autumn of 1939, Jiří left for Slovakia which still offered some prospects of escape. In return for bribes the Gestapo turned a blind eye when the Jews began to organize a route along the Danube to Istanbul and on to Palestine. The Danube passage was still to some extent neutral. More than a thousand refugees of all ages, from new-born babies to old people, found their way along this route at the beginning of November, in river steamers and subsequently in iron cargo barges pulled by tugs. Even at the slowest rate of sailing they were able to reach the Danube estuary within three weeks. Once in the Black Sea they were out of reach of the Gestapo. But on the river itself they were not safe. Their sluggish rate of progress was continually held up on all manner of pretexts. It was as though there was an outside force directing the movement of the ship. Even when the refugees reached the Danube delta, they were still not safe from Nazi fingers which might hold up the ship at Sulina harbour, a mere stone's throw from the freedom of the seas. To add to their misfortunes the fugitives encountered frosts that were unusually early for this part of the world. River and ship were held in the tightest grip. The iron barges became a prison and the refugees had sometimes to endure up to fifty degrees of frost without even the most primitive heating arrangements and with insufficient food. Dysentery, severe influenza and pneumonia, with all manner of complications, were rampant and occasioned innumerable deaths.

My brother wrote to me in Paris to tell me about the journey —it was something of a miracle that I ever received his letters— and to ask for help for all concerned. As it was the beginning of the war, the various international contacts and institutions were still functioning quite efficiently—the Red Cross, the Y.M.C.A., the Danube Transport Commission and a number of Jewish, Catholic and Quaker charitable organizations—and I got my friends busy on the matter wherever I could. But the most effective assistance came from our fellow-countrymen in Roumania, initiated by my brother-in-law, and from Jan Masaryk who prevailed upon the British Government to send out a relief ship. However, it was not until half-way through February that the refugees were delivered from their prison of ice and taken to Istanbul.

Jiří was among those rescued—if one can talk of rescue! Always a dreamer in everything he undertook, he had made no proper preparations for the voyage. His suitcases were filled with his favourite books—two hundred he took with him; consequently he had neither thought nor room for any warm clothing or a supply of food. He suffered even more than the other passengers from cold and starvation, and his pneumonia was early complicated by a severe inflammation of the kidneys. When at last he was carried on to the relief ship he was at the end of his strength. His nephritis soon became chronic and in due course brought about his death.

I learned of his life in Palestine from the letters he wrote to me in England. His health picked up somewhat after he had landed on the shores for which he had yearned so long and had spent some time receiving treatment in hospital at Tel Aviv. Life was far from easy. Like all the refugees from Czechoslovakia who were unable to work, he received a small grant from our authorities. But it was not long before his condition worsened and he had frequently to be readmitted to hospital. Fortunately, after the first difficulties caused by the war in this part of the world had been overcome, I was able to send him assistance from England. He translated his Chassidic legends into Hebrew and planned to write a further series of stories about the Chassidic saints in Czech. To bring himself some relief and a measure of joy amidst his gloomy reflections, he turned once again to Hebrew poetry and published his verses in various magazines. Among these was his poem about Prague and the Old-New Synagogue. The reception given by the public was warm and lively.

At times my brother was so weakened by illness that he was unable to read. The letters in which he described his suffering, often with a brave touch of humour, made a deeply moving effect on me, especially in the passages where he wrote of his hope of recovery and subsequent return to Czechoslovakia; he told of how he was looking forward to meeting me and my children, but as a doctor I was well aware that ... At least he had the advantage of living the last days of his life in the beneficial dry climate of Palestine and in a little piece of his long-cherished dream. He loved to get out of Tel Aviv into the country, he loved to make the journey to Jerusalem. Whenever he mentioned the beauties of the Palestinian countryside his writing became rapturous with adoration. He did not write a great deal about people, although he was held in much affection and both friends and strangers brought him flowers when he was in hospital. Among his closest friends were the writer, Max Brod, and his wife. Jiří had a great deal in common with Brod, and the two men were linked by their nostalgia for Bohemia and Prague. After Jiří had been laid to rest in the cemetery at Tel Aviv, Brod made all the necessary arrangements regarding his grave and literary estate, in particular his books which my brother had bequeathed to the Tel Aviv library. Jiří died on the 12th of March 1943. As he lay dying, though still in full command of his faculties, Max Brod brought him the proof-sheets of a book containing my brother's collected Hebrew poems, written in Palestine. It was plainly printed on plain paper. The title he had chosen for it indicated how great was the comfort and how soothing the balm which he derived from that meagre measure of poetry that life had vouchsafed to him in spite of all his tribulation. The name he gave to the book was *Me'at Tsori*, which means 'A Little Balsam'.

His grave at Tel Aviv is marked by a modest stone, erected by his friends. But in his *Nine Gates* he has created for himself a noble memorial. The book is a remarkable, original work which will bring glory to Czech literature. It is also a very authentic document in the history of the Jews and thus shares the two-fold excellence of the work of Israel Zangwill—certainly a significant analogy.

But it is as though *Nine Gates* has been endowed by destiny with still further significance, as though history has appointed an additional mission for it after its birth. For it has become an infinitely tragic memorial erected over the vast, sorrowful graveyard of the Chassidim. Since the time that my brother lived there, the towns, villages and countryside of the Chassidim—Belz, Ropshitz, Lizensk, Kotsk and many another place—have been submerged under more waves of war than anywhere else in the whole of Europe. Such was their destiny during the First World War, and even after the end of that war, when everywhere else there was peace. Defenceless Jewish quarters, albeit poor, have always been the easiest of trophies for armies and marauding hordes. During the Second World War the destruction began when the Germans invaded Poland and started murdering the Jews with the horrifying thoroughness of Nazism. There can be no doubt that, as with the other parts of Central Europe, more than 90 per cent of the Jews in these isolated areas perished in the concentration camps. And if some of them escaped, they were caught up in the death-dealing inundation of war which spread twice over these desolate plains. Today we are entirely without first-hand accounts of the fate that befell the Chassidic settlements. All the tiny villages, each like a little kingdom on its own, in which the rabbi-saints ruled in the name of God, all the synagogues and universities in the mean, squat cottages—everything was transformed into a scene of ruin or conflagration. All those poor, humble, happy little people, the most defenceless of all the defenceless, the most peace-loving community in the world, all these perished in war.

It may be that among the Jews in Israel or New York there are a few handfuls of the old Chassidic believers still adhering to the customs which they have brought from their old homes. But these are merely so many reminiscences of the past. The mystical reality of the Chassidim cannot last under the blue sky of Israel or amidst the bustle of the streets of Brooklyn. It could only exist in that utter isolation from the world and time which it enjoyed in Galicia, in that poverty in which all were equal, in that freedom in which they were subjected to nought save the will of God, and in that spiritual grandeur which came to dwell in their villages through the wisdom and miracles of their saintly rabbis. And thus it was that my brother Jiří depicted it for the last time in his sweet and smiling book, thereby erecting for the Chassidim an eternal monument to preserve their memory for all time.

WORKS OF JIRI LANGER

Die Erotik der Kabbala. Prague, 1923.
On the Function of the Jewish Doorpost Sign (Zur Funktion der jüdischen Türpfortenrolle). Vienna, 1928 (Imago XIV, 4).
Pijjutim ve-Shire Jedidut. Prague, 1929.
Jewish Phylacteries (Die jüdischen Gebetriemen-Phylakterien). With addendum: Affinity with African Ritual Circles. Fire. The Snake. Vienna, 1931 (Imago XVI).
Nine Gates (Devět Bran). Prague, 1937.
Talmud (Extracts and History). Prague, 1939.
Songs of the Rejected (Zpěvy zavrženych). Prague, 1938.
Me'at Tsori. Tel Aviv, 1942.

ACKNOWLEDGMENTS

I should like to thank the translator, Mr. Stephen Jolly, for having undertaken this difficult work and for having devoted so much care to my brother's book. I should also like to thank Mr. A. D. Millard, of James Clarke & Co. Ltd., for deciding to publish it. I have always believed that this work by my brother was predestined to become part of the world's literature, and I am therefore convinced that public interest in the book will fittingly reward them for what they have done to help it to achieve its rightful place.

FRANTIŠEK LANGER

I. I. 59

CONTENTS

	PAGE
FOREWORD BY FRANTIŠEK LANGER	vii
INTRODUCTION—A Youth from Prague among the Chassidim	3
GATE I—Of diamonds in the Lord's crown the costliest, the holy Reb Sholem of Belz	33
GATE II—Child of God, our dearest, the holy Mayerl of Przemysl	59
GATE III—Heart of our mirth, the holy Reb Naftali of Ropshitz	71
GATE IV—Blazing lion of the heavenly Academy, the holy Reb Urele of Strelisk (also the holy Reb Jude Hersch of Stretena)	85
GATE V—Two golden trombones in the angelic choir, the holy Rebe Reb Meshulem Sussya of Anipol and the holy Rebe Reb Melech of Lizensk	115
GATE VI—Mystic twain, the holy Rebe Reb Schmelke of Mikulov and the holy Rebe Reb Pinchas of Frankfurt	141
GATE VII—Three tall tamarisks in the broad plain, the holy Yismach Moyshe of Ihel—the holy Ohev Yisroel of Apta—and the Saint of Kalev	161
GATE VIII—Mystic shining mirror, the holy Reb Jacob Yitzhak, the Seer of Lublin (also the holy Dyvre Chayyim of Sanz)	179

CONTENTS

GATE IX—Most secret brain of Greatness and Wisdom,   199
the holy Reb Pinchas of Koritz (ah! the saints at
Slavuta)

THE CITY OF WISDOM—Gold and silver and pearls and all   223
the precious stones of Kotsk—or the holy Reb
Moyshe Yide Leib of Sassov—Reb Simche Binem
of Pzhysha—the Holy Jew—Mendele of Kotsk—
and the wise Rim of Gora Kalwariye.

Nine Gates

to the Chassidic mysteries

THE AUTHOR TO HIS READERS

When you have read my book seven times, you will say, perhaps with justice: "It is a bad book; however, one incident in it pleased me." Which?—Each of you will say something different. . . . Each according to the roots of his soul and the glimmer of the worlds through which his Earth flew on that night.

INTRODUCTION

I

A Youth from Prague Among the Chassidim

Scenes from everyday life are scarcely to be found in these pages. Rather you will feel that you have been transported for a while to some far-off, exotic country where different flowers grow and different stars shine, to some primeval age in which reality was a dream and a dream was reality.

Yet that is not quite how it is. Everything happened in our immediate neighbourhood and not so very long ago; almost, one might say, only a moment ago. For in literary creation, which can survey more than three thousand years in the mirror of history, seventy years or a hundred and fifty years are nothing more than a moment!

It is an impassable road to the empire of the Chassidim. The traveller who pushes his way through the thick undergrowth of virgin forests, inexperienced and inadequately armed, is not more daring than the man who resolves to penetrate the world of the Chassidim, mean in appearance, even repellent in its eccentricity.

Only a few children of the West have accomplished this journey, hardly as many—when I come to think of it—as there are fingers on the hand that writes these lines.

One summer's day in 1913, a nineteen-year-old youth, brought up like all the youth of his time in the dying traditions of the pre-war generation, left Prague inspired by a secret longing which even now after the passage of so many years he still cannot explain to himself, and set out for the east, for strange countries.

Had he a foreboding of what he was losing on that day?

European civilization with its comforts and achievements, its living successes called careers? Had he a foreboding that his soul

3

would no longer be capable of feeling poetry which up to that time he had been so fond of quoting, that, from the first moment when he heard the rhythms of the Chassidic songs, all the magic charms of music would be swamped once and for all, and all beautiful things which his eye had ever conceived would in the future be half hidden by the mystic veil of the knowledge of good and evil?

He hardly suspected that, at the very moment when he believed he had reached his goal, the most impassable part of his journey was only beginning. For the gate to the empire of the Chassidim never opens suddenly for anyone. It is closed by a long chain of physical and spiritual suffering. But he who has once looked inside will never forget the riches he has seen.

The rulers of this empire are hidden from the eyes of the world. Their miraculous deeds and all-powerful words are only, as it were, of secondary importance—they are merely the hem of the veil in which their being is wrapped, while their faces are turned away from us towards the distant calm of the Absolute. Only a faint reflection of their souls falls on our too material shadows. Yet, even today, years afterwards, these shapes haunt me one after the other. Not only those I knew personally but also those I have heard so much about and read about in the old Hebrew books; they rise again before me in all their greatness and strength. I feel overcome. Something compels me to take up my pen and faithfully write down everything as best I can.

It is a Friday afternoon. The small town of Belz, the Jewish Rome, is preparing to welcome the Sabbath.

Small towns in eastern Galicia have all had the same character for centuries. Misery and dirt are their characteristic outward signs. Poorly clad Ukrainian peasant men and women, Jews wearing side-whiskers, in torn caftans, rows of cattle and horses, geese and large pigs grazing undisturbed on the square. Belz is distinguished from other places only by its famous synagogue, its no less famous House of Study and the large house belonging to the town rabbi. These three buildings enclose the square on three sides. They are simply constructed. But in this poor, out-of-the-way region of the world they are truly memorable. Belz has somewhat more than three thousand inhabitants, half of whom are Jews.

It is a long summer afternoon. There are still six or seven hours before dusk, when the Sabbath begins and even the lightest work is strictly forbidden. In spite of this, the shops are already shut, the tailors are putting away their needles, and the casual labourers—wearing side-whiskers like the rest—their hoes and spades. The housewives in the cottages are adding the last touches to their preparations for the festival.

The men hasten to the baths. After a steam bath we dive—always several of us at the same time—into a small muddy swimming-pool, a *mikve*, or special ritual bath. As though in mockery of all the rules of hygiene, a hundred bodies are 'purged' from the spirit of the working day. The water, like all the water in Belz, smells of sulphur and petroleum. . . .

Although everybody is in a tearing hurry on this day, the whole community already knows that a *bocher*, or young lad, has come to Belz all the way from Prague. A hundred questions are fired at me from every side. I am embarrassed because I do not understand a single word. I have never heard 'Yiddish' spoken before, that bizarre mixture of mediaeval German and Hebrew, Polish and Russian. It was only later that I gradually began to learn it.

The Sabbath candles are already lit in the rabbi's house. I enter with the other guests—there is a long queue of them—to greet the saint for the first time. He has been told that I am the lad from Prague; indeed they have told him a very wonderful thing—that I have succeeded in plaiting (in the prescribed fashion, of course) four fringes to my *Leib-zidakl*, or vest, with my own hands. For this work of art he calls me to him once again. Once again he shakes my hand, this time lingeringly, and regards me kindly. He looks at me with only one eye. The other eye is blind. It seems to me that a ray of light shines from his seeing eye and pierces me to the heart.

He is a sturdy, tall, old man, with broad shoulders and an unusual, patriarchal appearance, dressed in a caftan of fine silk, wearing, like all the other men, a *shtreimel*, a round fur hat worn on the Sabbath, on his head, round which hang thirteen short sable tails of dark brown colour. (On weekdays, he wears a *spodek* which is a tall, heavy velvet cap, worn by rabbis, similar to a grenadier's cap.)

Such is the welcome the youth from Prague receives from Rabbi Yissochor Ber Rokach—may his memory be blessed—the grandson of the holy Rabbi Sholem and perhaps the only person still living who can remember the old man. He addresses me in a kindly voice. I realize that he is asking me about Prague. Many years ago he was there with his father, to pray in the Old-New Synagogue and to visit the grave of his famous ancestor, the Great Rabbi Loev.

The spacious Belz synagogue has meanwhile filled with people. There are a hundred lighted candles. In a way the interior reminds me of the Old-New Synagogue in Prague. The men, for the most part tall and well-built, old and young, await the arrival of the rabbi, talking quietly among themselves. In contrast to their weekday appearance, they are all absolutely clean. Their festive caftans of black silk reach down to the ground. On their heads the older ones wear *shtreimels*, which smell of the perfumed tobacco they carry in their tobacco pouches. Some are from Hungary, others from far away—from Russia. Owing to the bad state of the roads they have journeyed for weeks on end to get to Belz, and it may be that they will not be staying there more than a single day. The next day, Sunday, they will set out again on the wearisome journey home. Next Sabbath others will come in their place.

Dusk is already well advanced when the rabbi enters the synagogue. The crowd quickly divides, to let him pass. Perhaps the waters of the Red Sea once divided in the same way before Moses.

With long, rapid strides he makes straight for the *bimah*, or reading desk, and the strange Chassidic service begins.

"*O give thanks unto the Lord, for He is good; for His mercy endureth for ever.*"

These words from Psalm 107 are used every Friday by the Chassidim when they greet the coming Sabbath. So it was ordained by the holy Baal-Shem when he was delivered out of the hands of pirates on his abortive journey to the Holy Land.

"O give thanks unto the Lord, for He is good; for His mercy endureth for ever."

It is as though an electric spark has suddenly entered those present. The crowd which till now has been completely quiet, almost cowed, suddenly bursts forth in a wild shout. None stays in his place. The tall black figures run hither and thither round the synagogue, flashing past the lights of the Sabbath candles. Gesticulating wildly, and throwing their whole bodies about, they shout out the words of the Psalm. They knock into each other unconcernedly, for all their cares have been cast aside; everything has ceased to exist for them. They are seized by an indescribable ecstasy.

Do I dream?—I have never seen anything like this before! Or maybe I have? . . . Have I perhaps been here before? . . . Everything is so peculiar, so incomprehensible!

"O give thanks unto the Lord! . . . whom He hath redeemed from the hand of the enemy; and gathered them out of the lands, from the east, and from the west, from the north, and from the south."

The voice of the old man at the *bimah* is heard clearly above all the rest. It expresses *everything*—in immense, joyous humility, and at the same time in infinitely sad longing, as though it would flow into the Infinite, as though the king's son, after being cast out for six days, were returning to face his royal Father. With deep sobs he does penance for our sins.

"They wandered in the wilderness in a solitary way; they found no city to dwell in. Hungry and thirsty, their soul fainted in them."

At this moment the power of the saint's prayers brings deliverance to the souls of those who for their great sins have found no peace after death, and been condemned to wander through the world. The *sparks* of the holy Wisdom of God, which fell into Nothingness when God destroyed the mysterious worlds that preceded the creation of our world, these sparks are now raised from the abyss of matter and returned to the spiritual Source from which they originally came.

"*Then they cried unto the Lord in their trouble, and He delivered them out of their distresses. And He led them forth by the right way, that they might go to a city of habitation. Such as sit in darkness and in the shadow of death, being bound in affliction and iron. Because they rebelled against the words of God, and contemned the counsel of the Most High. Then they cried unto the Lord in their trouble, and He delivered them out of their distresses. O praise the Lord for His goodness, and for His wonderful works to the children of men!*"

The old man at the *bimah* raises his right hand as though to bless an unseen stranger. It is as though healing balsam flows from his quivering fingers.

"*They that go down to the sea in ships, that do business in great waters. He raiseth the stormy wind which lifteth up the waves thereof. They mount up to the heaven, they go down again to the depths. They stagger like a drunken man, and are at their wits' end. Then they cry unto the Lord in their trouble, and He bringeth them out of their distresses. Then they are glad because they be quiet; so He bringeth them unto a haven of hope. Oh that men would praise the Lord for His goodness and for His wonderful works to the children of men! . . . Come then, Beloved, come to meet thy Bride, let us hasten to greet the Sabbath! . . .*"

The old man throws himself about as though seized by convulsions. Each shudder of his powerful body, each contraction of his muscles is permeated with the glory of the Most High. Every so often he claps the palms of his hands together symbolically.

The crowd of the devout swirls and streams, hums and seethes like molten lava. Suddenly, as though at a word of command, all remain with their faces towards the west, towards the entrance of the synagogue, bowing their heads in expectation. It is at this moment that the invisible Queen of the Sabbath comes in, and brings to each of us a priceless heavenly gift: a second, new, festive *soul*.

"*Come in peace, oh crown of the Lord, in the joy and exultation within the true ones of the chosen people! Come, oh Bride, come, oh Bride, come, oh Bride, Sabbath, Queen!*"

Once again we raise our heads.

"Come, Beloved, come to meet thy Bride. . . ."

The service ends. The ecstasy is over, the mystic vision has melted. Gone is the ecstasy. Now we are again in this world. But the whole world has been made sublime. Joy sparkles in the people's eyes. There is a festive, carefree atmosphere—the peace of the Queen Sabbath.

We walk past the saint in single file and wish him "good Sabbath!"

How hungry we all are!—That is because of the "second soul" that comes on the Sabbath. . . . We hasten to the inns to have a quick meal, so as to be in time at the saint's table. The stars have long since come out in the deep sky above the Ukrainian steppe. They are large like oranges.

The women are not in the synagogue. Their duty is to light the sacred Sabbath candles at home and wait for the return of their husbands and sons. They do not come out till the Saturday morning. We run into groups of them on the square—wearing traditional costumes in which the predominant colours are green, yellow and white.

Let us not look at them too closely—neither the old women in their aprons and hoods, nor the girls, fair and dark, bareheaded! They might wrongly interpret our attention, and that would cause no small scandal!

. . . On weekdays I spend most of my time at the *Bes Hamidrash*, or House of Study. It is open day and night for all who thirst after knowledge. The high shelves round the walls are stuffed full of books from the floor to the ceiling. The tables are littered with a jumbled mass of folios. Anyone may take out any book he likes and study in the *Bes Hamidrash* whenever he wishes. Here of course there are only holy, theological Hebrew books. A devout man would not touch any other. Even to know a single Latin or Russian letter is an indelible stain upon the soul. I sit and study the books from morning till evening, leaving them only for a short while to go to evening prayers or meals. Yet even the nights are not made for rest but—as the Talmud says—

for the study of the Law of God. Spiteful insects remind me of this impressively enough as soon as I lie down. It is forbidden to kill insects. I already know that it would be a sin, so I prefer to go to the House of Study. I either study or listen to someone else, in another corner, reading aloud to himself in a drawling, plaintive chant. The *Shames*, or caretaker, hands us round candles. We hold the lighted candles in our hands so as not to fall asleep over our studies.

One afternoon I dive into the ritual bath in the same way as before prayer, for on this day I am going to the saint with my *kvitel*. A *kvitel* is a small piece of paper on which one of the saint's clerks writes the name of the suppliant and the name of his mother—not his father!—the suppliant's place of origin and, in a few concise words, the substance of what he is coming to ask of God. The Chassidim, it must be explained, do not bring their petitions to the saint by word of mouth but in writing. On my *kvitel* are written the words: "Mordecai ben Rikel mi-Prag, hasmodoh be-limud ve-yiras shomayim", which means that I am asking God "that I may persevere in my studies and in the fear of God". Not one word more. That was how the Chassidim advised me to write it. The saint's entrance hall and room are already crowded—in Belz it is always crowded—with scores of suppliants, mostly women. Some come to ask the saint to intercede with God for success in their business, others for recovery from an illness, others for advice for or against a marriage. The needs of the Chassidim are many and varied, and only *he*, the saint, can satisfy them through his intercession with the Most High. After reading some of the petitions, the saint asks for details before beginning to pray or give advice. He reads some petitions with obvious displeasure, especially those asking for cures. He scolds the suppliant and tells him to go to a doctor. But he wishes him a speedy recovery. Some bring a *matbeya*, that is, a coin which the saint will endow with secret power and which can then be used as a *kameo*, or amulet. The saint places the coin on the table and draws three circles round it. He does so with obvious reluctance. But once the coin has been consecrated by the saint's hand, the suppliant receives it back with an expression of radiant joy on his face. Besides the *kvitel*, we place a *pidyen* on the saint's table; this is a small sum of money according to one's means. The saint is *in duty bound* to accept gifts. This custom was instituted by the holy Baal-Shem, and it has a metaphysical background. When the saint intercedes with God on behalf of us unworthy people, the Lord asks him: "Of what importance is this sinner to you? Have you any obligation towards him, dearly beloved son?" And the saint can reply to God: "Yes, I have an obligation towards him. He has assisted me and my family." Our money offering is thus the only link, mean as it is, between us and the saint; it is the necessary prerequisite for our prayers to be heard. Hence the saint accepts gifts. But he returns the gifts of poor people immediately. From declared unbelievers he will not take any gifts at all. The devout who live outside Belz send their petitions and contributions to the saint's office by post, or if the matter is urgent, by telegram. The suppliant obtains relief as soon as the clerk unsticks the telegram even though the saint has not yet received the remittance. Those who come to Belz from Hungary kiss the saint's hand. The Poles do not. I am last in the queue. The saint reads my *kvitel* with undisguised delight. When I come out of his room, the Chassidim are waiting for me outside, to wish me luck: "Git gepoilt!"— "Well done!"

When the moon is full, the saint cures mental maladies. The people stand in a sad queue in his room while the saint pores over the Talmud by the light of large candles. I once knew a girl who was completely cured of melancholia in this way.

The saint never looks on the face of a woman. If he must speak to women—as, when he receives a *kvitel*—he looks out of the window while he speaks. He does not even look at his own wife, a somewhat corpulent woman, but still beautiful. On a later occasion, when the holy man was alone with his wife, it was only natural that the lad from Prague should seize this rare opportunity of peeping through the keyhole when no one was watching. She had come to ask her husband's advice about their domestic worries, of which they had their full share. Even on this occasion the saint looked out of the window, with his face turned away from her, as though he were talking to a strange woman, not his wife. The Talmud tells of one devout man who did not notice that his wife had a wooden stump instead of a leg, until her funeral. . . . That man was a teacher. Thus far the Talmud.

From the window of the entrance hall to the saint's apartment one can see far out across the Ukrainian steppe. For miles round there is nothing but a flat plain, without a single tree or hill to be seen. It is a fen with a narrow path made of boards running across it. In the distance a small bridge leads into a barren little field; then the path leads on across the bog into the unknown. When I am weary of the House of Study, I cross this bridge and lie down in the little field. This is the only bit of nature where one can find spiritual refreshment in all this wilderness!

I can endure it no longer. This life of isolation from the rest of the world is intolerable. I feel disgusted with this puritanism, this ignorance, this backwardness and dirt. I escape. I travel back to my parents in Prague. But not for long. I must perforce return to my Chassidim.

One night I cannot sleep. I am lying down, facing the kitchen door, which looks towards the East. I have left the door ajar. I have just been reading some holy Hebrew book in the kitchen. The kitchen windows are open, open towards the East, the East where Belz lies at the end of a train journey of a few hours more than a day and a night. . . . It is useless for me to close my eyes to induce sleep. Suddenly I am dazzled by a bright light penetrating into my dark bedroom through the half-open door. What is it?—I know that I have put out the lamp, and there is no one in the kitchen. I stare at the light, and in the middle of it, a few steps in front of me, I can see quite clearly through the half-open door—*the saint of Belz!* He is sitting in his room at Belz looking fixedly at me. On his expressive countenance shines that barely recognizable, sublime smile of his, full of wisdom. I have no idea how long the apparition lasts, but it is long enough to shake me.

So I travel to Belz a second time, this time firmly resolved. I am no longer alone as on my first pilgrimage. This time I have a companion, a Prague lad like myself, who has also decided for Chassidism.

My vision of the saint of Belz that night was a great favour. So the Chassidim said when I told them about it. To behold a living saint from far away and, moreover, while still awake, is not indeed an absolutely isolated phenomenon among the Chassidim, but it is a greater expression of God's favour than, for instance, a conversation with someone who is dead or with the prophet Elijah.

We "who are really in earnest" do not board at the inn like those who "merely journey" to the saint of Belz. We belong to our own society, or *chevre*, the members of which are called *Yoshvim*, or *sitting ones*, because they live, or sit in Belz permanently. Our society lives on small contributions earned with difficulty from the more wealthy visitors to Belz. We cook for ourselves. The dining-room is small. Deep holes yawn in the unplaned boards of the dirty floor. We crowd together round the table on a narrow bench. There is a great shortage of crockery. We young people often eat two out of one dish, with our hands, of course. To use a fork would be an indecent innovation. The menu is not very varied. For lunch we get a slice of heavy rye bread, a plate of vermicelli or potato soup, which of course we eat with a spoon, and a tiny piece of beef to which a large portion of broad beans must always be added. The older men drink vodka, all from the same bottle (though the Talmud, or rather the Shulchan Aruch forbids two people to drink from the same vessel on hygienic grounds). We often have the famous Belz *purée*, made from sweet-smelling brown buck-wheat flour, called *grapel*, which is remarkably tasty. Sometimes we have fish, small white fish full of treacherous little bones. It is my duty to help to scrape the fish in the kitchen when it comes to my turn.

On the Sabbath the crowd is even greater. It is a real squeeze. We do not eat in our mess, but press round the rabbi at his table, quite regardless of each other's comfort in our anxiety to obtain straight from his hands some morsel of food which he has first touched and tasted. Each little titbit of his sweet *kugel* (a hot pudding), each piece of his greasy *chaulnt* (chaud lit), each drop of his home-made raisin wine contains a complete paradise with all its accompanying celestial delights. He who eats of food which the saint has blessed is sure to obtain both earthly and eternal bliss. At the table the Chassidim sing their Sabbath songs in praise of Belz, songs whose changing rhythms are a dance of gaiety and sorrow, chaos and desire. Before the grace after the meal the rabbi expounds the Word of God. Every new truth which the saint brings out from the depths of the Law is fashioned by God into a new heaven. The saint's exposition is at the same time a sermon. I hear his deep mystic voice, but I cannot distinguish the words.

On festivals there is dancing. A hundred men take hold of each other's hands, or put their arms round each other's necks and form a large circle that rotates with a rocking dance-step, slowly at first and then faster and faster. The dancing begins in the *Bes Hamidrash*, but after a while the whole crowd spreads out on to the square and dances under the rabbi's window. A dance lasts uninterrupted for an hour, or maybe more, till the dancers are exhausted, intoxicated by the endless repetition of the same, mystically coloured, dance melody. In the same way the celestial spheres dance eternally round the glorious throne of the Lord. We young people are not allowed to take part in the sacred dance of the Chassidim. We look on and sing, clapping our hands in time to the rhythm. The rabbi dances only a short while during the morning service on the autumn festivals. He dances alone. In his hand he holds a palm branch or a parchment scroll of the Law. The sight of the saint's mystic dance fills us with godly fear.

We take very good care not to catch the saint's eye during a service. As he enters the House of Study we press together in one confused mass, to leave him as much free space as possible. No true Chassid comes within a distance of *four ells* (about eight feet) of him either during prayer or before it. If we are not sufficiently careful and agile he shouts at us—using words like "cattle!" or even "robbers!"—and sometimes he slips off his *gartel* (belt) and belabours the careless individual who has got in his way. But, surprisingly enough, his blows do not hurt in the least. Nor do his words. We laugh quietly to ourselves with joy, because we know that they are not insults but a high mark of honour, a secret blessing which he disguises with blows and rough words. For the Devil must not recognize them, or he may stop them from ascending to the throne of the Most High. Nevertheless we try to keep our distance from the saint; the farther we get away from him the better it is. Why?—Why do we take such care not to come close to him? Why does he warn us so sternly to keep away? After all he is well aware that not even with a whisper would we interrupt him but would only pray in the most devout fashion. It is not because we might say anything we ought not to, or knowingly disturb him, but because our *thoughts*—all those silly thoughts we carry in our heads, even though not expressed, even the most devout— would upset his spiritual, mystic concentration. For our thoughts are so material that they would sully his pure, mystic concentration and detract from the splendour of his thoughts, each of which is a glorious, living angel. Some Chassidim hide modestly behind the backs of those who happen to stand in front of them. That is foolish, for the saint knows about everybody—even those who are hiding or are far away.

The weekdays slip by monotonously. I continue my study of the Talmud. I have long been fond of these interminable discourses of the ancient Palestinian and Babylonian rabbis on ritual and law, their legends, moral teachings, proverbs, anecdotes, paradoxes, that go to form the Talmud. The Hebrew and Aramaic languages, with their ancient elegance and terseness, have never lost their charm for me. Those picturesque signs in Hebrew writing which even to this day are half hieroglyphic, without vowels or punctuation, have been my favourite reading matter almost from childhood. Now for the first time I can give myself up to this pleasure completely. I sit and learn. When I do not understand one of the complex Talmudic problems, I ask an older person to explain it for me. But mostly I study alone. I repeat each page at least six times as I have been recommended to do. I memorize the actual Talmudic text; I learn the remarkably exact mediaeval commentaries which are printed round the text on each page like a wreath of tiny flowers, the diminutive letters of a mediaeval rabbi's handwriting. Sometimes I use other large volumes containing notes about these commentaries to help me along.

Books are greatly respected here, worshipped in fact. Nobody, for instance, sits on a bench if there is a book anywhere on it. That would be an affront to the book. We never leave a book face downwards or upside down, but always face upwards. If a book falls to the ground we pick it up and kiss it. When we have finished reading we kiss the book before we put it away. To throw it aside, or put other things on top of it is a sin. Yet the books are nearly all woefully dilapidated by constant use. When a book is so badly torn that it cannot be used, the caretaker takes it to the cemetery and buries it. Even the smallest scrap of paper with Hebrew characters printed on it must not be left lying about on the floor, or trodden on; it must be buried. For every Hebrew letter is a name of God. We never leave books open except when we are actually learning from them. If we are obliged to slip away for a moment, and do not wish to close the book, we may leave it open so as not to lose the place, but we must cover it with a cloth. It anyone notices another person going away from a book without closing or covering it, he goes over and shuts it himself; but first he will look at the open page and read a few lines out of it. If he were to shut the book without reading it at all, his act of closing it would weaken *the power of memorizing* in the other person who left the book open. The parchment scroll of the Law, which is hand-written, is held in even greater respect than printed books.

I am gradually becoming acquainted with *Chassidic* literature. The first book I read is called "The Beginning of Wisdom" (Reshit Chochmah), a cabbalistic book of exercises for the ascetic. It inculcates humility and self-denial and is full of beautiful quotations from the mystical Zohar and a book called "The Duties of the Heart" by Bachya Ibn Pakuda. "Reshit Chochmah" is the work of a famous cabbalist named Elijah de Vidas who lived in Palestine at the end of the seventeenth century. Another book I read is "The Joys of Elimelech" (Noam Elimelech) by the "Rebe Reb" Melech of Lizensk (Elimelech). I shall be telling you something about this book and its wonderful author later on. The first of these books was recommended to me by the saint of Belz himself; the second was brought to my notice by the Chassidim. I early got to know other books, Chassidic, old Hebrew and, after a while, modern ones (see the note on Literature). But the first two are the dearest of all to me. They accompany me on all my journeys; I had them with me even when I was a soldier. When I am alone and no one can see me, I dip into cabbalistic writings which we young people have been forbidden to study.

My health is affected and I am conscious that I am becoming physically weaker every day. The daily bath before morning prayer, the bad food, the all too frequent voluntary fasts, the loss of sleep, and the lack of movement and air, considerably weaken the otherwise strong constitution of a youth who is not yet physically mature. But I force myself to face up to things. I will not give in.

Why in fact are we here at all? Why not serve God at home? Is it perhaps because we want to become rabbis, or perfect saints like the saint of Belz? No, not at all. Nothing like this ever occurs to us. We have no desire to be rabbis and we shall never become saints. We are quite convinced of that. All we want is to enjoy the glory of God's majesty which the personality of the saint sheds around him. We want to enjoy it throughout our lives, continuously and unceasingly. We know that when the day comes for him to bid us his last farewell, he will leave us his first-born son, no less a saint than himself and perhaps even greater. Many people are convinced of this already. Perhaps the future has proved them right; I cannot allow myself to decide about that. I would prefer to sketch another picture of Chassidic life.

. . . On weekdays, at Belz, we do not say morning prayers until noon when the rabbi comes into the House of Study with his sons. We pray at the synagogue only on the Sabbath. The weekday service, which in other places lasts nearly an hour, is completed in an almost miraculously fast time at Belz—fifteen or twenty minutes. This speed is very important for "no pig can penetrate a fence if the stakes are set close together"; in other words, no sinful thoughts can steal into prayers if the words are spoken quickly and without any pauses. "A person who cannot say a thousand words with one breath has no right to be called a saint."

(*Speed and agility* in bodily movements—especially, of course, in the performance of religious duties—are a great virtue and an excellent means of ennobling the soul and making the mind supple. This was emphasized by one of the *predecessors* of Chassidism, the Italian cabbalist and poet, Rabbi Moses Chayyim Luzzatto, in his ethical work, "Mesilat Yesharim". This ray of sunlight from Renaissance Italy has to this day given Belz Chassidism a particular character of its own, making it a striking exception in this somewhat dull-witted northern region. Indeed the other Chassidim cannot tolerate the brisk way we do things at Belz. They see something grotesque about it.)

I am still a foreigner. People are very polite and full of respect when they talk to me, but they are mistrustful. The mere fulfilment of religious injunctions, however precise and conscientious, is as little adequate to inspire confidence here as is the utmost zeal over one's study. Excessive religiosity is not welcomed. But now that my beard and side-whiskers are well grown, now that I am able to speak some Yiddish and have begun wearing a long *shipits* (an overcoat similar to a caftan) instead of a short coat, and ever since I have started wearing a black velvet hat on weekdays, as all the other Chassidim do, this ice-wall of mistrust has gradually begun to thaw. But why even now am I not completely like the others? For example, why am I not gay, all the time, as a true Chassid ought to be? . . .

At last, when my face is pallid from undernourishment and illness, and my emaciated body has acquired a stoop, it is clear to nearly all of them that "I am really in earnest". No longer will the gates of Chassidism be closed in front of the youth from Prague.

Meanwhile I have come to know a number of Chassidic truths. For example I already know that "the whole world hates the Jews, that all Jews hate the Chassidim, that all foreign Chassidim hate the Chassidim of Belz and that the Belz Chassidim (that is, those who 'merely journey' to see the saint of Belz) hate *us*, the true *yoshvim*, but that we, the *yoshvim* of Belz, are the pillar on which the whole world rests". I assimilate the mysteries of humility and modesty. Nothing can now deprive me of these fundamental Chassidic virtues. Nothing can tempt me away from them. My Hebrew name, Mordecai, prompts one of the *yoshvim* to quote some words from the book of Esther and apply them to me: "And Mordecai sat in the king's gate." It is meant well. It is a discreet form of praise for my having advanced so far as to sit in the gate of the King of kings, for my having become a real *yoishev* (*yoishev* means: sitting). But to me it does not seem to be any great compliment. I prefer to interpret it as a gentle reproach: I am only in the *gate* of the King; I have still a long way to go before I get to the chamber. . . .

The Chassidim are becoming kinder to me every day. My lot is being improved in every possible way. Better bread, and milk. But my weakened stomach resolutely refuses all these extra comforts. Moreover, the insects are becoming crueller all the time. They have absolutely no pity on me. The mice nibble at my clothes. I sleep on the ground on a heap of old straw. My whole outward appearance testifies that I am gradually turning into a complete *chnyok* and *katcherak*. These two words are untranslatable nicknames used by the Chassidim to mock any of their fellows who are totally indifferent to their outward appearance.

Meanwhile the scene itself has long since changed. But the difference is not very great. Instead of the Ukrainian steppe, there is now the Hungarian puszta. We are no longer in Polish Belz but in the no less dusty Hungarian town of Ratsfert (Ujféhérté), near Debrecin. The Belz rabbi came here for refuge with his entire court at the beginning of the war.

At this time, however, we do not even need to travel to Ratsfert to quench our thirst at the fount of Chassidism. Gunfire has swept the villages and towns, and thousands of bearded Jews are fleeing westwards, arousing contempt and disgust wherever they go. Some have succeeded in saving their holy books and old manuscripts. Prague is flooded with Jews from the east who have set up their own synagogues and schools. Among the thousands of refugees are a few dozen genuine Chassidim who have come from a great variety of places and from all possible directions. For the time being, Prague is part of the Chassidic Empire.

The saint of Belz has fallen ill. After a great deal of persuasion he has decided to visit Mariánské Lázně (Marienbad). We are carrying him there along the paths through the forest. At other times he is separated from us by his secretaries and servants, as God is separated from our souls by myriads of spheres and worlds. But here among the forest trees we can all approach him. Although he is seriously ill, he talks cheerfully to everybody. We are conscious that his are no ordinary words even when he is talking about things which appear to be everyday matters. All his words, however small, are to be understood metaphorically. The whole time his thoughts are concentrated exclusively on supernatural matters. He talks to us, but we are aware that we understand his words no better than the wooden gnomes adorning the forests of Mariánské Lázně. He converses with these distorted little figures as gaily and unconstrainedly as he does with us living people. When he is not speaking to anyone, he repeats the Talmud to himself, which he naturally knows by heart in its entirety—all thirty-six tractates in their twelve mighty volumes! Once, as we were walking through the forest, he remarked: "If I didn't have you, I would pray with these trees here." He has never made a secret of his pacifist opinions. We have often admired his outspokenness. Once, when he noticed a public collecting box for war contributions on one of the forest roads, he called out with passion: "Is that what we've got to do with our money—so still more people can be murdered?" And on another occasion he said: "The German says: The whole world belongs to me! The Englishman says: The whole sea belongs to me! But my Yossele—that was the name of the Chassid who led the prayers in those days—my Yossele sings so sweetly: The sea belongs to God, for He made it; the dry land belongs to God, for His hand created it."

Ever since this time I have felt profoundly indebted to the saint of Belz. I know that it is he alone whom I have to thank for my miraculous deliverance from Austrian military service. It was his intercession with God that brought this about. Everything is again as it used to be. My beard and side-whiskers, which I had to shave off whilst on active service, have grown again.

It is now quite a time since I last saw Gavril, my friend from Prague. He is settled at Hivnev, near Belz, and is making good progress with his studies. He is sure to be enjoying himself, having recently got married.

We are at Ratsfert again. The autumn holidays are over. It is 1918. All of us are very run down. Influenza is taking its toll. But a magic word is going through the world: Armistice—peace!

The woebegone lad from Prague is strangely excited. He does not himself understand what is happening to him, as on that day five years ago when he started out on his first journey to Belz. He bids farewell to the saint and the Chassidim. They do not try to hold him back. Everyone is excited, everyone is looking forward to getting home. They wish him every success and hope he will soon return to them in good health. Some of them go with him a short way. Mechale of Baiberk accompanies him to the station. They eat out of the same dish. A final warm handshake, and the youth from Prague leaves for Budapest and thence on to Vienna. Since then he has not returned to his Chassidim. Europe has not let him go. He returns to them only in this book....

The heroes of our story are the *Tsaddikim*, the rulers of the Chassidim. The word *tsaddik* means a perfect and just person, a saint. The word *chassid*, which becomes *chassidim* in the plural, means a deeply devout person who is wholeheartedly devoted to a particular *Tsaddik*. The founder of Chassidism was Rabbi Yisroel Baal-Shem-Tov who lived and worked in Poland in the middle of the eighteenth century. (He died about 1761.) To this day hundreds of thousands of Chassidic communities live almost totally isolated from the surrounding world, faithful to their unique traditions, and it would be true to say that in Eastern Europe they form states within states. Their *real* rulers are the grandsons and great-grandsons of the saints whom I shall be writing about in this book.

To relate stories from the lives of the saints is one of the most praiseworthy acts a Chassid can do. He will tell of them at every opportunity—during a meal, during his studies, on a train journey, but especially on the anniversary of a saint's death. He must never forget to add the word "holy", or the phrase, "May his merits protect us!", whenever he mentions the name of a saint. Woe to the listener who protests that he has already heard this or that episode before! Everybody is in duty bound to listen patiently to each story even if he has heard it a hundred times already. In this way, over the course of years, everything becomes imprinted on the memory—the heroes' names, their wives' names, the characters connected with them and the place where the various events took place.

Anyone can be a narrator. If you know a nice story about a saint, it will be gratefully accepted, and one of your listeners will immediately reward you with another story about the same saint, or a similar anecdote about another saint, or something a saint has said. If you make a mistake in any detail, you will immediately be corrected by your listeners, for of course they know it much better than you do! . . .

The story-teller does not speak with words alone. If his vocabulary proves inadequate, he can help himself along with gestures, miming or modulations of the voice. When relating something gloomy, he will lower his voice to a whisper. If he has a mystery to unfold he will content himself with hinting, breaking off in the middle of a sentence with a meaningful wink or squint. If he has to describe some supernatural beauty he will close his eyes and roll his head about in genuine ecstasy. In this way the listener can understand much more than if we were to paint everything in detail with the choicest and cleverest words. The narrator's style is absolutely simple, without any special pathos, and completely inconsequent. He often wanders from one saint to another—so do not be surprised if I sometimes do the same.

The Chassidim are aware that by no means everything they relate about their saints actually happened; but that does not matter. If a saint never really worked the miracle they describe, it must still have been one such as only he was capable of performing. Rabbi Nachman of Brazlav goes out of his way to point out that "not everything related about the holy Baal-Shem (for instance) is true, but even the things which are untrue are *holy* if told by devout people. The fact is (says Rabbi Nachman) that man is perpetually sunk in a magic sleep throughout his life and is unable to rouse himself except by narrating anecdotes about the saints."

It is as though the Chassidic saints had breathed their soul into the legends which the people tell of them. In consequence these Chassidic legends are perhaps more faithful in depicting the characters of their heroes than in recording the actual deeds performed or the actual words spoken.

If I do not use a tearful voice when telling about the Chassidic saints in this book, that is fully in keeping with the style of the Chassidic story-tellers who never avoid humour if it befits the occasion. May I be forgiven if in presenting the various stories I follow a different order than the chronological sequence. By way of excuse I would recall what the Talmud says, that "there is neither *before* nor *after* in the word of God". The verses at the head of each section of the book are modelled on the practice followed in old Hebrew books which used to have similar verses in praise of distinguished rabbis. No chapters in this book are specially devoted to the actual founder of Chassidism, Baal-Shem, whose spirit pervades all our stories. There is of course a purer strain of poetry in the legends about the Baal-Shem, and the truths revealed to him are deeper than the aphorisms of his successors. Above all I have aimed to introduce my readers to some of the more recent representatives of the Chassidic movement.[1] Furthermore I have been lured on by the realization that

[1] Literature (*A*). *Hebrew:*—Anonymous: Or 'Olam (Lvov s.a.)—Deutsch, Shimon: Hakme ha-Razim (Mukajevo 5696)—Horodetsky, S.A.: Ha-Hasiduth ve-ha-Hasidim (Berlin 5683)—Israel ben Simha: Eser Oroth (Pietrokov 5667)—

I have an opportunity in this book of publishing various stories which have possibly never been written down before—not even in Hebrew—and which I have learnt only from verbal tradition.

It is not the purpose of this book to present a philosophical analysis of Chassidic learning. Certainly it is easy enough to bore one's readers and misuse their patience, but it is not godly. My aim is rather to entertain the reader and at the same time to give him a truthful report. The remaining part of this chapter is not primarily intended for the ordinary layman. It is written more particularly by way of anticipating the ill-will of the learned philosophers and the most esteemed critics.

Chassidism is the Cabbala made accessible to the people. It is a particular type of pantheism with a popular appeal of its own and at the same time partly dogmatic, a pantheism which is shot through with the mystic magic of the *idea* of rabbinical Neo-Platonism and subtly interwoven with pseudo-Pythagorean threads, the whole ingeniously grafted on the old stock of Old Testament Talmudic Judaism. It grew up long, long ago in Palestine, Egypt or Mesopotamia, like a hardly discernible plant in the semi-darkness of unknown circumstances. It was then transplanted to the romantic environment of Catholic and Arab Spain and subsequently returned to Palestine. But it was not until the last two centuries, on the fertile soil of Slavonic north-eastern Europe, in the shade of the Carpathian forests and on the Ukrainian plains, that it developed into the present

Kaddish, Yo'es Kayyam: Siah Sarfe Kodesh (Lodz 5686)—Kahana, Abraham: Sefer ha-Hasiduth (Warsaw 5682)—Kahana, Abraham ("Abrech"): Deyoknaoth ve-Ikunim (Przemysl 5695)—Walden Aharon: Shem hag-Gedolim he-Hadash (Warsaw 5624)—Zeitlin Hillel: Ha-Hasiduth (Warsaw 5682). (B) *In other languages:*—Aescoly W. A.:—L'introduction à l'étude des hérésies religieuses parmi les Juifs. La Kabbale—Le Hassidisme (Paris 1928)—Bloch C.: Priester der Liebe (Vienna 1930)—Buber M.: Die chassidischen Bücher (Hellerau 1928)—Dubnow S.: Die Geschichte des Chassidismus (Berlin 1931)—Klein G.: Bidrag till Israels religions-historia, sex föredrag (Stockholm 1898)—Lehmann E.: Illustrerad religions-historia (Stockholm 1924)—Mosbech H.: Essaeismen et bidrag til senjdendommens religionshistorie (Copenhagen 1916)—Oesterley W. O. E.: The sacred dance, A study in comparative folklore (Cambridge 1923)—Ysander Torsten: Studien zum B'eshtschen Hasidismus (Upsala 1933).

fabulous, many-branched tree whose blooms are so remarkable in their variety. Not many reliable dates can be given. A fundamental problem is presented by the "Zohar", that most important of the cabbalistic books, in that it is not known when and where it was set down in writing. The book appears in Spain at the end of the thirteenth century, when it purported to be an ancient work of Palestinian origin. The dispute about this question—which has a certain analogy in the controversy over the Králové Dvůr and Zelená Hora manuscripts in Czechoslovakia —is not yet at an end. Yitzhak Luria Ashkenazi, who is designated in our stories by the sign *Holy ARI*, the great promulgator of cabbalistic doctrines, was born in Jerusalem in the year 1553 and died at Safed in 1572. His teaching, which was edited by Chayyim Vital Calabrese, a disciple of his, was of particular importance for the rise of Chassidism.

The Chassidic Cabbala is linked with Platonic and Neo-Platonic philosophy in a number of aspects—in its conception of "spheres", in its doctrine of the contraction of the Infinite before the creation of the world, its understanding of all phenomena in a symbolic way (likewise its allegorical interpretation of the Scriptures) and so on. The similarity with Pythagorean philosophy is to be seen in the cabbalists' belief in the creative power of figures (and letters) and in their teaching about the transmigration of souls. On the latter point there is a striking similarity to both Brahmanism and Buddhism. Unlike these two systems, however, the Lurian Cabbala teaches that the human soul can be incarnated not only in animals but also in plants, waters and minerals. The connection with the Indian Upanishads is to be seen in the doctrine of the worlds that preceded the creation of our world, while in its emphasis on the world-creating principles of manhood and womanhood the Cabbala reminds one of Chinese mysticism (Lao-Tse). The idea that man is created in the image of God leads the cabbalists to views about the microcosm similar to those found in Aristotle and Plato, or, for instance, in the Catholic mystic, Nicholas of Cusa. The emphasis on permanent joy as being the most important ethical principle of life links Chassidism with the mysticism of the Mohammedan Sufi, while the functional importance which the Cabbala attaches to the secret "names" of God and the angels brings us near to Ethiopian and even perhaps ancient Babylonian magic.

In popular Chassidic mysticism we find these elements so delicately diffused and elaborated that at first sight we are hardly aware of their presence. In consequence we cannot dismiss Chassidism as a mere inorganic fusion, or medley of mystical ideas culled from various world systems. It may be that Chassidism is a sea into which all mystical streams flow, but if this is so then the fusion took place deep in the subconsciousness of history. It would be possible, perhaps, to reconstruct the bridges linking Chassidism with the mystic centres farthest removed from it both in time and place. Nevertheless the overall impression it gives is so individual and particular that any doubts as to its independent growth are to a large extent dispelled. The Chassidim point out of course—and not altogether without justice—that in one form or another the elements of their teaching are contained in the ancient Talmud and also, in part, in the Holy Scriptures. In confirmation of this opinion it is pertinent to observe that some Christian theologians in the Middle Ages considered that certain Greek philosophical systems were actually of Jewish origin. In recent times, only Nietzsche has held the view that there is evidence of Jewish influence on the philosophy of Plato. In ancient times the Jewish Essenes were almost perfect Pythagoreans, as is clear from the records left by Flavius Josephus.

In time and place Chassidism is closer to the Orthodox Church than to any other denomination. To a certain extent this is also true, I think, in a cultural sense. However this opinion must be taken *cum grano salis* even if justified in certain details.

In support of this view I might instance the deification of the saints during their lifetime and the eating of food sanctified by their mouths, which are phenomena to be found not only among Orthodox Christians and in Chassidism, but also, for example, in far-off Tibet. It is clear from certain passages in the Talmud that similar customs have been considerably widespread among the Jews from oldest times.

Boundless faith, joy inspired by other-worldliness, humility, hope and love, but above all simplicity of soul—these are the qualities that form the foundation of the ethics and moral strength of this legendary Chassidic world. The Chassidic saints are filled with these virtues to an extent that is truly superhuman. Simplicity is not of course a primary quality in the complicated Jewish psychology. Nevertheless Chassidism succeeds in cultivating it by means of its rigid discipline. It is this simplicity which is the source of that naïve refinement and refined naïvety that give the Chassidic legend its peculiar charm and attraction. For although Chassidism profoundly respects Talmudic learning, it takes strict care to ensure that not even scholarship shall be achieved at the expense of simplicity and pureness of soul. For this reason the Chassidim have no love for the eccentric sophistry of the average Talmudist and forbid the reading of pseudo-rationalistic works written by mediaeval Jewish scholars under the influence of Aristotle. They do not even make an exception in the case of the philosophical writings of Maimonides although certain Chassidic saints have made a very careful study of them. In this the influence of the Chief Rabbi Loev of Prague is clearly seen. Loev would have nothing to do with the fruitless controversies of learned Talmudists and vigorously rejected the philosophical speculations of the mediaeval Jewish peripatetics. The influence of the Prague miracle-worker is also evident in the warm-heartedness felt by the Chassidim towards their saints.

In spite of differences between Talmudic Judaism and Chassidism, both in philosophical outlook and in the manner of studying the Talmud, it should be stressed that nowadays even the Talmudists do not look upon Chassidism as a heresy or as a sect in the usual sense. The differences in ritual are insignificant. Differences over dogma are virtually non-existent. Both consider the Old Testament and the Talmud, with all its annotations and decisions, as equally authoritative. The main difference between them lies in the fact that Chassidism has elevated occult lore, or the Cabbala, with all its implications, above everything else. It has made it accessible to the ordinary people, as we have already said, whereas for the rest of Orthodox European Jewry the Cabbala has, on the whole, a subordinate position and is virtually only of theoretical importance, being at best only one of the religious subjects studied by certain rabbis, and without any perceptible influence on religious life. In its positive attitude towards the Cabbala, Chassidism comes near to oriental Judaism, especially in the liturgical aspect and its doctrine of the transmigration of souls which is totally unknown in western Judaism.

The most beautiful Chassidic doctrine is undoubtedly that of the *spiritual nature* of all matter. According to Chassidism, all matter is *full of supernatural "sparks" of the holiness of God*, and purely human functions such as eating and drinking, bathing and sleeping, dancing and the act of love are dematerialized and considered as the *most sublime* actions *in the service of God*.

The Chassidic legend is not without its cloudy moods. On the whole however it can be said that the mysticism of the Chassidic legends is *bright and joyous*, which gives it a great charm and appeal without in any way detracting from its depth.

Chassidic first names are given in their Chassidic form and not as they are found in classical Hebrew. Thus, for instance: 'Sholem' not 'Shalom', 'Avrum' not 'Abraham', 'Yisrol' not 'Israel', 'Nachman' not 'Naaman'. For the most part the names appear with one or other of the diminutive endings in which the Yiddish language is very rich, for instance, -ele, -el, -nju, -tje, -ke.

The Hebrew word 'reb' has been preserved in referring to the rank of the man concerned. It is always used immediately before a proper name and never as an independent word. If the word 'rabbi' is to be used independently, the Hebrew word is 'rebe' (rabbi) or 'rov' (rab). Titles of works (except where they are used as their authors' names) are written in accordance with academic usage. Well-known biblical names are spelt in the accepted way.

(Where transliteration has been necessary, the following points should be observed: 'ch' is always guttural, as in the Scotch word 'loch', 'tch' is to be pronounced as in the English word 'catch', 'sh' is as in the English word 'shoe', 'h' is always aspirate, 'u' is always to be sounded as in the English word 'put', a final 'e' must always be pronounced as in the Italian word 'niente', 'j' is to be pronounced as a short 'ee' sound. Translator's note.)

How a silken young man was not fitted to go into business, or how the predictions of the Seer were fulfilled—a disputation between the Devil and a Messiah, or how our Redeemer was confounded by a woman—how the holy Reb Sholem built a House of God and how the holy Rebe Reb Shimon of Jaroslav visited it and kissed every stone in it—how the holy Reb Sholem lived with his consort Malkele as in paradise—how the holy Malkele expounded the Scriptures and healed a lame man—then it is related how the holy Reb Sholem was incarnated in a citron (*esrig*) and how a disciple unveiled a mystery—how our Chassidic stubbornness is our greatest virtue—how a sinner was punished by having to eat swine's flesh, and how another sinner was saved by his stubbornness—how the angels sought an intercessor and how they made the holy Reb Sholem their cantor—how the holy Reb Sholem settled a disturbance after his death, or how he tarries among us at our prayers.

All you, then, who wish to live, enter this gate with me, for there you shall read all this.

The First Gate

Of diamonds in the Lord's crown the costliest,
Shining jewel of humility,
In modesty the purest,
Source of peace and loyalty,
In faith the deepest.

To him thousands of Jacob's sheep have hastenèd,
Through him their thirsty souls have quenchèd,
And to his wisdom piously have listenèd,
Our teacher and our master, godly man perfected,
Light of all Israel eternally ahead.

THE HOLY REB SHOLEM OF BELZ

may his merits protect us eternally!

THE FIRST GATE

Old, very old, is the wondrous family of the Rokachs, Rabbis at Belz. We shall not here discuss whether or not it is likely that they are able to trace back their lineage to King David. We are restrained from so doing by our firm Chassidic faith. It is certain that bearers of the name of Rokach were learned Rabbis in Germany as early as the thirteenth century. On the distaff side the Belz Rokachs are descendants of Loev, the great Prague Rabbi, and the no less famous Chacham Tsvi of Amsterdam. Of this there is no doubt.

It was the holy Reb Sholem, the great-grandfather of the present Rabbi, who first started the family on the road to Chassidism.

Reb Sholem was a *silken* man. Silken?—Yes. In other words, he was an exceptionally learned man, perfect in godliness and richly endowed with all the virtues, a rare, exceedingly rare fellow, a silken fellow. *A zadener yinger mantchik*—it really is impossible to express it in any other way.

Reb Sholem did not want to become a Rabbi. Why not?—Out of modesty, evidently. He wanted to be a perfectly ordinary Jewish trader. But there was a stumbling-block, for the holy Reb Sholem—may the Light of his merits protect us—was a man of no mean gifts. Gifts for learning and meditation, of course. It has not been proved if he also had a bent for commerce. All his days he had spent brooding over the Talmud but now the time had come for him to start up in business. How does a person set about becoming a business man? Sholem had no idea. So he made friends with another young man, a trader in the true sense of the word, but an honourable, reliable fellow at the same time, in short, an ideal partner.

To begin with, the two enterprising young men wanted to know what the holy *Seer* would have to say about it because it was he who had been their teacher. So they went to Lublin to see him.

It was strange advice indeed that the Seer gave them. He recommended Sholem to go into business but warned his companion against entering into partnership with him. So the two men reconsidered what they should do, for the mysterious words of the Seer had not left them any the wiser. Finally they decided that at all events they would set up shop together. Sholem put all his small fortune into the concern.

But the business did not prosper. Both Sholem and his partner soon lost everything they had.

"Did I not tell you not to get involved in any business ventures with him?" the holy Seer asked Sholem's partner, when the two men came to Lublin a second time. Then turning to Sholem he said:

"As long as you had money, you did not want to become a Rabbi, even though you were predestined to be one. Now that you have nothing you will have to do so, whether you want to or not, to earn a livelihood for yourself and your wife. Now perhaps you understand why I advised you to go into business...."

And so the good Sholem had to become a Rabbi, as his forefathers had been before him, and take his place at Belz.

Although small, Belz is both ancient and famous. Before the holy Reb Sholem became Rabbi at Belz, the Rabbi's office had been managed by none other than a *Messiah*!

There is a Messiah in every generation. He leads a solitary life and no one knows of his existence. He may not reveal himself to the world because of our guilt. But at that time the whole world knew that a Messiah was there, living at Belz, and that his name was Aaron.

The whole world knew about it and was glad, both those on earth and those in heaven.

Only the Devil did not rejoice. He could not reconcile himself to the idea of having to bid farewell to his rule over the world and hand over his sceptre to a Messiah.

So the Devil changed himself into a woman, a woman of outstanding beauty and—this is what was unusual—wisdom. Thus disguised he set out on his road.

He went from town to town and wherever he came started learned discussions with distinguished Rabbis. No one surmised who this erudite woman could be. But all the savants whom she induced to talk with her were confounded by her arguments, whatever the subject discussed. Her fame flew round the world.

Reb Aaron Messiah also desired to cross swords with this wondrous woman.

Dear me, what an occasion that was, this battle of words between a Messiah and the Devil! It is a wonder they did not burn each other up with the fire of their breath. In their wit and wisdom they overturned rocks by their roots and ground each other to pulp.

Finally the woman produced a question which even the Messiah was unable to answer.

"I will tell you when we are alone," she said. "It's a great secret. No one must know it except us."

Not knowing whom he had before him, the Messiah ordered everyone present to leave the room. Not even a child was allowed to remain, so sublime was the secret!

It was not until he had shut the door after the last person that the Messiah saw his error. In the heat of the learned dispute he had forgotten the words of the holy scholars in the Talmud which forbid us to be alone with a strange woman for a single moment.

It was too late. The Messiah's holy mission had been profaned and his journey on this earth came to an end. It was the sixth day of the month of Tishri. The Devil celebrated his victory.

As a result we have longer to wait for our salvation. It will be a long time yet, a very long time, perhaps.

Only an old tombstone in the Belz cemetery shows us that a Messiah really lived there: Reb Aaron Messiah.

It was the holy Reb Sholem who succeeded the Messiah.

Reb Sholem acquired miraculous qualities through the merit of his wife, Malkele.

Reb Sholem devoted his days to the study of the Talmud. This was no secret and nothing out of the ordinary. In those times almost all devout men did nothing else but meditate on the Talmud the whole day long and leave the care of the family to their patient wives. The latter were well aware that they would be richly rewarded for this in the next world, that for their self-sacrifice they would be allowed to sit at golden tables in paradise with their husbands, in the company of the most famous scholars of Israel, and that they too would rejoice in the glorious light of the majesty of God.

Malkele however was not satisfied with this. She wanted her Sholem to sit on a throne of rubies and pearls among the most holy of the saints and the angels of the Lord, wearing the diamond crown of the purest merits, high, exceedingly high above the husbands of all her neighbours—and she at his side.

For this reason, as soon as everybody had gone to sleep in the evening, Malkele would let her husband out of the house. To make sure that no jealous soul should know of it he climbed out of the window with the help of a ladder. Sholem's new partner would be waiting for him in front of the house. As before with the shop, so now he had a partner with whom he secretly went off to study in the empty *Bes Hamidrash*. There the two young men would search the word of God and its sublime mysteries the whole night long. Night after night—except perhaps the night of the Sabbath—they did not get a wink of sleep. They spent altogether nine hundred and ninety-nine nights in this way.

On the thousandth night there was a terrible storm with heavy rain, hail and thunder, and the Devil himself came to bar their way to the *Bes Hamidrash*. Sholem's companion was profoundly scared and preferred to go home to his wife. But the holy Reb Sholem would not give in. However he did not spend that memorable stormy night alone in the Belz House of Study. The immortal prophet Elijah and the spirits of saints who had long since died came to initiate the dauntless Sholem into the inscrutable mysteries of the Cabbala and give him the keys of the celestial gates.

Such is the way Heaven rewards perseverance. A single night more—and Reb Sholem turned into a saint. A single night less —and his companion remained an ordinary human being!

So the Seer of Lublin was not Sholem's only teacher; there was none other than the prophet Elijah as well. Let us remember him, this wondrous man, let us sing his praises and he will bring us his blessing.

Elijah in Gilead had his place,/Happy the man who but dreams of his face,/Happy the man who has greeted him but once,/ Happier still if he returned him his glance,/A leather girdle round his loins is wound,/In the desert his food by ravens was found,/On horses of fire he ascended to heaven, He never knew death nor to the grave was given,/The hearts of the sons he returns to God's word,/And in evil times he is sent by the Lord,/ Or when the oppressor is strong./Brothers, to be sure, you know the old song.

The holy Reb Sholem never forgot what his Malkele had done for him.

When he was famous throughout the world for his holiness and for the miracles he performed, and when hundreds and thousands of devout persons journeyed from far and wide to his table at Belz, to fulfil obediently his every word, the slightest nod of his head, he would declare:

"If it were not for Malkele (which means *little queen*), Sholem would not be *king*!"

But when an inquisitive person once asked the holy Reb Sholem if it were true that he had watched through a thousand nights, Reb Sholem opened his holy eyes wide and repeated the words after him in amazement:

"A *thousand* nights?" . . .

Behold! How modest was the holy Reb Sholem!

The ladder by which Malkele let her husband out of the house is exhibited to this day. It stands as an eternal memorial at the Belz House of Prayer, which Reb Sholem caused to be built to a plan of his own. It is a wonderful House of Prayer. Through its doors the Messiah will come to this earth when His time is really come.

We ordinary mortals cannot even surmise the holy secrets Reb Sholem incorporated into the masonry of this House of God from his precious heart. Only a saint like the holy Rebe Reb Shimon of Jaroslav could feel their fervour.

One day after a wedding ceremony, a colleague of Reb Sholem's, the famous blind saint, the holy Rebe Reb Shimon of Jaroslav, visited Belz. (It was he who wrote the book "Nahalat Shimon", "The Legacy of Shimon".) The holy Rebe Reb Shimon entered the new synagogue. He crept along the walls and kissed each stone, each brick. But at one spot he removed his holy lips from the wall and started kissing again only when he had moved a few steps farther on.

"Forgive me, Master," the holy Reb Sholem apologized modestly, not in the least surprised by the strange behaviour of the blind saint. And pointing to that part of the wall which the saint had not kissed, he added: "I happened not to be present when this piece of wall was being built."

Naturally the Chassidim who built the House of Prayer had laid stone upon stone with the same piety as when they prayed. But the good bricklayers did not breathe their soul into the building nor infuse their hearts into the cold stones. Only their holy Reb Sholem could do that. But on one occasion this had not happened, and only the holy Rebe Reb Shimon of Jaroslav could be aware of that.

If the learned Reb Sholem was a worker of miracles, his devout wife Malkele was no less so. One day there arrived a man who had something seriously wrong with his feet. The doctors had been unable to help him. He had therefore travelled to Belz so that the saint might entreat the Most High to cure him.

"You needn't go to the Rabbi," Malkele told him. "Go to the House of Study and light a candle!" The cripple limped off and did as Malkele had advised him. Wonderful to relate, he was immediately cured. When Reb Sholem heard of it, he asked Malkele: "Who revealed to you the mystery by which a man can be made whole?"

"There's no mystery about it," exclaimed Malkele, "It's there for everybody to read in the Psalms of David: 'Thy word is a light unto my feet.' What else should that mean except that the light we use for studying the holy Law is good for feet?"

Such "mistakes" in interpreting the Word of God can of course only be made by the purest and simplest hearts, like the heart of the holy Malkele.

"God gives commandments and the saint breaks them," says the Talmud. Because the pious Malkele was also a saint, she too had something to say when God gave an order. The following incident is evidence of this:

One day a certain Chassid was travelling to Belz from a distant Galician town to see Reb Sholem. On the way he was obliged to spend the Sabbath at Przemysl. Naturally he would have considered it most reprehensible and discourteous not to visit the renowned saint of Przemysl, the holy Reb Mayerl. "You certainly didn't come here intending to see me," observed Reb Mayerl when he saw the Chassid's unfamiliar face. "You're on your way to Belz, I'm sure. When you get there, tell them that Mayerl likes to eat capons."

The holy Reb Mayerl always talked of himself in the third person and—like many other saints—avoided using the arrogant word "I".

The Chassid was unaware of the import of Reb Mayerl's words. However he hastened to deliver the message.

"All right," said Malkele when she heard the message. "Then we shall put it on the unclean birds" (meaning the birds we are not allowed to eat)!

Malkele's words were equally incomprehensible to the good Chassid. It was only later that he understood what they were all about, for soon afterwards all the crows and owls in the neighbourhood began to die off, as though shot by an unseen hand.

What had happened was this: A command had gone forth in heaven that a fatal disease was to attack the poultry that year, which was to exterminate them. However Malkele came to the conclusion that it would be quite enough if only the capons perished because very few people ate them in any case. Clearly she had forgotten the holy Reb Mayerl of Przemysl. Naturally he too knew what plans were being made in heaven and he was also aware of what Malkele had decided. Hence his message—which prompted Malkele at the last moment to intervene in heaven a second time, and so prevent the disastrous decision of the celestial court from descending upon the capons.

Worthy Malkele! Blessings upon you, you thoughtful house-wife!

Reb Sholem never withdrew himself from the company of his excellent wife. Contrary to the custom of all devout men he even ate at the same table with her. At first sight, it might seem that this was at variance with the practice of a real saint. Reb Sholem however was a man of such genuine piety that there could be no harm in it. That this was indeed the case was observed by a saint who once stayed as a guest at Reb Sholem's house: "Reb Sholem," he declared, "lives with his wife in a state of innocence, like Adam and Eve in paradise before the Fall." It was true. They did indeed live as in paradise.

To this day we Chassidim at Belz celebrate the memory of the holy Malkele every year. We observe the anniversary of her death on the 27th of the month of Adar with as much ostentation, if not with still greater piety, as when we commemorate the death of any other saint.

Now let us hear how deeply the holy Reb Sholem loved to fulfil the commandments of God! The Rabbi of Kamionka—also Sholem by name—came to Belz for the Feast of Tabernacles while he was still a disciple of Reb Sholem at Belz. He entered the House of Prayer at the precise moment when our Reb Sholem was saying the Halel prayer at the *bimah* with his Chassidim. The disciple heard the master's voice raised in fervent prayer and rejoiced. Naturally he also wanted to look at his teacher's holy face, where the light of the glory of God was continuously reflected. But his search for his master was in vain. The latter was nowhere to be seen. Finally he found him where clearly no ordinary person would think of looking. In his great humility and his love for God's commandments Reb Sholem of Belz had incarnated himself completely, every little bit of himself, in a citron, an *esrig*, which in accordance with the law of Moses he held in his hand during the solemn prayer (the esrog or ethrog is a kind of lemon imported from Palestine). So completely had he fitted himself into the *esrig* that he, a saint, was not to be seen at all.

Sholem of Kamionka of course was no ordinary disciple. A typical proof of this was the wonderfully prompt way in which he expounded the Scriptures. On one occasion his teacher, Reb Sholem of Belz, asked him:

"It is written (in the first book of Moses, Chapter 8, verse 13): 'And Thou didst say unto me, I will do thee *good, good. . . .*'" These were the words with which our forefather Jacob called upon the Lord, as literally quoted in the Hebrew text. "But is there any passage where we read of God having spoken like this to Jacob on a previous occasion?" the saint of Belz inquired of his disciple. "God never made him a promise that He would do him *good*. As for His having promised to do so twice, that surely is nowhere written in the Holy Scriptures!? How then could Jacob say: 'And Thou didst say unto me. . . ?'"

"It is written," returned Kamionka without a moment's hesitation, "It is written at the very beginning when God created the world. For the seven days of the beginning of all things are an expression of those seven qualities of God which are also represented by the Seven Shepherds: the first day, Sunday, is the Love of Abraham. Monday is the Strength of Isaac, Tuesday the Truth of Jacob. Wednesday is the Might of Moses, Thursday the Humility of Aaron, Friday the Faithfulness of Joseph and Saturday the Rule of David. For each day at the beginning of the first book of Moses it is written: And God saw that it was *good*. The only exception of course is Monday, for on Monday Hell was also created through the Strength of Isaac, and that is not exactly a good thing. We never start on a journey on a Monday since we are aware that it is not a lucky day. Tuesday, on the other hand, is the expression of the Truth of *Jacob*, and so it is written *twice* (verses 10 and 12): And God saw that it was *good*, and once again . . . and God saw that it was *good*. In very truth, then, God did promise our forefather Jacob—whose day is Tuesday—that He would show him good and again only good from the very creation of the world. Jacob therefore was quite *right* when he prayed: "And Thou didst say unto me: 'I will do thee *good*, *good*.' " He was recalling the actual words of the Creator.

Let it not be supposed that Sholem loved only the more learned disciples. He loved all the Chassidim and took them all under his protection. One day, for instance, some one protested that one of the Chassidim was a great glutton and would eat a whole goose at one sitting.

"Never mind," said the holy Reb Sholem in defence of the Chassid, "Let us not forget that that is the only passion he has." And indeed blessed is the man who has no worse passions!

It is true that no respectable person ought to be a glutton. But you often reproach us Chassidim with not being respectable people at all. How do you make out that we are not respectable? —Well, you say, a respectable man will keep his promise. He looks upon his pledged word as something sacred. But the Chassidim?—They are not put out in the least when they break a promise. Yes, you respectable people, when you promise something, even if it be to Satan himself, you do not hesitate to carry it out. I do not doubt that. And in the same way with us many a *silken* young man lets himself be persuaded now and again and promises the Tempter that he will commit this or that sin. But then he immediately reconsiders the matter, commits no sin and is quite unconcerned at having broken a promise he had made to the Tempter. So we Chassidim are not really respectable people. We gladly acknowledge it.

But to make up for this we have at least one virtue which you cannot boast of. We are obstinate people, as we ought to be, especially when we have some good deed to perform. The same is true of us in all matters of Faith in which no one can dissuade us and nothing can shake our determination. Yes, obstinacy, *akshones*, that is our finest virtue at Belz. Every Chassid must first and foremost be *akshen*—obstinate. This is our highest principle. How we put it into effect will be immediately clear to you from the example of Mordche Pelts.

The Chassidim at Belz had a profound belief in the magic power of the holy Reb Sholem, a belief as boundless as the ocean. One day a *Tsaddik* arrived at Belz who was a stranger to the town. The holy Reb Sholem invited him to go for a drive round the town. The two saints strictly forbade anybody to accompany them on this trip. Why?—Well, so that they could discuss the mysteries of the Cabbala without anybody disturbing them. To be sure, the holy Baal-Shem had also sometimes gone for drives in this way with his most trusted followers, and so had the holy ARI himself.

But such prohibitions had no effect on Mordche Pelts. Not for anything in the world would Mordche Pelts be separated from his master for a single moment. He was incessantly at the saint's heels. And now that he could not ride openly with the saint, he did not hesitate to use guile. He got into the carriage by stealth and covered himself with straw. To such lengths did the Chassidim carry their devotion in those days, overcoming conventions and express commands!

For some time Mordche Pelts travelled unnoticed in the straw, like a lord, until the moment came when he found himself in an unpleasant situation. If you have ever had occasion to hide yourself in straw you will understand his plight and will not be cross with him. Suddenly something began tickling his nose, and although he struggled like a lion, he could not hold out indefinitely. Finally a great sneeze burst forth from his pent up lungs: "He-tishu!" and the straw went flying in all directions.

"Get out!" shouted the visiting saint at poor Mordche Pelts, "Or I shall cast your soul into deepest Hell."

But Mordche Pelts would not give in.

"What if you do cast me into Hell?!" he retorted. "Our holy Reb Sholem will haul me out again immediately."

When the holy Reb Sholem—may his merits protect us—heard this answer, he smiled and said:

"You stay where you are, Mordche!"

And Mordche Pelts did stay where he was. Upon my soul, he did. What a magnificently obstinate fellow he was, and what faith he had!

It is a well known fact that a saint will lead his Chassidim all the way to the Garden of Eden in the other world. Moreover this will be quite a simple operation. The Chassidim will catch hold of his *gartel*, his belt I mean, and he will then pull them all into paradise hanging on to his belt.

There are other ways in which the belt is a very important instrument for a true Chassid. It is a thick cord of black silk which we wind round the waists of our *bekish* (caftans). The ends of the belt are ornamented with handsome fringes. It must be sufficiently long to encircle the waist three times. We wear it the whole day long. It is particularly important that we should not be without it at prayer, when we are studying the Law, and during meals. The Talmud declares that it is only the upper part of the human body—the head, chest and hands—which is created in the image of God. In the lower part, with its functions of digestion and secretion, a man is similar to an animal. The belt thus demarcates the boundary between the godly part and the animal part of a man and prevents *the heart from seeing shame*. When we put on our belts in the morning we say a charming benediction: "Blessed be the Lord our God, King of the world, who hast girt Israel about with strength and power!"

Take care that no one ever makes a knot in your belt! During prayer the Devil moves round a man's waist at his belt. If it has a knot in it he could stop there and snatch away your prayer.

Furthermore the letters in the word *sheker*, which means a *lie*, are the same as the letters in the word *kesher*, a *knot*. Everything about a Chassid has to be truthful. Therefore the genuine fervour of our prayers must not be disturbed, even by a small knot in our belts.

For a similar reason we Chassidim of Belz walk about with

our chests partially uncovered, both in winter and summer—to help us remember that *the heart must always be open.*

We are also careful to see that in taking our phylacteries off our arms, we do not cover the knot. The knot on the phylactery reminds us not of lies, but of the Truth. By its shape it recalls the first letter of the Hebrew word for God. This letter is called *yod* and looks exactly like a little knot. Similarly the word "Jew" in Yiddish sounds exactly like the first letter of the name of God: *Yod.* That is the reason why we may not cover the knot on the phylactery. For a Jew, a *Yod, has to be open and has always to act without guile.*

The phylactery is wound round the arm seven times. We Chassidim do the winding away from ourselves, away from our bodies. Our adversaries wind towards themselves, towards their bodies. They do it this way because they are selfish, and only think of themselves, whereas we think first and foremost of our neighbours and their happiness. That is the reason why we wind the phylacteries away from ourselves and towards our neighbours.

Phylacteries are an infinitely sacred commandment of God. If we were to place all the other commandments and laws on one side of the scale and put the phylacteries on the other, the latter would outweigh all the other commandments of God. By means of these black phylacteries, we bind on to our arms and heads four little paragraphs from the Holy Scriptures, sewn into little black leather cubes. Their beautifully written Hebrew letters radiate invisible rays which penetrate directly into our brains and hearts. They bring us closer to God and neutralize the harmful outside influences. He who does not bind them on himself incurs the grievous curses of the holy Rabbis. God also has His phylacteries.[1]

The phylacteries of course may only be worn by a person who is perfectly pure in body and soul. Does not each of those little black cubes contain parchment with holy writing wherein the most sacred name of God is repeated twenty-one times? When we

[1] Those who desire more detailed information on this subject should read my article on phylacteries in the international *Freudian* psychoanalytical journal *IMAGO*, Volume XVI, 1930, pages 435–85.

are wearing our phylacteries we must concentrate our thoughts totally and unceasingly on the content of this writing. This is not easy. Inside these cubes it is written how God permeates all the worlds with His holy power, how He redeems the faithful from the yoke of evil and how everywhere and for all time He remains undisturbed in His holy oneness. It is also written there that we are to love Him with all our heart, with all our soul and in all circumstances, and that we must faithfully fulfil His sacred commandments. There is also something written there about rewards and punishments. So we have plenty to think about when the phylacteries are on our bodies! If a person does not have all these things in his thoughts the whole time, the phylacteries are of no use to him: *It is as if he had bound stones to his head and arms!* At the same time, of course, we are required to think about the words of the prayers. But then it is only during services that the phylacteries are worn. How earnestly we have to think about the prayers! Before you can read this one page we should have read ten pages in the prayer book. Read them, did I say? No!—we fly through them. We pronounce every sound properly and yet fly from letter to letter, from world to world, like lightning. Our little soul jumps into each precious letter as one might jump into a swimming bath. It dives in with all its love and all its fear —those are its wings—with all its strength and feeling—those are its legs—and once again it jumps out of one letter like a flea and jumps into the next one. (An honest flea has no wings, do you say?—Then you don't know the Chassidic fleas, the little beasts!) And when the soul has flown through all these letters, all these thousands of worlds, it is purged and will be redeemed. That is how we Chassidim serve God every day of our lives. At the same time we do not think merely about the simple sense of the words and sentences! We also remember what the Talmud says about this or that place, and how a saint expounded this or that verse. We do not stop for a single moment. The whole time we keep rushing farther and farther, higher and higher. As for the saints—how much more do they think about during prayers: the sublime mysteries of the Cabbala which are so diffcult that it is impossible to describe them! You only have to take a look at the Holy ARI's commentary to the prayer book! Your head turns as though you were on a merry-go-round.

Through the ocean of substance we creep, useless *drops of evil-smelling drift.* more slowly and lazily than the clumsy shad-fish making its way through the slime at the bottom of deep pools. But prayers that spring from ecstasy—perhaps you too have sometimes experienced such moments—raise us above all worlds, material and spiritual, back to that original point in which everything is contained, all worlds, times and ages, all souls, all spirits, the entire law of God and all its mysteries, everything, every little thing, like the tree in the seed. Everything in one unique indivisible unity! And this original point is the first word of the mystic, sacred Scriptures: BEₖESHIS—At the Beginning. From this, from this word, all Creation has crept forth like the snail from his little house, and thither we flee for all eternity when times are at their worst for our souls. Only please do not think that in passing on to you this my cogitation about fleas, shad-fish and snails, these unclean and forbidden animals, I merely want to vex you. Know then that just as God has created us in His own holy image, so He has also created the unclean beasts in a particular likeness—that of mysterious worlds, and for the sole purpose of instructing us. Every animal in its own kind is created in the image of some former world, and before our world was created there was quite a number of these worlds. But do not expect me to tell you about this too because these things are great mysteries.

I do not want to bore you by repeating things that are well known. I have told you that already. But I must say a word about another very important commandment. This will help you to understand the very charming incident which the holy Reb Sholem used to relate. First of all, then, regarding the commandment.

It concerns the washing of hands. We perform this duty as follows: First we pour some clean water into a pot, but before doing so we must make sure that the pot is intact. It would never do to pour the water into a flower-pot—which has a hole in the bottom. Next, there must be no notches on the rim of the pot. The edge must be as even as the knife we use for killing animals. We take the pot of water in the right hand; from the right hand we put it into the left hand, and from the left hand we tip half the water over the right hand. We then take the pot into the right hand and with the right hand we pour the rest of the water over the left hand. We rub our hands together and bless God "that He has sanctified us with His commandments and ordered us to wash our hands", after which we wipe our hands thoroughly. Throughout the entire holy ceremony we carry a towel over the left arm. A proper Chassid always carries a towel in addition to a handkerchief. When wiping our hands we must keep the left hand continuously covered by the towel. Not everybody knows this, but it is very important. Only when we have washed our hands in this way and wiped them really thoroughly and conscientiously can we finally bless the bread and eat.

If you do not cut your nails every Friday before the Sabbath, you must examine them before washing your hands, to make sure they are not dirty; if they are the least bit dirty your act of washing could be considered invalid. When you cut your nails, you must be careful to see that not a single piece of nail gets lost; all the bits must be burnt at once, otherwise you will have to look for them after you are dead. When burning your nails you must not forget to put two small pieces of wood in with them as witnesses.

There are great and sublime mysteries in the washing of hands. Any one who dips into the mystic writings of the Holy ARI will soon realize this, always granting of course that he understands them.

There is one great secret in the washing of hands which you will not find even in the writings of the Holy ARI. In every generation there is only one saint whom Heaven has inspired to know this secret.

If you do not wash your hands before eating in the way laid down by the law you put yourself in dire danger. The Talmud warns us of this when it relates the terrible story of what happened to a certain guest.

This individual came to an inn and ordered dinner. The innkeeper noticed that he did not wash his hands before partaking of bread and inferred from this that the man was not a Jew but a Greek or Armenian, in short, a Gentile. He therefore gave him pork and green vegetables. This ghastly mistake only became apparent after the meal.

It can thus be seen that every sin leads directly to another, still worse sin.

He who is negligent in the washing of hands will incur grievous punishment after death—a punishment inflicted only on murderers who have spilt the blood of an innocent man. The souls of such persons will be spirited away to a waterfall. In summer and winter torrential water will stream down on them without interruption, without relief. Special *malignant* messengers from God will be entrusted with the task of watching over the poor condemned souls, to make sure that they are not able for a single moment to escape their just sentence, until their guilt has been washed away and atoned for.

On the other hand, the man who throughout his life has properly observed the commandment concerning the washing of hands in all its details will obtain rewards in paradise which cannot be taken away from him.

The holy Reb Sholem used to tell the following story: "There was once a great sinner. Throughout his life this sinner did not do a single good deed. He sinned continuously and forgot about God. However there was one commandment which he always obeyed faithfully, as his mother had taught him in childhood: the washing of hands before meals. Strange to relate, he clung to this commandment pertinaciously.

"One day he went on a far journey and became very hungry. He had plenty of bread with him but no water for washing his hands. He knew there was a spring in the forest not far away, but he also knew that this forest was infested with robbers who killed without mercy all who came within their reach. So the unfortunate sinner preferred to continue his journey without having anything to eat. But his hunger pressed ever more cruelly upon him.

" 'Suppose I die of hunger?' he thought. 'How foolish I am, still refusing to eat with unwashed hands at a time like this! After all, it's only a small, unimportant commandment of the Rabbis, and I have many, many worse sins on my conscience. Besides, the Law allows us to eat anything if it means saving our lives.'

"So the poor man took a slice of bread out of his knapsack and was just about to bite into it, but in the last moment his courage failed him and his hand dropped.

" 'No, no,' he said to himself. 'This is the only commandment I have never yet broken. I will not do so now, whatever happens! I would prefer to take the risk and go into the forest. If they kill me—they kill me. But I will not eat bread with unwashed hands!'

"Nor did he. He went into the forest for water and there he was killed.

"Thus it came about that his sinful soul appeared before the court of Heaven.

"When a person leaves this world for all eternity, in that very hour all his deeds go on before him. They say to him: You did this and this on such and such a day, at such and such a place. And he answers: Yes. And they say to him: Sign!—And he signs. So it is written in the holy Talmud.

"So it was with this sinner; all his deeds accompanied him. They were terrible sins indeed. There was no end to them. But because all his life he had observed the commandment about the washing of hands, even to the point of sacrificing his life for it, everything was forgiven him. The gate of Mercy was opened to him and he was received among the righteous."

"If such a hardened sinner as this man was received into paradise," the holy Reb Sholem would conclude, "if such a man was allowed into paradise for no other reason than that he had sacrificed his life for a single commandment, how great is the reward awaiting those who devote their whole lives to the performance of good deeds, as God and His holy men of learning have commanded us!"

I have already had occasion to show how Reb Sholem of Belz never became arrogant on account of his learning which, he said, he had acquired through his faithful Malkele. Nor did his knowledge of the fact that there were so many famous men among his ancestors incline him to become haughty. On the contrary: the very realization of this served him as a source of humility and modesty.

One day he received a visit from a learned man who was himself also perfect—for he was a *Tsaddik*—only his parents and all his ancestors had been simple folk. This "self-made man" had got it into his head that Reb Sholem had cut him, and had ascribed this to his humble origin. In reality, of course, this had only seemed to be the case. The kindly Reb Sholem never cut any one. How much less would he behave so discourteously towards a man who had himself attained such virtues as this *Tsaddik*! Nevertheless the latter still continued to bear a grudge in his heart. With the intuitiveness of his holy spirit Reb Sholem sensed that his guest still harboured resentment. "Our learned men of blessed memory," he remarked to the *Tsaddik*, "have told us in the Talmud that it is always our duty to ask ourselves this question: 'When do my deeds approach the greatness of the deeds of my ancestors?' From this it is clear that a man whose ancestors were neither holy nor learned is happier than a man with distinguished ancestors. The former never needs to feel ashamed in front of his ancestors. For me, however, it is more difficult," continued Reb Sholem, "I did have ancestors of distinction, so I must always feel ashamed in front of them, for I know that I am still very far from approaching their perfection."

If the holy Reb Nachman of Brazlav declares that true humility is only attained by a man who can say of himself with a pure conscience that he is humble, this statement is true in full measure of our holy Reb Sholem. When Reb Jacob Yitzhak, the Seer of Lublin, was still an ordinary Chassid, a saint once came to Lublin to see him.

"Is it true," the saint inquired of the Seer of Lublin, "that one nificant controversy.[5] These debates were fueled in the 1970s by challenges to state marriage laws, and in the late 1980s by the spread of AIDS, which made clear the value of monogamous relationships. The legislative and judicial context of the current debate will likely require a more formal resolution than was required by those earlier contexts.

When court proceedings become the focal point of competing large-scale interests of citizens—as was earlier true of the *Griswold* and the *Bowers* proceedings—the resultant decisions become definitive for the lives of citizens far beyond those directly involved in the case. In the 1973 case *Roe* v. *Wade,* the parameters within which Americans dealt with abortion were fixed in a way very different from the way they had been prior to the *Roe* decision. The *Griswold* and *Bowers* cases likewise set parameters within which Americans have subsequently lived. The same is sure to be true also of the ultimate judicial resolution of the same-sex marriage issue. In November 1996, print and broadcast media hurried to exploit the fashionability of the issue. *Newsweek's* cover for November 4, 1996, featured singer Melissa Etheridge and her pregnant partner, Julie Cypher, in a mutual embrace and staring defiantly toward the camera; the caption on the cover read, "We're Having a Baby," with subcaptions "Can Gay Families Gain Acceptance?" and "What It's Like for the Kids." Similarly, *Harper's* magazine for November 1996 featured a cover picture of two gay men nuzzling each other: the title of *Harper's* cover story was "Wedded to an Illusion: Do Gays and Lesbians Really Want the Right to Marry?" Likewise, television "news magazines" have recently done features on same-sex marriage. Political attention to the issue has also been much in the news, resulting in the Defense of Marriage Act. Cultural controversy about this issue seems, as of this writing, near its apex, but the final judicial decision remains to be made, Whatever the outcome of those proceedings, its impact on American society will be great, perhaps as great as the *Roe* decision. As legal abortion has become common throughout American society, likewise a judicial resolution favoring same sex marriage likely would result eventually in social acceptance of lesbians and gays in stable relationships; they could live together among other American families and pursue their own versions of the American dream, including parenting their own children.

The goal of this volume of essays is to present a representative sample of diverse and well-informed opinion. The perspectives represented in this collection cover the views of the radical gays and lesbians, of conventional heterosexuals who think their fundamental traditions are undermined by homosexual relationships of any kind, and of those gay and lesbian couples who desire legal legitimacy for their relationships.

We have divided the collection into four parts. The first contains the text of the Defense of Marriage Act, along with two senators' responses, one in opposition and one in support.

Part Two, "Emotional Dimensions of the Debate," seeks to capture the more personal, emotional, and occasionally visceral ways this issue affects individuals. Its dimensions are those people actually live with when they are confronted with sexually significant same-sex relationships in their own lives, or when they face the imminent prospect of having married same-sex couples as neighbors.

Part Three, "The Philosophical Arguments," focuses on considerations frequently brought forward in justification of the various perspectives people take on the issue of same-sex marriage. These considerations include different kinds of religious perspectives; philosophical arguments; and a wide variety of moral, social, political, and cultural arguments. We have not tried to divide this section into more specific subsections primarily because we believe that most of the selections dealing with this issue in what might be conventionally called "a philosophical manner" are essays in which these different perspectives crisscross and overlap in ways that make very difficult the sorting of them as primarily "philosophical," "religious," "political," and so on. We have chosen here from a wide variety of perspectives and from authors who are fervent in representing their respective views and constituencies. This section we take to be the heart of the collection, because it makes available a representative sample of the arguments advanced in defense of the various perspectives.

Part Four, "The Hawaii Case," makes available some prominent materials that represent judicial thought about same-sex marriage to date. Of special interest in this section is the Report of the Hawaii Commission on Sexual Orientation and the Law, which was appointed by the Hawaii legislature to make recommendations to the legislature about the issue; included also is the minority report of the commission.

As with previous volumes in this Contemporary Issues series, we hope these selections will be taken seriously by a wide variety of Americans. Each of us, after all, should be able to acknowledge that most of our fellow citizens, including those who have interests and traditions different from our own, are at least well intentioned in seeking to understand and accommodate, to the extent they are able to do so, the interests and traditions of Americans unlike themselves.

NOTES

1. Lobel was quoted in a press release on the National Gay and Lesbian Task Force web site. Contacts listed on the press release were Robert Bray (rbray@ngltf.org) and Tracey Conaty (tconaty@ngltf.org).

2. Knight was quoted in a press release on the Family Research Council web site. The contact listed on the release was Kristi S. Hamrick—202 393-2100 x3017.

3. One lesbian thinker who would likely have this perspective is Monique Wittig. See her "The Straight Mind," in *The Straight Mind and Other Essays,* quoted in Cheshire Calhoun, "Separating Lesbian Theory from Feminist Theory," *Ethics* 104 (April 1994): 558–81. (See especially 563–66.)

4. An edited version of *Bowers* v. *Hardwick* that makes clear the Court's reasoning is available in *Homosexuality: Debating the Issues* (Amherst, N.Y.: Prometheus Books, 1995), pp. 97–102.

5. See Infanti's "*Baehr* v. *Lewin*: A Step in the Right Direction for Gay Rights?" *Law and Sexuality: A Review of Lesbian and Gay Legal Issues* 4 (1994): 3.

Part One

THE DEFENSE OF MARRIAGE ACT

1.

THE TEXT

ONE HUNDRED FOURTH CONGRESS
SECOND SESSION
JANUARY 3, 1996

Be it enacted by the Senate and House Representatives of the United States of America in Congress assembled,

Section 1. Short Title.

This act may be cited as the 'Defense of Marriage Act'.

Sec. 2. Powers Reserved to the States.

(a) IN GENERAL—Chapter 115 of title 28, United States Code, is amended by adding after section 1738B the following:

Sec. 1738C. Certain acts, records, and proceedings and the effect thereof

No State, territory, or possession of the United States, or Indian tribe, shall be required to give effect to any public act, record, or judicial proceeding of any other State, territory, possession, or tribe respecting a relationship between persons of the same sex that is treated as a marriage under the laws of such other State, territory, possession, or tribe, or a right or claim arising from such relationship. . . .

Sec. 3. Definition of Marriage.

(a) IN GENERAL—Chapter 1 of title 1, United States Code, is amended by adding at the end the following:

Sec. 7. Definition of 'marriage' and 'spouse'

In determining the meaning of any Act of Congress, or of any ruling, regulation, or interpretation of the various administrative bureaus and agencies of the United States, the word 'marriage' means only a legal union between one man and one woman as husband and wife, and the word 'spouse' refers only to a person of the opposite sex who is a husband or a wife.

2.

THE HON. HENRY A. WAXMAN: IN OPPOSITION

Thursday, July 11, 1996

The House in Committee of the Whole House on the State of the Union had under consideration the bill (H.R. 3396) to define and protect the institution of marriage:

Mr. WAXMAN. Mr. Chairman, I rise in strong opposition to H.R. 3396, the so-called Defense of Marriage Act, and ask my colleagues to reject this mean-spirited legislation.

The proponents of H.R. 3396 would have us believe that this legislation is necessary to save the institution of marriage. The real purpose of H.R. 3396 is to create a wedge issue for Republicans for the upcoming elections.

In a shameless attempt to divide the American public, the Republican party is espousing official bigotry. It is promoting discrimination against individuals who seek the same responsibilities and opportunities other Americans seek when they form a lifelong union with someone they love. It is scapegoating a segment of our society to fan the flames of intolerance and prejudice. And it is doing this to try to improve its standings in the polls.

Discrimination against people who are gay and committed to one another does nothing to defend marriage or to strengthen family values. It does, however, continue to deny them legal rights that married couples simply take for granted—inclusion in a spouse's health insurance plan, pension and tax benefits, the ability to participate in medical decisions, and the right to visit a dying spouse in the hospital.

Our nation's families deserve better from their leaders than this cynical effort to raise fears and create divisions for political gain. They need leaders who will recognize the true needs of families and who are willing to work for adequate healthcare, access to educational opportunities, a decent wage, and a livable environment.

Let's work together on the real challenges we face as a nation. Let's not allow our Republican leaders to create scapegoats to distract the public's attention from the failure of this Congress to address issues the American public cares about.

I urge my colleagues to stand up to bigotry and discrimination. I urge you to vote against this mean-spirited legislation.

3.

THE HON. JESSE HELMS: IN SUPPORT

September 9, 1996

Mr. HELMS. Mr. President, during my years in the Senate I have been privileged on many occasions to work with a substantial number of ministers whose Washington churches today are referred to as "African-American."

The day before the Senate adjourned for the August recess, I ran into one of these fine ministers over in the Russell Building. His church is Baptist. He has a booming, cheerful voice. And when I heard that voice, I knew who it was. He was saying, "Are you going home tomorrow?" And I told him I thought I was since the Senate probably would recess for the month of August.

I asked him, Mr. President, if he had a message for the folks back home. And he said, "I sure do. Tell them that God created Adam and Eve—not Adam and Steve."

Some may chuckle at this good-natured minister's humor. But he meant exactly what he was saying. In fact, it was a sort of sermonette. The truth is, he was hitting the nail on the head, if you want to use that cliché, or telling it like it is. However one may choose to describe this minister's getting down to the nitty-gritty, it was no mere cliché, Mr. President. There could not have been, as a matter of fact, a better way to begin this debate in favor of the Defense of Marriage Act, which is H.R. 3396. The formal debate will begin tomorrow morning in this Chamber, the U.S. Senate.

Now, then, let there be no mistake about it, this bill in no way, to any degree, is the kind of legislation which homosexual and lesbian leaders have disdainfully described as a, to use their words, "hate-driven bill."

In fact, it is precisely the critics of H.R. 3396 who are demanding that homosexuality be considered as just another lifestyle—these are the people who seek to force their agenda upon the vast majority of Americans who reject the homosexual lifestyle.

Indeed, Mr. President, the pending bill—the Defense of Marriage Act—will safeguard the sacred institutions of marriage and the family from those who seek to destroy them and who are willing to tear apart America's moral fabric in the process.

Isn't it disheartening, Mr. President, that Congress must clarify the traditional definition of marriage? But inch by inch, little by little, the homosexual lobby has chipped away at the moral stamina of some of America's courts and some legislators, in order to create the shaky ground that exists today that prompts this legislation being the subject of debate tomorrow morning in the U.S. Senate.

Just think, the prospect of a sovereign state's being compelled to recognize same-sex marriages sanctioned in another state is incredibly stark. If Hawaii's supreme court legalizes same-sex marriages in Hawaii, does the full faith and credit clause of the Constitution compel the other forty-nine states to recognize the new marriage law within their jurisdictions? I say no.

Such a suggestion, Mr. President, is a cockeyed interpretation of the Constitution, and this is one of so many times that I have wished the late, great Senator Sam J. Ervin, Jr., were here to cut it down to size. Homosexuals and lesbians boast that they are close to realizing their goal—legitimizing their behavior.

Mr. President, Bill Bennett has championed the cause of preserving America's culture; he contends that we are already reaping the consequences of the devaluation of marriage. And he warns that "it is exceedingly imprudent to conduct a radical, untested, and inherently flawed social experiment on an institution that is the keystone and the arch of civilization."

Bill Bennett is everlastingly right, and I believe the American people in the majority understand that the Defense of Marriage Act is vitally important. It will establish a simple, clear federal definition of marriage as the legal union of one man and one woman, and it will exempt sovereign states from being compelled by a half-baked interpretation of the U.S. Constitution to recognize same-sex marriages wrongfully legalized in another state.

If the Senate, tomorrow, makes the mistake of approving the Employment Nondiscrimination Act proposed by the senator from Massachusetts,* it will pave the way for liberal judges to threaten the business policies of countless American employers, and, in the long run, put in question the legality of the Defense of Marriage Act. The homosexual lobby knows this and that is why there is such a clamor favoring adoption of the Kennedy bill.

Mr. President, at the heart of this debate is the moral and spiritual survival of this nation. Alexis de Tocqueville said a century and a half ago that America had grown great because America was good. Mr. de Tocqueville also warned

---

*I.e., Senator Edward Kennedy (D-Mass.)

that if America made the mistake of ceasing to be good, America would cease to be great.

So, we must confront the question posed long ago: "Quo Vadis, America?"

The Senate is about to answer that question. We will decide whither goeth America. It is solely up to us.

Part Two

THE EMOTIONAL DIMENSIONS OF THE DEBATE

4.

A (PERSONAL) ESSAY ON SAME-SEX MARRIAGE

Barbara J. Cox

Very little since Stonewall,* and the break from accepting the status quo that those riots symbolize, has challenged the lesbian and gay community as much as the debate we have had over the past several years on whether seeking the right to marry should be the focus of our community's efforts, political influence, and financial resources. As is often true in most such political debates, both "sides" to the debate make important arguments about the impact that the right to marry will have on each member of our community, on the community as a whole, and on our place in society. . . .

One way to expand this debate is to read the interviews of lesbian and gay couples, some of whom have chosen to have public ceremonies celebrating their commitment and some of whom have chosen to keep their commitment private.

The debate continues to rage, as seen from the recent articles contained in the *Virginia Law Review*'s symposium issue. Without resolving the debate here, it seems clear that obtaining the right to marry will drastically impact the lesbian and gay civil rights movement. My response to the debate is best expressed in the following short (and personal) essay, explaining the vital political change that can result from the simple (and personal) act of same-sex marriage.

Yes, I know that weddings can be "heterosexual rituals" of the most repressive and repugnant kind. Yes, I know that weddings historically symbolized the loss of the woman's self into that of her husband's, a denial of her ex-

This article originally appeared as notes 10, 11, and 12 in Barbara J. Cox, "Same-Sex Marriage and Choice-of-Law: If We Marry in Hawii, Are We Still Married When We Return Home?" *Wisconsin Law Review* (1994): 1033. Copyright 1994 by the Board of the Regents of the University of Wisconsin System. Reprinted by permission of the Wisconsin Law Review.

*The gay and lesbian riot began early in the morning of June 28, 1969, when police raided the Stonewall bar in Greenwich Village. It sparked gay and lesbian activity around the world. (Eds.)

istence completely. Yes, I know that weddings around the world continue to have that impact on many women and often lead to lives of virtual slavery. Yes, I know. Then how could a feminist, out, radical lesbian like myself get married a year ago last April? Have I simply joined the flock of lesbians and gay men rushing out to participate in a meaningless ceremony that symbolizes heterosexual superiority?

I think not.

When my partner and I decided to have a commitment ceremony, we did so to express the love and caring that we feel for one another, to celebrate that love with our friends and family, and to express that love openly and with pride. It angers me when others, who did not participate or do not know either of us, condemn us as part of a mindless flock accepting a dehumanizing ceremony. But more, it distresses me that they believe their essentialist vision of weddings explains all—because they have been to weddings, both straight and queer, they can speak as experts on their inherent nature.

Perhaps these experts should consider the radical aspect of lesbian marriage or the transformation that it makes on the people around us. As feminists, we used to say that "the personal is political." Have we lost that vision of how we can understand and change the world?

My commitment ceremony was not the mere "aping" of the bride that I supposedly spent my childhood dreaming of becoming. (In fact, I was a very satisfied tomboy who never once considered marriage.) My ceremony was an expression of the incredible love and respect that I have found with my partner. My ceremony came from a need to speak of that love and respect openly to those who participate in my world.

Some of the most politically "out" experiences I have ever had happened during those months of preparing for and having that ceremony. My sister and I discussed for weeks whether she would bring her children to the ceremony. Although I had always openly brought the women I was involved with home with me, I had never actually sat down with my niece and nephews to discuss those relationships. My sister was concerned that her eldest son, particularly, might scorn me, especially at a time when he and his friends tended toward "faggot" jokes. After I expressed how important it was for me to have them attend, she tried to talk with her son about going to this euphemistically entitled "ceremony." He kept asking why my partner and I were having a "ceremony" and she kept hedging. Finally he just said, "Mom, Barb's gay, right?" She said yes, they all came, and things were fine. Her youngest son sat next to me at dinner after the ceremony trying to understand how it worked. "You're married, right?" "Yes." "Who's the husband?" "There is no husband." "Are you going to have children?" "No." "So there's no husband and no children but you're married, right?" "Yes." "Okay," and he happily turned back to his dinner.

My partner invited her large Catholic family to the ceremony. We all know how the pope feels about us. Despite that, her mother and most of her siblings, some from several states away, were able to attend. Her twin brother later told us that our ceremony led him to question and resolve the discomfort that had plagued his relationship with his sister for many years.

As a law professor leaving town early for the ceremony, I told my two classes (one of ninety-five and one of twenty students) that I was getting "married" to my partner, who is a woman. (I actually used "married" because saying I was getting "committed" just didn't quite have the right ring to it.) The students in one of my classes joined together to buy my partner and myself a silver engraved frame that says "Barb and Peg, Our Wedding." My colleagues were all invited to the ceremony and most of them attended. One of them spoke to me of the discussion they had within their family explaining to their children that they were going to a lesbian wedding.

How can anyone view these small victories in coming out and acceptance as part of flocking to imitate, or worse join, an oppressive heterosexual institution? Is it not profoundly transformative to speak so openly about lesbian love and commitment? The impact was so wide-ranging, not just on my partner and myself, but on our families, our friends, and even the clerks in the jewelry stores when we explained we were looking for wedding rings for both of us. Or on the two hundred people who received my mother's annual xeroxed Christmas letter with a paragraph describing the ceremony. Or the clerk in the store who engraved the frame for my students. Or the young children who learned that same-sex marriage exists.

Yes, we must be aware of the oppressive history that weddings symbolize. We must work to ensure that we do not simply accept whole-cloth an institution that symbolizes the loss and harm felt by women. But I find it difficult to understand how two lesbians, standing together openly and proudly, can be seen as accepting that institution. What is more anti-patriarchal and rejecting of an institution that carries the patriarchal power imbalance into most households than clearly stating that women can commit to one another with no man in sight? With no claim of dominion or control, but instead of equality and respect. I understand the fears of those who condemn us for our weddings, but I believe they fail to look beyond the symbol and cannot see the radical claim we are making.

5.

ADAM AND EVE, NOT ADAM AND HENRY

Jeffrey Hart

Being nasty to homosexuals is certainly not on the agenda of any decent person. Whatever it is homosexuals do in private is best left private. Our problem at the moment, however, is homosexual cultural aggression.

One major segment of that is the drive to make homosexual companionships legally "marriages." The focus has been the recent legal fight in Hawaii.*

But before we get into that, a point about the nature of language:

Language is normative. Its meanings and connotations communicate values. Thus everyone knows what the word "marriage" means. It means what it has always meant.

Millennia of human experience have demonstrated that marriage is the best arrangement for bringing up children and communicating to them the substance of a culture.

Recently, the old truths have been reinforced by researchers, who have marked the disastrous results of single-parent upbringing, dysfunctional families and so forth.

Aside from the civilizational value of marriage, it does not take much experience to discern that females and males are naturally complementary.

But along comes Hawaii, where a state court is expected this summer [1996] to legalize homosexual "marriages."

If the state court does hand down the decision, it likely would be appealed to the Supreme Court, where no one knows what will result.

If homosexual "marriages" become legal in Hawaii, the other forty-nine states might well have to honor—if that is the word—such arrangements. The U.S. Constitution requires that each state afford "full faith and credit" to "the public acts, records and judicial proceedings of every other state."

*See chapter 26.

Viewing that prospect with distaste, nineteen state legislatures are considering legislation that would bar out-of-state homosexual marriages.

Just what is at stake?

Currently, homosexuals living together can avail themselves of most of the practical benefits of a genuine marriage arrangement. They can endorse any sort of a legal contract binding upon both of them, such as agreed-upon penalties if they stop living together. They can put one another in their wills, or they can agree to leave joint property to any charity or trust they desire. They can own property together, under agreed-upon terms about what happens to it. They can make each other the beneficiary of life insurance.

The homosexuals pushing for legalized "marriage" know all that. What they want is legal and social equality with what has always been understood to be marriage.

Homosexuality in virtually all cultures has been frowned upon and sometimes condemned. The universal vote of human experience has gone against it.

It certainly is true throughout the Hebrew Bible. The paradigmatic couple in Genesis is named "Adam and Eve." The representation is valid not just because it is in the Bible, but in the Bible because it is valid. It is amusing to imagine what would have been the response from the rabbis in the Temple of Jerusalem if a theological poet had shown up with a proposal for Genesis featuring a first couple named "Adam and Henry."

In Canto XV of Dante's *Inferno,* he writes a great poem of personal love and pity for his older master in literature, Brunetto Latini. He loves Brunetto for his writing, but pities him and condemns him for his crime against nature. He is in Dante's *Inferno* because in life he was in his private inferno.

In Elizabethan England, homosexual acts were punishable by death.

Perhaps strange to say, Oscar Wilde can be understood as participating in the general negative judgment. His paradoxical wit consisted of jokes against the norm. He said things such as "Niagara Falls would be more interesting if it flowed upward." If Dante's Brunetto was tragic, Wilde's sense of homosexuality was comic. In his homosexual persona he was a society clown.

Human culture, for millennia, has been "homophobic"—a strange new coinage that tries to make disapproval of homosexuality equivalent to an illness, or phobia. That is, the normal is "ill."

No one would worry much about homosexuals today if so many of them had not become so aggressive. They want their aberration projected into education at all levels, celebrated in popular culture and honored in so-called marriages.

Well, the cup runneth over. It is time for legal, political, and cultural resistance to homosexual aggression.

6.

A LESBIAN FAMILY

Lindsy Van Gelder

Sarah is in most ways your basic five-year-old: a watcher of Charlie Brown videos, a reader of Richard Scarry books, a crayoner of cotton-puff clouds and fat yellow suns with Tinkertoy-spoke rays. Like every other piece of kindergarten artwork ever made, her portrait of "My Family" contains stick-figurey construction paper people, all holding hands and looking jolly. Except her family is a little different: there's Sarah, there's "Daddy," there's "Mommy" . . . and there's Amy, Mommy's lover.

Sarah's "cubby' at school is special, too. While the other kids hang their windbreakers and lunch boxes next to photos of one parent, or two, Sarah has three. She takes this embarrassment of riches in stride—which is to say, without any embarrassment at all.

Not that she isn't a very savvy little girl about the precisely calibrated degrees to which the many adults in her life fit into the larger scheme of things. If you ask her about the members of her "whole" (i.e., extended) family, she will tick off various grandmothers and cousins on her fingers. "Francis [her biological mother's ex-lover and now best friend] is in my family, too" she adds. "But Richard [her father's new boyfriend] isn't *exactly* in my family . . . yet." The adults around her would probably say the same thing, in many more words.

. . . [Sarah's] biological mother, Nancy, had interviewed a dozen potential gay and straight sperm donors before she and Amy met Doug and his then-boyfriend. Unlike many lesbian couples who decide to have a child, Nancy has no particular quarrel with the notion that a parent of each gender is a desirable thing. But in the original scenario, the women weren't necessarily looking for anything much more enduring than a turkey baster deposit. They simply wanted someone they could point to on the day their daughter asked where Daddy was.

This is an edited version of an article that originally appeared in *Ms.*, March/April 1991, pp. 44–47. Reprinted by permission of the author.

But something unexpected happened: a flowering of feeling that turned the American Gothic nuclear family progression on its head. Instead of two people meeting, falling in love, and having a baby, four people met, had a baby, and then became good friends.

In fact, their whole lives became entwined. At the time Nancy got pregnant, all the adults were entering their forties, both Amy and Doug were at career crossroads, and both couples were sick of the expense and hassle of living in New York City. The baby was both a symbol of the changes the adults were ready for and a catalyst to more. . . . The men had moved to the Southwest, where Doug spent his childhood, and the women were talking about following. Although it wasn't part of their original agreement, Doug insisted on helping with Sarah's financial support. . . . Recently, . . . we found Amy, Nancy, Sarah, and their two cats living down the street from Doug in an adobe house with a yard full of mesquite trees. Amy and Doug have pooled their resources and opened a café. He does most of the cooking; she takes care of most of the business end. Nancy meanwhile teaches at a nearby college. All three contribute to Sarah's expenses, although Amy—because she lives with Sarah and has a more flexible schedule than Nancy—is the primary caregiver in terms of time at the moment.

"It confuses the hell out of people," Amy notes cheerfully. "People come into the restaurant, and they see that Doug and I are partners, and then they see this little kid running around after school relating to both of us. Not surprisingly, they assume that Doug and I are married—which, of course, we both hate. Usually, I sit them down and just explain the story." Some people still don't quite get it. "I'm thinking of having palm cards made up," she jokes, "Maybe like, *Good afternoon, you have entered a Strange Other World.*"

Amy, Nancy, and Doug are completely out of the closet in their dealings with the straight community. They grudgingly elected to use pseudonyms in this article only after Nancy's mother asked them to. Nancy's mother has told all her relatives that Sarah was born out of a liaison between Nancy and a married man. "Somehow that's better than being in a happy, committed, lesbian relationship," Nancy sighs.

"I think it behooves us to be out, and even to boast about it, to show that it can work," says Doug. For Sarah's sake, the adults tend to like to deal with the gay issue up front, where it can be defused if need be. "When it came time to get a pediatrician, all three of us marched in—we didn't want some situation later on where the doctor didn't realize that all of us were in on this. It's the same thing now that we've been looking at elementary schools for next year. At interviews, our position is, 'This is our situation, and it's very important that Sarah get support on that if she needs it.' " At one school they considered, they got more than they asked for—several faculty members discreetly came out to them. . . .

Sarah's parents have had some rough times, however. The biggest rupture in their lives occurred when Doug and his longtime boyfriend messily broke up two years ago. Aside from the immediate trauma, the women worried that

Doug might find small-city gay single life intolerable and leave. "For a while he was dating someone here we were not crazy about as stepdaddy material, either," they confide. Then Doug met Richard, an elementary school substitute teacher who loves children. The two men are about to start living together.

"It sounds crass, but part of my getting together with Richard is about Sarah," Doug says. "If I were thirty-six, I probably would have cashed in my chips and left town. But at forty-six, I have different needs." In fact, Richard is now talking seriously with a lesbian woman—a close friend of Amy and Nancy, as it happens—about adding another child to the extended family. . . .

Not surprisingly, the adults in Sarah's life don't always agree. The funniest example was the time that Sarah snookered her father into buying her a "Wet 'n' Wild Barbie," only mentioning once they were safely past the checkout counter that the item wouldn't be remotely welcome at her house. The crisis was resolved by keeping Barbie at Daddy's. There have also been many, many jokes about possible Birkenstocks and flannel shirts that one might add to Barbie's wardrobe. Sarah later made all the adults laugh when she bought her father his own Ken doll for his birthday. Of course, now that Doug has Richard, Sarah has Ken. She is not a dumb kid.

Doug and Richard have occasionally hinted that Sarah gets away with too much at Nancy and Amy's house, and the women have occasionally felt a financial pinch when Doug is casual about paying his share of the child support money on time. But the splits are minor, and they're by no means consistently Boys Versus Girls. Amy and Doug are currently pushing for Sarah to go to private or Episcopal parochial school next year; Nancy thinks "every justification for sending kids to private school sounds just like what white people in the South historically use as excuses. Okay, maybe the reading scores in the public schools are lower, but maybe it's because a lot of the kids are Mexican Americans who grew up bilingual. It doesn't necessarily mean the education is worse."

Nancy also strenuously objected to the "girls in skirts" dress code required by the school Doug and Amy favor—a rule Amy wasn't thrilled with either. The three parents brought it up with the administration and ascertained that if Sarah were to wear a nice blouse and a pair of dressy pants instead of a skirt, the school wouldn't object. "But she'll wear a dress anyway, because she likes them," Doug smirks. "She's very femme."

One of the worst parts of parenting for Amy and Nancy is that their schedules leave them very little time to be alone together. Nancy's teaching requires her to be out of the house several nights a week, as well as on Sunday, the one day the café is closed. Doug previously took care of Sarah on a fairly irregular basis, and he unabashedly notes: "I never thought I had to deal with her shitty diapers to bond with her. I wanted the fun parts." But when Nancy and Amy asked him if he would keep Sarah every Sunday night, he was glad to help.

"I told Doug I was asking him this as a personal favor, having nothing to do with his relationship to Sarah," Amy jokes. "I told him that as his friend that he works with, I'll be a lot happier, and therefore he'll be a lot happier. Now when I come in Monday morning, there's lots of leering, and lots of *gee, Sarah and I went to McDonald's last night—what did YOU guys do, hmmmm?*"

But Amy and Nancy are quick to note that almost all their minor difficulties—from scheduled sex to sporadic conflicts about child-raising—are typical of those encountered by all parents. "There's almost nothing so far that's wrong because we're gay," says Nancy, "and a lot of what's right is because we're gay." For one thing, there's no ancient sexual bitterness between Sarah's biological mother and father of the sort that mars so much postdivorce parental jockeying.

One gay problem is health insurance: none of them has it. "We've talked about supplying benefits here at the restaurant," says Doug, "but that would only help Amy and me. We have no legal relationship, in the eyes of the insurance companies, with Nancy and Sarah."

"There's also weird stuff you have to think about," says Amy. "Like, when Sarah goes to other kids' houses, sometimes the kids take a bath together. Her friends' parents seem to be cool about us, but it's still the sort of thing I'd think twice about doing, because you just know it would only take one asshole to turn Naked Kids in Lesbian Home into something really sordid and horrible."

But when you ask them all if there's anything they would do over differently, the answer is: not much. "I'm glad I did it with a father that I know, and not a sperm bank," says Nancy. When Sarah was an infant, Nancy did go through a spell of jealousy of Doug's relationship with their child. "I didn't want to share her with him; I hardly knew him," she admits. "Then I told myself to just cool out and think of what was best for Sarah." Nancy adds that she might be less enthusiastic if Doug were an absentee father. "There's this whole Daddy Thing; Daddy gets to be Daddy, and all that that represents, no matter what he does or doesn't do, and kids—all kids—just plug into that. But in fact, Doug *is* lovely with her."

Nancy and Amy have also been lucky in other ways. Seven or eight years ago, when they began their search for a donor, AIDS was an established fact, but it was less discussed than it is now. Despite urgings from their friends, the women thought it would be presumptuously rude to ask Doug to take an HIV test. Recently, Nancy was reading the *New York Times* and happened upon the name of another man she'd asked to be a donor—someone who inexplicably stopped taking her calls. Now there he was on the obit page, dead of AIDS.

Of all the adults in Sarah's life, Amy is the one in the most vulnerable position. She has no legal claim on Sarah if she and Nancy ever break up (although gay civil rights groups are fighting for the rights of nonbiological lesbian mothers who are thus left with no recourse). Nancy and Doug's wills specify that if they were to die, they would want Amy to have custody, but it's a wish that grandparents or even the state could challenge in court. "It's too devastating to think about," says Amy. "So I don't."

She also finds terminology a problem. "I'll be at the grocery store and some clerk will ask me if Sarah's mine. Well, she is, damn it, even if that's not what they meant. I periodically sit Sarah down to make sure she's okay with this stuff. Like I recently said to her, 'You know, I'm not your mother, but I'm sort of like your parent.' She nodded and said, 'Right. Mommy is my mother. But I *am* your daughter.' "

At the preschool Sarah currently attends, the other kids tend to announce "Your Amy is here to pick you up." There are several other children in Sarah's class who have gay parents, and in one of the more open families, the nonbiological mother also happens to be named Amy. It's becoming a sort of generic honorific: Sarah and her friend Rex both go off after school with their Amys.

Perhaps things will be more awkward when Sarah is older, the adults say. But perhaps they won't be. Or, more likely, they will be, but only because most teenagers find *something* about their parents that's, like, totally gross. So far, so good.

Sarah's only recorded worry about the future is one that she shared with Nancy one day when she was trying to figure out how she could be a doctor and stay home with her own sick child. Nancy assured her that such things were eminently doable; she herself could baby-sit. Sarah sighed with relief, her grownup life secured.

"But," she suddenly asked, "where will I find a Daddy and an Amy?"

7.

I LEFT MY HUSBAND FOR THE WOMAN I LOVE

*Jane Doe**

"Are you going to marry the person you left him for?" she asked.

"The person is a woman," I said.

"How wonderful for you," she said. "But you don't fit the script. No one would know to look at you."

I have heard this many times. Even if nobody else said it, I would know it is true. Neither my appearance nor my "script" betrays that after twenty-five years of family life, I have left my marriage to live with the woman I love.

I wore a pink tutu with sequins when I was nine. At the prom I wore the required crinoline under my white, spaghetti-strapped prom formal. My first love was the captain of the football team, and I could not have been more crazy about him. With him I learned the ways of the body in wild scenes in the sail lockers at the end of the dock near where I lived. I had a typical suburban teenage career "making out" in convertibles.

Then I got married. At the wedding, there were my proud, ambivalent parents, who had protested the marriage, ironically because they had heard that my intended might be homosexual.

Once married, I finished various degrees, made soufflés, learned to use eye makeup, traveled from New York to Nepal, and changed lots of diapers.

Though I was too young to know what mature love was, I did love my husband when I married him. But a few years ago, as we sat eating prawns overlooking the Mediterranean, I wondered what would be left between us when the kids left home. I had known for years that I no longer loved him. My analyst had said, "Couldn't you try?" But how can you *try* to love someone? My eleven-year-old understood right away when I said I had not planned it this way. "No one can change love," he said.

This article originally appeared in *Ms.*, January 1988.

*Jane Doe is a pseudonym.

But most of the time the rapid pace of days took over and obliterated the question of whether love could last and whether it was necessary or important. I never thought that love and marriage were synonymous. For me, as long as there was no lasting outside love, the family came first. There was richness in family life, vitality and interest and fun. I was not looking for escape. I was not angry with my husband or disillusioned about love. Now, though I am not leaving the kids, the pain of breaking apart this family sometimes tears at my gut. I hate to see their sadness.

But when there is no love in marriage, and there *is* a lasting love outside it, everything changes. The center of the family is empty and the children know it. It is no favor to them to live a charade "for their sake." Ultimately it undermines their sense of emotional truth. What model for a child is a mother who stays to "serve" her children, sacrificing her inner life in a spirit of self-denial for kids she hopes will find their own full lives? I have seen that if you are honest with kids about feelings, though it may not be easy, they will understand even the act of leaving their father for someone of the same sex.

I did not leave, as some think, because I chose women over men. I have never thought that women are better than men, or that men have betrayed me. If I can pinpoint the important lack in my marriage, it is that my particular husband did not have the full range of emotional expression I need. I filled the gap with friends and other loves. I found that I felt things for others I did not feel for him. Until now, I never found one person with all the qualities that mattered to me, but I did find a kind of balance of riches among the people I cared about.

People who knew me as a woman with a twenty-five-year-old marriage and two kids have asked what it is like to love a woman. A male friend said he could understand everything but that part, since he could never love a man. I told him I love certain *people,* men and women, and this woman is the person I love best. I never closed out the idea that women are as interesting and lovable as men. I have known intense, passionate women, and I know that it was not their womanhood but their intensity and passion that attracted me.

The woman I love is the only person I have met with that combination of qualities I want in love. (I cannot answer whether a man could have them, too. Only that I have never met a man who does.) She is gentle and fiery, intelligent and sensitive, imaginative and energetic, wide awake and dreamy, funny and emotional, loving and clear-visioned. When I see her in bed next to me, I wonder by what miracle such a human being, man or woman, exists at all, and exactly how she got in my bed. Real love just is, without reason or motive.

People want to know if *our* sex is different from sex with men. Someone said, "Isn't it like making love to yourself?" To me, in spite of our both being female, we do not seem the same. We both know what it is like to love men and women. We feel the other as different. We listen closely to every nuance. It is not the physical difference from sex with men but the love in every gesture that makes it different. We have seen women couples who assume the roles of nurtured and nurturer, of stronger and weaker, of star and servant. We have no roles. We exchange moments of strength and vulnerability, of giving care and of being cared for. It's rich and sometimes difficult, maybe more difficult than if we had roles, because things are not always clear. Subtleties need attention. But then we both pay attention.

Today my friends and family know about my personal life because I have expressed in public something that previously was there only in private. I find it troublesome when people think I have changed, when all that has happened is that they know more about me.

Although my choice of lover is not a political or public statement but the natural consequence of feeling, the disclosure of it has produced a kind of Rorschach test of possible responses. People ask, "How did you dare to love this woman when it didn't fit with your life?" Among the members of my family of origin I have heard:

"I have trouble thinking of you as a lesbian."

"I have learned a lot of things about you that I might have preferred not to know."

"What kind of people do you socialize with now?"

"I can't imagine your kids with you and another woman. It's not my idea of a family."

A friend of my parents, a famous psychoanalyst I thought was forbidding, said, "You were always a pioneer."

A woman psychiatrist said, "Why do you *need* to carry on this relationship?"

Some friends have understood; others have found it a problem. One said, "I have to call you secretly because my husband cannot deal with your story." Another asked, "Are you getting help?" Still others have said, "You have a lot of guts." "You will get hurt." "If two people can love each other it's a miracle."

I am sitting at lunch with my friend the French professor. She knows my family well. "Have you thought of how your mother was the strong one and your father dresses flamboyantly? Did role switches have anything to do with it?" If there is an influence from childhood, it could as easily be from the intensity of my mother's friendships with women, the feeling I came to recognize as a kind of love, long before I met my lover.

I met her the day she came to rent the apartment in our house. We started talking one day, and now, more than two years later, we have not stopped. In the middle of our first talk, one of my kids called out that he had had a nightmare. She and I spoke of our own adult nightmares. Once I was in the kitchen when she returned from the movies crying, so I asked her to have a cup of tea. We talked about sorrows and loves. When she got up to go, many hours later, we grabbed hands and then somehow we were hugging. It could have been a hug between friends, but there was so much feeling in it that we were both stunned, as we told each other only later.

A few days later she was reading the paper in our pantry as I came to fix dinner. I said, "Did you have a nice day?" and she said, "No. I ran into a Cadillac on my bicycle." I invited her to have dinner with the family. When the others left the table she and I practically jumped out of our seats at each other.

"Why do I feel so comfortable with you?" she asked when we were alone.

"Why not?" I said. And we kissed for the first time. And asked each other whether if you touch you risk the rest. Finally, some time later, in a house by the sea, with waves tearing around the rocks, we made love over and over.

Then we started building our own history.

On a vacation on a Caribbean island, a steel band played to the staccato beats of lizards and tree frogs, rousing thumps and tunes, but the middle-aged, middle-American crowd would not budge. We were shy about dancing, but finally we could not resist, so we started on the edge. Soon the rest of the crowd was on the floor, waitresses, barmen, and the stodgy guests. Then two women came on the dance floor and moved together, bumping noses; the hotel manager and, yes, her girlfriend. We started something.

Together we have read Dostoyevski and Donald Duck. We have been to the Parthenon, Harlem, Paris, Disney World, and we've celebrated New Year's Eve in Times Square.

One summer weekend my friend, my eleven-year-old, my father, and I are eating lobsters at sunset on an island off the New England coast. My son finds a huge yellow moon hanging over the water, opposite the rosy sun. Later my friend and I go to say good night to my father, who is dozing in his bed. He looks at us, and smiles. I think they are tears of understanding rolling down his face.

It has not been easy. In the same year, I ended a long marriage and my friend's mother died. I have had family problems, she has visa problems. We still cannot be sure how much of the year we can be together. When she told a U.S. Embassy official abroad that she had compelling reasons to stay in this country, he quipped, "Then get married."

When my husband learned that I love this woman, he was very angry and said extreme things in front of the kids and my parents and to others. He said, "You are not a mother any more." He threatened to take the kids from me and drag me to court. Though my younger son found a way to keep out of these scenes, my older son, eighteen, did not. He exploded about my breaking up the family, betraying his father, and loving a woman. Since then, he has not come to our house for more than a few minutes. Although he is beginning to understand, this has been agonizing for me. I can only tell him that I hope he will come to accept my choice and that I love him as much as I always have.

One day he took a photo of the whole family—grandparents, aunts, nieces—from the hallway table and put it in his room, saying, "This was the last time we were a happy family." He wants to keep the family inside him. I try to tell him he will not lose the love, but he feels that my loving another has taken something from him. What happened to change the picture, I try to say, had been there for a long time. Pictures leave things out.

When he got angry, he mostly shouted and stormed. But one night he came home hungry and tired, smelling sweaty from hockey practice. He taunted me about my friend, who happened to call as we were eating dinner. I took my plate to the other room. He followed me with a mouthful of steak and peas. I had not asked him how he felt about my loving someone else, he shouted, starting to cry. I grabbed him, all six feet, and put my arms around him, as he cried his tears of lost innocence and childhood love and peas into my torn jogging jersey and faded sweatpants that used to be his.

"This is the first time I have cried about it," he said, and he cried and cried and hugged me like a child. "How I feel about it is sad."

"Yes," I said, through my own tears.

My eleven-year-old says, "It's hard for me to get used to seeing that you love someone else." Tears drop off his cheeks like beads. We talk about this new claim on my attention, about the sadness of losing a family. I tell him about people who gain strength and wisdom from sadness, about the wise saying that only the wounded physician heals. I tell him a great novelist had a sad childhood.

"Who?" he asks.

"Dickens."

He smiles. One night he asks me to sing a lullaby, and we both start to cry.

He watched a TV show in which two women living together win custody of the son of one of them. He says he is happy it ends that way. He watched it with his father's housekeeper, who said, "I hate that word 'lesbian.'" He does not like her saying this. Sometimes he thrusts himself between my friend and me on the street and holds our hands so we will not hold each other's. But at night when he is going to sleep he seems glad when we both tell him we love him.

So my friend and my younger son and I live together. Two writers, one student. My son has his room, where he lies on the floor making charts of how fruit holds water. At dinner we light candles. Afterward, we read the *Just So Stories* together, about the "great, gray-green, greasy Limpopo River, all set about with fever-trees." There is love in the house; it is the first time my son has lived with grown-ups who love each other. My friend is European, has no kids, has never been married. It is not easy to blend the two cultures, two very different histories, an unconventional way of life, and one child.

"How do you know it will last?" someone asks. It is hard to answer. My friend and I are not kids; we've had experience, we know about risk. We have looked for oracles and found none. We tell ourselves only this: if anything promises to last forever, we do.

8.

MARRIAGE FROM GOD, NOT COURTS

Cal Thomas

The decision by one judge in Hawaii that the state may not prohibit same-sex "marriages" goes against the author of marriage, legal precedent, the will of an estimated 75 percent of Hawaii's citizens and what used to be called common sense.

But it is not the victory the gay lobby claims. It is what Alliance for Traditional Marriage chairman Mike Gabbard calls "a preliminary decision. The main event is the upcoming 1997 legislative session, where a constitutional amendment defending marriage as the legal union between a man and a woman will be introduced and hopefully passed with the required two-thirds majority in both the House and Senate."

The reason Hawaii and the rest of the nation are having problems not only with same-sex "marriage" but also a host of other moral issues is that we've forgotten or ignored certain definitions. If gay "marriage" is allowed, there will be no stopping others who wish to strike down what remains of foundational truths once thought to be self-evident. Even the dictionary will have to be rewritten, because it says to marry "is to join as husband and wife according to law or custom." The U.S. Supreme Court has understood this definition to mean that marriage occurs when a man and a woman enter into a legal and spiritual relationship ordained by God.

"For this reason, a man will leave his father and mother, and be united to his wife, and they will become one flesh." That's from the Old Testament Book of Genesis (chapter 2, verse 24, to be precise), a book that has been receiving some attention on television, in *Time* magazine, and in the bookstores in recent weeks. That notion of male-female marriage is repeated in the New Testament and given a further dimension when St. Paul describes it as an earthly manifestation of the Trinity.

So, God is the author of marriage, not a university sociologist, or think tank and certainly not the courts. But what happens when a nation forgets God and what he has created for our benefit? All things then become possible, even probable. If gay "marriage" becomes possible, then there is nothing stopping polygamists, or anyone else, seeking redress of unique grievances. Where will the line be drawn, who will draw it and on what standard will it be based?

Besides, homosexuals can and do change. My files bulge with stories of those who once engaged in sex with people of the same gender, but no longer do. They testify to the possibility of change for those who want to. Along with our own history and the history of nations that tolerated licentiousness, it is the greatest legal argument against granting the right of marriage to same-sex couples.

Fortunately, Congress has passed and President Clinton signed the Defense of Marriage Act, allowing states the right not to recognize same-sex marriages. But this will be challenged under the Constitution's "equal protection" clause.

The tyranny of some courts continues. The will of the majority and even precedent can be set aside by the power of a single judge. But the battle isn't over. The gay lobby will continue its attempt to intimidate all who stand in the way (including columnists). Those opposed to gay "marriage" believe they will prevail in the Hawaii legislature with their proposed constitutional amendment.

It will probably be close. While Hawaii has long been on the liberal fringe of many social issues, the struggle to maintain what remains of the social fabric will ultimately determine whether we will continue to follow ancient Rome on the road to destruction, or come to our senses, turn around and re-enter a harbor of safety ordained by God for our own protection.

Turning Benjamin Franklin's categorical statement into a question, the gay "marriage" debate is about whether God any longer governs in the affairs of men—but what happens to us if he doesn't?

9.

COUNSELING SAME-SEX COUPLES

Douglas Carl

Once coupled, gays and lesbians face myriad problems, some not so unlike those experienced by heterosexual couples, some very different. Needless to say, all couples today face the specter of bleak statistics: 48 percent of all first marriages fail, while 47 percent of all second marriages end in divorce. We have no accurate figures for same-sex couples. However, in these statistics lies an ingrained prejudice or two that we need to explore before we go any further.

We as a culture seem to assume that coupled is best. True happiness, it is written, lies in wending your way down life's highway together. Real fulfillment, popular myth has it, comes from finding the right mate and designing a life that fits the two of you. I remember as a child that my parents had something of a pitying regard for two groups: those unmarried (particularly women, who certainly would not *choose* to remain single) and those who were married but childless (another condition no person would choose willingly).

Attitudes have changed in the last several decades, but most of us still aspire to finding the one *right* relationship that will help make our lives fulfilling. I find no fault in this aspiration per se, but I prefer to believe that, even though coupling will remain the preferred mode of lifestyle in the foreseeable future, we need to look at it as a popular option among several options open to us. In other words, we do ourselves and our clients a disservice with any implicit assumption that coupling is best. It may prove best for some or for most, but marriage-style coupling does not automatically spell happiness. Many single people can and do find real fulfillment in a variety of lifestyles, but we often fail to credit that fact. In addition, there are those who maintain their coupled relationships in less conventional ways that are rewarding to them; from these individuals we can garner ideas that could expand everyone's options. Some of these ideas will emanate from same-sex couples, who need not always be bound by social conventions, even though sometimes unwittingly they are.

The second myth we often buy into is that longevity is best. As a culture we honor and revere long-surviving marriages. I remember taking a genogram from a client whose grandparents had just celebrated their sixtieth wedding anniversary. "That's terrific," I exclaimed. "What's so terrific about it?" he replied. "They haven't talked to each other in twenty years!" Less acceptable and less recognized in our culture are serial relationships—a series of shorter-term relationships that may better fill the needs of individuals as they face the demands of fast-moving, ever-changing lifestyles (something that happens quite often in practice without really being recognized). Childless relationships, without the same issues of consistency and stability for the progeny, could sometimes benefit from this serial orientation.

I do not wish to convey the idea that I am anti-marriage or anti-relationship, longterm or otherwise. Far from it! Still, I feel that we do clients a disservice by accepting prevailing ideas of what is best in life and not exploring to the fullest what might work best for *them.* Longterm marriage at the end of the twentieth century does not seem to work for large numbers of people. For some, this represents difficulty with commitment or pressures from a rapidly changing world. Perhaps, some feel, the culprit is an erosion of moral/spiritual values. All these things and more merit exploration. Another option is to evaluate conditions as they appear and to think about relationships in terms of how they might fit changing social conditions.

Gays and lesbians approach relationships with the same preconceptions as prevail in the heterosexual world. Most of them have only marriage models as road maps for how their relationships should function, but these maps, based on a different assessment of the landscape, often lead them and their therapists in the wrong direction.

MARRIAGE: RITUAL, BOUNDARIES, ROLES

Just as it is more difficult to function in the world as a gay individual than it is as a straight individual, it is more difficult to function as a same-sex couple than it is as a heterosexual couple. That is simply reality. One major reason for this has to do with marriage and its deeply rooted implications in our culture.

First, there is marriage ritual. In its most elaborate expression, marriage ritual involves family, friends, church or synagogue, the legal system, and a new status. For same-sex couples there usually is none of this. No planning for the big day by friends, family, coworkers, etc. No parties. No gifts. No introduction of families to each other or to the prospective partner. No ceremony (although a limited number of gay men and women do manage to carry out a ritual ceremony for friends and some family but without any official religious or legal significance). No honeymoon. Often, the joining together just happens gradually, and at some point there is recognition of couple status by the participating individuals through communication about the couple's identity between partners and to others, agreements about sex, and *sometimes* a merging of households. Legally, no state recognizes the union, nor do most official religious institutions (some individual churches will "sanctify" or celebrate the union). There are signs of some small changes in this area. Recently the United Methodist Church voted to accept all members without regard to race, sex, or sexual orientation. And the San Francisco city council passed an ordinance in 1989 that effectively grants spousal equivalency to members of same-sex couples in terms of legal issues of property and employment benefits. Of course, San Francisco is a far cry from the rest of the United States.

More important is what marriage and the surrounding ritual represent. Marriage in our society creates boundaries. It says to family and to the world that there is the beginning of a new nuclear family. Think about traditional ritual: The father of the bride walks her down the aisle, "gives her away" to the bridegroom, and then sits down. Families may sooner or later transgress these boundaries, but "right" is on the side of the married partners to conduct their lives as they see fit. Generally, families back off, give them their space, and see them as a separately functioning unit.

For the same-sex couple, bonding often magnifies the issues of emotional cutoffs. It now becomes more difficult to deny one's homosexuality, unless the couple status remains secret. If so, then emotional cutoffs intensify. Often, coupling signals the need to deal with family and friends. *In fact, gays and lesbians may avoid a real commitment because they cannot face that very issue.*

Generally, same-sex couples do not reap the boundary benefits generated by the married couple. Usually, this happens because of lack of recognition of the legitimacy of their relationship. Sometimes it happens just because friends and family simply have not been informed about the significance of the relationship.

Jennifer and Ione had been together nearly three years when they came into therapy. Jennifer struggled with Ione around closeness. After three years, she expected more from her partner. Ione came from an Italian-Catholic family. She had always seen her family as intrusive, and she had worked very hard to fend off what she saw as interfering overtures. In doing so, she had established a pattern she used with her partner, where she defended against closeness that she was afraid would suffocate her.

At my gentle urging, she scheduled a session with her parents. Seeing them together it became clear that the father's motive was to look after his unmarried daughter in his accustomed "old world" way. He knew nothing of his daughter's relationship with Jennifer. Even if he had, there was some question whether he would have respected the boundary created by their relationship. Clearly, he would have treated the relationship differently than he would a "real" marriage. (It is possible in working with such families to "legitimize" the relationship in a way that eventually establishes boundaries between the family of origin and the couple.) This represented a major issue between Jennifer and Ione that definitely called for a broader, systemic approach, which would include additional work with family members, either in person or "on paper."

Pete and Larry were friends, not clients. They had recently celebrated eight years together and generally seemed to have a good, supportive relationship, but not one without friction. A major source of that friction (but certainly not directly cause and effect) involved Pete's relationship with his family of origin. His parents were upper-class Bostonians, with the requisite money and social connections. Even after eight years, they did not recognize Pete and Larry's relationship. It was not clear whether they chose not to or whether they were just naive, because when Pete was in college they found out that Pete and Larry were intimate. That was seven years earlier. They threatened to cut off Pete's tuition and expense money unless the two men stopped sharing an apartment and ceased seeing each other. Pete felt that he had no choice but to present the appearance of compliance. Since that incident, seven years before, there had been no discussion about Larry, Pete's sexual orientation, or his social lifestyle.

For Pete and Larry, the issue still lurked behind the scenes. For that next year in college, they kept the relationship as secret as they could. A year after graduation, they again took up residence together, unbeknownst to Pete's parents. Even now, Larry never answered the telephone in his own apartment for fear that it might be Pete's parents. The parents' shadow continued to influence the relationship from a great distance because Pete's inheritance was at stake.

Larry and his family also played a part in the scenario. They knew about the relationship between the two men and, even though they did not openly support it, at least they showed implicit indifference. Larry could at least mention Pete and their vacations, their friends, and their successes. They all avoided anything that smacked of the conflictual.

Both of Larry's parents were over seventy years old. They had both suffered declining health in recent years, and since they lived five hours by car from their son, they felt free to call on him at any time should they require his presence. During a recent summer Larry had spent six weeks at his parents' home tending to their care and their business affairs when his mother was hospitalized. He spent that six weeks apart from Pete, with only two brief visits between them. Larry's married sister, who lived a bit closer with her husband and child, was never asked by her parents to help.

Both men had boundary issues with families of origin that contributed to tension in their relationship. The tension was not likely to dissipate without some sort of systemic intervention. The prevailing myth was that death would eventually resolve the issues in both families. However, too often the prevailing patterns will continue despite the demise of an older generation.

*   *   *

Tony and Rob would have said that their situation differed a lot from that of Pete and Larry. They had coupled five years ago with the full understanding of both families. Tony's father lived a good distance away and his mother was dead. Rob's family lived within a few miles of the two men, who owned a lovely home in a fashionable city neighborhood. Holidays and family gatherings always found Tony included with Rob's family. Rob had an older brother who lived nearby with his wife. The two brothers and their mates socialized fairly frequently.

Then, suddenly, Rob's father developed cancer. In three months he had died. During the illness and in the time following his death, the family called on Rob for endless errands and commitments and energy, not because this had been his previous role in the family, but because he was perceived as being available. On several occasions the message came through loud and clear from his mother, "I would ask your brother to do it, but he has things to take care of for Sally."

Whether or not Tony and Rob would have recognized it, in the final analysis, boundaries held up very much the same in the two different situations. . . .

In the context of marriage and couple relationships, we all carry preconceptions of how roles should and do operate. Gay men and lesbians share the same preconceptions, many of which may not be relevant to their particular contexts: the "supplemental" nature of the woman's income, the male's primary role as "breadwinner," the woman's role as primary manager of the household economy, issues of power and dominance, issues of emotional support, etc. Although roles in marriage have changed somewhat in the last several decades, there still exist fairly clear-cut guidelines and expectations for how roles sort out in marriage. Sometimes these marital-role expectations cause difficulty for heterosexual couples, such as when spouses decide to reverse the traditional roles.

One such situation was reported to me several years ago. A married couple decided over a several-year period and two children that they would both continue to work, but that she would focus on advancing her career, while he would just work a job and take more responsibility for home and kids. Before too long she had advanced up the corporate ladder and was making more money than he was. One night a neighbor dropped by and in the course of conversation inquired earnestly, "How can you let your wife make more money than you do?"

Gay men and lesbians enter relationships without benefit of clear role expectations because role models remain so invisible. There are advantages and disadvantages to this situation. On the plus side, there is much less likelihood that any well-meaning neighbor will inquire about an income differential. On the minus side, there is the push/shove of reinventing the wheel. Through the years I have found that same-sex couples need some help in negotiating these role issues, *but they do not emerge as stated sources of conflict in most relationships.* In fact, the lack of rigid role delineation often leaves room for creativity in these couples.

There may be one important exception. Sociologists Philip Blumstein and Pepper Schwartz have recently come up with some interesting findings in their research on couples. They studied cohabiting and married heterosexual couples and, as controls because they washed out gender differences, gay and lesbian couples. Basically, their research showed that money equals power, that in heterosexual, lesbian, and gay couples, the person making the lesser amount of money deferred to the person making more. The person with the greater income (and status) interrupted more and, among heterosexuals and lesbians, the person with the smaller income generally supported the ideas and opinions of the greater-status mate ("uh-huh, well said, well done"). However, in gay male couples *no one took the supportive role.* Now, because men make more money than women, they generally have more power, too. But even in the small number of heterosexual couples where the woman made more money, the men took something of a supportive role. This seems to say that men will do the supporting for women, but they will not provide this support for other men. This has interesting implications for working with gay male couples, implications that need to be more fully explored. . . .

Sometimes rigid sexual roles [are] observed in gay and lesbian couples. In my experience, these sexual roles do not necessarily carry over into other parts of the relationship. In other words, the man who is sexually passive in a gay relationship does not necessarily assume more traditional feminine duties in other aspects of the relationship. The same seems true for lesbian couples.

For example, issues of household economy, traditionally a female preserve in marriage, may get attended to by either partner (or both), irrespective of roles he or she plays in bed. What you may see is a struggle between two men or two women who *both* want responsibility in this area. I have seldom seen same-sex couples coming into therapy because they could not sort out who would "play" husband and who would "play" wife. The struggle in the sexual arena represents another matter.

THE ISSUE OF CHILDREN

Another qualitative difference exits between same-sex and opposite-sex couples: One will never produce children together, while in the other it is almost always at least a consideration (discounting age). In fact, the opportunity to produce children is a major reason for religious and legal sanction of marriage and a major reason why the culture glorifies longterm relationships. Even the rules surrounding proper conduct in marriage stem from concerns regarding pregnancy and illegitimacy in the bloodline.

Gay males do not couple with the intent of producing children nor will the decision not to have them constitute a common bond. Neither will the presence of children produced in common produce the guilt and conflict present in many divorce situations—making this aspect of separation easier for gay men.

The circumstances for lesbians are changing. Lesbians do have the option of pregnancy, although obviously not for biologically mutual progeny. However, there are at least opportunities to decide together whether to have children. One couple I heard about recently opted to use donor sperm from the brother of one partner to impregnate the other. Biologically, this is as close as one can get to the process in heterosexual unions; even the family bond with the grandchildren is perpetuated.

Adoption has theoretically always been an option for same-sex couples, but in practice this process is extremely difficult for anyone identified as being homosexual. Adoption, in fact, may prove a tortuous process for qualifying heterosexual couples.

Still, the vast majority of gay and lesbian couples do not make conscious or even subconscious decisions to have children, and this fact means that this bonding factor is unavailable to them.

It is not unusual for one or both partners in gay or lesbian relationships to bring children from a marriage into the same-sex relationship. Such an arrangement brings up two major issues, one common to heterosexual recouplings and one unique to same-sex marriages. The universal blended family issues present in all recombinations present a force to be reckoned with for homosexuals and heterosexuals alike, but the issue of how and when to deal with children around your sexual orientation represents a distinctly homosexual problem.

Many books have already been written on the challenges and strategies of dealing with blended family issues. . . . Much less has been explored concerning coming out to the children and all of the implications involved in that process. . . .

As a therapist, I have experienced a much more subtle issue impacting same-sex couples, one that may affect gay males more than lesbians. I have been impressed with a qualitative difference between gay men who have been married, especially those who have been married with children, and those who have never experienced heterosexual marriages. When you think about it, the implications are obvious: Those who have been married have experienced firsthand all the supports and role expectations that go with marriage in our culture. So it is not surprising that their expectations in gay relationships come tinged with these feelings and attitudes.

Darryl and Don split up after five years together. The breakup was congenial and could be traced to a number of issues. A major, largely unspoken, issue involved Don's incomprehension of the powerful emotional bond that existed between Darryl and his ex-wife and child. In fact, Darryl, who had maintained a very positive relationship with his ex-wife, admitted that when he visited them in their home town, he enjoyed the three of them going out as a family, just like in the old days. "Kind of like having your cake and eating it, too," he exclaimed. Don did not resent this bond intellectually, but emotionally it upset him quite a bit. He felt on the outside of a major force in Darryl's life—and, in truth, he was.

Many major cities have support groups or networks for gays and lesbians who have been married, since so often they feel out of sync with never-married gays. "I feel so much better understood around other gay men with kids," Darryl reported. While lesbians may feel just as strongly about this kind of support or lack of it, this has not represented my experience with them. Somehow it *may* be that, since women tend to be more child-focused as a group, there exists more support and understanding in the lesbian culture in general.

DUAL CAREERS

The vast majority of same-sex couples face the issues of dual careers that many heterosexual marriages face. (This is one area where a heterosexual relationship issue, one that has received a good deal of attention in recent years, *does* generalize to the same-sex couple.) Almost always, both participants in a same-sex relationship work at jobs or careers rather than one person staying home as homemaker. Some of the issues confronting any dual-career couple concern where to locate or relocate, coordination of work and time together, and satisfaction from longterm career goals. . . .

In many dual-career marriages, the traditional obstacles of male/female position and status in the marriage plus the demands on one spouse to combine childcare, housework, and career provide fodder for conflict and cry out for resolution. Gay male and lesbian unions do not have to face these concerns. Same-sex couples, though, may experience an obstacle concerning the fruits of their labors, since, because of previous experiences and sociological conditions discussed earlier, there is not necessarily the assumption that "what's mine is ours," as one tends to find in a marriage. In fact, the rampant cynicism concerning lack of permanence in these relationships also contributes to difficulties in sharing resources. However, sometimes the reverse is true: A couple works so hard to stay together just to show that it *can* be done and resources are shared so completely that there is little room for individual use of financial resources (perhaps an extreme embrace of traditional marital values).

Jay, who earned $35,000 per year, complained that he could not even buy a shirt that he might see and want because there was no money left over from the joint budget administered by his lover, Steve, who earned considerably less. These two men adhered strongly to a fairly traditional marital household management philosophy, but there was still resentment caused by the disparity in incomes. The "what's mine is ours" dictum did not work for them, even though they tried to operate like a traditional marriage in many ways.

Another major issue common to dual-career couples is the "whither thou goest" dilemma. Traditionally, families move when the husband gets transferred, but with a more professionally egalitarian arrangement couples need to prepare to decide when career demands for *either* spouse may dictate a move. Over the years, I have seen a small number of gay male couples split up over this issue: "It was time for us to go our separate ways anyway," Charles said. "We'd been together four years and things were starting to feel stale. We had more time together than most of my friends have had, after all." This couple split when Charles's lover, Phil, took a job across the country. Charles was not willing to give up his job and his friends to make the move. Their expectations regarding impermanence of gay relationships also contributed to the outcome.

This issue may take a slightly different twist for lesbians, since in traditional marriages women most often give in around this issue. Lesbians may struggle with whether they have the *right* to ask a partner to move, while men may assume they have the right implicitly. As was discussed earlier, men also tend to display more open competitiveness around professional accomplishments than their lesbian counterparts, making their actual process around this issue a more vigorous and even hostile one. Coupled men with unequal incomes and potentials will likely experience competition and friction eventually.

THE FUSION ISSUE

[G]ender issues . . . also get played out in relationship styles that are fundamentally different for gay men and for lesbians. We have hinted at some of this operating in other areas, such as dual careers and support for having children. A more basic difference seems to operate in terms of style.

Krestan and Bepko, in a classic 1980 *Family Process* article, present the case for what they call "lesbian fusion." According to the authors, women's socialization tends to make them more homebound, to erode boundaries between them, and to fuse them dysfunctionally under stress. They describe this as a "two against the world" posture. Men, on the other hand, tend to distance under stress, staying away from home, involving themselves in other activities, including sexual ones.

This major difference really is not too surprising when we consider that women in our culture tend to be the ones who hold families together, keeping the home fires burning and providing the lion's share of the emotional support in families. Men are the ones who typically go out to earn a living and to intermingle with a broader world. These differences manifest themselves markedly in therapy. . . .

INTRARELATIONSHIP DIFFERENCES

Several years ago, one of my partners asked me this question: "How come," she said, "most of the heterosexual couples I see come from the same or similar socioeconomic background, and so many of the gay couples I see come from such unlike backgrounds?" I do not know whether her observations would hold up statistically, but my observations have been somewhat the same. Seemingly, more gays and lesbians come from dissimilar cultural, educational, and economic backgrounds. If this is true, we might attribute it to the fact that the pool of available partners is smaller for gays and lesbians and *as a group gay men and lesbians are thrown together only because they share the same "deviant" sexual orientation.* So the son of a sharecropper from Alabama finds himself in a bar with a corporate attorney's son from New York. They find each other attractive, have sex, and may end up as a couple. Since meeting places for gay men in particular have been limited and reasonably isolated, the selection of partners of unlike backgrounds becomes more likely.

Another observation that may not hold up statistically: I have observed more same-sex relationships with fairly great differences in age than I have in heterosexual relationships. The need for role models in the coming-out process, cutoffs from family, the small pool of eligible partners, and various other reasons may account for this phenomenon. For the therapist, it means another consideration in therapy: different experiences and developmental stages.

Interracial considerations may also play more of a part in therapy. In Atlanta, for example, an organization called Black and White Men Together provides support for a fairly sizable number of interracial couples. Interracial coupling should logically be easier with gays and lesbians, since so many are already cut off from families of origin and having children is usually not a major consideration.

LEGAL ISSUES

There are few legal protections for same-sex couples. Their sexual acts are illegal in most states. They may not file joint income tax returns, claim each other as deductions, qualify as dependents on insurance policies, collect a "spouse's" Social Security, or, in some cases, be named as life insurance beneficiaries. We have mentioned the difficulty with adoption. Gays and lesbians may be barred from visitation with their own biological children, and they experience difficulty gaining custody in divorce proceedings.

Monty, thirty-four, had been married for eight years and divorced over three. He has three children, two sons, nine and seven, and a daughter, four. Since the divorce, his middle child, Alex, has presented problems for his mother. She has remarried and lives 150 miles from her ex-husband. Whenever Alex becomes particularly difficult, his mother sends him to his father to live. Sometimes this has happened with advance notice, sometimes more spontaneously. After several months, she misses Alex, feels guilty about abandoning him to his father, and takes steps to get him back. Since she never has surrendered custody, this gets accomplished with little difficulty. Monty has repeatedly asked for custody, but his ex-wife always puts him off. He is afraid to go to court because the issue of his homosexuality may come up and, in his old home town, there is some likelihood that the judge would deny visitation altogether. Obviously this situation is detrimental to Alex. It also puts a burden on Monty's relationship with his partner, since the blended family issues never really get addressed. . . .

AIDS has sharpened the focus on legal protections or rights for spouses. Anecdotal information is replete with examples of a surviving spouse losing everything the two of them had worked for to a deceased lover's next of kin. For most couples, where one partner has contracted AIDS, negotiation around wills, power of attorney, use of life support measures, and legal issues around death and burial becomes essential in the relationship.

In general, same-sex couples must work at what married couples take for granted as legal rights. Of course, the absence of legal bonds makes it easier for partners to move on with relative legal ease. It may also contribute to the attitude of not really taking the relationship seriously. Some couples may use legal commitments such as joint ownership of property, wills, and life insurance to formalize their bonds.

Part Three

THE PHILOSOPHICAL ARGUMENTS

10.

THE MORALITY OF HOMOSEXUAL MARRIAGE

Daniel Maguire

For a significant minority of persons in the human community, erotic desire is focused, primarily or exclusively, on persons of the same sex. Psychiatrists are divided on whether to label this *de facto* variation pathological or not. Similarly, moralists are divided as to whether this orientation is an inclination to moral perversion, or a simple variation in the human quest for intimacy. If it is pathology, medical science should look for a cure; if it is an ingrained tilt toward unconscionable behavior, ethicists must counsel its containment.

The psychiatric or ethical position that sees homosexuality as clinical or moral pathology is blessed with striking simplicity. Clearly, pathologies are not to be encouraged under the specious claim of freedom or self-fulfillment. We find in the human sexual lexicon such manifestly pathological conditions as zoophilia, pedophilia, necrophilia, fetishism, sadistic or masochistic sex, exhibitionism, voyeurism, and rape. If homosexuality fits somewhere in that listing, we need not labor long in discussing its moral or psychological status. We do not speak of a well-adjusted necrophiliac, nor do we consider necrophiliacs as having a moral and civil right to access to corpses. There is no cry for rapist or fetishist liberation. Some things are abnormal and harmful at least to the agent who acts out on them. Is this the case for homosexuality?

Those who say yes face two critical difficulties: (1) they must show that those who act in any way on their homosexual orientation victimize themselves or others and (2) they must show that celibacy is good for all nonheterosexual persons.

First, regarding the harm, it is empty nominalism to name something harmful in the absence of identifiable harm. It is illogical to speak of a moral

This article originally appeared in *A Challenge to Love: Gay and Lesbian Catholics in the Church*, edited by Robert Nugent, and with an introduction by Bishop Walter F. Sullivan (New York: The Crossroad Publishing Company, 1983). Reprinted by permission.

or psychological cure for a harmful condition if we cannot show what harm the cure is to address. Illness is known by its symptoms. In the absence of symptoms, we assume persons are well. If psychiatry would label homosexuality a pathology or illness, it must show how it adversely affects persons who express their intimacy-needs homosexually. The delineations of these adverse effects must also show that these are due to the orientation itself and not to the sociocultural effects of seeing the condition as an illness. If a society falsely imputes negative meaning to a sexual orientation, this will adversely affect persons who act out on that orientation, though the fault would be with the social stigmatizing and not with the orientation itself.

Clearly, then, psychiatry and ethics must pass the "show-me" test when they speak of homosexuality as a malady in need of a remedy. The test is not met simply by stating that homosexuality is a "disorder" because it is a minority phenomenon or because anatomy and reproductive needs suggest male-female coitus as the unexceptionable norm. Minority status does not of itself mean objectionable deviance. Indeed, the presence of minority status is the spice of variety and thus of life. But is not anatomy destiny? The penis and the vagina do enjoy a congenial fit, and the species' need for reproduction relies on that. But sex rarely, in any lifetime, has to do with reproduction, and not even heterosexual persons are limited to coitus for sexual fulfillment. Also, the species' need for reproductive sex is being met and often overmet.

In ethics, the term *biologism* refers to the fallacious effort to wring a moral mandate out of raw biological facts. The male-female coital fit and its relationship to reproduction are basic biological facts. The biologistic error would leap from those facts to the moral imperative that all sexual exchange must be male-female coital in kind. The leap could only become likely if you reduce human sexuality to the biological simplicities of the stud farm. Given the infinity of meanings beyond baby-making involved in human eroticism and sexuality, such a leap is misdirected and, literally, unreal.

No. If homosexuality is an illness requiring cure, if it is an orientation to sin, it is because it is harmful to persons. If that harm cannot be pinpointed, the charge of sin or illness must be reconsidered.

George Bernard Shaw reminded us that it is the way of barbarians to think of the customs of their tribe as the laws of nature. Is the homosexually oriented quest for intimacy contrary to the laws of nature or simply to the current customs of our tribe? That question is regularly sent to go a-begging. The discussion, however, depends on facing it squarely.

The second question confronting those who see homosexuality as pathology regards celibacy as the only moral option for nonheterosexuals. Moralists of this position say that the condition of being homosexually oriented is not evil in itself since it seems irreversible in many or most instances. (Some deviant Christian fundamentalists see homosexuality as a contumacious and wicked option that can be cast out by prayer and fasting. In the absence of any supportive data, we commend such a position to its own embarrassment.) The evil would be in acting out one's homosexual proclivities. The morally good homosexual, in this view, is the celibate homosexual. This position has inherent contradictions. Implicitly it is reducible to the position of the deviant Christian fundamentalists since it says: You may be homosexual but, with prayer and fasting, you will never have to express it. It insists that there is nothing wrong with being a homosexual as long as you do not act on it. That is too tidy. There is a lot wrong with being a homosexual if all the values that attach to sexual expression are denied you. Sex is more than orgasms; it is an important avenue to many personal values. If the sexual avenue is categorically closed off to gay persons, that is no slight impairment. It makes the condition itself an abridgment of personality.

This "be-but-don't-do" position rests on three errors: (1) a materialistic and narrow view of sex; (2) a stunted epistemology; and (3) a departure from biblical good sense. First, then, it views sex narrowly and materialistically, missing its linkage to such deeply felt human needs as intimacy, trust, and friendship. It would be gratuitous to say that a celibate cannot meet those human needs—that sex is necessary for human fulfillment—but it is equally gratuitous to say that a whole class of persons involving as much as 4 or 5 percent of the human population can be barred morally from the only kind of access to sexuality that attracts them.

1. Erotic desire is deeply interwoven into the human desire and need for closeness and for trusting relationships. The desire for a significant other with whom we are uniquely conjoined is not a heterosexual but a basic human desire. The programmatic exclusion of gay persons from the multiple benefits of erotic attraction, which often opens the way to such a union, is arbitrary, harmful, cruel, and therefore sinful.

Again, I am not saying that marriage or sexual activity are necessary for human fulfillment or psychological normalcy. Voluntary and involuntary celibacy is more common than is generally noted in a time of sexual overemphasis. Celibacy, voluntary or not, does not exclude human fulfillment. Sexually unfulfilled persons may be very fulfilled humanly. However, I stress that the sweeping exclusion of all gay persons from this important access route to meeting intimacy needs could only be based on a narrow and, I must insist, macho-masculine conception of what sex is and how it functions in human personal development.[1]

2. This position also lumps together without distinction all manifestations of homosexuality. Basically, the position is anthropologically naive. Few areas of human life are as variegated as sexual activity. This holds also for homosexuality. Some manifestations of homosexuality are harmful to human personal and social good. A moral argument opposed to homosexual activity in those instances can be made. However, to claim to know, by some encyclopedic intuition, that only celibacy befits homosexuals in any culture, clime, or time is—to say the least—immodest. More accurately, it is epistemologically absurd. It involves a kind of *essentialist* approach to knowing. Thus, even be-

fore all the data is in on what homosexuality is, how it develops, what it means in persons and societies, how it interrelates with other aspects of human relating, etc.—before all of that is known, a formula-panacea has been found that exhausts the moral meaning of homosexuality by prescribing celibacy.

Such essential thinking in ethics has a poor track record. Once we thought we had intuited the nature of money so clearly that we could say that all interest taking was sinful regardless of circumstances. Once we thought that we had so intuited the nature of sex that we could know that all contraceptive sexual exchange was wrong. We also believed that we had so thoroughly plumbed the meaning of speech that even to prevent serious harm such as murder we could not speak untruth. All of these essentialist visions have been humbled. The road to truth is longer and more tortuous than we thought. But now, regarding homosexuality, we are again told that the nature of homosexuality can be so perfectly intuited (especially by heterosexuals) that we can, with majestic calm, make a transcultural judgment that any expression of it anywhere is wrong and dehumanizing. Such arrogance is not the hallmark of truth.

Any position about the complexities of human behavior and development that ignores the witness of experience is suspect. The position that asserts that homosexuality is all right as long as you do not act on it is innocent of and apparently unconcerned with the experience of homosexually oriented persons. The more one looks into that experience and hears sensitive witness from gay persons, the less comfortable one can be with the glib "be-but-don't-do" approach to this human mystery. This approach gratuitously and stubbornly assumes that homosexuality fits with such things as pedophilia and obsessive voyeurism. It assumes with signal cruelty that homoeroticism has no more humanizing possibilities than incest or zoophilia. In this view, homoeroticism is, like all of these demonstrably noxious realities, sick. Since the conclusion of this error is a prescription of universal celibacy for all gays, the burden is clearly upon those who would so prescribe. Instead we receive poor exegesis of religious texts, biologisms, and warmed-over biases in place of argument. Neither ethics nor persons are well served by such careless intuitionism and empirically bereft moralizing.

Jean-Paul Sartre has told us that the greatest evil of which persons are capable is to treat as abstract that which is concrete. That is precisely what the "be-but-don't-do" school does to homosexuality. It takes the infinitely diverse experiences of homosexual persons and classifies them without distinction as evil. Such a globular approach does not commend itself to intelligence.

3. The final error of the "be-but-don't-do" position relates particularly to Christians who should be nourished by the earthy wisdom of the Bible. Facile urgings of celibacy for persons who do not happen to be heterosexual fly in the face of biblical good sense. Saint Paul, in his celebrated First Letter to the Corinthians, talks about the possibility of celibacy. Even though he is writing in a state of high eschatological expectation, and with the expressed conviction that it is better not to have sex (1 Cor. 7:1), he allows that sexual needs are such

that it would be better to marry (7:12). He concedes that persons may lack self-control (7:15), and so even married persons would be better advised not to be sexually abstinent for long. He would prefer all to be celibate but notes that each one has his/her own gift from God (7:17), implying very clearly that not all have the gift of celibacy. Again, he would prefer the unmarried and widowed to stay celibate but, once more, allows for the possible lack of "self-control" and concludes that "it is better to marry than to burn" (7:19).

The "be-but-don't-do" position would certainly allow, with Paul, that it is better for heterosexuals to marry than to burn. But, apparently their message for our homosexual brothers and sisters is: "Burn, burn!" We should not be terribly surprised that gay persons do not see this as "the good news." They can point out that Paul in this passage is reflecting the good sense of Jesus, who also said of voluntary celibacy: "Let him accept it who can" (Matt. 19:12). The Church itself, in the Second Vatican Council, has taken up this sensible idea, describing voluntary celibacy as "a precious gift," not as something indiscriminately given to whole classes of peoples.[2] The council points out that chastity will be very difficult, that it will face "very severe dangers" even for seminarians and religious with all the safeguards built into their lifestyle.[3] Those who would embark on a life of celibacy "should be very carefully trained for this state."[4] The council calls voluntary celibacy a "counsel," not a mandate, "a precious gift of divine grace which the Father gives to *some* persons," but not to all.[5] This gift of "total continence" is seen as worthy of special honor and as something "unique."[6] Celibate chastity "deserves to be esteemed as a surpassing gift of grace . . . which liberates the human heart in a unique way."[7] Persons entering religious orders should be warned in advance that celibacy, even in the sacred confines of religious life, is not easy. Involved in the celibate project are "the deeper inclinations of human nature." Candidates for a celibate religious life should have "a truly adequate testing period" to see if "they have the needed degree of psychological and emotional maturity." They should be warned of "the dangers confronting chastity."[8]

To all of which, our gay brothers and sisters might reply: "If total continence is so difficult for nuns and priests, why is it so easy for us? If it is a counsel for them, why is it a precept for us? These are good questions. If celibacy is so difficult that only some heterosexuals can undertake it—and then with the most extraordinary systems of support—how can we say that all gays have this "unique" talent for self-containment? If celibacy is seen as it is in a religious context as a special charism, are all gays charismatically blessed with celibate graces? Is this not a radical theological restatement of the position that "gay is good"? It is a traditional axiom of Catholic moral theology that no one is held to the impossible (*nemo ad impossible tenetur*). Are gays, nevertheless, held to what is impossible for nongays? For nongays, in this view, celibacy is a gifted feat that symbolizes the special, generous presence of the power of God. For gays, it is just a way of life, and the least that they can do. There are problems here that even minimal insight and honesty could see and should admit.

The pastoral position resulting from this contorted ethical position is equally strained. The only advice it leaves for gays is this: Pray and repress your erotic tendencies. God does not demand the impossible, and so God will give you the strength to do what moral theology, written by heterosexuals, has decided God wants you to do. If you fall from grace, appeal to God for forgiveness and your pastoral counselor will receive you with kindness and compassion.

Such pastoral advice embodies the theological error of "tempting God." It also harkens back to the medieval "ordeal," which contrived tests and put God on notice to come up with the response dictated by the test. If the fire burned you, you were evil. In this ordeal which we impose on gay persons, ethicists have boxed themselves into an arbitrary theological position which requires total celibacy from all gays and then leaves it up to God to pull off this implausible feat through prayer, sacraments, and pastoral counseling. Poor theology always puts God on the spot.

When we do theological ethics, we are painting a picture of our God. To say that something is good or bad is to say that it is in agreement or disagreement with the perceived will of God. In the position under discussion, we have God asking one thing from gays and considerably less from heterosexuals. If gay persons accept this particular ideological position on the ethics of homosexuality as the mind of God, *and* if they find it in contradiction to their own experience of reality, they have been pushed into the position of having to accept themselves *or* God. It is a position calculated to do precisely what pastoral theology should not do—alienate persons from the experience of God. Even at some risk to their professional situation, pastoral counselors are required not to offer either formal or material cooperations with a position that is so insensitive and religiously devastating.

MARRIAGE AS AN OPTION FOR HOMOSEXUALS

Marriage is the highest form of interpersonal commitment and friendship achievable between sexually attracted persons. Nothing in that definition requires that the sexually attracted persons who are conjoined in committed, conjugal friendship must be heterosexual. Neither is the capacity for having children required. Reproductive fertility is not of the essence of genuine marriage. Even in the Roman Catholic tradition, sterile persons are permitted to marry, and, as a recent celebrated case in the Diocese of Joliet, Illinois, illustrated, even male impotence is no barrier to marriage. This means that the basic sense of the current Catholic position on the relationship of marriage and childbearing is this: If there are to be children, they should be born within the confines of marriage. Yet, even fertile heterosexual persons do not have an obligation to have children. As Pope Pius XII taught, there can be a variety of reasons—social, economic, and genetic—for excluding children from a marriage entirely. Marriage clearly has more goods than the "good of children," the *bonum prolis*. And those other goods, in themselves, are enough to constitute marriage as a fully "human reality and saving mystery."[9]

The Second Vatican Council produced a major statement on the dignity and value of married life. The council Fathers were, of course, speaking of marriage between heterosexual persons. In fact, however, aside from the "good of offspring," which they stress is not essential for a genuine marriage, the goods and values they attach to marriage are not exclusively heterosexual in kind. The needs that marriage fulfills are human needs. The values that marriage enhances are integral to humanity as such and not to humanity as heterosexual. In fact, the *indispensable* goods of marriage are those that do not relate intrinsically to heterosexuality. The *dispensable* good—offspring—is the only good that does relate to heterosexuality.

Let us look to the council's statement on marriage and see what "good news" we might find there for gay persons who seek a humanizing and holy expression of their God-given orientation.

The image that the council gives of marriage is, on the whole, very positive and sensitive to personal needs. Marriage is seen as "an unbreakable compact between persons" of the sort that must "grow and ripen."[10] "Marriage persists as a whole manner and communion of life, and maintains its value and indissolubility, even when offspring are lacking."[11] Married persons should "nourish and develop their wedlock by pure conjugal love and undivided affection."[12] The council continues in a decidedly personalist tone:

> This love is an eminently human one since it is directed from one person to another through an affection of the will. It involves the good of the whole person. Therefore it can enrich the expressions of body and mind with a unique dignity, ennobling these expressions as special ingredients and signs of the friendship distinctive of marriage. This love the Lord has judged worthy of special gifts, healing, perfecting, and exalting gifts of grace and of charity.
>
> Such love, merging the human with the divine, leads the spouses to a free and mutual gift of themselves, a gift proving itself by gentle affection by deed. Such love pervades the whole of their lives. Indeed, by its generous activity it grows better and grows greater. Therefore it far excels mere erotic inclination which, selfishly pursued, soon enough fades wretchedly away.[13]

To make married love prosper, the couple are urged to "painstakingly cultivate and pray for constancy of love, largeheartedness, and the spirit of sacrifice."[14] The married couple are to become no longer two, but one flesh by rendering "mutual help and service to each other through an intimate union of their persons and their actions. Through this union they experience the meaning of their oneness and attain to it with growing perfection day by day." The goal of marriage is "unbreakable oneness."[15] Such "multifaceted love" mirrors the love of God for the Church. It will be marked by "perpetual fidelity through mutual self-bestowal." It should lead to the "mutual sanctification" of the two parties and "hence contribute jointly to the glory of God."[16]

The council does not look on this love as angelic and asexual. In fact, it stresses that this mutually satisfying and sanctifying love "is uniquely expressed and perfected through the marital act."[17] Sexual expression is extolled: "The acts themselves which are proper to conjugal love and which are exercised in accord with genuine human dignity must be honored with great reverence."[18] Again, reflecting the biblical sense of the natural goodness of sexual liturgy and its importance to conjugal love, the council warns that "where the intimacy of married life is broken off, it is not rare for its faithfulness to be imperiled and its quality of fruitfulness ruined."[19] Abstinence from sex, therefore, is viewed cautiously.

All of these texts of the council show a keen sense of the kinds of needs that are met in marital love. Married love will not survive on the thrills of early eroticism. What persons seek in marriage is total acceptance of all aspects of the self, the corrigible and the incorrigible, the lovely and the unlovely, the strong and the weak. Married love is not a selfish investment but an adventure in self-sacrificing, creative love. It is a school of holiness where persons may grow closer to God as they grow closer to one another and where their conjugal love may fuel their passion for justice and love for all people.

By what reasoning should values such as these be reserved for the heterosexual majority and denied to our gay brothers and sisters? By what twisted logic could we assume that gay persons would not experience the advantage of a love that produced such an "unbreakable oneness?" Why would gay persons in love be forbidden to aspire to and pray for "constancy of love, large-heartedness, and the spirit of sacrifice" to sustain their love? If erotic love between heterosexuals "is uniquely expressed and perfected" through sexual language, why would homoerotic love be judged moral only if sexually mute?

TWO OBJECTIONS TO HOMOSEXUAL MARRIAGE

Two immediate objections might be these: (1) gay persons do not display the psychological stability and strength necessary for lifelong commitment in marriage, and (2) the data indicate that gay persons prefer promiscuity to closed one-to-one relationships, showing that marriage is a heterosexual ideal being imperiously imposed on homosexuals.

How stable are gays psychologically? In a recent important study, Professors Alan Bell and Martin Weinberg bring extensive research to bear on the common stereotypes our society maintains regarding homosexual persons. At the heart of the stereotyping is the belief that homosexuals are "pretty much alike." Accordingly, it is significant that Bell and Weinberg entitle their study *Homosexualities: A Study of Diversity among Men and Women.* According to the stereotype, the homogeneous homosexuals are marked by "irresponsible sexual conduct, a contribution to social decay, and, of course, psychological pain and maladjustment."[20] The study presents strong evidence that "relatively few homosexual men and women conform to the hideous stereotype most people have of them." The authors describe as their "least ambiguous finding" that "homosexuality is not necessarily related to pathology."[21]

Regarding the psychological adjustment of homosexual men, Bell and Weinberg discovered that only one or two of the homosexual subgroups compared adversely to heterosexual men as to psychological adjustment. "The remaining subgroups tended to appear as well adjusted as the heterosexuals or, occasionally, even more so."[22] One quasi-marital subgoup, which the study styles "close-coupled" fared more than well in comparison to heterosexuals. "They felt no more tense, and were even happier than the heterosexual men."[23] Lesbians differed even less than male homosexuals in measures of psychological adjustment. In fact, close-coupled lesbians came out better in some regards than comparably situated heterosexual women.[24]

These findings are remarkable when we consider the stresses gay persons are subjected to in an antihomosexual society. All adolescents are vulnerable in their self-image. They are normally moving out from the nurturing closeness of family life, where their value has been consistently and reliably affirmed. In coping with this the adolescent vacillates between shrillness and bombast and shyness and tears. If, in the delicate move from familial to somewhat broader social endorsement, the young persons discover that a profound aspect of their personality is loathsome to the dominant majority, a painful crisis ensues. The discovery that one is a "queer," a "faggot," and a "pervert" is terrifying news to the delicate emergent ego. The news is so frightening that some self-protectively blind themselves to their own sexual identity in an amazing feat of denial. Others cope, often alone, with little or no solace or support. Even those on whom they have most depended up till now are normally of no help. Parents and siblings usually give clear witness to their detestation of homosexuality. Sexual awareness, then, brings the homosexual adolescent into a terrible loneliness. That so many of them bear this solitary suffering so well and arrive at such high levels of psychological adjustment is a striking tribute to the resilience of the human spirit. Heterosexual youths have their own tensions, but normally nothing comparable to the crushing rejection that greets the young gay person with the onset of puberty.

In view of all this, it is both arrogant and unjust for the heterosexual and dominant majority to perpetuate the myth that gay persons are psychologically unsound when these persons have passed more tests of psychological adjustment than many heterosexuals are ever required to do. There is simply no evidence that the psychological state of gays disqualifies them *as a class* from deeply committed and specifically conjugal relationships. The gratuitous assertion or assumption that they are lamed in this respect constitutes, in terms of traditional Catholic moral theology, a mortal sin of calumny. It is also a sin of injustice requiring restitution. Few of us heterosexuals are without sin in this regard, and so we are required by the virtues of justice and veracity to take the trouble to know better the actual situation of our gay brothers and sisters and to make appropriate reparatory responses to their needs.

The second objection to marital friendship for homosexual persons rests on their alleged preference for promiscuous sexual lifestyles. Again, studies do not support these stereotypes. Lesbians are particularly prone to form lasting marriagelike relationships. Even among male homosexuals, where promiscuity is more common, prolonged "affairs" are common. The Bell-Weinberg study reaches this conclusion:

> Our data indicate that a relatively steady relationship with a love partner is a very meaningful event in the life of a homosexual man or woman. From our respondents' descriptions, these affairs are apt to involve an emotional exchange and commitment similar to the kinds that heterosexuals experience, and most of the homosexual respondents thought that they and their partners had benefited personally from their involvement and were at least somewhat unhappy when it was over. The fact that they generally went on to a subsequent affair with another partner seems to suggest a parallel with heterosexuals' remarriage after divorce rather than any particular emotional immaturity or maladjustment. In any case, most of our homosexual respondents spoke of these special relationships in positive terms and clearly were not content to limit their sexual contacts to impersonal sex.[25]

There is, of course, evidence that homosexual men are more promiscuous than any other group. This fact, however, must be put in context to be evaluated. A major factor is the high availability of sex in the male homosexual world, and homosexual men are men. As the psychologist, Dr. C. A. Tripp writes: "The variety of sex the heterosexual male usually longs for in fantasy is frequently realized in practice by the homosexual. . . . There is no indication that homosexual promiscuity is any greater than its heterosexual equivalent would be in the face of equal opportunity."[26] There are other reasons that account for the promiscuous pattern among many male homosexuals. Two men do not have the same social freedom to live together that women enjoy. It often amounts to revelation of one's orientation with all the hazards that entails in a biased society. The prejudice of the community and of traditional Catholic moral theology discourages stable relationships and indirectly opens the way to promiscuity. Homosexual unions also usually lack children. As the Vatican Council noted, "children contribute in their own way to making their parents holy."[27] Part of that holiness is the holiness of fidelity and stable, enduring love. By excluding any serious consideration of mature and stable gay couples adopting children, or of lesbian couples having children by artificial insemination, we block, without due ethical process, this inducement to healthy relationships among gays. Another factor that inclines to promiscuity among gays is the fact that they are more likely to find partners that are more culturally diverse, which makes for greater likelihood of incompatibility on the long haul.

Therefore, we may not simply look from a distance at the statistics of greater male homosexual promiscuity without distinguishing the various groupings of homosexuals and without recognizing the pressures against marital relationships in the life situation of many gays.

THE MARRIAGE OPTION AND SOLIDLY PROBABLE OPINION

Within the confines of Roman Catholicism, there is division on the ethics of homosexual behavior. A number of moralists hold the traditional "be-but-don't-do" position and a number of others are open to humane expressions of gay sexual love. The hierarchical magisterium seems firm on the "be-but-don't-do" position. The theological magisterium is divided. The hierarchical position is admittedly noninfallible and is not an obstacle to open debate as long as there is due account of and study of that position. What tools for such a pluralistic situation did the Roman Catholic tradition provide? The answer is that the tradition provided an excellent moral system known as probabilism for precisely such a situation. The system has been in a state of disuse, and this represents a major loss of a traditional Catholic treasure.

Probabilism, like all good things, was abused, but the theological achievement that it represents was significant and, until we see how it relates to the charismatic theology of Paul and John and to the concept of the moral inspiration of the Holy Spirit in Augustine and Saint Thomas Aquinas, it has not been given its theological due. Another reason for bringing probabilism down from the Catholic attic is that after Vatican II's recognition of the truly ecclesial quality of Protestant Christian churches, neoprobabilism could be the test of ecumenism. Is our ecumenism merely ceremonial or can we really begin to take Protestant moral views into account in discussing liceity in doubtful matters? The older probabilism did not even face such a question.

The triumph of probabilism in the Church was an achievement of many of our long-suffering theological forebears and we do well to harken back to their work. Let me briefly repeat what probabilism is all about. Probabilism arose, and finally gained prominence over competing systems, as a way of solving practical doubt about the liceity of some kind of behavior. In practice, it confronted a situation in which a rigorous consensus claiming the immorality of certain behavior was challenged. The question was: At what point does the liberty-favoring opinion attain such respectability in the forum of conscience that a person could follow it in good faith? Those who said that even frivolous reasons would justify departure from rigorous orthodoxy were condemned as laxists by Popes Innocent XI and Alexander VII. At the other extreme were the absolute tutiorists who taught that you could never follow the liberal opinion unless it was strictly certain. Even being most probable (*probabilissima*) was not enough. In graph form the situation was like this:

A   /**B**

A represents the dominant rigorous opinion claiming that certain activity could never be moral. B represents the liberal dissent. Laxism claimed that the most tenuous B would override A. Absolute tutiorism claimed that until B replaced A and was beyond challenge, it could not be followed. The Jansenists found absolute tutiorism attractive, but Alexander VIII did not, and he condemned it on December 7, 1690. Thus between the two banned extremes of laxism and absolute tutiorism, the Catholic debate raged with probabilism gradually becoming dominant.

Probabilism proceeded from the twin insights that a doubtful obligation does not bind as though it were certain, and that where there is doubt there is freedom. It held that a solidly probable opinion could be followed even though more probable opinions existed. To be solidly probable, a liberal opinion had to rest upon cogent though not conclusive reasons (intrinsic probability) or upon reliable authority (extrinsic probability). As Tanquerey puts it in his manual of moral theology, to be probable, an opinion could not be opposed to a "definition of the Church" or to certain reason and should retain its probability when compared with opposing arguments.[28] Since there is no "definition of the Church" regarding homosexuality and since furthermore it is clear that the Church does not have the competence to define such issues infallibly,[29] that condition cannot stand in the way of using probabilism.

Intrinsic probability, where one followed one's own lights to a solidly probable opinion, was not stressed in the history of probabilism, but it was presented as a possibility. Stress fell upon extrinsic probability where one found "five or six" moralists known for their "authority, learning and prudence." Even one extraordinary preeminent teacher alone could constitute probability. What this meant is that minority B on our graph became solidly probable through private insight or through the insight of five or six learned experts even though the enormous majority of theologians disagreed. Note well that the basis of probabilism is insight—one's own or that of reliable experts. Insight is an achievement of moral intelligence. It cannot be forbidden, neither does it await permission to appear.

Note also that probabilism does not require a consensus or certitude. As Father Henry Davis writes, "when I act on the strength of a probable opinion, I am always conscious that though I am morally right in so acting, since I act prudently, nevertheless, the opinion of others who do not agree with me may be the true view of the case."[30] Obviously, the perennial debate will be between those who argue that the defenders of probability in a particular case are actually crypto-laxists and those who argue that the deniers of probability are disguised absolute tutiorists.

Probabilism was a remarkable development, and represents a high point in Catholic moral thought. It recognized that the apparent safety of absolute tutiorism was only apparent. The acceptance of such a rigorous position, as Father Tanquerey explained, would impose an impossible burden on the faithful contrary to the mind of the Gospel, which promises that the yoke will be sweet and the burden light; it would thus increase sins, generate despair, and drive many from the practice of religion.[31] Those reasons and probabilism itself are still relevant today.

To dismiss probabilism as the legalistic bickerings of the sixteenth and seventeenth centuries, is theologically shortsighted. In the heyday of the debate, extravagant claims were made. Caramuel, who became known as the "prince of the laxists," taught that Adam and Even used probabilism successfully to excuse themselves from many sins, until their wits and their probabilism failed them and they did fall. Vigorous efforts were made to trace the formal doctrine of probabilism to Augustine, Jerome, Ambrose, Gregory of Nazianzen, Basil, and Thomas Aquinas. One need not become party to such adventures to insist on and argue how compatible probabilism is with deep Christian traditions. The early Church was remarkably sanguine about the presence of the illumining Spirit in the hearts of the faithful. As Vatican II says:

> The Spirit dwells in the Church and in the hearts of the faithful as in a temple (cf. 1 Cor. 3:16; 6:19). In them He prays and bears witness to the fact that they are adopted sons (cf. Gal. 4:6; Rom. 8:15–16, 26). The Spirit guides the Church into the fullness of truth (cf. John 16:13) and gives her a unity of fellowship and service. He furnishes and directs her with various gifts, both hierarchical and charismatic, and adorns her with the fruits of His grace (cf. Eph. 4:11–12; 1 Cor. 12:4; Gal. 5:22).[32]

The Church has shared the confidence of Saint Paul when he said that the spiritual man "is able to judge the value of everything."[33] Augustine and Thomas manifest in strong theological language this exuberant confidence in the presence in all Christians of the illumining Spirit of God. Augustine asked: "What are the laws of God written by God in our hearts but the very presence of the Holy Spirit?"[34] And Thomas Aquinas, arguing that the new law is not anything written (including the New Testament), cites Jeremiah's promise that in the future testament God will put his law into the minds of his people and inscribe it on their hearts. In its primary meaning, then, the new law for Thomas is not the writings of biblical authors, Church officers, or theologians, all of which are secondary, but the instructive grace of the Holy Spirit.[35]

This, admittedly, is a heady doctrine which called for and did historically elicit a theology of the discernment of the Spirit. One must test one's claimed inspiration against all the witnesses to truth within the community. And yet this heady doctrine, with all of its perils, is not a private preserve of the current charismatic movement in the Church, but is rather *bona fide* mainstream Catholic thought. It is also, I believe, eminently congenial with the spirit of the debate that led to the championing of probabilism. The debate on probabilism in many ways seems a curious and stilted period piece, but it would be ungrateful and unconservative of us to reject this achievement of the Catholic tradition. And reject it, in effect, we did. Of course, it maintained its presence in the manuals, but in practice it was rendered nugatory. This was done by simply ignoring the genuine possibility of intrinsic probability and by controlling the theological enterprise in such ways that any theologians favoring a liberal opinion that did not square with the contemporary Vatican view were quickly deemed neither learned nor prudent. Thus did extrinsic probability pass. And thus were the doors thrown open to a juridical positivism based on the hierarchical magisterium.

The neoprobabilism for which I call would have to be extended to include Protestant witnesses to moral truth. Vatican II said of Protestant Christians that "in some real way they are joined with us in the Holy Spirit, for to them also He gives his gifts and graces, and is thereby operative among them with His sanctifying power."[36] It becomes unthinkable, therefore, if those words mean anything, that we accept that solid probability could not also be achieved through the witness of Protestant Christians, who are also subjects of the "gifts and graces" of our God. I submit that if that thought is unpalatable, our ecumenism is superficial and insincere.[37]

Obviously, within Protestant and Catholic Christianity, there is considerable support for the possibility of moral, humane, and humanizing sexual expression by gay persons. Extrinsic probability does obtain. Intrinsic probability is within the reaches of mature persons. There is no reason why this traditional tool of Catholic thought should not be used by pastoral counselors. Obviously the acceptance of the ideal of marriage for gay persons is not something that could be celebrated with public liturgy at this point in the history of the Church since such a celebration would imply a general consensus that as yet does not exist. The celebration of private liturgies, however, to conjoin two gays in permanent and committed love would seem commendable, and well within the realm of the principles and spirit of probabilism. The marital good of exclusive, committed, enduring, generous, and faithful love is a human good. We have no moral right to declare it off limits to persons whom God has made gay.

NOTES

1. On the negative qualities of the macho-masculine, see Daniel C. Maguire, "The Feminization of God and Ethics," *Christianity and Crisis* 42 (March 1983): 59–67.

2. See Walter M. Abbott, general ed., *The Documents of Vatican II* (New York: Herder and Herder, 1966), p. 447, in the *Decree on Priestly Formation.*

3. Ibid.

4. Ibid., p. 446.

5. Ibid., p. 71, in the *Dogmatic Constitution on the Church.* Emphasis added.

6. Ibid., pp. 71–72.

7. Ibid., p. 474, in the *Decree on the Appropriate Renewal of the Religious Life.*

8. Ibid., p. 475.

9, The phrase "human reality and saving mystery" is from Edward Schillebeeckx's book *Marriage: Human Reality and Saving Mystery* (New York: Sheed and Ward, 1965).

10. Abbott, *Documents of Vatican II, The Church Today,* p. 255.

11. Ibid.

12. Ibid., p. 252.

13. Ibid., pp. 252–53.

14. Ibid., p. 253.

15. Ibid., pp. 250–51.

16. Ibid., p. 251.

17. Ibid., p. 253.

18. Ibid., p. 256.

19. Ibid., p. 255.

20. Alan P. Bell and Martin S. Weinberg, *Homosexualities: A Study of Diversity among Men and Women* (New York: Simon & Schuster, 1978), pp. 229–30.

21. Ibid., pp. 230–31

22. Ibid., p. 207.

23. Ibid., p. 208.

24. Ibid., p. 215.

25. Ibid., p. 102.

26. C. A. Tripp, *The Homosexual Matrix* (New York: McGraw 1975), p. 153.

27. Abbott, *Documents of Vatican II*, p. 252.

28. ". . . ei nec definitio Ecclesiae nec certa ratio adversetur. . . ." See Adolphe Tanquerey, *Theologia moralis fundamentalis: De virtutibus et praceptis* (Paris: Desclée, 1955), 2: 293.

29. See my "Moral Absolutes and the Magisterium," in which I argued that it is not meaningful to say that the Church is infallible in specific issues of morality, in *Absolutes in Moral Theology?* ed. C. Curran (Washington, D.C.: Corpus Books, 1968).

30. Henry Davis, *Moral and Pastoral Theology* (London and New York: Sheed and Ward, 1949), 1: 107.

31. See Tanquerey, *Theologia Moralis*, p. 287.

32. Abbott, *Documents of Vatican II*, p. 17.

33. 1 Cor. 2:15.

34. *De spiritu et littera*, C 21, M.L. 44,222.

35. "Ed ideo dicendum est quod principaliter nova lex est lex indita, secundario autem est lex scripta," *Summa Theologica* I–II, q. 106, a. 1, in corp.

36. Abbott, *Documents of Vatican II*, p. 34.

37. See Daniel C. Maguire, "*Human Sexuality*: The Book and the Epiphenomenon," in *Proceedings of the Thirty-Third Annual Convention of the Catholic Theological Society of America* (June 1978), ed. Luke Salm, F.S.C., pp. 71–75, from which this description of probabilism is taken.

11.

IS IT WRONG TO DISCRIMINATE ON THE BASIS OF HOMOSEXUALITY?

Jeff Jordan

Much like the issue of abortion in the early 1970s, the issue of homosexuality has exploded to the forefront of social discussion. Is homosexual sex on a moral par with heterosexual sex? Or is homosexuality in some way morally inferior? Is it wrong to discriminate against homosexuals—to treat homosexuals in less favorable ways than one does heterosexuals? Or is some discrimination against homosexuals morally justified? These questions are the focus of this essay.

In what follows, I argue that there are situations in which it is morally permissible to discriminate against homosexuals because of their homosexuality. That is, there are some morally relevant differences between heterosexuality and homosexuality which, in some instances, permit a difference in treatment. The issue of marriage provides a good example. While it is clear that heterosexual unions merit the state recognition known as marriage, along with all the attendant advantage—spousal insurance coverage, inheritance rights, ready eligibility of adoption—it is far from clear that homosexual couples ought to be accorded that state recognition.

The argument of this essay makes no claim about the moral status of homosexuality per se. Briefly put, it is the argument of this essay that the moral impasse generated by conflicting views concerning homosexuality, and the public policy ramifications of those conflicting views justify the claim that it is morally permissible, in certain circumstances, to discriminate against homosexuals.[1]

This article originally appeared in the *Journal of Social Philosophy* 25, no. 1 (Spring 1995). Reprinted by permission of the *Journal of Social Philosophy*.

1. THE ISSUE

The relevant issue is this: does homosexuality have the same moral status as heterosexuality? Put differently, since there are no occasions in which it is morally permissible to treat heterosexuals unfavorably, whether because they are heterosexual or because of heterosexual acts, are there occasions in which it is morally permissible to treat homosexuals unfavorably, whether because they are homosexuals or because of homosexual acts?

A negative answer to the above can be termed the "parity thesis." The parity thesis contends that *homosexuality has the same moral status as heterosexuality.* If the parity thesis is correct, then it would be immoral to discriminate against homosexuals because of their homosexuality. An affirmative answer can be termed the "difference thesis" and contends that there are morally relevant differences between heterosexuality and homosexuality which justify a difference in moral status and treatment between homosexuals and heterosexuals. The difference thesis entails that *there are situations in which it is morally permissible to discriminate against homosexuals.*

It is perhaps needless to point out that the difference thesis follows as long as there is at least one occasion in which it is morally permissible to discriminate against homosexuals. If the parity thesis were true, then on no occasion would a difference in treatment between heterosexuals and homosexuals ever be justified. The difference thesis does not, even if true, justify discriminatory actions on every occasion. Nonetheless, even though the scope of the difference thesis is relatively modest, it is, if true, a significant principle which has not only theoretical import but important practical consequences as well.[2]

A word should be said about the notion of discrimination. To discriminate against X means treating X in an unfavorable way. The word "discrimination" is not a synonym for "morally unjustifiable treatment." Some discrimination is morally unjustifiable; some is not. For example, we discriminate against convicted felons in that they are disenfranchised. This legal discrimination is morally permissible even though it involves treating one person unfavorably different from how other persons are treated. The difference thesis entails that there are circumstances in which it is morally permissible to discriminate against homosexuals.

2. AN ARGUMENT FOR THE PARITY THESIS

One might suppose that an appeal to a moral right, the right to privacy, perhaps, or the right to liberty, would provide the strongest grounds for the parity thesis. Rights talk, though sometimes helpful, is not very helpful here. If there is reason to think that the right to privacy or the right to liberty encompasses sexuality (which seems plausible enough), it would do so only with regard to private acts and not public acts. Sexual acts performed in public (whether heterosexual or homosexual) are properly suppressible. It does not take too much imagination to see that the right to be free from offense would soon be offered as a counter consideration by those who find homosexuality morally problematic. Furthermore, how one adjudicates between the competing rights claims is far from clear. Hence, the bald appeal to a right will not, in this case anyway, take one very far.

Perhaps the strongest reason to hold that the parity thesis is true is something like the following:

1. Homosexual acts between consenting adults harm no one. And,

2. respecting persons' privacy and choices in harmless sexual matters maximizes individual freedom. And,

3. individual freedom should be maximized. But,

4. discrimination against homosexuals, because of their homosexuality, diminishes individual freedom since it ignores personal choice and privacy. So,

5. the toleration of homosexuality rather than discriminating against homosexuals is the preferable option since it would maximize individual freedom. Therefore,

6. the parity thesis is more plausible than the difference thesis.

Premise (2) is unimpeachable: if an act is harmless and if there are persons who want to do it and who choose to do it, then it seems clear that respecting the choices of those people would tend to maximize their freedom.[3] Step (3) is also beyond reproach: since freedom is arguably a great good and since there does not appear to be any ceiling on the amount of individual freedom—no "too much of a good thing"—(3) appears to be true.

At first glance, premise (1) seems true enough as long as we recognize that if there is any harm involved in the homosexual acts of consenting adults, it would be harm absorbed by the freely consenting participants. This is true, however, only if the acts in question are done in private. Public acts may involve more than just the willing participants. Persons who have no desire to participate, even if only as spectators, may have no choice if the acts are done in public. A real probability of there being unwilling participants is indicative of the public realm and not the private. However, where one draws the line between private acts and public acts is not always easy to discern, it is clear that different moral standards apply to public acts than to private acts.[4]

If premise (1) is understood to apply only to acts done in private, then it would appear to be true. The same goes for (4): discrimination against homosexuals for acts done in private would result in a diminishing of freedom. So

(1)–(4) would lend support to (5) only if we understand (1)–(4) to refer to acts done in private. Hence, (5) must be understood as referring to private acts; and, as a consequence, (6) also must be read as referring only to acts done in private.

With regard to acts which involve only willing adult participants, there may be no morally relevant difference between homosexuality and heterosexuality. In other words, acts done in private. However, acts done in public add a new ingredient to the mix; an ingredient which has moral consequence. Consequently, the argument (1)–(6) fails in supporting the parity thesis. The argument (1)–(6) may show that there are some circumstances in which the moral status of homosexuality and heterosexuality are the same, but it gives us no reason for thinking that this result holds for all circumstances.[5]

3. MORAL IMPASSES AND PUBLIC DILEMMAS

Suppose one person believes that X is morally wrong, while another believes that X is morally permissible. The two people, let's stipulate, are not involved in a semantical quibble; they hold genuinely conflicting beliefs regarding the moral status of X. If the first person is correct, then the second person is wrong; and, of course, if the second person is right, then the first must be wrong. This situation of conflicting claims is what we will call an "impasse." Impasses arise out of moral disputes. Since the conflicting parties in an impasse take contrary views, the conflicting views cannot all be true, nor can they all be false.[6] Moral impasses may concern matters only of a personal nature, but moral impasses can involve public policy. An impasse is likely to have public policy ramifications if large numbers of people hold the conflicting views, and the conflict involves matters which are fundamental to a person's moral identity (and, hence, from a practical point of view, are probably irresolvable) and it involves acts done in public. Since not every impasse has public policy ramifications, one can mark off "public dilemma" as a special case of moral impasses: those moral impasses that have public policy consequences. Public dilemmas, then, are impasses located in the public square. Since they have public policy ramifications and since they arise from impasses, one side or another of the dispute will have its views implemented as public policy. Because of the public policy ramifications, and also because social order is sometimes threatened by the volatile parties involved in the impasse, the state has a role to play in resolving a public dilemma.

A public dilemma can be actively resolved in two ways.[7] The first is when the government allies itself with one side of the impasse and, by state coercion and sanction, declares that side of the impasse the correct side. The American Civil War was an example of this: the federal government forcibly ended slavery by aligning itself with the Abolitionist side of the impasse.[8] Prohibition is another example. The Eighteenth Amendment and the Volstead Act allied the state with the Temperance side of the impasse. State-mandated affirmative action programs provide a modern example of this. This kind of resolution of a public dilemma we can call a "resolution by declaration." The first of the examples cited above indicates that declarations can be morally proper, the right thing to do. The second example, however, indicates that declarations are not always morally proper. The state does not always take the side of the morally correct; nor is it always clear which side is the correct one.

The second way of actively resolving a public dilemma is that of accommodation. An accommodation in this context means resolving the public dilemma in a way that gives as much as possible to all sides of the impasse. A resolution by accommodation involves staking out some middle ground in a dispute and placing public policy in that location. The middle ground location of a resolution via accommodation is a virtue since it entails that there are no absolute victors and no absolute losers. The middle ground is reached in order to resolve the public dilemma in a way which respects the relevant views of the conflicting parties and which maintains social order. The Federal Fair Housing Act and, perhaps, the current status of abortion (legal but with restrictions) provide examples of actual resolutions via accommodation.[9]

In general, governments should be, at least as far as possible, neutral with regard to the disputing parties in a public dilemma. Unless there is some overriding reason why the state should take sides in a public dilemma—the protection of innocent life, or abolishing slavery, for instance—the state should be neutral, because no matter which side of the public dilemma the state takes, the other side will be the recipient of unequal treatment by the state. A state which is partial and takes sides in moral disputes via declaration, when there is no overriding reason why it should, is tyrannical. Overriding reasons involve, typically, the protection of generally recognized rights.[10] In the case of slavery, the right to liberty; in the case of protecting innocent life, the right involved is the negative right to life. If a public dilemma must be actively resolved, the state should do so (in the absence of an overriding reason) via accommodation and not declaration since the latter entails that a sizable number of people would be forced to live under a government which "legitimizes" and does not just tolerate activities which they find immoral. Resolution via declaration is appropriate only if there is an overriding reason for the state to throw its weight behind one side in a public dilemma.

Is moral rightness an overriding reason for a resolution via declaration? What better reason might there be for a resolution by declaration than that it is the right thing to do? Unless one is prepared to endorse a view that is called "legal moralism"—that immorality alone is a sufficient reason for the state to curtail individual liberty—then one had best hold that moral rightness alone is not an overriding reason. Since some immoral acts neither harm nor offend nor violate another's rights, it seems clear enough that too much liberty would be lost if legal moralism were adopted as public policy.[11]

Though we do not have a definite rule for determining a priori which moral impasses genuinely constitute public dilemmas, we can proceed via a case by case method. For example, many people hold that cigarette smoking is harmful and, on that basis, is properly suppressible. Others disagree. Is this a public dilemma? Probably not. Whether someone engages in an imprudent action is, as long as it involves no unwilling participants, a private matter and does not, on that account, constitute a public dilemma. What about abortion? Is abortion a public dilemma? Unlike cigarette smoking, abortion is a public dilemma. This is clear from the adamant and even violent contrary positions involved in the impasse. Abortion is an issue which forces itself into the public square. So, it is clear that, even though we lack a rule which filters through moral impasses designating some as public dilemmas, not every impasse constitutes a public dilemma.

4. CONFLICTING CLAIMS ON HOMOSEXUALITY

The theistic tradition, Judaism and Christianity and Islam, has a clear and deeply entrenched position on homosexual acts: they are prohibited. Now it seems clear enough that if one is going to take seriously the authoritative texts of the respective religions, then one will have to adopt the views of those texts, unless one wishes to engage in a demythologizing of them with the result that one ends up being only a nominal adherent of that tradition.[12] As a consequence, many contemporary theistic adherents of the theistic tradition, in no small part because they can read, hold that homosexual behavior is sinful. Though God loves the homosexual, these folk say, God hates the sinful behavior. To say that act X is a sin entails that X is morally wrong, not necessarily because it is harmful or offensive, but because X violates God's will. So, the claim that homosexuality is sinful entails the claim that it is also morally wrong. And, it is clear, many people adopt the difference thesis just because of their religious views: because the Bible or the Koran holds that homosexuality is wrong, they too hold that view.

Well, what should we make of these observations? We do not, for one thing, have to base our moral conclusions on those views, if for no other reason than not every one is a theist. If one does not adopt the religion-based moral view, one must still respect those who do; they cannot just be dismissed out of hand.[13] And, significantly, this situation yields a reason for thinking that the difference thesis is probably true. Because many religious people sincerely believe homosexual acts to be morally wrong and many others believe that homosexual acts are not morally wrong, there results a public dilemma.[14]

The existence of this public dilemma gives us reason for thinking that the difference thesis is true. It is only via the difference thesis and not the parity thesis, that an accommodation can be reached. Here again, the private/public distinction will come into play.

To see this, take as an example the issue of homosexual marriages. A same-sex marriage would be a public matter. For the government to sanction same-sex marriages—to grant the recognition and reciprocal benefits which attach to marriage—would ally the government with one side of the public dilemma and against the adherents of religion-based moralities. This is especially true given that, historically, no government has sanctioned same-sex marriages. The status quo has been no same-sex marriages. If the state were to change its practice now, it would be clear that the state has taken sides in the impasse. Given the history, for a state to sanction a same-sex marriage now would not be a neutral act.

Of course, some would respond here that by not sanctioning same-sex marriages the state is, and historically has been, taking sides to the detriment of homosexuals. There is some truth in this claim. But one must be careful here. The respective resolutions of this issue—whether the state should recognize and sanction same-sex marriage—do not have symmetrical implications. The asymmetry of this issue is a function of the private/public distinction and the fact that marriage is a public matter. If the state sanctions same-sex marriages, then there is no accommodation available. In that event, the religion-based morality proponents are faced with a public, state sanctioned matter which they find seriously immoral. This would be an example of a resolution via declaration. On the other hand, if the state does not sanction same-sex marriages, there is an accommodation available: in the public realm the state sides with the religion-based moral view, but the state can tolerate private homosexual acts. That is, since homosexual acts are not essentially public acts, they can be, and historically have been, performed in private. The state, by not sanctioning same-sex marriages, is acting in the public realm, but it can leave the private realm to personal choice.[15]

5. THE ARGUMENT FROM CONFLICTING CLAIMS

It was suggested in the previous section that the public dilemma concerning homosexuality, and in particular whether states should sanction same-sex marriages, generates an argument in support of the difference thesis. The argument, again using same-sex marriages as the particular case, is as follows:

7. There are conflicting claims regarding whether the state should sanction same-sex marriages. And,

8. this controversy constitutes a public dilemma. And,

9. there is an accommodation possible if the state does not recognize same-sex marriages. And,

10. there is no accommodation possible if the state does sanction same-sex marriages. And,

11. there is no overriding reason for a resolution via declaration. Hence,

12. the state ought not sanction same-sex marriages. And,

13. the state ought to sanction heterosexual marriages. So,

14. there is at least one morally relevant case in which discrimination against homosexuals, because of their homosexuality, is morally permissible. Therefore,

15. the difference thesis is true.

Since proposition (14) is logically equivalent to the difference thesis, then, if (7)–(14) are sound, proposition (15) certainly follows.

Premises (7) and (8) are uncontroversial. Premises (9) and (10) are based on the asymmetry that results from the public nature of marriage. Proposition (11) is based on our earlier analysis of the argument (1)–(6). Since the strongest argument in support of the parity thesis fails, we have reason to think that there is no overriding reason why the state ought to resolve the public dilemma via declaration in favor of same-sex marriages. We have reason, in other words, to think that (11) is true.

Proposition (12) is based on the conjunction of (7)–(11) and the principle that, in the absence of an overriding reason for state intervention via declaration, resolution by accommodation is the preferable route. Proposition (13) is just trivially true. So, given the moral difference mentioned in (12) and (13), proposition (14) logically follows.

6. TWO OBJECTIONS CONSIDERED

The first objection to the argument from conflicting claims would contend that it is unsound because a similar sort of argument would permit discrimination against some practice which, though perhaps controversial at some earlier time, is now widely thought to be morally permissible. Take mixed-race marriages, for example. The opponent of the argument from conflicting claims could argue that a similar argument would warrant prohibition against mixed-race marriages. If it does, we would have good reason to reject (7)–(14) as unsound.

There are three responses to this objection. The first response denies that the issue of mixed-race marriages is in fact a public dilemma. It may have been so at one time, but it does not seem to generate much, if any, controversy today. Hence, the objection is based upon a faulty analogy.

The second response grants for the sake of the argument that the issue of mixed-race marriages generates a public dilemma. But the second response points out that there is a relevant difference between mixed-race marriages and same-sex marriages that allows for a resolution by declaration in the one case but not the other. As evident from the earlier analysis of the argument in support of (1)–(6), there is reason to think that there is no overriding reason for a resolution by declaration in support of the parity thesis. On the other hand, it is a settled matter that state protection from racial discrimination is a reason sufficient for a resolution via declaration. Hence, the two cases are only apparently similar, and, in reality, they are crucially different. They are quite different because,clearly enough, if mixed-race marriages do generate a public dilemma, the state should use resolution by declaration in support of such marriages. The same cannot be said for same-sex marriages.

One should note that the second response to the objection does not beg the question against the proponent of the parity thesis. Though the second response denies that race and sexuality are strict analogues, it does so for a defensible and independent reason: it is a settled matter that race is not a sufficient reason for disparate treatment; but, as we have seen from the analysis of (1)–(6), there is no overriding reason to think the same about sexuality.[16]

The third response to the first objection is that the grounds of objection differ in the respective cases: one concerns racial identity; the other concerns behavior thought to be morally problematic. A same-sex marriage would involve behavior which many people find morally objectionable; a mixed-race marriage is objectionable to some, not because of the participants' behavior, but because of the racial identity of the participants. It is the race of the marriage partners which some find of primary complaint concerning mixed-race marriages. With same-sex marriages, however, it is the behavior which is primarily objectionable. To see this latter point, one should note that, though promiscuously Puritan in tone, the kind of sexual acts that are likely involved in a same-sex marriage are objectionable to some, regardless of whether done by homosexuals or heterosexuals.[17] So again, there is reason to reject the analogy between same-sex marriages and mixed-race marriages. Racial identity is an immutable trait and a complaint about mixed-race marriages necessarily involves, then, a complaint about an immutable trait. Sexual behavior is not an immutable trait and it is possible to object to same-sex marriages based on the behavior which would be involved in such marriages. Put succinctly, the third response could be formulated as follows: objections to mixed-race marriages necessarily involve objections over status, while objections to same-sex marriages could involve objections over behavior. Therefore, the two cases are not analogues since there is a significant modal difference in the ground of the objection.

The second objection to the argument from conflicting claims can be stated so: if homosexuality is biologically based—if it is inborn[18]—then how can discrimination ever be justified? If it is not a matter of choice, homosexuality is an immutable trait which is, as a consequence, morally permissible. Just as it would be absurd to hold someone morally culpable for being of a certain race, likewise it would be absurd to hold someone morally culpable for being a homosexual. Consequently, according to this objection, the argument from conflicting claims "legitimizes" unjustifiable discrimination.

But this second objection is not cogent, primarily because it ignores an important distinction. No one could plausibly hold that homosexuals act by some sort of biological compulsion. If there is a biological component involved in sexual identity, it would incline but it would not compel. Just because one naturally (without any choice) has certain dispositions, is not in itself a morally cogent reason for acting upon that disposition. Most people are naturally selfish, but it clearly does not follow that selfishness is in any way permissible on that account. Even if it is true that one has a predisposition to do X as a matter of biology and not as a matter of choice, it does not follow that doing X is morally permissible. For example, suppose that pyromania is an inborn predisposition. Just because one has an inborn and, in that sense, natural desire to set fires, one still has to decide whether or not to act on that desire.[19] The reason that the appeal to biology is specious is that it ignores the important distinction between being a homosexual and homosexual acts. One is status; the other is behavior. Even if one has the status naturally, it does not follow that the behavior is morally permissible, nor that others have a duty to tolerate the behavior.

But, while moral permissibility does not necessarily follow if homosexuality should turn out to be biologically based, what does follow is this: in the absence of a good reason to discriminate between homosexuals and heterosexuals, then, assuming that homosexuality is inborn, one ought not discriminate between them. If a certain phenomenon X is natural in the sense of being involuntary and nonpathological, and if there is no good reason to hold that X is morally problematic, then that is reason enough to think that X is morally permissible. In the absence of a good reason to repress X, one should tolerate it since, as per supposition, it is largely nonvoluntary. The argument from conflicting claims, however, provides a good reason which overrides this presumption.

7. A SECOND ARGUMENT FOR THE DIFFERENCE THESIS

A second argument for the difference thesis, similar to the argument from conflicting claims, is what might be called the "no-exit argument." This argument is based on the principle that:

A. no just government can coerce a citizen into violating a deeply held moral belief or religious belief.

Is (A) plausible? It seems to be since the prospect of a citizen being coerced by the state into a practice which she finds profoundly immoral appears to be a clear example of an injustice. Principle (A), conjoined with there being a public dilemma arising over the issue of same-sex marriages, leads to the observation that if the state were to sanction same-sex marriages, then persons who have profound religious or moral objections to such unions would be legally mandated to violate their beliefs since there does not appear to be any feasible "exit right" possible with regard to state sanctioned marriage. An exit right is an exemption from some legally mandated practice, granted to a person or group, the purpose of which is to protect the religious or moral integrity of that person or group. Prominent examples of exit rights include conscientious objection and military service, home-schooling of the young because of some religious concern, and property used for religious purposes being free from taxation.

It is important to note that marriage is a public matter in the sense that, for instance, if one is an employer who provides health care benefits to the spouses of employees, one must provide those benefits to any employee who is married. Since there is no exit right possible in this case, one would be coerced, by force of law, into subsidizing a practice one finds morally or religiously objectionable.[20]

In the absence of an exit right, and if (A) is plausible, then the state cannot morally force persons to violate deeply held beliefs that are moral or religious in nature. In particular, the state morally could not sanction same-sex marriages since this would result in coercing some into violating a deeply held religious conviction.

8. A CONCLUSION

It is important to note that neither the argument from conflicting claims nor the no-exit argument licenses wholesale discrimination against homosexuals. What they do show is that some discrimination against homosexuals, in this case refusal to sanction same-sex marriages, is not only legally permissible but also morally permissible. The discrimination is a way of resolving a public policy dilemma that accommodates, to an extent, each side of the impasse and, further, protects the religious and moral integrity of a good number of people. In short, the arguments show us that there are occasions in which it is morally permissible to discriminate on the basis of homosexuality.[21]

NOTES

1. The terms "homosexuality" and "heterosexuality" are defined as follows. The former is defined as sexual feelings or behavior directed toward individuals of the same sex. The latter, naturally enough, is defined as sexual feelings or behavior directed toward individuals of the opposite sex.

Sometimes the term "gay" is offered as an alternative to "homosexual." Ordinary use of "gay" has it as a synonym of a male homosexual (hence, the common expression, "gays and lesbians"). Given this ordinary usage, the substitution would lead to a confusing equivocation. Since there are female homosexuals, it is best to use "homosexual" to refer to both male and female homosexuals, and reserve "gay" to signify male homosexuals, and "lesbian" for female homosexuals in order to avoid the equivocation.

2. Perhaps we should distinguish the weak difference thesis (permissible discrimination on *some* occasions) from the strong difference thesis (given the relevant moral differences, discrimination on *any* occasion is permissible).

3. This would be true even if the act in question is immoral.

4. The standard answer is, of course, that the line between public and private is based on the notion of harm. Acts which carry a real probability of harming third parties are public acts.

5. For other arguments supporting the moral parity of homosexuality and heterosexuality, see Richard Mohr, *Gays/Justice: A Study of Ethics, Society and Law* (New York: Columbia University Press, 1988); and see Michael Ruse, "The Morality of Homosexuality" in *Philosophy and Sex*, eds. R. Baker & F. Elliston (Amherst, N.Y.: Prometheus Books, 1984), pp. 370–90.

6. Perhaps it would be better to term the disputing positions "contradictory" views rather than "contrary" views.

7. Resolutions can also be passive in the sense of the state doing nothing. If the state does nothing to resolve the public dilemma, it stands pat with the status quo, and the public dilemma is resolved gradually by sociological changes (changes in mores and in beliefs).

8. Assuming, plausibly enough, that the disputes over the sovereignty of the Union and concerning states' rights were at bottom disputes about slavery.

9. The Federal Fair Housing Act prohibits discrimination in housing on the basis of race, religion, and sex. But it does not apply to the rental of rooms in single-family houses, or to a building of five units or less if the owner lives in one of the units. See 42 U.S.C. Section 3603.

10. Note that overriding reasons involve generally recognized rights. If a right is not widely recognized and the state nonetheless uses coercion to enforce it, there is a considerable risk that the state will be seen by many or even most people as tyrannical.

11. This claim is, perhaps, controversial. For a contrary view see Richard George, *Making Men Moral* (Oxford: Clarendon Press, 1993).

12. See, for example, Leviticus 18:22, 21:3; and Romans 1:22–32; and Koran IV:13

13. For an argument that religiously based moral views should not be dismissed out of hand, see Stephen Carter, *The Culture of Disbelief. How American Law and Politics Trivialize Religious Devotion* (New York: Basic Books, 1993).

14. "Two assumptions are these: that the prohibitions against homosexual activity are part of the religious doctrine and not just an extraneous addition; second, that if X is part of one's religious belief or religious doctrine, then it is morally permissible to hold X. Though this latter principle is vague, it is, I think, clear enough for our purposes here (I ignore here any points concerning the rationality of religious belief in general, or in particular cases).

15. This point has implications for the moral legitimacy of sodomy laws. One implication would be this: the private acts of consenting adults should not be criminalized.

16. An *ad hominem* point: if this response begs the question against the proponent of the parity thesis, it does not beg the question any more than the original objection does by presupposing that sexuality is analogous with race.

17. Think of the sodomy laws found in some states which criminalize certain sexual acts, whether performed by heterosexuals or homosexuals.

18. There is some interesting recent research which, though still tentative, strongly suggests that homosexuality is, at least in part, biologically based. See Simon LeVay, *The Sexual Brain* (Cambridge, Mass.: MIT Press 1993), pp. 120–22; and J. M. Bailey and R. C. Pillard "A Genetic Study of Male Sexual Orientation," *Archives of General Psychiatry* 48 (1991): 1089–96; and C. Burr, "Homosexuality and Biology," *The Atlantic* 271/3 (March, 1993): 64; and D. Hamer, S. Hu, V. Magnuson, N. Hu, A. Pattatucci, "A Linkage Between DNA Markers on the X Chromosome and Male Sexual Orientation," *Science* 261 (July 16, 1993): 321–27; and see the summary of this article by Robert Pool, "Evidence for Homosexuality Gene," *Science* 261 (July 16, 1993): 291–92.

19. I do not mean to suggest that homosexuality is morally equivalent or even comparable to pyromania.

20. Is the use of subsidy here inappropriate? It does not seem so since providing health care to spouses, in a society where this is not legally mandatory, seems to be more than part of a salary and is a case of providing supporting funds for a certain end.

21. I thank David Haslett, Kate Rogers, Louis Pojman, and Jim Fieser for helpful and critical comments.

12.

THE CASE FOR GAY MARRIAGE

Richard D. Mohr

I. INTRODUCTION: MARITAL STORIES

The climax of Harvey Fierstein's 1979 play, *Torch Song Trilogy*, is a dialogue—well, shouting match—between mother and son about traditional marriage and its gay variant. As is frequently the case, the nature and function of an institution flashes forth only when the institution breaks down or is dissolved—here by the death of Arnold's lover.

> *Arnold:* [I'm] widowing. . . .
>
> *Ma:* Wait, wait, wait, wait, wait. Are you trying to compare my marriage with you and Alan? Your father and I were married for thirty-five years, had two children and a wonderful life together. You have the nerve to compare yourself to that? . . .
>
> What loss did you have? . . . Where do you come to compare that to a marriage of thirty-five years? . . .
>
> It took me two months until I could sleep in our bed alone, a year to learn to say "I" instead of "we." Are you going to tell me you were "widowing." How dare you!
>
> *Arnold:* You're right, Ma. How dare I. I couldn't possibly know how it feels to pack someone's clothes in plastic bags and watch the garbage-pickers carry them away. Or what it feels like to forget and set his place at the table. How about the food that rots in the refrigerator because you forgot how to shop for one? How dare I? Right, Ma? How dare I?
>
> *Ma:* May God strike me dead! Whatever I did to my mother to deserve a child speaking to me this way. The disrespect!

This article originally appeared in the *Notre Dame Journal of Law, Ethics & Public Policy* 9, no. 1 (1995). Reprinted by permission of the publisher.

Arnold: Listen, Ma, you had it easy. You have thirty-five years to remember, I have five. You had your children and friends to comfort you, I had me! My friends didn't want to hear about it. They said "What're you gripin' about? At least you had a lover." 'Cause everybody knows that queers don't feel nothin'. How dare I say I loved him? You had it easy, Ma. You lost your husband in a nice clean hospital, I lost mine out there. They killed him there on the street. Twenty-three years old, laying dead on the street. Killed by a bunch of kids with baseball bats. Children. Children taught by people like you. 'Cause everybody knows that queers don't matter! Queers don't love! And those that do deserve what they get![1]

In its representation both of the day-to-day nature of gay relationships and of the injustices which beset these relationships because they are not socially, let alone legally, acknowledged as marriages, Fierstein's moving fictional account has its roots deep in the real life experience of lesbian and gay couples. Consider three true-life stories of gay couples:

Years of domesticity have made Brian and Ed familiar figures in the archipelago of middle-aged, middle-class couples who make up my village's permanent gay male community. Ed drives a city bus. Brian is a lineman for the power company—or rather he was until a freak accident set aflame the cherry-picker atop which he worked. He tried to escape by leaping to a nearby tree, but lost his grip and landed on his head. Eventually, it became clear that Brian would be permanently brain-damaged. After a few awkward weeks in the hospital, Brian's parents refused to let Ed visit anymore. Eventually they moved Brian to their village and home, where Ed was not allowed.

A similar case garnered national attention. In Minnesota, Karen Thompson fought a seven-year legal battle to gain guardianship of her lover, Sharon Kowalski. Sharon was damaged of body and mind in a 1983 car accident, after which Sharon's parents barred Karen for years from seeing her.[2] Although the Minnesota tragedy made headlines, the causes of such occurrences are everyday stuff in gay and lesbian lives. In both Sharon and Karen's and Brian and Ed's cases, if the government had through marriage allowed the members of each couple to be next-of-kin for each other, the stories would have had different endings—ones in keeping with our cultural belief that in the first instance those to whom we as adults entrust our tendency in crisis are people we choose, our spouses, who love us because of who we are, not people who are thrust upon us by the luck of the draw and who may love us only in spite of who we are.[3]

On their walk back from their neighborhood bar to the Victorian which, over the years, they had lovingly restored, Warren and Mark stopped along San Francisco's Polk Street to pick up milk for breakfast and for Sebastian, their geriatric cat. Just for kicks, some wealthy teens from the Valley drove into town to "bust some fags." Warren dipped into a convenience store, while Mark had a smoke outside. As Mark turned to acknowledge Warren's return, he was hit across the back of the head with a baseball bat. Mark's blood and vomit splashed across Warren's face. In 1987, a California appellate court held that under no circumstance can a relationship between two homosexuals—however emotionally significant, stable, and exclusive—be legally considered a "close relationship," and so Warren was barred from bringing any suit against the bashers for negligently causing emotional distress.[4]

Gay and lesbian couples are living together as married people do, even though they are legally barred from getting married. The legally aggravated injustices contained in the stories above suggest both that this bar deserves a close examination and that the law, if it aims at promoting justice, will have to be attentive and responsive to the ways couples actually live their lives rather than, as at present, preemptively and ignorantly determining which relationships are to be acknowledged and even created by it. America stands at a point where legal tradition is largely a hindrance to understanding what the law should be.

In this article, I advocate the legalization of gay marriage.[5] My analysis does not in the main proceed by appeal to the concept of equality; in particular, nothing will turn on distinctive features of equal protection doctrine. Rather, the analysis is substantive and turns on understanding the nature and meaning of marriage itself.

To count as a marriage, a relation must fulfill certain normative conditions. Marriage is norm-dependent. In the first half of the article, I examine this aspect of marriage. First, in Part II-A, I examine the going social and legal definitions of marriage and find them all wanting. I then in Part II-B tender a substantive, nonstipulative definition of marriage that is centered and analytically based on the norms which inform the way people actually live as couples. I go on to show that gay couples in fact meet this definition.

But marriage is also norm-invoking: when a relation is determined to be a marital one, that property, in turn, has normative consequences. In particular, it invokes a certain understanding of the relation of marriage to government. And so, Part III of this article examines, along several dimensions, various normative consequences and legal reforms that are suggested by the values that inform marriage. Along the way, I suggest that the lived experience of gay couples not only shows them as fulfilling the norms of marriage but can even indicate ways of improving marital law for everyone. The article concludes in Part IV with an examination of the social, religious, and legal reforms that are under way toward the recognition and support of gay marital relationships. Part of the chore of plumping for radical legal reform is to show that the reform is in fact possible—and that it does not cause the skies to fall.

II. DEFINITIONS OF MARRIAGE: ITS NORMATIVE CONTENT

A. Definitional Failures

1. Social and Legal Attempts to Define Marriage

Usually in religious, ethical, and legal thinking, issues are settled with reference to a thing's goodness. Yet oddly, the debate over gay marriage has focused not on whether the thing is good but on whether the thing can even exist. Those opposing gay marriage say that the very definition of marriage rules out the possibility that gay couples can be viewed as married.[6]

If one asks the average Jo(e) on the street what marriage is, the person generally just gets tongue-tied. Try it. The meaning of marriage is somehow supposed to be so obvious, so entrenched and ramified in daily life, that it is never in need of articulation.

Standard dictionaries, which track and make coherent common usages of terms, are unhelpfully circular. Most commonly, dictionaries define marriage in terms of spouses, spouses in terms of husband and wife, and husband and wife in terms of marriage.[7] In consequence, the various definitions do no work in explaining what marriage is and so simply end up assuming or stipulating that marriage must be between people of different sexes.

Legal definitions of marriage fare no better. Many state laws only speak of spouses or partners and do not actually make explicit that people must be of different sexes to marry.[8] During the early 1970s and again in the early 1980s, gays directly challenged these laws in four states, claiming that in accordance with common law tradition, whatever is not prohibited must be allowed, and that if these laws were judicially construed to require different-sex partners, then the laws constituted unconstitutional sex or sexual-orientation discrimination.[9] Gays lost all these cases, which the courts treated in dismissive, but revealing, fashion.[10]

The courts would first claim that the silence of the law notwithstanding, marriage automatically entails gender difference. The best known of these rulings is the 1974 case *Singer* v. *Hara,* which upheld Washington's refusal to grant a marriage license to two males. The case defined marriage as "the legal union of one man and one woman" as husband and wife.[11] This definition has become *the* legal definition of marriage, since it has been taken up into the standard law dictionary, *Black's Sixth Edition,* where the case is the only citation given in the section on marriage.[12]

Yet, the *Singer* definition tells us nothing whatever of the content of marriage. First, the qualification "as husband and wife" is simply circular. Since "husband" and "wife" mean people who are in a marriage with each other, the definition, as far as these terms go, presupposes the very thing to be defined. So what is left is that marriage is "the legal union of one man and one woman."

Now, if the term "legal" here simply means "not illegal," then notice that a kiss after the prom can fit its bill: "the legal union of one man and one woman." We are told nothing of what "the union" is that is supposed to be the heart of marriage. The formulation of the definition serves no function other than to exclude from marriage—whatever it is—the people whom America views as destroyers of the American family, same-sex couples and polygamists: "*one* man and *one* woman." Like the ordinary dictionary definitions, the legal definition does no explanatory work.[13]

Nevertheless, the courts take this definition, turn around, and say that since this is what marriage *means,* gender discrimination and sexual-orientation discrimination is built right into the institution of marriage; therefore, since marriage itself is permitted, so, too, must be barring same-sex couples from it. Discrimination against gays, they hold, is not an illegitimate discrimination in marriage, indeed it is necessary to the very institution: No one would be married if gays were, for then marriage wouldn't be marriage. It took a gay case to reveal what marriage is, but the case reveals it, at least as legally understood, to be nothing but an empty space, delimited only by what it excludes—gay couples. And so the case has all the marks of being profoundly prejudicial in its legal treatment of gays.

2. Gender in Marital Law

If we shift from considering the legal definition of marriage to the legal practices of marriage, are there differences of gender that insinuate themselves into marriage, so that botched definitions aside, marriage does after all require that its pairings be of the male-female variety? There used to be major gender-based legal differences in marriage, but these have all been found to be unjust and have gradually been eliminated through either legislative or judicial means. For example, a husband used to have an obligation to take care of his wife's material needs without his wife (no matter how wealthy) having any corresponding obligation to look after her husband (however poor). Now both spouses are mutually and equally obliged.[14] At one time a husband could sell his wife's property without her consent; the wife had no independent power to make contracts. But these laws have not generally been in force since the middle of the last century and are now unconstitutional.[15] It used to be that a husband *by definition* could not rape his wife—one could as well rape oneself, the reasoning went. Now, while laws governing sexual relations between husbands and wives are not identical to those governing relations between (heterosexual) strangers, they are nearly so, and such differences as remain are in any case cast in gender-neutral terms.[16] Wives are legally protected from ongoing sexual abuse from husbands—whatever the nonlegal reality.

Now that gender distinctions have all but vanished from the legal *content* of marriage, there is no basis for the requirement that the legal form of marriage unite members of different sexes. The legal definition of marriage—

"union of one man and one woman"—though doggedly enforced in the courts, is a dead husk that has been cast off by marriage as a living legal institution.[17]

3. Babies in Marital Law

Perhaps sensing the shakiness of an argument that rests solely on a stipulative definition of little or no content, the courts have tried to supplement the supposedly obvious requirement for gender disparity in access to marriage with appeal to reproduction. By assuming that procreation and rearing of children is essential to married life, the courts have implicitly given marriage a functional definition designed to eliminate lesbians and gay men from the ranks of the marriageable.[18] "As we all know" (the courts self-congratulatorily declare), lesbians are "constitutionally incapable" of bearing children by other lesbians, and gay men are incapable of siring children by other gay men.

But the legally acknowledged institution of marriage in fact does not track this functional definition. All states allow people who are over sixty to marry each other, with all the rights and obligations marriage entails, even though biological reality dictates that such marriages will be sterile. In Hawaii, the statute that requires women to prove immunity against rubella as a condition for getting a marriage license exempts women "who, by reason of age or other medically determined condition are not and never will be physically able to conceive children."[19] In 1984, Hawaii also amended its marriage statute to delete a requirement that "neither of the parties is impotent or physically incapable of entering into the marriage state."[20] This statutory latitude belies any claim that the narrow purpose of marriage is to promote and protect propagation.[21]

The functional definition is too broad as well. If the function of marriage is only to bear and raise children in a family context, then the state should have no objection to the legal recognition of polygamous marriages. Male-focused polygamous families have been efficient bearers of children; and the economies of scale afforded by polygamous families also make them efficient in the rearing of children.[22] So given the actual scope of legal marriage, reproduction and child rearing cannot be its purpose or primary justification.

This finding is further confirmed if we look at the rights and obligations of marriage, which exist independently of whether a marriage generates children and which frequently are not even instrumental to childbearing and rearing. While mutual material support might be viewed as guarding (indirectly) the interests of children, other marital rights, such as the immunity against compelled testimony from a spouse, can hardly be grounded in child-related purposes. Indeed, this immunity is waived when relations with one's own children are what is at legal stake, as in cases of alleged child abuse.[23]

The assumption that childrearing is a function uniquely tethered to the institution of heterosexual marriage also collides with an important but little acknowledged social reality. Many lesbian and gay male couples already are raising families in which children are the blessings of adoption, artificial insemination, surrogacy, or prior marriages. The country is experiencing something approaching a gay and lesbian baby boom.[24] Many more gays would like to raise or foster children. A 1988 study by the American Bar Association found that eight to ten million children are currently being raised in three million gay and lesbian households.[25] This statistic, in turn, suggests that around 6 percent of the U.S. population is made up of gay and lesbian families with children.[26] We might well ask what conceivable purpose can be served for these children by barring to their gay and lesbian parents the mutual cohesion, emotional security, and economic benefits that are ideally promoted by legal marriage.[27]

4. Marriage as a Creature of the State

If the desperate judicial and social attempts to restrict marriage and its benefits to heterosexual parents are conceptually disingenuous, unjust, and socially inefficient, the question arises: what is left of marriage? Given the emptiness of its standard justifications, should marriage as a legal institution simply be abolished? Ought we simply to abandon the legal institution in favor of a family policy that simply and directly looks after the interests of children, leaving all other possible familial relations on the same legal footing as commercial transactions?

Not quite; but to see what is left and worth saving, we need to take a closer look at the social realities of marriage. Currently, state-sanctioned marriage operates as a legal institution that defines and creates social relations. The law creates the status of husband and wife; it is not a reflection of or response to spousal relations that exist independently of law. This notion that the law "defines and creates social relations" can be clarified by looking at another aspect of family law, one which ordinary people might well find surprising, even shocking. If Paul consensually sires a boy and raises the boy in the way a parent does, then we are strongly inclined to think that he is the boy's father in every morally relevant sense. And we expect the law to reflect this moral status of the father. But the law does not see things this way; it does not reflect and respond to moral reality. For if it turns out that at the time of the boy's birth, his mother was legally married not to Paul but to Fred, the boy is declared by law to be Fred's son, and Paul is, legally speaking, a stranger to the boy. If the mother subsequently leaves Paul and denies him access to the child, Paul has no right at all even to explore legally the possibility that he might have some legislated rights to visit the boy—or so the Supreme Court declared in 1989.[28] Here the law defines and creates the relation of father and son—which frequently, but only by legal accident, happens to accord with the moral reality and lived experience of father and son.

Similarly, in the eyes of the law, marriage is not a social form that exists independently of the law and which marriage law echoes and manages. Rather, marriage is entirely a creature of the law—or as Hawaii's Supreme Court recently put it: "Marriage is a state-conferred legal partnership status."[29]

If we want to see what's left in the box of marriage, we need to abandon this model of legal marriage as constitutive of a status, and rather look at marriage as a form of living and repository of norms independent of law, a moral reality that might well be helped or hindered, but not constituted by the law.[30] Further, current legal marriage, at least as conceptualized by judges, with its definitional entanglements with gender and procreation, is likely to distract us from perceiving lived moral reality.

B. Marriage Defined

What is marriage? Marriage is intimacy given substance in the medium of everyday life, the day-to-day. Marriage is the fused intersection of love's sanctity and necessity's demand.

Not all loves or intimate relations count or should count as marriages. Culturally, we are disinclined to think of "great loves" as marriages. Antony and Cleopatra, Tristan and Isolde, Catherine and Heathcliff—these are loves that burn gloriously but too intensely ever to be manifested in a medium of breakfasts and tire changes. Nor are Americans inclined to consider as real marriages arranged marriages between heads of state who never see each other, for again the relations do not grow in the earth of day-to-day living.

Friendships, too, are intimate relations that we do not consider marital relations. Intimate relations are ones that acquire the character they have—that are unique—because of what the individuals in the relation bring to and make of it; the relation is a distinctive product of their separate individualities. Thus, intimate relations differ markedly from public or commercial transactions. For instance, there is nothing distinctive about your sales clerk that bears on the meaning of your buying a pair of socks from him. The clerk is just carrying out a role, one that from the buyer's perspective nearly anyone could have carried out. But while friendships are star cases of intimate relationships, we do not count them as marriages; for while a person might count on a friend in a pinch to take her to the hospital, friendly relations do not usually manifest themselves through such necessities of life. Friendships are for the sake of fun, and tend to break down when put to other uses. Friendships do not count as marriages, for they do not develop in the medium of necessity's demand.

On the other hand, neither do we count roommates who regularly cook, clean, tend to household chores and share household finances as married, even though they "share the common necessities of life." This expression is the typical phrase used to define the threshold requirement for being considered "domestic partners" in towns that have registration programs for domestic partners.[31] Neither would we even consider as married two people who were roommates and even blended their finances if that is all their relationship comprised. Sharing the day-to-day is, it best, an ingredient of marriage.

Marriage requires the presence and blending of both necessity and intimacy. Life's necessities are a mixed fortune: on the one hand, they frequently are drag, dross, and cussedness, yet on the other hand, they can constitute opportunity, abidingness, and prospect for nurture. They are the field across which, the medium through which, and the ground from which the intimacies which we consider marital flourish, blossom, and come to fruition.

III. THE NORMATIVE AND LEGAL CONSEQUENCE OF MARRIAGE

A. The Legal Rights and Benefits of Marriage

This required blend of intimacy and everyday living explains much of the legal content of marriage. For example, the required blend means that for the relationship to work, there must be a presumption of trust between partners; and, in turn, when the relationship *is* working, there will be a transparency in the flow of information between partners—they will know virtually everything about each other. This pairing of trust and transparency constitutes the moral ground for the common law right against compelled testimony between spouses, and explains why this same immunity is not extended to (mere) friends.[32]

The remaining vast array of legal rights and benefits of marriage fit equally well this matrix of love and necessity—chiefly by promoting the patient tendency that such life requires (by providing for privacy, nurture, support, persistence) and by protecting against the occasions when necessity is cussed rather than opportune, especially when life is marked by crisis, illness, and destruction.[33]

First and foremost, state-recognized marriage changes strangers-at-law into next-of-kin with all the rights which this status entails. These rights include: the right to enter hospitals, jails and other places restricted to "immediate family"; the right to obtain "family" health insurance and bereavement leave; the right to live in neighborhoods zoned "single family only"; and the right to make medical decisions in the event a partner is injured or incapacitated.

Both from the partners themselves and from the state, marriage provides a variety of material supports which ameliorate, to a degree, necessity's unfriendly intervals. Marriage requires mutual support between spouses. It provides income tax advantages, including deductions, credits, improved rates, and exemptions. It provides for enhanced public assistance in times of need. It governs the equitable control, division, acquisition, and disposition of community property. At death, it guarantees rights of inheritance in the absence of wills—a right of special benefit to the poor, who frequently die intestate. For the wealthy, marriage virtually eliminates inheritance taxes between spouses, since spouses as of 1981 can make unlimited untaxed gifts to each other even at death.[34] For all, it exempts property from attachments resulting from one partner's debts. It confers a right to bring a wrongful death suit. And it confers the right to receive survivor's benefits.

Several marital benefits promote a couple's staying together in the face of changed circumstances. Included in the benefits are the right to collect unemployment benefits if one partner quits her job to move with her partner to a new location because the partner has obtained a new job there, and the right to obtain residency status for a noncitizen partner. Currently lesbians and gay men are denied all of these rights in consequence of being barred access to legal marriage, even though these rights and benefits are as relevant to committed gay relationships as to heterosexual marriages.

B. The Structuring of Lesbian and Gay Relationships

The portraits of gay and lesbian committed relationships that emerge from ethnographic studies suggest that in the way they typically arrange their lives, gay and lesbian couples fulfill in an exemplary manner the definition of marriage developed here.[35]

In gay relationships, the ways in which the day-to-day demands of necessity are typically fulfilled are themselves vehicles for the development of intimacy. It is true that gay and lesbian relationships generally divide duties between the partners—this is the efficient thing to do, the very first among the economies of scale that coupledom affords. But the division of duties is in the first instance a matter of personal preference and joint planning, in which decisions are made in part with an eye to who is better at doing any given task and who has free time—say, for ironing or coping with car dealerships. But adjustments are made in cases where one person is better at most things, or even everything. In these cases, the relation is made less efficient for the sake of equality between partners, who willingly end up doing things they would rather not do. Such joint decisions are made not from a sense of traditionally assigned duty and role, but from each partner's impulse to help out, a willingness to sacrifice, and a commitment to equality.[36] In these ways, both the development of intimacy through choice and the proper valuing of love are interwoven in the day-to-day activities of gay couples. Choice improves intimacy. Choice makes sacrifices meaningful. Choice gives love its proper weight.

C. Weddings and Licensing Considered

If this analysis of the nature of marriage is correct, then misguided is the requirement, found in most states, that beyond securing from government a marriage license, the couple, in order to be certifiably married, must also undergo a ceremony of solemnization, either in a church or before a justice of the peace.[37] For people are mistaken to think that the sacred valuing of love is something that can be imported from the outside, in public ceremonies invoking praise from God or community.[38] Even wedding vows can smack of cheap moral credit, since they are words, not actions. The sacred valuing of love must come from within and realize itself over time through little sacrifices in day-to-day existence. In this way, intimacy takes on weight and shine, the ordinary becomes the vehicle of the extraordinary, and the development of the marital relation becomes a mirror reflecting eternity. It is more proper to think of weddings with their ceremonial trappings and invocations as bon voyages than as a social institution which, echoing the legal institution of marriage, defines and confers marital status. In a gay marriage, the sanctifications that descend instantly through custom and ritual in many heterosexual marriages descend gradually over and through time—and in a way they are better for it. For the sacred values and loyal intimacies contained in such a marriage are a product of the relation itself; they are truly the couple's own.

The model of marriage advanced here is highly compatible with, indeed it recommends, what has been, until recently, by far the most usual form of marriage in Western civilization, namely, common-law marriage—in which there is no marriage license or solemnization. Currently only about one-fourth of the states legally acknowledge common-law marriages, but over the largest stretches of Western civilization, legally certifiable marriage was an arrangement limited almost exclusively to the wealthy, the noble—in short, the few.[39]

In a common-law arrangement, the marriage is at some point, as the need arises, culturally and legally acknowledged in retrospect as having existed all along. It is important to remember that as matter of law, the standard requirement of living together seven years is entirely evidentiary and not at all constitutive of the relation as a marriage.[40] So, for example, a child born in the third year of a common-law marriage is legitimate from the moment of its birth and need not wait four years as Mom and Dad log seven years together. The marriage was there in substance all along. The social and legal custom of acknowledging common-law marriage gives an adequately robust recognition to marriage as a lived arrangement and as a repository of values.

The securing of a marriage license is something the state may well want to encourage as a useful device in the administration of the legal benefits of marriage. But the licensing should not be seen as what legally constitutes the marriage when questions arise over whether the marriage in fact exists (say, in paternity, custody, or inheritance disputes). In turn, it is completely legitimate for the state to terminate marital benefits if in fact the couple gets a license but is not fulfilling the definition of marriage as a living arrangement. The state already investigates such cases of fraud when marriage licenses are secured simply to acquire an enhanced immigration status for one of the licensees.[41] Indeed, that immigration fraud through marriage licenses is even conceptually possible is a tacit recognition that marriage *simpliciter* is marriage as a lived arrangement, while legally certified marriage is and should be viewed as epiphenomenonal or derivative—and not vice versa.

D. The Relation between Love and Justice

If intimate or private relations of a certain quality provide the content of marriage, what can the law and public policy provide to marriage? Why do we need legal marriage at all? Folk wisdom has it that both love and justice are blind. But they are blind in different ways, ways which reveal possible conflicts and tensions between love and justice in practice.[42]

Justice is blind—blindfolded—so that it may be a system of neutral, impersonal, impartial rules, a governance by laws, not by idiosyncratic, biased, or self-interested persons. Principles of justice in the modern era have been confected chiefly with an eye to relations at arm's length and apply paradigmatically to competitions conducted between conflicting interests in the face of scarce resources. Equal respect is the central concern of justice.[43]

Love is blind—(as the song goes) blinded by the light—because the lover is stutteringly bedazzled by the beloved. In love, we overlook failings in those whom we cherish. And the beloved's happiness, not the beloved's respect, is love's central concern.

Within the family, we agree that the distribution of goods should be a matter of feeling, care, concern, and sacrifice rather than one conducted by appeal to impartial and impersonal principles of equity. Indeed, if the impersonal principles of justice are constantly in the foreground of familial relations, intimacy is destroyed. If every decision in a family requires a judicial-like determination that each member got an equal share, then the care, concern, and love that are a family's breath and spirit are dead. Justice should not be front and center in family life.

But love may lead to intolerable injustices, even as a spinoff effect of one of its main virtues. In the blindness of love, people will love even those who beat them and humiliate them. Conversely, aggressors in these cases will feel more free to aggress against a family member than a stranger exactly because the family is the realm of love rather than of civic respect. Some of these humiliations are even occasioned by the distinctive opportunities afforded by traditional family life—in particular, society's misguided notion that everything that occurs behind the family's four walls is private, and so beyond legitimate inquiry.

Conflicts between love and justice can be relieved if we view marriage as a legal institution that allows for appeals to justice when they are needed. Justice should not be the motivation for loving relations, but neither should love and family exist beyond the reach of justice. Justice needs to be a reliable background and foundation for family life. Therefore, legal marriage should be viewed as a nurturing ground for social marriage, and not (as now) as that which legally defines and creates marriage and so tends to preclude legal examination of it.

E. The Contribution of Minorities to Family Law Reform

Marriage law should be a conduit for justice in moments of crisis—in financial collapse, in illness, at death—to guard against exploitation both in general and in the distinctive forms that marriage allows.

And, indeed, family law reform has generally been moving in this direction. State-defined marriage is an evolving institution, not an eternal verity. As noted, inequitable distributions of power by gender have been all but eliminated as a legally enforced part of marriage.[44] People at the margins of society have frequently provided the beacon for reform in family law. Already by the 1930s, black American culture no longer stigmatized children born out of wedlock, though whites continued to do so.[45] In 1968, the Supreme Court belatedly came to realize that punitively burdening innocent children is profoundly unjust, and subsequently, through a series of some thirty Supreme Court cases, illegitimacy has all but vanished as a condition legally affecting children born out of wedlock.[46] Further, black Americans provided to the mainstream the model of the extended family with its major virtue of a certain amount of open texture and play in the joints. In 1977, this virtue, too, was given constitutional status when the Supreme Court struck down zoning laws that discriminated against extended, typically black, families.[47]

Currently society and its discriminatory impulse make gay coupling very difficult. It is hard for people to live together as couples without having their sexual orientation perceived in the public realm, which in turn targets them for discrimination. Sharing a life in hiding is even more constricting than life in a nuclear family. Members of nongay couples are here asked to imagine what it would take to erase every trace of their own sexual orientation for even one week. Still, despite oppressive odds, gays have shown an amazing tendency to nest.[48] And those lesbian and gay male couples who have persevered show that the structure of more usual couplings is not a matter of destiny, but of personal responsibility. The so-called basic unit of society turns out not to be a unique immutable atom; it can adopt different parts, and be adapted to different needs.

F. Gay Couples as Models of Family Life

Gay life, like black culture, might even provide models and materials for rethinking family life and improving family law. I will now chart some ways in which this might be so—in particular drawing on the distinctive experience and ideals of gay male couples.[49]

Take sex. Traditionally, a commitment to monogamy—to the extent that it was not simply an adjunct of property law, a vehicle for guaranteeing property rights and succession—was the chief mode of sacrifice imposed upon or adopted by married couples as a means of showing their sacred valuing of their relation. But gay men have realized that while couples may choose to restrict sexual activity in order to show their love for each other, it is not necessary for this purpose; there are many other ways to manifest and ritualize commitment. And so monogamy (it appears) is not an essential component of love and marriage. The authors of *The Male Couple* found that:

> [T]he majority of [gay male] couples, and *all* of the couples together for longer than five years, were not continuously sexually exclusive with each other. Although many had long periods of sexual exclusivity, it was not the ongoing expectation for most. We found that gay men *expect* mutual emotional dependability with their partners [but also believe] that relationship fidelity transcends concerns about sexuality and exclusivity.[50]

Both because marital sacrifices must be voluntary to be meaningful and because sexual exclusivity is not essential to marital commitment, the law should not impose monogamy on married couples. And, indeed, half the states have decriminalized adultery.[51]

Other improvements that take their cue from gay male couplings might include a recognition that marriages evolve over time. *The Male Couple* distinguishes six stages that couples typically pass through: blending (year one), nesting (years two and three), maintaining (years four and five), building (years six though ten), releasing (years eleven through twenty), and renewing (beyond twenty years).[52] Relations initially submerge individuality, and emphasize equality between partners, though the equality usually at first takes the form of complementarity rather than similarity.[53] With the passage of years individuality reemerges. Infatuation gives way to collaboration. The development of a foundational trust between the partners and a blending of finances and possessions, interestingly enough, occurs much later in the relationship—typically after ten years.[54] While the most important factor in keeping men together over the first ten years is finding compatibility, the most important factor for the second decade is a casting off of possessiveness, even as the men's lives become more entwined materially and by the traditions and rituals they have established.

The fact that relations evolve makes the top-down model of legal marriage as creator of relations particularly inappropriate for human life. Currently at law, the only recognition that marriages change and gather moral weight with time, is the vesting of one spouse's (typically the wife's) interests in the other's Social Security benefits after ten years of marriage.[55] More needs to be explored along these lines. For example, one spouse's guaranteed share of the other's inheritance might rise with the logging of years, rather than being the same traditionally fixed, one-third share, both on day one of the marriage and at its fiftieth anniversary.[56] Men's relations also suggest, however, that the emphasis that has been put on purely material concerns, like blended finances, as the marks of a relation in domestic partnership legislation and in a number of gay family law cases is misguided and fails to understand the dynamics and content of gay relations.[57]

In gay male relations, the relation itself frequently is experienced as a third element or "partner" over and above the two men.[58] This third element frequently has a physical embodiment in a home, business, joint avocation, or companion animal, but also frequently consists of joint charitable, civil, political, or religious work. The third element of the relation both provides a focus for the partners and relieves some of the confining centrifugal pressures frequently found in small families. Whether this might have legal implications deserves exploration—it certainly provides a useful model for small heterosexual families.

All longterm gay male relationships, *The Male Couple* reports, devise their own special ways of making the relations satisfying: "Their styles of relationship were developed without the aid of visible role models available to heterosexual couples."[59] This strongly suggests that legal marriage ought not to enforce any tight matrix of obligations on couples if their longterm happiness is part of the laws' stake. Rather the law ought to provide a ground in which relations can grow and change and even recognize their own endings.

IV. CONCLUSION: RELIGIOUS AND LEGAL REFORMS AFOOT

Given the nature of marriage and the nature of gay relations, it is time for the law to let them merge. And, indeed, there have been some general legal, social, and cultural shifts in the direction of acknowledging and supporting gay marriages. On January 1, 1995, gay marriages [became] legal in Sweden; they [became] legal in Denmark in 1989 and Norway in 1993.[60]

In 1993, Hawaii's Supreme Court ruled that Hawaii's marriage laws, which the court interpreted as requiring spouses to be of different sexes, presumptively violate Hawaii's Equal Rights Amendment, which bars sex discrimination. The court ruled that the laws could only be upheld on remand if shown to be necessary to further a compelling state interest.[61] The court preemptively found illegitimate the two standard justifications that have been used in other jurisdictions to claim state interests in restricting marriage to different-sex couples—namely, appeals to the very definition of marriage and to procreation.[62] It looks promising, then, that the court will strike down the ban on same-sex marriages. And if one is married in Hawaii, one is married everywhere—thanks both to common-law tradition and to the U.S. Constitution's full faith and credit clause.[63]

As a matter of general cultural perception, recognitions of same-sex domestic partnerships are baby steps toward the legalization of gay marriage. A number of prestigious universities (including Harvard, Columbia, Stanford, the University of Chicago, and the University of Iowa), and prestigious corporations (including AT&T, Bank of America, Levi Strauss and Company, Lotus Development Corp., Apple Computer, Inc., Warner Brothers, MCA/Universal Inc., the *New York Times* and *Time* magazine) have extended to their employees' same-sex partners domestic partnership benefits, which include many of the privileges extended to their employees' heterosexual spouses.[64] These benefits typically include health insurance. Approximately thirty municipalities, beginning with Berkeley in 1984 and including San Francisco, Seattle, and New York City, have done the same, establishing in some cases a system of civic registrations for same-sex couples.[65]

In June 1994, Vermont became the first state to extend health insurance coverage to the same-sex partners of its state workers.[66] In August 1994, the California legislature passed a bill to establish a registry of domestic partners for both mixed-sex and same-sex couples and gave the partners three legal rights: (1) access to each other when one of them is hospitalized; (2) the use of California's short form will to designate each other as primary beneficiaries, and, most importantly; (3) the establishment of one's partner as conservator if one is incapacitated.[67] On September 11, Governor Pete Wilson vetoed the legislation, issuing a veto message that failed even to acknowledge the bill's impact on the lives of California's gay couples.[68]

In 1984, the General Assembly of the Unitarian-Universalist Association voted to "affirm the growing practice of some of its ministers in conducting services of union of gay and lesbian couples and urges member societies to support their ministers in this important aspect of our movement's ministry to the gay and lesbian community."[69]

In October 1993, the General Assembly of the Union of American Hebrew Congregations—which is the federation of U.S. and Canadian Reform synagogues—adopted a resolution calling for the legal and social recognition and support of gay domestic partners.[70]

Mainline Protestant denominations have ceased full scale attacks on gay and lesbian relationships and are struggling with the issue of blessing them.[71] In June 1994, the General Assembly of the Presbyterian Church (U.S.A.) came within a few votes of permitting ministers to bless same-sex unions.[72] Also in June 1994, a draft proposal by the Episcopal bishops, after describing homosexuality as an orientation of "a significant minority of persons" that "cannot usually be reversed," went on to say that sexual relationships work best within the context of a committed life-long union: "We believe this is as true for homosexual relationships as for heterosexual relationships and that such relationships need and should receive the pastoral care of the church."[73] In October 1993, a draft report by a national Lutheran study group on sexuality had called for the blessing and even legal acknowledgment of loving gay relationships.[74]

These actions addressing the material dimensions of gay relationships through domestic partnership legislation and the spiritual dimensions of gay relationships through holy union ceremonies constitute true moral progress if they are steps toward the full legal and religious recognition of gay marriages. They are morally suspect, though, if they simply end up establishing and then entrenching a system of gay relations as separate but equal to heterosexual ones. To move from a position of no gay blessings and privileges to a structure of separate blessings and privileges is to traverse only the moral ground from the Supreme Court's 1857 *Dred Scott* ruling upholding the form of white supremacy under which blacks could not marry at all—slavery—to its 1896

Plessy v. *Ferguson* ruling upholding the reign of white supremacy that allowed blacks to marry blacks but not to marry whites.[75]

Whether domestic partnership legislation is a steppingstone or a distracting impediment to gay marriage cannot be known categorically. Whether it is one or the other depends on a number of factors: the specific content of the legislation, the social circumstances of its passage, and the likely social consequences of its passage. I conjecture that states will take the route of domestic partnership legislation until they find out that a "separate but equal" structuring of gay and nongay relationships is hopelessly unwieldy. Then states will resort to the benefits of simplicity and recognize gay marriages straight out.

If the analysis of marriage in this article is correct, then marriage, like knowledge, is a common good, one which any number of people can share without its diminution for any one of the sharers. So heterosexuals have nothing to lose from the institutionalization of gay marriage. And the legalization of gay marriage is a moral advance over mere civil rights legislation. For civil rights legislation tends to treat gayness as though it were a property, like having an eye color or wearing an earring, which one could have in isolation from all other people. But gay marriage is an acknowledgement that gayness, like loving and caring, is a relational property, a connection between persons, a human bonding, one in need of tendance and social concern.

NOTES

1. Harvey Fierstein, *Torch Song Trilogy* (New York: Villard Books, 1983; c. 1979), pp. 144–46.

2. See Karen Thompson and Julie Andrzejewski, *Why Can't Sharon Kowalski Come Home?* (San Francisco: Spinsters/Aunt Lute, 1988).

3. Eventually, Thompson did get guardianship of Kowalski, but only after Kowalski's parents withdrew from the field of battle. A Minnesota appeals court held that "this choice [of guardianship] is further supported by the fact that Thompson and Sharon are a family of affinity, which ought to be accorded respect." In re Guardianship of Kowalski, 478 N.W.2d 790, 796 (Minn. 1991).

4. *Coon* v. *Joseph*, 237 Cal. Rptr. 873, 877–78 (Cal. Ct. App. 1987).

5. As a subsidiary matter, I also advocate domestic partnership legislation to the extent that such legislation is a determinate step toward the realization of gay legal marriage and not a distraction from or new hurdle to this goal. See below, part IV.

6. See, e.g., *Adams* v. *Howerton,* 486 F. Supp. 1119, 1123 (C.D. Cal. 1980) (holding that under the immigration and Nationality Act a gay man could not be considered an 'immediate relative" of another with whom he had lived for years and had had a marriage ceremony), "Thus there has been for centuries a combination of scriptural and canonical teaching under which a 'marriage' between persons of the same sex was unthinkable and, by definition, impossible." Id.

Similarly, in 1991, Hawaii's Director of the Department of Health argued before Hawaii's Supreme Court: "The right of persons of the same sex to marry one another does not exist because marriage, by definition and usage, means a special relationship between a man and a woman." Baehr v. *Lewin,* 852 P.2d 44, 61 (Haw. 1993).

7. *The Concise Oxford Dictionary* (3d ed., 1964), pp. 594, 746, 1241, 1478, 1493, for example, offers the following definitions:

"Marriage: relation between married persons, wedlock."
"Married: united in wedlock."
"Wedlock: the married state."
"Spouse: husband or wife."
"Husband: man joined to woman by marriage."
"Wife: married woman esp. in relation to her husband."

8. For example, "Kentucky statutes do not specifically prohibit marriage between persons of the same sex, nor do they authorize the issuance of a marriage license to such persons." *Jones v. Hallahan,* 501 S.W.2d 588, 589 (Ky. 1973). One of the very first gay marriage cases—one from Minnesota—also dealt with a state statute that failed to expressly prohibit same-sex marriages. *Baker v. Nelson,* 191 N.W.2d 185 (Minn. 1971), appeal dismissed, 409 U.S. 810 (1972).

9. *De Santo v. Barnsicy,* 476 A.2d 952 (Pa. 1984) (two persons of the same sex cannot contract a common-law marriage notwithstanding the state's recognition of common law marriages between persons of different sexes); *Singer v. Hara,* 522 P.2d 1187 (Wash. 1974); *Jones,* 501 S.W.2d at 588; *Baker,* 191 N.W.2d at 185.

10. Other cases that, in one way or another, have held that gays cannot marry are *Adams,* 486 F. Supp. at 1119; Succession of Bascot, 502 So. 2d 1118, 1127–30 (La. 1987) (holding that a man cannot be a "concubine" of another man); *Slayton v. Texas,* 633 S.W.2d 934, 937 (Tex. 1982) (stating that same-sex marriage is impossible in Texas); *Jennings v. Jennings,* 315 A.2d 816, 820 n.7 (Md. 1974) (explaining that "Maryland does not recognize a marriage between persons of the same sex"); *Dean v. District of Columbia,* No. CA 90-13892, slip op. at 18–21 (D.C. Super. Ct. Dec. 30, 1991) (invoking passages from Genesis, Deuteronomy, Matthew, and Ephesians to hold that "societal recognition that it takes a man and a woman to form a marital relationship is older than Christianity itself"); In re Estate of Cooper, 564 N.Y.S.2d 684, 687 (N.Y. Sup. Ct. 1990) (refusing to "elevat(e) homosexual unions to the same level achieved by the marriage of two people of the opposite sex"); *Anonymous v. Anonymous,* 325 N.Y.S.2d 499, 500 (N.Y. Sup. Ct. 1971) (stating that "[m]arriage is and always has been a contract between a man and a woman").

11. *Singer,* 522 P.2d at 1193.

12. *Black's Law Dictionary* (6th ed. 1990), p. 972.

13. Even the highly analytical historian John Boswell, in his recent book on the history of gay marriage, fares no better in coming up with a definition of marriage: "It is my understanding that most modern speakers of English understand the term 'marriage' to refer to what the partners expect to be a permanent and exclusive union between two people, which would produce legitimate children if they chose to have children, and which creates mutual rights and responsibilities, legal, economic, and moral." John Boswell, *Same-Sex Unions in Premodern Europe* (New York: Villard Books, 1994), p. 10; cf. Boswell, p. 190. But if one asks "what partners?" "what union?" "what rights?" and "what responsibilities?" I fear the answer in each instance must be "marital ones," in which case the definition goes around in the same small circle as the law. And legitimate children just are children of a marriage, so, that component of the definition is circular as well.

14. Harry D. Krause, *Family Law in a Nutshell,* 2d ed. (St. Paul, Minn.: West Publishing Co., 1986), p. 92 (hereinafter *Family Law*).

15. Ibid., pp. 96–103. See, e.g., *Kirchberg v. Feenstra,* 450 U.S. 455 (1981) (invalidated Louisiana's community property statute that gave the husband, as the family's "head and master," the unilateral right to dispose of property jointly owned with his wife without her consent).

16. *Family Law,* pp. 127–29.

17. "However unpleasant, outmoded or unnecessary, whatever sex discrimination remains in family law is trivial in comparison with the inequality of spouses that result from family facts, from the traditional role division which places the husband into the money-earner role and the wife into the home where she acquires neither property nor marketable skills." *Family Law,* p. 146.

18. See *Singer v. Hara,* 522 P.2d 1187, 1195 (Wash. 1974).

19. *Baehr* v. *Lewin,* 852 P.2d 44, 50 n.7 (Haw. 1993) (quoting *Haw. Rev. Stat.* § 572-7[a] [Supp. 1992]).

20, Id. at 48 n.1 (quoting Raw. Rev. Stat. 580–21 [1985]).

21. Id. at 48.

22. See Dirk Johnson, "Polygamists Emerge from Secrecy, Seeking Not Just Peace, But Respect," *New York Times,* April 9, 1991, p. A22.

23. *Family Law,* p. 131.

24. See, e.g., Susan Chira, "Gay and Lesbian Parents Grow More Visible," *New York Times,* September 30, 1993, p. A1; Daniel Coleman, "Gay Parents Called No Disadvantage, *New York Times,* December 2, 1992, p. B7; "Homosexuality Does Not Make Parent Unfit, Court Rules," *New York Times,* June 22, 1994, p. A8.

25. Editors of the *Harvard Law Review, Sexual Orientation and the Law* 119 (1990).

26. Craig R. Dean, "Legalize Gay Marriage," *New York Times,* September 28, 1991, § 1, p. 19.

27. Andrew Sullivan, "Here Comes the Groom: A (Conservative) Case for Gay Marriage," *New Republic,* August 1989, p. 22.

28. *Michael H.* v. *Gerald D.,* 491 U.S. 110 (1989).

29. *Baehr* v. *Lewin,* 852 P.2d 44, 58 (Haw. 1993).

30. The Supreme Court's three "right to marry" cases implicitly acknowledge that marriage is a social reality and repository of norms, indeed of rights, independent of statutory law, since the right to marry is a substantive liberty right which overrides, trumps, and voids statutory marital law. *Loving* v. *Virginia,* 388 U.S. 1, 12 (1967) (voiding laws barring blacks and whites from marrying each other); *Zablocki* v. *Redhail,* 434 U.S. 374 (1978) (voiding law barring child support scofflaws from marrying); *Turner* v. *Safley,* 482 U.S. 78, 94–99 (1987) (voiding regulation barring prisoners from marrying).

31. See, e.g., City of Berkeley, California, Domestic Partnership Policy, Statement of General Policy, December 4, 1984, quoted in Harry D. Krause, *Family Law: Cases, Comments and Questions,* 3rd ed. (1990), p. 159.

32. See *Family Law,* pp. 131–32.

33. *Baehr,* 852 P.2d at 59 (catalogues the most salient rights and benefits that are contingent upon marital status). The benefits discussed in this section are drawn from this case and from a catalogue of marital privileges given in a 1993 Georgia Supreme Court case, *Van Dyck* v. *Van Dyck,* 425 S.E.2d 853 (Ga. 1993) (Sears-Collins, J., concurring) (holding that a state law authorizing cutoff of alimony payments to a former spouse who enters into a voluntary cohabitation does not apply when the cohabitation in question is a lesbian one). See also 1 Hayden Curry and Denis Clifford, *A Legal Guide for Lesbian and Gay Couples,* R. Leonard, ed., 6th ed. (Berkeley, Calif.: Nole Press, 1991), p. 2.

34. *Family Law,* p. 107.

35. See Alan P. Bell and Martin S. Weinberg, *Homosexualities: A Study of Diversity among Men and Women* (New York: Simon and Schuster, 1978); Philip Blumstein and Pepper Schwartz, *American Couples: Money, Work, Sex* (New York: Morrow, 1983); David McWhirter and Andrew M. Mattison, *The Male Couple: How Relationships Develop* (Englewood Cliffs, N.J.: Prentice-Hall, 1984); Suzanne Sherman, *Lesbian and Gay Marriages: Private Commitments, Public Ceremonies* (Philadelphia: Temple University Press, 1992); Kath Weston, *Families We Choose: Lesbians, Gays, Kinship* (New York: Columbia University Press, 1991).

36. See Weston, *Families We Choose,* pp. 149–50.

37. *Family Law,* pp. 47–48.

38. On sacred values, see generally Douglas MacLean, "Social Values and the Distribution of Risk," in *Values at Risk,* Douglas MacLean, ed. (Totowa, N.J.: Rowman & Allanheld, 1986), pp. 85–93.

39. *Family Law,* p. 50. For a review of the literature on the vagaries of marriage as an institution, see Lawrence Stone, "Sex in the West: The Strange History of Human Sexuality," *New*

Republic, July 8, 1985, p. 25–37. See also Boswell, *Same-Sex Unions in Premodern Europe,* pp. 32–33, 35.

40. *Family Law,* p. 49.

41. Ibid. p. 47.

42. This section draws on some ideas in Claudia Mills and Douglas MacLean, "Love and Justice," *QQ: Report from the Institute for Philosophy and Public Policy,* Fall 1989, pp. 12–15.

43. For a classic statement of this position, see Ronald Dworkin, *Taking Rights Seriously* (Cambridge, Mass.: Harvard University Press, 1978), pp. 180–83, 272–78.

44. Ibid., 1944; text accompanying notes 14–17.

45. Gunnar Myrdal, *An American Dilemma* (New York: Harper & Row, 1944; 1962), p. 935.

46. *Family Law,* pp. 154–55.

47. *Moore* v. *City of East Cleveland, Ohio,* 431 U.S. 494 (1977).

48. Ibid., note 35 (studies of gay couples).

49. Lesbian legal theorists have generally supposed marriage too sexist an institution to be salvaged, and lesbian moral theorists also have found traditional forms of coupling highly suspect. Some recommend communal arrangements as the ideal for lesbians. Others have proposed that lovers should not even live together. See Paula L. Ettelbrick, "Since When Is Marriage a Path to Liberation?" *OUT/LOOK,* Fall 1989, pp. 9, 14–17; Nancy D. Polikoff, "We Will Get What We Ask For: Why Legalizing Gay and Lesbian Marriage Will Not 'Dismantle Legal Structure of Gender in Every Marriage,' " *Virginia Law Review* 79 (1993): 1535; Sarah Lucia Hoagland, *Lesbian Ethics: Toward New Value* (1988); Claudia Card, *Lesbian Choices* (1994).

50. McWhirter and Mattison, *The Male Couple,* p. 285.

51. *Family Law,* p. 130.

52. McWhirter and Mattison, *The Male Couple,* pp. 15–17.

53. Ibid., pp. 31–33.

54. Ibid., pp. 104–105.

55. *Family Law,* pp. 369, 386.

56. Ibid., p. 104.

57. I am thinking in particular of the 1989 case *Braschi* v. *Stahl,* 543 N.E.2d 49 (N.Y. 1989), in which New York's highest court ruled that two men who had been living together for years with blended finances—whom the court called "unmarried lifetime partners"—qualified as "family members" for the purposes of New York's law governing succession rights on apartment leases. At the time, this was considered the most progressive gay family law case of record. And in one regard the case was progressive. It proposed that the concept "family" should be given an operational definition: if it waddles, flaps, and quacks like a family, then it is a family. But then the case went on to dwell almost exclusively on the material and monetary side of life, so much so that in the end it appeared almost to be a case promoting property fights rather than familial relations. And, indeed, this case has had no progeny.

Two years later, the same court abandoned any effort to define family relationships operationally or functionally and held that a lesbian had no rights at all to visit a daughter whom she had jointly reared with the girl's biological mother. *Alison D.* v. *Virginia M.,* 572 N.E.2d 27 (N.Y. 1991). Here only biology mattered. The same court held later that year that grandparents do have a right to visit their grandchildren even over the objections of both parents. In re *Emanuel S.,* 577 N.E.2d 77 (N.Y. 1991). Clearly much work remains to be done in bring law into accord with what families and marriages functionally are and operationally do. Mere reference to the material circumstances of marriage will not do that work.

58. McWhirter and Mattison, *The Male Couple,* p. 285.

59. Ibid., p. 286.

60. "A Swede Deal for Couples," *Advocate,* July 12, 1994, p. 16.

61. *Baehr* v. *Lewin,* 852 P.2d 44, 60–68 (Haw. 1993). Subsequently, Hawaii's legislature voted that marriages in Hawaii must have mixed-sex partners; but since the court had already

evaluated this condition in its constitutional analysis of Hawaii's laws, the legislature's vote seems to be a case of moral grandstanding and political posturing. "Hawaii Legislature Blocks Gay Marriage," *New York Times,* April 27, 1994, at A18.

62. *Baehr,* 852 P.2d at 48 n.1, 61 (Haw. 1993).

63. "Full Faith and Credit shall be given in each State to the public Acts, Records, and judicial Proceedings of every other State." *U.S. Const.* art. IV, § 1.

Gay marriage is also gradually coming into law through the back door of same-sex second parent adoptions. At least six states have allowed the lesbian partner of a woman with a child to adopt—become the second mother of—the child. But if Heather has at law two moms, what is the relation between her two parents? Strangers at law? Surely not. "Court Grants Parental Rights to Mother of Lesbian Lover," *New York Times,* September 12, 1993, § 1, p. 42.

64. "Two Universities Give Gay Partners Same Benefits as Married Couples," *New York Times,* December 24, 1992, p. A10; "Domestic Partnership Benefits Found Not to Increase Employer Costs," *Windy City Times,* June 4, 1992, p. 9; *Frontiers* (Los Angeles), October 7, 1994, p. 16.

65. "Workers' Partners Get Benefit of Health Plan," *New York Times,* October 31, 1993, § 1, p. 40.

66. "Vermont Union Wins Benefits for Partners," *New York Times,* June 13, 1994, p. A12. In some jurisdictions, including Vermont, such benefits are also extended to unmarried but cohabiting heterosexual couples.

67. "Senate Passes Historic Domestic Partners Bill," *Frontiers* (Los Angeles), September 9, 1994, p. 17.

68. "Domestic Partner Bill Vetoed in California," *New York Times,* September 13, 1994, p. A6; see *Frontiers* (Los Angeles), October 7, 1994, p. 36.

69. Paul H. Landen, "Unitarian-Universalist Views on Issues in Human Sexuality" (unpublished Ph.D. thesis, Michigan State University, 1992), p. 134.

70. General Assembly, Union of American Hebrew Congregations, Recognition for Lesbian and Gay Partnerships (October 21–25, 1993).

71. See William N. Eskridge, Jr., "A History of Same-Sex Marriage," *Virginia Law Review* 79 (1993): 1419, 1497–1502.

72. Presbyterians Try to Resolve Long Dispute, *New York Times,* June 17, 1994, p. A9.

73. "Episcopal Draft on Sexuality Tries to Take a Middle Course," *New York Times,* June 26, 1994, § 1, p. 9.

74. "Lutherans to Decide Whether to Sanction Homosexual Unions," *New York Times,* October 21, 1993, p. A1; "Lutheran Church Stalled in Drafting Sex Statement," *New York Times,* November 26, 1993, p. A14.

In marked contrast, the Catholic Church has dug in its heels on the issue. In February 1994, Pope John Paul II issued a hundred-page "Letter to Families." Among other things, the letter sent a message to Catholics to refrain from supporting the notion of gay and lesbian marriages, calling such unions "a serious threat to the family and society" and viewing them as "inappropriately conferring an institutional value on deviant behavior." The pope's own definition of marriage, however, seems to be as circular in its exclusion of gays as those definitions explored above (See above Part II, A.1): "Marriage . . . is constituted by the covenant whereby a man and a woman establish between themselves a partnership for their whole life." "Pope Calls Gay Marriage Threat to Family," *New York Times,* February 23, 1994, p. A2. The complete English language text of the Letter is published in *Origins: CNS Documentary Service* 23:37 (March 3, 1994): 637–59.

75. *Dred Scott* v. *Sandford,* 60 U.S. (19 How.) 393 (1857); *Plessy* v. *Ferguson,* 163 U.S. 537 (1896). In 1883, the Supreme Court in a cursory opinion had upheld against constitutional challenge anti-miscegenation laws. *Pace* v. *Alabama,* 106 U.S. 583 (1883). These laws were finally struck down in 1967. *Loving* v. *Virginia,* 388 U.S. 1 (1967).

13.

THE STAKES IN THE GAY-MARRIAGE WARS

Richard D. Mohr

Two questions: Why have gays suddenly come to view access to marriage as the paramount issue in achieving justice? And why is society's opposition to the legal recognition of gays' love so intense?

To answer these questions I want to draw a distinction between marriage viewed as a way of experiencing the world—of interacting with others and conducting one's affairs—and marriage viewed as a cultural ideal, one tethered to people's identities. Marriage viewed as a way of experiencing the world explains gays' sudden interest in the issue, while marriage viewed as a cultural ideal explains the strength of the backlash against gay marriage. The unfortunate result is that in this battle of the cultural wars the combatants are not even fighting on the same field.

Gays are gradually coming to an awareness that gayness matters in the way we lead our lives; that it is not some insignificant factor in life like a preference for grapes over strawberries. Nor is gayness a property, like having an eye color or wearing an earring, that a person could have in splendid isolation from all others. Being gay situates a person in the world in an ongoing day-to-day way. It's not something one does just on Saturday night or in the sack.

All this was denied by traditional civil rights approaches to justice. Such approaches analogized gayness to skin color and viewed gayness as a property that is fundamentally irrelevant to people's lives. If it *is* fundamentally irrelevant, then presumptively it is irrelevant to teaching a class, flying a plane, or being a cop. On this account, job discrimination is unjust since it is based on something that isn't the basis of anything. This alluring, if limited, model dominated the gay movement from its inception through at least the first decade of the AIDS crisis.

But now consider marriage. Marriage can acknowledge the importance of gayness by affording a way to incorporate gayness into a person's everyday affairs. Viewed as a way of experiencing the world, marriage is the development of love and intimacy through the medium of everyday living. Marriage develops the sanctity of love through the very means by which people meet the day-to-day necessities of life. Marriage converts houses into homes, the consumption of food into customs of nurturance, and sex into filiation. This intersection of gayness and the everyday at marriage explains why gays have rightly shot marriage to the top of the gay rights agenda.

The bad news, though, is that marriage plays an important role not simply in people's experience of living but also in our culture's received ideals.

At the end of May [1996], as part of a House subcommittee hearing on the so-called Defense of Marriage Act, Barney Frank grilled DOMA co-sponsor Henry Hyde to revelatory result. Frank got Hyde to admit that if gays got married, they would take absolutely nothing away from Hyde's own marriage nor, by extension, from any other current American marriage. No heterosexual couple would lose any legal right or material benefit if gays were allowed to get legally married. But what then, Frank queried, was Hyde trying to protect through the Defense of Marriage Act? Hyde's answer: "It demeans the institution. The institution of marriage is trivialized by same-sex marriage." But note that the institution of marriage here has become completely detached from any actual marriage. It is only the concept or ideal of marriage—marriage wholly in the abstract—that concerns Hyde. Here we have left the realm of traditional social policy and entered the realm of cultural symbols. But symbols matter: it is chiefly in terms of symbols that people define their lives and have identities.

To put it bluntly: marriage, viewed now as a symbolic event, enacts, institutionalizes, and ritualizes the social meaning of heterosexuality. Marriage is the chief means by which culture maintains heterosexuality as a social identity. Don Juan, Casanova, and Lothario are now cultural tropes for homosexual denial rather than heterosexual affirmation. One does not become a heterosexual by having heterosexual sex. Rather, marriage is the social essence of heterosexuality. In consequence, on the plane of symbols and identities, if one did not marry, one would not be fully heterosexual. And here's the kicker: if others were allowed to get married, one wouldn't be fully heterosexual either. This analysis explains why the courts, the president, and Congress can claim that marriage—by definition—is the union of one man and one woman as husband and wife, even though this definition is circular, lacks any content, and explains nothing. Its function is not to clarify or explain; its function is to assure heterosexual supremacy as a central cultural form.

What political strategy does this analysis suggest? Standard civil rights strategies that appeal to fairness and equality will do no good. Since the problem is chiefly cultural rather than political, we must adopt a cultural strategy. We need to be able to assure straights that they can be as heterosexual as they want to be—even if gay marriage is legalized. Once we get them to realize, as Frank seems nearly to have done for Hyde, that the issue is a symbolic, if still important, one for them, one wrapped up with their self-conception rather than their well-being, then we can begin to mobilize religious analogies rather than racial analogies as our chief strategy.

Consider: Catholics, but not Protestants, believe that the bread and wine which a priest holds up are literally the body and blood of Christ and this belief is central to their identities as Catholics. In light of the carnage of the Thirty Years War between Protestant and Catholic governments, the world decided that the state is not the proper vehicle for enforcing through law the symbols by which individuals establish themselves as having identities. And Catholics now believe that they can be as Catholic as they want to be, hold as articles of faith the beliefs that define them as Catholics, even if Protestants do not hold or live by these same tenets. Similarly our aim should be to convince straights that they may have an abiding religious-like faith in the rightness of heterosexuality for their lives, but that it is not a proper function of government to enforce that faith on everyone, any more than it is right for the government to impose a belief in transubstantiation on all citizens.

14.

HOW DOMESTIC PARTNERSHIPS AND "GAY MARRIAGE" THREATEN THE FAMILY

Robert H. Knight

For several years, homosexual activists have promoted the extension of marital benefits to same-sex couples (and, in some cases, unmarried heterosexual couples) in corporations and in the law. This practice, called "domestic partnerships" is billed as an extension of tolerance and civil rights, but would actually undermine the institutions of marriage and family.

So, too, is the drive to confer actual marital status on same-sex relationships through the legalization of so-called gay marriage.

Policies and laws that confer partner benefits or marital status on same-sex couples should be opposed because they:

- send a clear signal that companies or cities no longer consider marriage a priority worth encouraging above other kinds of relationships;

- deny the procreative imperative that underlies society's traditional protection of marriage and family as the best environment in which to raise children;

- seek to legitimize same-sex activity and homosexuals' claim that they should be able to adopt children, despite the clear danger this poses to children's development of healthy sexual identities;

- injure the crucial kinship structure, which is derived from marriage and family and imparts continuity, community, and stability to societies;

- violate freedom of religion, as more and more devout Christian, Jewish and Muslim employees and citizens are told that they must accept as "moral" what their faiths teach is immoral;

This article originally appeared in *Insight,* June 1994. Reprinted by permission of the Family Research Council and the author.

- mock the idea of commitment, since most domestic partner laws allow for easy dissolution of the relationship and the registry of several partners (consecutively) a year;

- breed cynicism, because they defy common understanding about the relative worth of particular relationships. Societies must have intact families to survive; societies do not need any homosexual relationships in order to flourish. To equate them is to lie about them.

Furthermore, the drive for homosexual status is undergirded by faulty assertions of scientifically based findings, such as the now-discredited, Kinsey-derived 10 percent estimate of homosexuality in the population; the media-touted but unproven "genetic link" to homosexual behavior; and the deliberate misinterpretation of key psychological studies about homosexuality.

A GROWING CAMPAIGN

Across America, cities, corporations and universities are being lobbied or intimidated into conferring marital benefits on same-sex couples.

- Several cities, including Seattle, Madison (Wisconsin) and the California cities of Los Angeles, San Francisco, Berkeley, Laguna Beach, Santa Cruz and West Hollywood, have extended employee family benefits to same-sex partners. In the District of Columbia, the City Council voted in 1992 to add domestic partners to the city's health insurance policy, but the policy was deleted by Congress in an appropriations bill. Proponents plan to try again to enact the extension.[1]

- In 1990, Stanford University adopted rules granting unmarried couples, including homosexuals, access to dormitories and other campus facilities. Later, "family housing," which had been set aside primarily for married couples with children, was officially opened to homosexuals. Several other campuses have extended benefits such as campus housing to same-sex couples, including the University of Chicago, Harvard, Columbia, Dartmouth, Iowa, Iowa State, the University of Wisconsin, Minnesota, Northwestern, Indiana, and the Massachusetts Institute of Technology.[2]

Several corporations have extended family benefits to same-sex partners, although most corporations have resisted doing so. Only six of the Fortune 1000 companies have instituted domestic partner plans, and about seventy companies nationwide permit unmarried partners to join company health plans.[3] The co-chair of the National Gay and Lesbian Task Force, Elizabeth Birch, is also senior litigation counsel at Apple Computer. She says, "No area has more potency than the advancement of gay rights in the workplace.[4] Companies/institutions with same-sex benefits include Time Warner, Levi-Strauss, Apple, Lotus, Microsoft, MCA, Inc., Viacom Inc., Oracle Systems Corp., Digital, Ben & Jerry's, Minnesota Public Radio, Montefiore Hospital in New York, the *Village Voice* newspaper, Borland International Inc., and the Federal National Mortgage Association.[5] Institutions that promote homosexuality through diversity training and officially sanctioned homosexual employees' groups include many major universities, AT&T (with a 1,000-member homosexual employees group), U.S. West, Xerox, and federal agencies, such as the departments of Transportation, Agriculture, Health and Human Services, and Housing and Urban Development.

- In Hawaii, the state Supreme Court has ruled that the state must show a "compelling interest" in denying marital status to homosexual couples. A constitutional conflict looms should the Hawaii court legalize "gay marriage," because under the U.S. Constitution's full faith and credit clause, states must accord reciprocity to other states in such matters as marriage and drivers' licenses. So, theoretically, a homosexual couple could marry in Honolulu, move to California, and demand that the Golden State recognize their "marriage."

THE HOMOSEXUAL AGENDA

Why is all this happening right now? It seems like only yesterday that homosexual activists wanted only "tolerance," demanding no special rights to compete with the prevailing moral order. But now, activists are on the verge of actually changing the definitions of marriage and family.

Homosexual activist Michelangelo Signorile speaks with a candor not found in most media portrayals of the issue. Discussing ways to advance homosexuality, he urges activists:

> ... to fight for same-sex marriage and its benefits and then, once granted, redefine the institution of marriage completely, to demand the right to marry not as a way of adhering to society's moral codes but rather to debunk a myth and radically alter an archaic institution that as it now stands keeps us down. The most subversive action lesbians and gay men can undertake—and one that would perhaps benefit all of society—is to transform the notion of "family" entirely.[6]

Signorile is right about the subversive nature of the goal of "gay marriage," but homosexuals would not have to go to any lengths to "redefine" marriage once granted that status. The very act of obtaining recognition for same-sex relationships on a par with marriage would transform the notion of "family" entirely.

While Signorile might be dismissed as just one voice, his views are in keeping with those of other high-profile homosexual activists. Franklin Kameny, a Washington, D.C.-based leader of the homosexual rights movement for three decades, has this to say about families:

> ... the "traditional" family has been placed upon such a lofty pedestal of unquestioning and almost mindless, ritualistic worship and endlessly declared but quite unproven importance that rational discussion of it is often well-nigh impossible. ... There is no legitimate basis for limiting the freedom of the individual to structure his family in nontraditional ways that he finds satisfying.[7]

Thomas Stoddard, leader of the drive to lift the military's ban on homosexuals and former president of the Lambda Legal Defense Fund, now known as the Lambda Legal Defense and Education Fund, a homosexual legal foundation, sees marriage as the prime vehicle to advance societal acceptance of homosexuality:

> I must confess at the outset that I am no fan of the "institution" of marriage as currently constructed and practiced. ... Why give it such prominence? Why devote resources to such a distant goal? Because marriage is, I believe, the political issue that most fully tests the dedication of people who are not gay to full equality for gay people, and also the issue most likely to lead ultimately to a world free from discrimination against lesbians and gay men. Marriage is much more than a relationship sanctioned by law. It is the centerpiece of our entire social structure, the core of the traditional notion of "family."[8]

Lesbian activist Paula Ettelbrick, former legal director of the Lambda Legal Defense and Education Fund and now policy director for the National Center for Lesbian Rights, supports the "right" of homosexuals to marry, but opposes marriage as oppressive in and of itself. She says homosexual marriage does not go far enough to transform society:

> Being queer is more than setting up house, sleeping with a person of the same gender, and seeking state approval for doing so. ... Being queer means pushing the parameters of sex, sexuality, and family, and in the process, transforming the very fabric of society. ... As a lesbian, I am fundamentally different from non-lesbian women. ... In arguing for the right to legal marriage, lesbians and gay men would be forced to claim that we are just like heterosexual couples, have the same goals and purposes, and vow to structure our lives similarly. ... We must keep our eyes on the goals of providing true alternatives to marriage and of radically reordering society's views of reality.[9]

MARRIAGE, DOMESTIC PARTNERSHIPS AND THE LAW

No jurisdictional unit in the United States—town, city, or state—recognizes same-sex couples as "married." Protections favoring marriage are built into the law and the culture because of the central importance of the family unit as the building block of civilization. In 1888, the U.S. Supreme Court described marriage "as creating the most important relation in life, as having more to do with the morals and civilization of a people than any other institution."[10]

However, some jurisdictions are moving toward redefining the family to include same-sex relationships, and there is a movement within the legal community to overhaul the definitions of marriage and family. A note in the *Harvard Law Review* in 1991 advocated replacing the formal definition of family with an elastic standard based "mainly on the strength or duration of emotional bonds," regardless of sexual orientation. The note recommends redefining the family through "domestic partner" or family "registration" statutes that go beyond the limited benefits now conferred by existing domestic partnership laws so as to "achieve parity" between marriage and other relationships.[11]

In 1990, San Francisco Mayor Art Agnos appointed lesbian activist Roberta Achtenberg (currently assistant secretary of the U.S. Department of Housing and Urban Development) to chair the Mayor's Task Force on Family Policy. The final report of the task force defines the family this way:

> A unit of interdependent and interacting persons, related together over time by strong social and emotional bonds and/or by ties of marriage, birth, and adoption, whose central purpose is to create, maintain, and promote the social, mental, physical and emotional development and well-being of each of its members.[12]

In this definition, which could reasonably be described as a formulation by homosexual activists, marriage is no longer the foundation for families but secondary to "strong social and emotional bonds." This definition is so vague that multiple-partner unions are not excluded, nor any imaginable combination of persons, including a fishing boat crew. The whole point is to demote marriage to a level with all other conceivable relationships.

The Task Force's definition of "domestic partners" is almost as vague, but limits the relationship to two partners: "Two people who have chosen to share all aspects of each other's lives in an intimate and committed relationship of mutual caring and love."

The District of Columbia City Council legislation defines "domestic partner" as "a person with whom an individual maintains a committed relationship," which is defined as "a familial relationship between two individuals characterized by mutual caring and the sharing of a mutual resident." One of the partners must be a city employee "at least eighteen years old and is competent to contract"; "not be related by blood closer than would prohibit marriage in the District"; "be the sole domestic partner of the other person"; and "not be married."[13]

Applicants would qualify by signing a "declaration of domestic partnership" to be filed with the mayor, and which could be terminated by filing a termination statement with the mayor, which takes effect six months after filing. After that, another partner could be registered. Benefits include granting of sick leave, health insurance, and funeral leave.[14]

Domestic partnership laws have been imposed or enacted by governmental agencies without much say from the public. When citizens do get a chance to give their views, they reject the notion. In May 1994, the city of Austin, Texas, became the first U.S. jurisdiction to overturn an existing domestic partners law when the citizenry voted 62 percent to 38 percent to undo what the city council had enacted. In other jurisdictions, notably Cincinnati, Tampa, and Lewiston, Maine, voters overwhelmingly voted to roll back homosexual rights laws, which are the foundation of the claim for the "right" of domestic partnership status. Even in liberal San Francisco, voters rejected domestic partnerships in 1991, although the policy was later approved.

In the courts, the issue has returned repeatedly since 1976, when the famous "palimony" case of *Marvin* v. *Marvin* held that a property agreement between two unmarried adults who live together and engage in sex is enforceable in a court of law.[15] In most cases, judges, with some notable exceptions, have rejected claims made by homosexual partners to marital-type recognition concerning property allocation and custody of children. In September 1993, a Virginia judge awarded custody of a boy to his grandmother, removing him from his mother's lesbian household.[16] An appeals court overturned that ruling, however, and the case is making its way toward the Supreme Court. In California, a lesbian lost her bid to enforce a "co-parenting" agreement with a biological mother after the couple terminated their relationship.[17] In West Virginia, the state supreme court in July 1993 granted a lesbian mother a stay of an order to remand custody of her children to their father. A circuit court had issued the order, citing as cause that the mother had moved in with her lesbian companion.[18]

HAWAII

In May 1993, the Hawaiian Supreme Court ruled three to one that the state's exclusion of same-sex couples from marital status may be unconstitutional because it amounts to sex discrimination. Marriage is a civil right, the court said, and when the state says who may marry (and by implication, who may not), it violates the guarantee of equal protection under the law. The court invited the state to offer compelling reasons why marriage should be limited to opposite-sex couples.

In April 1994, the state legislature overwhelmingly passed a bill defining marriage in the traditional sense and defending it as the time-honored foundation for procreating and raising children. But many observers expect the liberal Hawaiian court to mandate "gay marriage." Also pending in Hawaii is a domestic partnership bill, which State Senator Ann Kobayashi, a homosexual rights supporter, praised as "a foot in the door" toward legalization of same-sex "marriage."[19]

Homosexual activists, including those in Hawaii, often compare their quest for marital status with an interracial couple's legal victory in *Loving* v. *Virginia.* In that 1967 case, the Supreme Court struck down laws preventing marriage between people of different races as violating the equal protection and due process clauses of the Fourteenth Amendment to the Constitution.

But the court never came close to redefining the institution of marriage itself, which is what would have to occur for same-sex relationships to be accorded marital status. The false equation of a benign, nonbehavioral characteristic such as skin color with an orientation based precisely on behavior finds no support within the law.

In the 1970s, homosexuals unsuccessfully challenged marriage laws in Minnesota, Kentucky, and Washington state. In the Minnesota case, the state supreme court noted, "The institution of marriage as a union of man and woman, uniquely involving the procreating and rearing of children within a family, is as old as the book of Genesis. . . . This historic institution is more deeply founded than the asserted contemporary concept of marriage and societal interests for which petitioners contend."[20]

Other relationships have not been accorded the same status as marriage because they do not contribute in the same way to a community. To put it bluntly, societies can get along quite well without homosexual relationships, but no society can survive without heterosexual marriages and families. In fact, because the term "heterosexual marriage" is redundant, the term "marriage" will mean in this paper what it has always meant: the social, legal, and spiritual union of a man and a woman. "Gay marriage" is an oxymoron, an ideological invention designed to appropriate the moral capital of marriage and family toward the goal of government-enforced acceptance of homosexuality.

THE IMPORTANCE OF DEFINITION

Marriage \ a: the state of being united to a person of the opposite sex as husband or wife ‖ b: the mutual relation of husband and wife: wedlock ‖ c: the institution whereby men and women are joined in a special kind of social and legal dependence for the purpose of founding and maintaining a family.—*Webster's Third New International Dictionary of the English Language Unabridged,* Merriam-Webster Inc., Springfield, Mass., 1981, p. 1284.

To place domestic partner relationships on a par with marriage denigrates the marital imperative. But to describe such relationships as "marriage" destroys the definition of marriage altogether. When the meaning of a word becomes more inclusive, the exclusivity that it previously defined is lost. For instance, if the state of Hawaii decided to extend the famous—and exclusive—"Maui onion" appellation to all onions grown in Hawaii, the term "Maui onion" would lose its original meaning as a specific thing. Consumers would lack confidence in buying a bag of "Maui onions" if all onions could be labeled as such. The same goes for any brand name or even wine from Bordeaux as opposed to wine from California. Likewise, if "marriage" in Hawaii ceases to be the term used solely for the social, legal and spiritual bonding of a man and a woman, the term "marriage" becomes useless. Other states rightly could challenge Hawaii's marriage licenses as meaning something entirely different from what is meant in Pennsylvania or California.

Homosexual activist Tom Stoddard acknowledges that "enlarging the concept to embrace same-sex couples would necessarily transform it into something new. . . . Extending the right to marry to gay people—that is, abolishing the traditional gender requirements of marriage—can be one of the means, perhaps the principal one, through which the institution divests itself of the sexist trappings of the past."[21]

In other words, while many homosexual spokesmen say they want only to be left alone to enjoy the benefits of marriage, Stoddard rightly sees the expanded definition as a way of attacking the institution itself.

Once the "one man, one woman" definition is abandoned, there is no logical reason for limiting it to two people or even to people. Back to the Maui onion example: Hawaii's garlic growers could demand that the exclusive use of the term "Maui onions" gives onion farmers an advantage, and is therefore "discrimination." Of course, garlic growers could qualify for the "Maui onion" label by growing onions in Maui under the Maui requirements. Likewise, homosexuals are not denied the right to marry. Like anybody else, they can qualify for the appellation of marriage by fulfilling its requirements. But they cannot call same-sex relationships "marriage" since they are lacking a basic requirement; they are missing an entire sex. The joining of the two sexes in permanence is the very essence of marriage. Once the "one man, one woman" definition is abandoned, there is no logical reason for limiting "marriage" to two people or even to people. Why not have three partners? Or why not a man and his daughter? Or a man and his dog? The logical reason to extend "marriage" to homosexual couples has nothing to do with marital integrity, but only reflects the fact that homosexuals want the same status regardless of its real meaning. Anything less, they say, is a denial of human rights. If so, then a threesome or a foursome seeking marital status can similarly claim that their sexual proclivities must be recognized by society and the law as the equal of marriage or they are facing discrimination.

Destroying definitions does enormous damage not only to marriage but to the idea of truth. Calling two lesbians a "marriage" is telling a lie, and official recognition of this lie breeds the sort of cynicism found in totalitarian societies, where lies are common currency.

THE MYTH OF HOMOSEXUAL MONOGAMY

In 1992, organizers of the homosexuals' 1993 March on Washington met in Texas to draft a platform of demands. Known as "the Texas platform," it was later toned down to make it more palatable to a mass audience. The original section on "family," however, is revealing as to the intentions of the movement. In addition to Demand No. 40, "the recognition and legal protection of all forms of family structures," the writers called for Demand No. 45, "legalization of same-sex marriages," and Demand No. 46, "legalization of multiple partner unions."[22]

An enormous body of research indicates that monogamy is not the norm for the average homosexual.[23] But even when it is, the result is not necessarily healthier behavior. A study published in the journal *AIDS* found that men in steady relationships practiced more anal intercourse and oral-anal intercourse than those without a steady partner.[24] In other words, the exclusivity of the relationship did not diminish the incidence of unhealthy behavior that is the essence of homosexual sexual activity. Curbing promiscuity would help curb the spread of AIDS and the many other sexually transmitted diseases that are found disproportionately among homosexuals, but there is little evidence that "monogamous" homosexual relationships function that way. An English study also published in the journal *AIDS* found that most "unsafe" sex acts occur in steady relationships.[25]

In April 1994, the homosexual-oriented magazine *Genre* examined current practices among male homosexuals who live with partners. The author concluded that the most successful relationships are possible largely because the partners have "outside affairs."[26]

An excerpt:

> "I think we are seeing a new phenomenon in the gay community," announces Guy Baldwin, an L.A.-based psychologist whose practice is mostly comprised [*sic*] of gay men. "It is the appearance of the well-adjusted open gay marriage." Historically, Baldwin argues, gay men have always engaged in erotic experiences outside a primary relationship, "but they have done so with a great deal of trepidation, soul-searching, and lots of beating up on themselves." For Baldwin's part, what's new is that gay men are no longer holding themselves up to the rigorous standards offered by mainstream society, which equates emotional fidelity with erotic exclusivity. . . . "With all the talk about legalizing marriage for gays, there's an assumption in the minds of most people I talk to that only rarely does that legalization include monogamy."

According to the *Genre* article, in 1993, David P. McWhirter and Andrew M. Mattison, authors of *The Male Couple,* "reported that in a study of 156 males in loving relationships lasting from one to thirty-seven years, only seven couples considered themselves to have been consistently monogamous. Most understood outside sex, and even outside love, as the norm.[27] 'It should be recognized that what has survival values in a heterosexual context may be destructive in a homosexual context,' argues a couple in the McWhirter and Mattison study. They add, 'Life-enhancing mechanisms used by heterosexual men and women should not necessarily be used as a standard by which to judge the degree of a homosexual's adjustment.' In other words, to adapt heterosexual models to homosexual relations is more than just foolhardy; it's an act of oppression."[28]

Former homosexual William Aaron explains why "monogamy" has a different meaning among homosexuals:

> In the gay life, fidelity is almost impossible. Since part of the compulsion of homosexuality seems to be a need on the part of the homophile to "absorb" masculinity from his sexual partners, he must be constantly on the lookout for [new partners]. Consequently the most successful homophile "marriages" are those where there is an arrangement between the two to have affairs on the side while maintaining the semblance of permanence in their living arrangement.[29]

SEXUAL REVOLUTION: LEVELER OF CIVILITY

As the research of the late Harvard sociologist Pitirim Sorokin reveals, no society has loosened sexual morality outside of marriage and survived. Analyzing studies of cultures spanning several thousand years on several continents, Sorokin found that virtually all political revolutions that brought about societal collapse were preceded by sexual revolutions in which marriage and family were no longer accorded premiere status.[30] To put it another way, as marriage and family ties disintegrated, the social restraints learned in families also disintegrated. Chaos results, and chaos ushers in tyrants who promise to restore order by any means, Sorokin notes.

Self-governing people require a robust culture founded on marriage and family, which nurture the qualities that permit self-rule: deferred gratification, self-sacrifice, respect for kinship and law, and property rights. These qualities are founded upon sexual restraint, which permits people to pursue longterm interests, such as procreating and raising the next generation, and securing benefits for one's children.

According sex outside marriage the same protections and status as the marital bond would destroy traditional sexual morality, not merely expand it. One can no more "expand" a definition or moral principle than one can continually expand a yardstick and still use it as a reliable measure.

The drive to delegitimize marriage by hijacking its status for other relationships, including unmarried opposite-sex couples, is being funded and directed by the homosexual rights movement. Lawsuits filed against landlords unwilling to rent to unmarried couples out of religious conviction are largely the work of the Lambda Legal Defense and Education Fund, the American Civil Liberties Union's homosexual legal project, and other homosexual activist organizations intent on using government power to force acceptance of their agenda. If the rights of landlords to refuse to aid and abet what they consider sinful behavior are abridged, it is a small legal step to force landlords, even in households with children, to rent to anyone regardless of sexual orientation. In this way, freedom for homosexuals would be expanded, but at the expense of the freedom of those who find homosexuality destructive, immoral, and unhealthy.

So far, the courts have rejected the claims of homosexuals and unmarried couples in this regard. In a series of recent cases, the courts have ruled that landlords cannot be compelled by law to betray their religious objections to fornication. In May 1994, a California appeals court ruled that the California Fair Employment and Housing Commission erred in fining a sixty-one-year-old landlady, Evelyn Smith, $954 for refusing to rent a duplex to an unmarried couple. The agency had also required Mrs. Smith to post a sign saying she would not discriminate against unmarried people.[31] The three-judge panel found that the order "penalizes [Mrs. Smith] for her religious belief that fornication and its knowing facilitation are sinful."

The Boston-based Gay and Lesbian Advocates and Defenders had filed an amicus brief in the case, and Lambda Legal Defense Fund senior staff attorney Evan Wolfson denounced the verdict, saying that religious beliefs should retreat "when it comes to public good, such as public housing and access to public housing."[32] In saying this, Mr. Wolfson ignored the distinction between government-run "public housing" and private property, as owned by Mrs. Smith.

Courts also have upheld the rights of landlords in Massachusetts, Minnesota, Illinois, and in other California jurisdictions.[33]

THE IMPORTANCE OF FAMILY TIES

For thousands of years, in all successful cultures, homosexuality has been discouraged through social norms and legal prohibition. Cultures have always found it necessary to encourage new marriages and protect existent marriages by extending rewards and privileges for this productive behavior and by extending sanctions and stigmas to unproductive behavior, such as promiscuous sex and homosexual sex. Research and common sense show that the health of any given society depends largely on the number of intact, mom-and-dad families. People living in other arrangements benefit from the social order derived from the marital order.

Marriage-based kinship is essential to stability and continuity. A man is more apt to sacrifice himself to help a son-in-law than some unrelated man (or woman) living with his daughter. Kinship entails mutual obligations and a commitment to the future of the community. Homosexual relationships are a negation of the ties that bind—the continuation of kinship through procreation of children. To accord same-sex relationships the same status as a marriage is to accord them a value that they cannot possibly have. Marriages benefit more than the two people involved, or even the children that are created. Their influence reaches children living nearby, as young minds seek out role models.

The stability they bring to a community benefits all. And the best chance for having a successful, strong marriage is to grow up in a family with a strong marriage as its foundation. This does not mean that people in divorced families or single-parent homes are unable to achieve their own strong family, just that it is more difficult since their role models did not reflect the mom-and-dad family on a daily, longterm basis. A homosexual household compounds the problem by not only lacking one entire sex in the household's foundational relationship but by presenting an aberrant form of sexuality as something "normal."

PROTECTING CHILDREN

A major reason for discouraging societal recognition of homosexual relationships on the partnership level or as "marriages" is the boost such arrangements give to the concept of homosexual adoption of children. Currently, only two states, Florida and New Hampshire, have laws preventing homosexuals from adopting children.[34] This is because it has been considered unthinkable and unnecessary, not because people favor adoption of children by homosexuals. Polls over the past two decades indicate strong societal disapproval of homosexual adoptions. But approval of same-sex relationships undermines much of the moral argument against same-sex couples adopting children. If two same-sex people are seen as the equivalent of husband and wife, it becomes easier for homosexuals to argue, falsely, that a same-sex couple provides the same environment for raising children.

BREAKING MORE WINDOWS

The purpose of marriage is to stabilize sexuality and to provide the best environment in which to procreate and raise children. Sex outside marriage traditionally has been discouraged not only because of the dangers of sexually transmitted diseases and out-of-wedlock births but also because of the dangers it poses to stable families. Crime scholar James Q. Wilson describes "the broken window effect," in which failure to curb breaches in civil order leads to more breaches. He noticed that a building in a tough part of a city had all its windows intact, unlike others around it. After one window was broken, however, all the other windows soon met the same fate. Likewise, if a culture does not discourage extramarital sexuality, the stable marriages are threatened because of the erosion of cultural, social, and, finally, legal support. Plagued by a high rate of divorce, teen pregnancies and STD epidemics, America can only unravel the social fabric further by legitimizing homosexuality.

CONCLUSION

"Domestic partnerships" and "gay marriages" are being advocated as an extension of tolerance and as a matter of civil rights, but these are really wedges designed to overturn traditional sexual morality, as is acknowledged by many homosexual activists themselves. There is little or no support within the law for such formulations, and there is no U.S. jurisdiction that recognizes homosexual "marriage." Voters and corporations should resist the demands made upon them to equate family life with behavior that has been deemed unhealthy, immoral, and destructive to individuals and societies in cultures the world over.

NOTES

1. "D.C. Officials Seek to Revive Domestic Partners Initiative," *Washington Post,* March 1, 1993, p. D-5.
2. "Report of the 14.06 Task Force," University of Michigan, March 29, 1994, pp. 3–5.
3. David J. Jefferson, "Gay Employees Win Benefits for Partners at More Corporations," *Wall Street Journal,* March 18, 1994, p. A-1. Also, Ken McDonnell of the Employee Benefit Research Institute in Washington, D.C., estimates about fifty companies have adopted partner benefits, cited in Robert Bellinger, " 'Domestic-Partner Benefits' Emerge," *Electronic Engineering Times,* November 8, 1993, p. 75.
4. Bellinger, " 'Domestic-Partner Benefits' Emerge."
5. Jefferson, "Gay Employees Win Benefits," and Thomas A. Stewan, "Gay in Corporate America," *Fortune,* December 16, 1991, p. 50; also Ann Merrill, "Domestic Partners: Many Companies Talking about Issue, But Few Have Done Anything about It," Minneapolis *Star-Tribune,* January 26, 1994, p. 1-D.
6. Michelangelo Signorile, "Bridal Wave," *Out,* December/January 1994, p. 161.
7. Franklin E. Karneny, "Deconstructing the Traditional Family," *The World & I,* October 1993, pp. 383–95.
8. Thomas Stoddard, "Why Gay People Should Seek the Right to Marry," in *Lesbians, Gay Men and the Law,* William B. Rubenstein, ed. (New York: The New Press, 1993), pp. 398, 400.
9. Paula Ettelbrick, "Since When Is Marriage a Path to Liberation?" in Rubenstein, *Lesbians, Gay Men and the Law,* pp. 401–405. See chapter 20 in this volume.
10. *Maynard v. Hill,* 125 U.S. 190, 205 (1888).
11. "Legal Definition of the Family," *Harvard Law Review* 104 (1991): 1640.
12. Roberta Achtenberg et al., "Approaching 2000: Meeting the Challenges to San Francisco's Families," The Final Report of the Mayor's Task Force on Family Policy, City and County of San Francisco, June 13, 1990, p. 1.
13. "Health Care Benefits Expansion Act of 1992," District of Columbia City Council, 1992, Sections 2 and 3.
14. Ibid., Sections 4 and 5.
15. *Marvin v. Marvin,* 18 Cal. 3d 660, 557 P.2d 106, 134 Cal. Rptr. 815 (1976).
16. The case is now on appeal as *Sharon Lynne Bottoms v. Pamela Kay Bottoms,* No. 1930-93-2, Court of Appeals of Virginia at Richmond, November 15, 1993.
17. *Georgia P. v. Kerry B.,* cited in "Lesbian Co-Parenting," National Center for Lesbian Rights *Newsletter,* Spring 1994, p. 4.
18. *Wanda J. v. Steven Wayne J.,* Lesbian Custody, National Center for Lesbian Rights *Newsletter,* Spring 1994, p. 4.

19. "Senator Attends Marriage Rights Meeting, *Island Lifestyle,* April 1994, p. 15.

20. *Baker* v. *Nelson* (1971), as cited in Stoddard, "Why Gay People Should Seek the Right to Marry," p. 400.

21. Ibid.

22. "Texas Platform Agreement for Next Year's March," *Washington Blade,* May 22, 1992.

23. See, for instance, Leon McKusick et al., "AIDS and Sexual Behavior Reported by Gay Men in San Francisco," *American Journal of Public Health* 75, no. 5 (May 1985): 493–96; A. P. Bell and M. S. Weinberg, *Homosexualities: A Study of Diversity Among Men and Women,* New York: Simon and Schuster, 1978, pp. 308–309. Also, M. Pollak, "Male Homosexuality," in *Western Sexuality: Practice and Precept in Past and Present Times,* ed. P. Aries and A. Bejin, New York: Basil Blackwell, 1985, pp. 40–61, cited in Joseph Nicolosi, *Reparative Therapy of Male Homosexuality* (Northvale, N.J.: Jason Aronson Inc., 1991), pp. 124–25.

24. A. P. M. Coxon et al., "Sex Role Separation in Diaries of Homosexual Men," *AIDS,* July 1993, pp. 877–82.

25. G. J. Hart et al., "Risk Behaviour, Anti-HIV and Anti-Hepatitis B Core Prevalence in Clinic and Nonclinic Samples of Gay Men in England, 1991–1992," *AIDS,* July 1993, pp. 863–69, as cited in "Homosexual Marriage: The Next Demand," Position Analysis paper by Colorado for Family Values, Colorado Springs, May 1994.

26. Doug Sadownick, "Open Door Policy," *Genre,* April 1994, p. 34.

27. Ibid, p. 35.

28. Ibid, pp. 35, 36.

29. William Aaron, *Straight* (New York: Bantam Books, 1972), p. 208, cited in Nicolosi, *Reparative Therapy of Male Homosexuality,* p. 125.

30. Pitirim Sorokin, *The American Sex Revolution* (Boston: Porter Sargent Publishers, 1956), pp. 77–105.

31. Nancy E. Roman, "Unmarried Couple Lose Rental Case," *Washington Times,* June 3, 1994, p. A-1.

32. Ibid, p. A-8.

33. Ibid.

34. The laws were enacted in 1989. Nan D. Hunter et al., *The Rights of Lesbians and Gay Men,* An American Civil Liberties Union Handbook (Carbondale: Southern Illinois University Press, 1992), p, 106.

15.

MARRIAGE'S TRUE ENDS

Commonweal Editorial

There is every likelihood that Hawaii's Supreme Court will soon overturn that state's prohibition on same-sex marriage. The court's reasoning will be simple enough: Hawaii's constitution forbids discrimination on the basis of sex, and for the state to deny the benefits of marriage to same-sex couples without demonstrating a "compelling state interest" does precisely that. Should Hawaii license same-sex marriage, other states may be bound to recognize those marriages under the Full Faith and Credit clause of the Constitution. The U.S. Supreme Court, it seems certain, will eventually be asked to rule on the constitutionality of the heterosexual exclusivity of marriage.

For the state to license same-sex unions will entail a fundamental reappraisal of the nature of marriage and the balance struck between rights of individual self-determination and the integrity of basic social institutions such as the family. American society has much to gain from a fair-minded debate about such questions, and much to lose if we retreat further from reasoning together about the nature and aims of our common life.

Whether there are compelling enough reasons to preserve the heterosexual exclusivity of marriage is a question that arises in the wake of profound changes in how we think about sexual morality, procreation, and marriage. Historically, marriage forged a powerful connection between sexual love, procreation, and the care of children. However, contemporary understandings of marriage increasingly stress the primacy of individual self-fulfillment, not intergenerational attachments. Moreover, contraception and abortion have essentially severed any unwilled connection between sex and procreation. That connection has been further attenuated by technological advances allowing us

---

This article originally appeared in *Commonweal,* May 17, 1996. Reprinted by permission of the publisher.

to separate biological, gestational, and relational parenting at will. In this context, marriage's meaning seems anything but secure.

But is a further erosion of marriage's traditional linkage between sexual love and human procreation desirable? Advocates of same-sex marriage advance two arguments. First, denying same-sex couples the marriage rights enjoyed by heterosexual persons is discriminatory, an imposition of unjustified inequality. Second, same-sex marriage is presented as an embrace of, not an assault on, what is acknowledged to be a uniquely valuable social institution. If society wishes to promote the human goods of marriage—emotional fulfillment, lifelong commitment, the creation of families, and the care of children—marginalizing homosexuals by denying civil standing to their publicly committed relationships makes little sense, advocates argue.

In modern democratic societies wide latitude is given to individuals and groups pursuing often conflicting and incompatible conceptions of the good. Still, a broad tolerance and a high regard for individual autonomy cannot result in the equal embrace of every private interest or social arrangement. Economic freedom, for example, must be balanced against environmental concerns. Parents' rights to instill their own values in their children must accommodate the state's mandate to set educational standards for all children. The exclusive legal status of monogamous marriage, it is useful to remember, was once challenged by Mormon polygamy. But polygamy was judged inimical to the values of individual dignity and social comity that marriage uniquely promotes.

Now we must weigh the implicit individual and social benefits of heterosexual marriage against those of same-sex unions. In this light, advocates of same-sex marriage often argue that laws prohibiting it are analogous to miscegenation statutes. But the miscegenation analogy fails. Miscegenation laws were about racial separation, not about the nature of marriage. Legalizing same-sex unions will not remedy a self-evident injustice by broadening access to the traditional goods of marriage. Rather, same-sex marriage, like polygamy, would change the very nature and social architecture of marriage in ways that may empty it of any distinctive meaning.

Recent social history can guide us here. Proponents of no-fault divorce argued that the higher meaning of marriage, and even the health of children, would be better served in making marriage easier to dissolve. Yet the plight of today's divorced women and their children refutes such claims. In fact, the loosening of marital bonds and expectations has contributed to the devaluation and even the abandonment of the marriage ideal by many, while encouraging unrealistic expectations of marriage for many more. How society defines marriage has a profound effect on how individuals think and act. And how individuals fashion their most intimate relationships has an enormous impact on the quality of our common life. The dynamic involved is subtle, but real.

Should marriage be essentially a contractual arrangement between two individuals to be defined as they see fit? Or does marriage recognize and embody larger shared meanings that cannot be lightly divorced from history, society, and nature—shared meanings and social forms that create the conditions in which individuals can achieve their own fulfillment? Popular acceptance of premarital sex and cohabitation gives us some sense of the moral and social trajectory involved. Both developments were welcomed as expressions of greater honesty and even better preparations for marriage. Yet considerable evidence now suggests that these newfound "freedoms" have contributed to the instability and trivialization of marriage itself, and have not borne the promises once made for them of happier lives. Similarly, elevating same-sex unions to the same moral and legal status as marriage will further throw into doubt marriage's fundamental purposes and put at risk a social practice and moral ideal vital to all.

The heterosexual exclusivity of marriage can be defended in the same way social policy rightly shows a preference for the formation of intact two-parent families. In both cases, a normative definition of family life is indispensable to any coherent and effective public action. Certainly, mutual love and care are to be encouraged wherever possible. But the justification and rationale for marriage as a social institution cannot rest on the goods of companionship alone. Resisting such a reductionist understanding is not merely in the interests of heterosexuals. There are profound social goods at stake in holding together the biological, relational, and procreative dimensions of human love.

"There are countless ways to 'have' a child," writes theologian Gilbert Meilaender of the social consequences and human meaning of procreation. "Not all of them amount to doing the same thing. Not all of them will teach us to discern the equal humanity of the child as one who is not our product but, rather, the natural development of shared love, like to us in dignity. . . . To conceive, bear, give birth to, and rear a child ought to be an affirmation and a recognition: affirmation of the good of life that we ourselves were given; recognition that this life bears its own creative power to which we should be faithful."[1]

Is there really any doubt that in tying sexual attraction to love and love to children and the creation of families, marriage fundamentally shapes our ideas of human dignity and the nature of society? Same-sex marriage, whatever its virtues, would narrow that frame and foreshorten our perspective. Marriage, at its best, tutors us as no other experience can in the given nature of human life and the acceptance of responsibilities we have not willed or chosen. Indeed, it should tutor us in respect for the given nature of homosexuality and the dignity of homosexual persons. With this respect comes a recognition of difference—a difference with real consequences.

Still, it is frequently objected that if the state does not deny sterile or older heterosexual couples the right to marry, how can it deny that right to homosexual couples, many of whom are already rearing children?

Exceptions do not invalidate a norm or the necessity of norms. How some individuals make use of marriage, either volitionally or as the result of some incapacity, does not determine the purpose of that institution. In that context, heterosexual sterility does not contradict the meaning of marriage in the way same-sex unions would. If marriage as a social form is first a procreative bond in the sense that Meilaender outlines, then marriage necessarily presupposes sexual differentiation, for human procreation itself presupposes sexual differentiation. We are all the offspring of a man and a woman, and marriage is the necessary moral and social response to that natural human condition. Consequently, sexual differentiation, even in the absence of the capacity to procreate, conforms to marriage's larger design in a way same-sex unions cannot. For this reason sexual differentiation is marriage's defining boundary, for it is the precondition of marriage's true ends.

NOTE

1. Gilbert Meilaender, *Body, Soul, and Bioethics* (Notre Dame, Ind.: University of Notre Dame Press, 1996).

16.

VIRTUALLY NORMAL

Andrew Sullivan

The centerpiece of [the] new [homosexual] politics . . . is equal access to civil marriage. . . .

This is a question of formal public discrimination, since only the state can grant and recognize marriage. If the military ban deals with the heart of what it means to be a citizen, marriage does even more so, since, in peace and war, it affects everyone. Marriage is not simply a private contract; it is a social and public recognition of a private commitment. As such, it is the highest public recognition of personal integrity. Denying it to homosexuals is the most public affront possible to their public equality.

This point may be the hardest for many heterosexuals to accept. Even those tolerant of homosexuals may find this institution so wedded to the notion of heterosexual commitment that to extend it would be to undo its very essence. And there may be religious reasons for resisting this that, within certain traditions, are unanswerable. But I am not here discussing what churches do in their private affairs. I am discussing what the allegedly neutral liberal state should do in public matters. For liberals, the case for homosexual marriage is overwhelming. As a classic public institution, it should be available to any two citizens.

Some might argue that marriage is by definition between a man and a woman; and it is difficult to argue with a definition. But if marriage is articulated beyond this circular fiat, then the argument for its exclusivity to one man and one woman disappears. The center of the public contract is an emotional, financial, and psychological bond between two people; in this respect, heterosexuals and homosexuals are identical. The heterosexuality of marriage is intrinsic only if it is understood to be intrinsically procreative; but that definition has long been abandoned in Western society. No civil marriage license is granted on the condition that the couple bear children; and the marriage is no less legal and no less defensible if it remains childless. In the contemporary West, marriage has become a way in which the state recognizes an emotional commitment by two people to each other for life. And within that definition, there is no public way, if one believes in equal rights under the law, in which it should legally be denied homosexuals.

Of course, no public sanctioning of a contract should be given to people who cannot actually fulfill it. The state rightly, for example, withholds marriage from minors, or from one adult and a minor, since at least one party is unable to understand or live up to the contract. And the state has also rightly barred close family relatives from marriage because familial emotional ties are too strong and powerful to enable a marriage contract to be entered into freely by two autonomous, independent individuals; and because incest poses a uniquely dangerous threat to the trust and responsibility that the family needs to survive. But do homosexuals fall into a similar category? History and experience strongly suggest they don't. Of course, marriage is characterized by a kind of commitment that is rare—and perhaps declining—even among heterosexuals. But it isn't necessary to prove that homosexuals or lesbians are less—or more— able to form longterm relationships than straights for it to be clear that at least some are. Moreover, giving these people an equal right to affirm their commitment doesn't reduce the incentive for heterosexuals to do the same.

In some ways, the marriage issue is exactly parallel to the issue of the military. Few people deny that many homosexuals are capable of the sacrifice, the commitment, and the responsibilities of marriage. And indeed, for many homosexuals and lesbians, these responsibilities are already enjoined—as they have been enjoined for centuries. The issue is whether these identical relationships should be denied equal legal standing, not by virtue of anything to do with the relationships themselves but by virtue of the internal, involuntary nature of the homosexuals involved. Clearly, for liberals, the answer to this is clear. Such a denial is a classic case of unequal protection of the laws.

But perhaps surprisingly, . . . one of the strongest arguments for gay marriage is a conservative one. It's perhaps best illustrated by a comparison with the alternative often offered by liberals and liberationists to legal gay marriage, the concept of "domestic partnership." Several cities in the United States have domestic partnership laws, which allow relationships that do not fit into the category of heterosexual marriage to be registered with the city and qualify for benefits that had previously been reserved for heterosexual married couples. In these cities, a variety of interpersonal arrangements qualify for health insurance, bereavement leave, insurance, annuity and pension rights, housing rights (such as rent-control apartments), adoption and inheritance rights. Eventually, the aim is to include federal income tax and veterans' benefits as well. Homosexuals are not the only beneficiaries; heterosexual "live-togethers" also qualify.

The conservative's worries start with the ease of the relationship. To be sure, potential domestic partners have to prove financial interdependence, shared living arrangements, and a commitment to mutual caring. But they don't need to have a sexual relationship or even closely mirror old-style marriage. In principle, an elderly woman and her live-in nurse could qualify, or a pair of frat buddies. Left as it is, the concept of domestic partnership could open a Pandora's box of litigation and subjective judicial decision making about who qualifies. You either are or you're not married; it's not a complex question. Whether you are in a domestic partnership is not so clear.

More important for conservatives, the concept of domestic partnership chips away at the prestige of traditional relationships and undermines the priority we give them. Society, after all, has good reasons to extend legal advantages to heterosexuals who choose the formal sanction of marriage over simply living together. They make a deeper commitment to one another and to society; in exchange, society extends certain benefits to them. Marriage provides an anchor, if an arbitrary and often weak one, in the maelstrom of sex and relationships to which we are all prone. It provides a mechanism for emotional stability and economic security. We rig the law in its favor not because we disparage all forms of relationship other than the nuclear family, but because we recognize that not to promote marriage would be to ask too much of human virtue.

For conservatives, these are vital concerns. There are virtually no conservative arguments either for preferring no social incentives for gay relationships or for preferring a second-class relationship, such as domestic partnership, which really does provide an incentive for the decline of traditional marriage. Nor, if conservatives are concerned by the collapse of stable family life, should they be dismayed by the possibility of gay parents. There is no evidence that shows any deleterious impact on a child brought up by two homosexual parents; and considerable evidence that such a parental structure is clearly preferable to single parents (gay or straight) or no effective parents at all, which, alas, is the choice many children now face. Conservatives should not balk at the apparent radicalism of the change involved, either. The introduction of gay marriage would not be some sort of leap in the dark, a massive societal risk. Homosexual marriages have always existed, in a variety of forms; they have just been euphemized. Increasingly they exist in every sense but the legal one. As it has become more acceptable for homosexuals to acknowledge their loves and commitments publicly, more and more have committed themselves to one another for life in full view of their families and friends. A law institutionalizing gay marriage would merely reinforce a healthy trend. Burkean conservatives should warm to the idea.

It would also be an unqualified social good for homosexuals. It provides role models for young gay people, who, after the exhilaration of coming out, can easily lapse into short-term relationships and insecurity with no tangible goal in sight. My own guess is that most homosexuals would embrace such a goal with as much (if not more) commitment as heterosexuals. Even in our society as it is, many lesbian and gay male relationships are virtual textbooks of monogamous commitment; and for many, "in sickness and in health" has become a vocation rather than a vow. Legal gay marriage could also help bridge the gulf often found between homosexuals and their parents. It could bring the essence of gay life—a gay couple—into the heart of the traditional family in a way the family can most understand and the gay offspring can most easily acknowledge. It could do more to heal the gay-straight rift than any amount of gay rights legislation.

More important, perhaps, as gay marriage sank into the subtle background consciousness of a culture, its influence would be felt quietly but deeply among gay children. For them, at last, there would be some kind of future; some older faces to apply to their unfolding lives, some language in which their identity could be properly discussed, some rubric by which it could be explained—not in terms of sex, or sexual practices, or bars, or subterranean activity, but in terms of their future life stories, their potential loves, their eventual chance at some kind of constructive happiness. They would be able to feel by the intimation of a myriad examples that in this respect their emotional orientation was not merely about pleasure, or sin, or shame, or otherness (although it might always be involved in many of those things), but about the ability to love and be loved as complete, imperfect human beings. Until gay marriage is legalized, this fundamental element of personal dignity will be denied a whole segment of humanity. No other change can achieve it.

Any heterosexual man who takes a few moments to consider what his life would be like if he were never allowed a formal institution to cement his relationships will see the truth of what I am saying. Imagine life without a recognized family; imagine dating without even the possibility of marriage. Any heterosexual woman who can imagine being told at a young age that her attraction to men was wrong, that her loves and crushes were illicit, that her destiny was singlehood and shame, will also appreciate the point. Gay marriage is not a radical step; it is a profoundly humanizing, traditionalizing step. It is the first step in any resolution of the homosexual question—more important than any other institution, since it is the most central institution to the nature of the problem, which is to say, the emotional and sexual bond between one human being and another. If nothing else were done at all, and gay marriage were legalized, 90 percent of the political work necessary to achieve gay and lesbian equality would have been achieved. It is ultimately the only reform that truly matters.

So long as conservatives recognize, as they do, that homosexuals exist and that they have equivalent emotional needs and temptations as heterosexuals, then there is no conservative reason to oppose homosexual marriage and many conservative reasons to support it. So long as liberals recognize, as they do, that citizens deserve equal treatment under the law, then there is no liberal reason to oppose it and many liberal reasons to be in favor of it. So long as intelligent people understand that homosexuals are emotionally and sexually attracted to the same sex as heterosexuals are to the other sex, then there is no human reason on earth why it should be granted to one group and not the other. . . .

[L]ifting the marriage bar [is] simple, direct, and require[s] no change in heterosexual behavior and no sacrifice from heterosexuals. [It would] represent a politics that tackles the heart of prejudice against homosexuals while leaving bigots their freedom. This politics marries the clarity of liberalism with the intuition of conservatism. It allows homosexuals to define their own future and their own identity and does not place it in the hands of the other. It makes a clear, public statement of equality while leaving all the inequalities of emotion and passion to the private sphere, where they belong. It does not legislate private tolerance; it declares public equality. It banishes the paradigm of victimology and replaces it with one of integrity. . . .

It has become a truism that in the field of emotional development, homosexuals have much to learn from the heterosexual culture. The values of commitment, of monogamy, of marriage, of stability are all posited as models for homosexual existence. And, indeed, of course, they are. Without an architectonic institution like that of marriage, it is difficult to create the conditions for nurturing such virtues, but that doesn't belie their importance.

It is also true, however, that homosexual relationships, even in their current, somewhat eclectic form, may contain features that could nourish the broader society as well. Precisely because there is no institutional model, gay relationships are often sustained more powerfully by genuine commitment. The mutual nurturing and sexual expressiveness of many lesbian relationships, the solidity and space of many adult gay male relationships, are qualities sometimes lacking in more rote, heterosexual couplings. Same-sex unions often incorporate the virtues of friendship more effectively than traditional marriages; and at times, among gay male relationships, the openness of the contract makes it more likely to survive than many heterosexual bonds. Some of this is unavailable to the male-female union: there is more likely to be greater understanding of the need for extramarital outlets between two men than between a man and a woman; and again, the lack of children gives gay couples greater freedom. Their failures entail fewer consequences for others. But something of the gay relationship's necessary honesty, its flexibility, and its equality could undoubtedly help strengthen and inform many heterosexual bonds.

In my own sometimes comic, sometimes passionate attempts to construct relationships, I learned something of the foibles of a simple heterosexual model. I saw how the network of gay friendship was often as good an emotional nourishment as a single relationship, that sexual candor was not always the same as sexual license, that the kind of supportive community that bolsters many gay relationships is something many isolated straight marriages could benefit from. I also learned how the subcultural fact of gay life rendered it remarkably democratic: in gay bars, there was far less socioeconomic stratification than in heterosexual bars. The shared experience of same-sex desire cut through class and race; it provided a humbling experience, which allowed many of us to risk our hearts and our friendships with people we otherwise might never have met. It loosened us up, and gave us a keener sense, perhaps, that people were often difficult to understand, let alone judge, from appearances. My heterosexual peers, through no fault of their own, were often denied these experiences. But they might gain from understanding them a little better, and not simply from a position of condescension.

As I've just argued, I believe strongly that marriage should be made available to everyone, in a politics of strict public neutrality. But within this model, there is plenty of scope for cultural difference. There is something baleful about the attempt of some gay conservatives to educate homosexuals and lesbians into an uncritical acceptance of a stifling model of heterosexual normality. The truth is, homosexuals are not entirely normal; and to flatten their varied and complicated lives into a single, moralistic model is to miss what is essential and exhilarating about their otherness.

This need not mean, as some have historically claimed, that homosexuals have no stake in the sustenance of a society, but rather that their role is somewhat different; they may be involved in procreation in a less literal sense: in a society's cultural regeneration, its entrepreneurial or intellectual rejuvenation, its religious ministry, or its professional education. Unencumbered by children, they may be able to press the limits of the culture or the business infrastructure, or the boundaries of intellectual life, in a way that heterosexuals, by dint of a different type of calling, cannot. Of course, many heterosexuals perform similar roles; and many homosexuals prefer domesticity to public performance; but the inevitable way of life of the homosexual provides an opportunity that many intuitively seem to grasp and understand.

Or perhaps their role is to have no role at all. Perhaps it is the experience of rebellion that prompts homosexual culture to be peculiarly resistant to attempts to guide it to be useful or instructive or productive. Go to any march for gay rights and you will see the impossibility of organizing it into a coherent lobby: such attempts are always undermined by irony, or exhibitionism, or irresponsibility. It is as if homosexuals have learned something about life that makes them immune to the puritanical and flattening demands of modern politics. It is as if they have learned that life is fickle; that there are parts of it that cannot be understood, let alone solved; that some things lead nowhere and mean nothing; that the ultimate exercise of freedom is not a programmatic journey but a spontaneous one. Perhaps it requires seeing one's life as the end of a biological chain, or seeing one's deepest emotions as the object of detestation, that provides this insight. But the seeds of homosexual wisdom are the seeds of human wisdom. They contain the truth that order is in fact a euphemism for disorder; that problems are often more sanely enjoyed than solved; that there is reason in mystery; that there is beauty in the wild flowers that grow randomly among our wheat.

17.

THE MARRYING KIND

Elizabeth Kristol

What would life be like if we were not allowed to marry? That is the question at the heart of Andrew Sullivan's first book, *Virtually Normal.* In a sharp departure from the brash tone of the *New Republic,* the political weekly he edits, Sullivan here takes a sober look at the public debate over homosexuality and offers a moving, often lyrical, plea for the legalization of same-sex marriage.

Virtually Normal should be of special interest to conservatives. For one thing, Sullivan has occasionally described himself as such. Second, he is a Roman Catholic who has always taken matters of faith and the teachings of his Church seriously. Finally, Sullivan's thesis hinges on the claim that legalizing homosexual marriage would have a conservatizing influence on society as a whole.

Sullivan begins his book with a poignant memoir of growing up gay. He describes the pain and embarrassment he experienced in his struggles to come to terms with his homosexuality; his determination, once his desires became undeniable, to remain celibate in accordance with his faith; the explosive mix of joy and confusion he experienced when he had his first homosexual experience at age twenty-three.

From this autobiographical opening, Sullivan turns to what he considers the four prevailing attitudes toward homosexuality. These range from the authoritarian "prohibitionists," who consider homosexuality an abomination warranting legal punishment, to the anarchistic "liberationists," who reject the very distinction between homosexuality and heterosexuality as merely semantics. In between lie the "conservatives," who combine private tolerance of homosexuals with public disapproval of homosexuality; and the "liberals," who speak a language of victimhood and look to the state to enforce private tolerance.

This review of Andrew Sullivan, *Virtually Normal: An Argument about Homosexuality* (see chapter 16) originally appeared in *First Things: A Monthly Journal of Religion and Public Life,* No. 59 (January 1996). Reprinted by permission of the publisher.

Sullivan analyzes each of these attitudes and concludes that they have all proven ineffective in developing a workable public position on homosexuality. Instead, he offers a political remedy that he claims will transcend the divisiveness. His solution is unique, Sullivan explains, in focusing exclusively on the actions of the "public neutral state." The state—but only the state—would have to treat homosexuals and heterosexuals with perfect equality. This would mean repealing antisodomy laws, permitting homosexuals to serve in the military on the same terms as heterosexuals, including lessons about homosexuality in public school sex-education programs, and legalizing homosexual marriage and divorce.

Sullivan claims that, since he does not seek to bar discrimination against homosexuals in the private sector, there would be "no cures or reeducation, no wrenching private litigation, no political imposition of tolerance; merely a political attempt to enshrine formal public equality, whatever happens in the culture and society at large." This solution, he adds, has the virtue of respecting religion; as part of the "private sector," churches can take whatever positions they like on homosexuality.

Is there such a thing as a purely "public" solution to the question of homosexuality that leaves the "private" realm untouched? We know Sullivan does not really believe this, because his entire argument in favor of legalized homosexual marriage hinges on the recognition that public law is the most powerful tool for shaping individual attitudes. The core assumption of *Virtually Normal*—and a compelling one, too—is that the *absence* of public laws granting homosexuals full equality has helped create a culture in which homosexuality is considered dirty or sinful, and in which homosexuals are deemed incapable of loving each other with dignity and commitment. As Sullivan rightly observes, the surest way to reverse the trickle-down effect of this message would be to stand the current law on its head. Far from being a simple matter of what the "neutral liberal state should do in public matters," then, public law is for Sullivan the crucial tool of social transformation.

Thus Sullivan notes that the existence of gay marriage would be an "unqualified social good" for homosexuals in providing role models for children coming to terms with their sexuality. As gay marriage

> sank into the subtle background consciousness of a culture, its influence would be felt quietly but deeply among gay children. For them, at last, there would be some kind of future; some older faces to apply to their unfolding lives, some language in which their identity could be properly discussed, some rubric by which it could be explained—not in terms of sex, or sexual practices, or bars, or subterranean activity, but in terms of their future life stories, their potential loves, their eventual chance at some kind of constructive happiness.

The influence of gay marriage, Sullivan believes, would not only make it easier to grow up gay, but would actually change how adult homosexuals conduct their lives. He acknowledges that many homosexual men are self-centered and promiscuous. According to Sullivan, though, "there is nothing inevitable at all about a homosexual leading a depraved life." Homosexuals simply lack the proper "social incentives" not to be depraved. Once same-sex marriage is the law, Sullivan predicts, most homosexuals would enter into marriage "with as much (if not more) commitment as heterosexuals."

But is that really true? Sullivan does not address the fact that most lesbians, who grow up facing the same stigmas and the same lack of role models as male homosexuals, live conventional lives and form longterm monogamous relationships. Why, with gay men, are quasi-marriages the exception to the rule? On this key point, Sullivan sends us a mixed message.

On the one hand, *Virtually Normal* presents a very sanitized picture of male homosexual life; there are no details of the gay subculture to repel heterosexual readers and make them less amenable to Sullivan's political proposals. Even Sullivan's chapter on "The Liberationists" does not include those we have come to associate with that term (the strident gay-rights activists or flamboyant gay liberationists) but focuses instead on a ragtag group of theoreticians influenced by French philosophy. Sullivan makes every effort to portray homosexuals as sharing the same emotions, longings, and dreams as heterosexuals.

Yet in the closing pages of his book, Sullivan undermines his own argument. In the final chapter he returns to the opening chapter's personal tone and reflects on some of the strengths he sees in the contemporary homosexual community. He asserts that "homosexual relationships, even in their current, somewhat eclectic form, may contain features that could nourish the broader society as well." The "solidity and space" of gay relationships "are qualities sometimes lacking in more rote, heterosexual couplings." Moreover, the "openness of the contract makes it more likely to survive than many heterosexual bonds." As Sullivan puts it, there is "more likely to be a greater understanding of the need for extramarital outlets between two men than between a man and a woman; and again, the lack of children gives gay couples greater freedom."

Sullivan suggests that gay marriage would do well to retain some of this "openness":

> I believe strongly that marriage should be made available to everyone, in a politics of strict public neutrality. But within this model, there is plenty of scope for cultural difference. There is something baleful about the attempt of some gay conservatives to educate homosexuals and lesbians into an uncritical acceptance of a stifling model of heterosexual normality. The truth is, homosexuals are not entirely normal; and to flatten their varied and complicated lives into a single, moralistic model is to miss what is essential and exhilarating about their otherness.

Rote? Stifling? Moralistic? These are strange epithets to come upon in the final pages of a book whose goal is to convince readers that homosexuals want to marry and deserve to marry; that homosexual love is as dignified as heterosexual love; that it is inhumane not to allow the dignity of this love to find fruition in marriage; that marriage is so venerable an institution that it is single-handedly capable of leading men out of lives of empty promiscuity into unions of commitment and fidelity. Suddenly we learn, almost as an afterthought, that the institution of marriage may have to change to accommodate the special needs of homosexuals.

At first glance, it seems odd that Sullivan would be so eager to support an institution for which he seems to have serious reservations. But Sullivan is more interested in marriage as a symbol than as an institution. On its most fundamental level, *Virtually Normal* is not about politics or ideas, but about emotions: Sullivan's overwhelming priority is to spare future generations the suffering he experienced. His argument for gay marriage is memorable, not as a cry for equal access to the covenant of marriage, but as a fervent hope that some day the stigma may be removed from homosexuality.

Sullivan is probably right that his proposals would make it easier for young homosexuals to accept themselves. But it could make adolescence a rougher time for everyone: children confronted with two equally legitimate images of adult sexual roles would be rudderless for many years, and no one knows what personal or social toll would result from this prolonged period of sexual confusion.

Nor does Sullivan take seriously the question of how children would be raised by same-sex parents, and what longterm effects this upbringing might have on their emotional and sexual development. Sullivan addresses only one sentence to this complicated subject: "There is no evidence that shows any deleterious impact on a child brought up by two homosexual parents." He does not discuss the practical implications of his reform for foster care, adoption, child-custody suits, and the like.

And while Sullivan would presumably not consider this a social "cost," policymakers would have to grapple with the fact that legalizing gay marriage would probably increase the number of homosexuals overall. Any societal influence that is strong enough to be "felt deeply" by children who are destined to become homosexual is also going to be felt by children whose sexual orientation is less certain. Even if Sullivan is correct in guessing that an individual's sexual orientation is firmly established by the age of five or six (a debatable point), this would hardly mean that sexual orientation is immune from social influence.

Finally, as many of Sullivan's "conservative" thinkers point out, placing gay marriage on an equal footing with heterosexual marriage might end up weakening marriage as an institution. Sullivan offers a particularly unsatisfying response to this concern. Because homosexuals "have no choice but to be homosexual," he declares, "they are not choosing that option over heterosexual marriage; and so they are not sending any social signals that heterosexual family life should be denigrated."

This answer misses the point of the pro-family argument. Conservatives do not fear that legalizing gay marriage would send heterosexuals the message that they are settling for second best. Conservatives are concerned that the more society broadens the definition of "marriage"—and some would argue that the definition has already been stretched to the breaking point—the less seriously it will be taken by everyone.

If *Virtually Normal* is any indication, this fear is warranted. When all is said and done, Sullivan is not just interested in admitting a new group of people to marriage (although that would be revolutionary enough). He wants to redefine marriage to accommodate a particular lifestyle. Sullivan's willingness to jettison the monogamous aspect of marriage (and what more important aspect is there?), and his suggestion that heterosexuals should rethink their own "moralistic" and "stifling" notions of marriage: these are the "social signals" that worry conservatives. In short, Sullivan's book beautifully engages our sympathy for the difficulties homosexuals encounter in our society, but it is unpersuasive in its argument that gay marriage would be a conservatizing force.

18.

AGAINST HOMOSEXUAL MARRIAGE

James Q. Wilson

Our courts,which have mishandled abortion, may be on the verge of mishandling homosexuality. As a consequence of two pending decisions, we may be about to accept homosexual marriage.

In 1993 the supreme court of Hawaii ruled that, under the equal-protection clause of that state's constitution, any law based on distinctions of sex was suspect, and thus subject to strict judicial scrutiny.[1] Accordingly, it reversed the denial of a marriage permit to a same-sex couple, unless the state could first demonstrate a "compelling state interest" that would justify limiting marriages to men and women. A new trial is set for early this summer. But in the meantime, the executive branch of Hawaii appointed a commission to examine the question of same-sex marriages; its report, by a vote of five to two, supports them. The legislature, for its part, holds a different view of the matter, having responded to the court's decision by passing a law unambiguously reaffirming the limitation of marriage to male-female couples.

No one knows what will happen in the coming trial, but the odds are that the Hawaiian version of the equal-rights amendment may control the outcome. If so, since the United States Constitution has a clause requiring that "full faith and credit shall be given to the public acts, records, and judicial proceedings of every other state," a homosexual couple in a state like Texas, where the population is overwhelmingly opposed to such unions, may soon be able to fly to Hawaii, get married, and then return to live in Texas as lawfully wedded. A few scholars believe that states may be able to impose public-policy objections to such out-of-state marriages—Utah has already voted one in, and other states may follow—but only at the price of endless litigation.

Reprinted from *Commentary,* March 1996, by permission of James Q. Wilson and *Commentary* magazine. All rights reserved.

That litigation may be powerfully affected by the second case. It concerns a Colorado statute, already struck down by that state's supreme court, that would prohibit giving to homosexuals "any claim of minority status, quota preferences, protected status, or claim of discrimination." The U.S. Supreme Court is now reviewing the appeals. If its decision upholds the Colorado supreme court and thus allows homosexuals to acquire a constitutionally protected status, the chances will decline of successful objections to homosexual marriage based on considerations of public policy.

Contemporaneous with these events, an important book has appeared under the title *Virtually Normal*.[2] In it, Andrew Sullivan, the editor of the *New Republic*, makes a strong case for a new policy toward homosexuals. He argues that "all *public* (as opposed to private) discrimination against homosexuals be ended. . . . *And that is all.*" The two key areas where this change is necessary are the military and marriage law. Lifting bans in those areas, while also disallowing antisodomy laws and providing information about homosexuality in publicly supported schools, would put an end to the harm that gays have endured. Beyond these changes, Sullivan writes, American society would need no "cures [of homophobia] or reeducations, no wrenching private litigation, no political imposition of tolerance."

It is hard to imagine how Sullivan's proposals would, in fact, end efforts to change private behavior toward homosexuals, or why the next, inevitable, step would not involve attempts to accomplish just that purpose by using cures and reeducations, private litigation, and the political imposition of tolerance. But apart from this, Sullivan—an English Catholic, a homosexual, and someone who has on occasion referred to himself as a conservative—has given us the most sensible and coherent view of a program to put homosexuals and heterosexuals on the same public footing. His analysis is based on a careful reading of serious opinions and his book is written quietly, clearly, and thoughtfully. In her review of it in *First Things* (January 1996),* Elizabeth Kristol asks us to try to answer the following question: what would life be like if we were not allowed to marry? To most of us, the thought is unimaginable; to Sullivan, it is the daily existence of declared homosexuals. His response is to let homosexual couples marry.

Sullivan recounts three main arguments concerning homosexual marriage, two against and one for. He labels them prohibitionist, conservative, and liberal. (A fourth camp, the "liberationist," which advocates abolishing all distinctions between heterosexuals and homosexuals, is also described—and scorched for its "strange confluence of political abdication and psychological violence.") I think it easier to grasp the origins of the three main arguments by referring to the principles on which they are based.

The prohibitionist argument is in fact a biblical one; the heart of it was stated by Dennis Prager in an essay in the *Public Interest* ("Homosexuality, the

---

*See chapter 17 of this volume (Eds.)

Bible, and Us," Summer 1993). When the first books of the Bible were written, and for a long time thereafter, heterosexual love is what seemed at risk. In many cultures—not only in Egypt or among the Canaanite tribes surrounding ancient Israel but later in Greece, Rome, and the Arab world, to say nothing of large parts of China, Japan, and elsewhere—homosexual practices were common and widely tolerated or even exalted. The Torah reversed this, making the family the central unit of life, the obligation to marry one of the first responsibilities of man, and the linkage of sex to procreation the highest standard by which to judge sexual relations. Leviticus puts the matter sharply and apparently beyond quibble:

> Thou shalt not live with mankind as with womankind; it is an abomination. . . . If a man also lie with mankind, as he lieth with a woman, both of them have committed an abomination; they shall surely be put to death; their blood shall be upon them.

Sullivan acknowledges the power of Leviticus but deals with it by placing it in a relative context. What is the nature of this "abomination"? Is it like killing your mother or stealing a neighbor's bread, or is it more like refusing to eat shellfish or having sex during menstruation? Sullivan suggests that all of these injunctions were written on the same moral level and hence can be accepted or ignored *as a whole*. He does not fully sustain this view, and in fact a refutation of it can be found in Prager's essay. In Prager's opinion and mine, people at the time of Moses, and for centuries before him, understood that there was a fundamental difference between whom you killed and what you ate, and in all likelihood people then and for centuries earlier linked whom you could marry closer to the principles that defined life than they did to the rules that defined diets.

The New Testament contains an equally vigorous attack on homosexuality by St. Paul. Sullivan partially deflects it by noting Paul's conviction that the earth was about to end and the Second Coming was near; under these conditions, all forms of sex were suspect. But Sullivan cannot deny that Paul singled out homosexuality as deserving of special criticism. He seems to pass over this obstacle without effective retort.

Instead, he takes up a different theme, namely, that on grounds of consistency many heterosexual practices—adultery, sodomy, premarital sex, and divorce among others—should be outlawed equally with homosexual acts of the same character. The difficulty with this is that it mistakes the distinction alive in most people's minds between marriage as an institution and marriage as a practice. As an institution, it deserves unqualified support; as a practice, we recognize that married people are as imperfect as anyone else. Sullivan's understanding of the prohibitionist argument suffers from his unwillingness to acknowledge this distinction.

The second argument against homosexual marriage—Sullivan's conservative category—is based on natural law as originally set forth by Aristotle and Thomas Aquinas and more recently restated by Hadley Arkes, John Finnis, Robert George, Harry V. Jaffa, and others. How it is phrased varies a bit, but in general its advocates support a position like the following: man cannot live without the care and support of other people; natural law is the distillation of what thoughtful people have learned about the conditions of that care. The first thing they have learned is the supreme importance of marriage, for without it the newborn infant is unlikely to survive or, if he survives, to prosper. The necessary conditions of a decent family life are the acknowledgment by its members that a man will not sleep with his daughter or a woman with her son and that neither will openly choose sex outside marriage.

Now, some of these conditions are violated, but there is a penalty in each case that is supported by the moral convictions of almost all who witness the violation. On simple utilitarian grounds it may be hard to object to incest or adultery; if both parties to such an act welcome it and if it is secret, what differences does it make? But very few people, and then only ones among the overeducated, seem to care much about mounting a utilitarian assault on the family. To this assault, natural-law theorists respond much as would the average citizen—never mind "utility," what counts is what is right. In particular, homosexual uses of the reproductive organs violate the condition that sex serve solely as the basis of heterosexual marriage.

To Sullivan, what is defective about the natural-law thesis is that it assumes different purposes in heterosexual and homosexual love: moral consummation in the first case and pure utility or pleasure alone in the second. But in fact, Sullivan suggests, homosexual love can be as consummatory as heterosexual. He notes that as the Roman Catholic Church has deepened its understanding of the involuntary—that is, in some sense genetic—basis of homosexuality, it has attempted to keep homosexuals in the church as objects of affection and nurture, while banning homosexual acts as perverse.

But this, though better than nothing, will not work, Sullivan writes. To show why, he adduces an analogy to a sterile person. Such a person is permitted to serve in the military or enter an unproductive marriage; why not homosexuals? If homosexuals marry without procreation, they are no different (he suggests) from a sterile man or woman who marries without hope of procreation. Yet people, I think, want the form observed even when the practice varies; a sterile marriage, whether from choice or necessity, remains a marriage of a man and a woman. To this Sullivan offers essentially an aesthetic response. Just as albinos remind us of the brilliance of color and genius teaches us about moderation, homosexuals are a "natural foil" to the heterosexual union, "a variation that does not eclipse the theme." Moreover, the threat posed by the foil to the theme is slight as compared to the threats posed by adultery, divorce, and prostitution. To be consistent, Sullivan once again reminds us, society would have to ban adulterers from the military as it now bans confessed homosexuals.

But again this misses the point. It would make more sense to ask why an alternative to marriage should be invented and praised when we are having enough trouble maintaining the institution at all. Suppose that gay or lesbian marriage were authorized; rather than producing a "natural foil" that would "not eclipse the theme," I suspect such a move would call even more seriously into question the role of marriage at a time when the threats to it, ranging from single-parent families to common divorces, have hit record highs. Kenneth Minogue recently wrote of Sullivan's book that support for homosexual marriage would strike most people as "mere parody," one that could further weaken an already strained institution.

To me, the chief limitation of Sullivan's view is that it presupposes that marriage would have the same, domesticating, effect on homosexual members as it has on heterosexuals, while leaving the latter largely unaffected. Those are very large assumptions that no modern society has ever tested.

Nor does it seem plausible to me that a modern society resists homosexual marriages entirely out of irrational prejudice. Marriage is a union, sacred to most, that unites a man and woman together for life. It is a sacrament of the Catholic Church and central to every other faith. Is it out of misinformation that every modern society has embraced this view and rejected the alternative? Societies differ greatly in their attitude toward the income people may have, the relations among their various races, and the distribution of political power. But they differ scarcely at all over the distinctions between heterosexual and homosexual couples. The former are overwhelmingly preferred over the latter. The reason, I believe, is that these distinctions involve the nature of marriage and thus the very meaning—even more, the very possibility—of society.

The final argument over homosexual marriage is the liberal one, based on civil rights.

As we have seen, the Hawaiian supreme court ruled that any state-imposed sexual distinction would have to meet the test of strict scrutiny, a term used by the U.S. Supreme Court only for racial and similar classifications. In doing this, the Hawaiian court distanced itself from every other state court decision—there are several—in this area so far.* A variant of the suspect-class argument, though, has been suggested by some scholars who contend that denying access to a marriage license by two people of the same sex is no different from denying access to two people of different sexes but also different races. The Hawaiian Supreme Court embraced this argument as well, explic-

---

*Minnesota refused a claim for a marriage license by two gay men even though the relevant state statute does not mention sex; the federal Ninth Circuit rejected a claim that Congress, in defining a spouse in the Immigration and Naturalization Act of 1982, meant to include same-sex spouses. In Pennsylvania a court refused to allow a same-sex couple to contract a common-law marriage. A Kentucky court did the same in the case of two lesbians applying for a marriage license, as did a Washington court in the case of two gay men. The District of Columbia Court of Appeals acted similarly (by a divided vote) in 1995.

itly comparing its decision to that of the U.S. Supreme Court when it over-turned state laws banning marriages involving miscegenation.

But the comparison with black-white marriages is itself suspect. Beginning around 1964, and no doubt powerfully affected by the passage of the Civil Rights Act of that year, public attitudes toward race began to change dramatically. Even allowing for exaggerated statements to pollsters, there is little doubt that people in fact acquired a new view of blacks. Not so with homosexuals. Though the campaign to aid them has been going on vigorously for about a quarter of a century, it has produced few, if any, gains in public acceptance, and the greatest resistance, I think, has been with respect to homosexual marriages.

Consider the difference. What has been at issue in race relations is not marriage among blacks (for over a century, that right has been universally granted) or even miscegenation (long before the civil-rights movement, many Southern states had repealed such laws). Rather, it has been the routine contact between the races in schools, jobs, and neighborhoods. Our own history, in other words, has long made it clear that marriage is a different issue from the issue of social integration.

There is another way, too, in which the comparison with race is less than helpful, as Sullivan himself points out. Thanks to the changes in public attitudes I mentioned a moment ago, gradually race was held to be not central to decisions about hiring, firing, promoting, and schooling, and blacks began to make extraordinary advances in society. But then, in an effort to enforce this new view, liberals came to embrace affirmative action, a policy that said that race *was* central to just such issues, in order to ensure that *real* mixing occurred. This move created a crisis, for liberalism had always been based on the proposition that a liberal political system should encourage, as John Stuart Mill put it, "experiments in living" free of religious or political direction. To contemporary liberals, however, being neutral about race was tantamount to being neutral about a set of human preferences that in such matters as neighborhood and schooling left groups largely (but not entirely) separate.

Sullivan, who wisely sees that hardly anybody is really prepared to ignore a political opportunity to change lives, is not disposed to have much of this either in the area of race or in that of sex. And he points out with great clarity that popular attitudes toward sexuality are anyway quite different from those about race, as is evident from the fact that wherever sexual orientation is subject to local regulations, such regulations are rarely invoked. Why? Because homosexuals can "pass" or not, as they wish; they can and do accumulate education and wealth; they exercise political power. The two things a homosexual cannot do are join the military as an avowed homosexual or marry another homosexual.

The result, Sullivan asserts, is a wrenching paradox. On the one hand, society has historically tolerated the brutalization inflicted on people because of the color of their skin, but freely allowed them to marry; on the other hand, it has given equal opportunity to homosexuals, while denying them the right to marry. This, indeed, is where Sullivan draws the line. A black or Hispanic child, if heterosexual, has many friends, he writes, but a gay child "generally has no one." And that is why the social stigma attached to homosexuality is different from that attached to race or ethnicity—"because it attacks the very heart of what makes a human being human: the ability to love and be loved." Here is the essence of Sullivan's case. It is a powerful one, even if (as I suspect) his pro-marriage sentiments are not shared by all homosexuals.

Let us assume for the moment that a chance to live openly and legally with another homosexual is desirable. To believe that, we must set aside biblical injunctions, a difficult matter in a profoundly religious nation. But suppose we manage the diversion, perhaps on the grounds that if most Americans skip church, they can as readily avoid other errors of (possibly) equal magnitude. Then we must ask on what terms the union shall be arranged. There are two alternatives—marriage or domestic partnership.

Sullivan acknowledges the choice, but disparages the domestic-partnership laws that have evolved in some foreign countries and in some American localities. His reasons, essentially conservative ones, are that domestic partnerships are too easily formed and too easily broken. Only real marriages matter. But—aside from the fact that marriage is in serious decline, and that only slightly more than half of all marriages performed in the United States this year will be between never-before-married heterosexuals—what is distinctive about marriage is that it is an institution created to sustain child-rearing. Whatever losses it has suffered in *this* respect, its function remains what it has always been.

The role of raising children is entrusted in principle to married heterosexual couples because after much experimentation—several thousand years, more or less—we have found nothing else that works as well. Neither a gay nor a lesbian couple can of its own resources produce a child; another party must be involved. What do we call this third party? A friend? A sperm or egg bank? An anonymous donor? There is no settled language for even describing, much less approving of, such persons.

Suppose we allowed homosexual couples to raise children who were created out of a prior heterosexual union or adopted from someone else's heterosexual contact. What would we think of this? There is very little research on the matter. Charlotte Patterson's famous essay, "Children of Gay and Lesbian Parents" (*Journal of Child Development,* 1992), begins by conceding that the existing studies focus on children born into a heterosexual union that ended in divorce or that was transformed when the mother or father "came out" as a homosexual. Hardly any research has been done on children acquired at the outset by a homosexual couple. We therefore have no way of knowing how they would behave. And even if we had such studies, they might tell us rather little unless they were conducted over a very long period of time.

But it is one thing to be born into an apparently heterosexual family and then many years later to learn that one of your parents is homosexual. It is quite another to be acquired as an infant from an adoption agency or a parent-for-hire and learn from the first years of life that you are, because of your family's position, radically different from almost all other children you will meet. No one can now say how grievous this would be. We know that young children tease one another unmercifully; adding this dimension does not seem to be a step in the right direction.

Of course, homosexual "families," with or without children, might be rather few in number. Just how few, it is hard to say. Perhaps Sullivan himself would marry, but, given the great tendency of homosexual males to be promiscuous, many more like him would not, or if they did, would not marry with as much seriousness.

That is problematic in itself. At one point, Sullivan suggests that most homosexuals would enter a marriage "with as much (if not more) commitment as heterosexuals." Toward the end of his book, however, he seems to withdraw from so optimistic a view. He admits that the label "virtually" in the title of his book is deliberately ambiguous, because homosexuals as a group are not "normal." At another point, he writes that the "openness of the contract" between two homosexual males means that such a union will in fact be more durable than a heterosexual marriage because the contract contains an *"understanding of the need for extramarital outlets"* (emphasis added). But no such "understanding" exists in heterosexual marriage; to suggest that it might in homosexual ones is tantamount to saying that we are now referring to two different kinds of arrangements. To justify this difference, perhaps, Sullivan adds that the very "lack of children" will give "gay couples greater freedom." Freedom for what? Freedom, I think, to do more of those things that heterosexual couples do less of because they might hurt the children.

The courts in Hawaii and in the nation's capital must struggle with all these issues under the added encumbrance of a contemporary outlook that makes law the search for rights, and responsibility the recognition of rights. Indeed, thinking of laws about marriage as documents that confer or withhold rights is itself an error of fundamental importance—one that the highest court in Hawaii has already committed. "Marriage," it wrote, "is a state-conferred legal-partnership status, the existence of which gives rise to a multiplicity of rights and benefits. . . ." A state-conferred legal partnership? To lawyers, perhaps; to mankind, I think not. The Hawaiian court has thus set itself on the same course of action as the misguided Supreme Court in 1973 when it thought that laws about abortion were merely an assertion of the rights of a living mother and an unborn fetus.

I have few favorable things to say about the political systems of other modern nations, but on these fundamental matters—abortion, marriage, military service—they often do better by allowing legislatures to operate than we do by deferring to courts. Our challenge is to find a way of formulating a policy with respect to homosexual unions that is not the result of a reflexive act of judicial rights-conferring, but is instead a considered expression of the moral convictions of a people.

NOTES

1. *Baehr et al.* v. *Lewin,* 852 P.2d 44.

2. Andrew Sullivan, *Virtually Normal: An Argument about Homosexuality* (New York: Alfred A. Knopf, 1995). See chapter 16 of this volume.

19.

BLESS THE TIE THAT BINDS: A PURITAN-COVENANT CASE FOR SAME-SEX MARRIAGE

Dwight J. Penas

INTRODUCTION

An increasing number of legal scholars and students, practicing attorneys, lobbyists and legislators, and private individuals are calling for the legal recognition of gay and lesbian marriages. Those writers claim that the denial of legal status for such marriages violates basic legal and moral guarantees of American law. They also argue that full legal recognition of same-sex marriage would be good for society as a whole. The commentators advance various rationales for their arguments. Absent, however, from their analyses is attention to one significant authority. That overlooked authority is Puritan[1] ideology[2]—specifically, the concept of *covenant* in Puritan theology and social thought. As ironic as it may seem, Puritan values—and especially those embodied in the notion of covenant—encourage reversal of the hostility which contemporary marriage law manifests toward same-sex couples.

The Puritans were a principal influence on American thought and polity during America's formative decades. Puritan concepts and metaphors guided those who led the War for Independence and who designed the political structures of the nascent republic. According to one scholar, "[t]he remarkable coherence of the American revolutionary movement and its successful conclusion in the constitution of a new civil order are due in considerable part to the convergence of the Puritan covenant pattern [of thought] and the Montesquieuan republican pattern."[3] Another scholar has said, "[w]ithout some understanding of Puritanism, . . . there is no understanding of America."[4]

A critical component in legal analysis is a sense of history. "We find our vi-

---

This is an edited form of an article that originally appeared in *Law and Inequality* 8, no. 3 (July 1990). Reprinted by permission of the publisher.

sions of good and evil . . . in the experience of the past, in our tradition. . . ."[5]
That is not to suggest that the past determines the present and the future—in law
any more than in psychology or history. But it does point out that in legal
analysis it is necessary to account for both written sources of law (e.g., the Constitution) and ideologies that lie behind those texts. As Justice Holmes explained:

> The law embodies the story of a nation's development through many centuries.
> . . . In order to know what it is, we must know what it has been, and what it tends
> to become. We must alternately consult history and existing theories of legisla-
> tion. But the most difficult labor will be to understand the combination of the two
> into new products at every stage.[6]

Such a "pragmatic" approach is not enslaved to history, but it recognizes the
importance of history. That courts—most notably the United States Supreme
Court—take history into account is clear. Any effort to explain, justify, or
change current legal positions must comprehend historical events, doctrines,
and developments. The appreciation of history implicates historically important social theories.

Puritan ideology is one of the essential sources of American law, and as
such it is a valuable and authoritative source of insight for resolving difficult
legal issues. Puritan thought provides a historical balance to other theoretical
arguments—e.g., "original intentionalism" or majoritarian rule or "neutral principles"—that claim historical authority. Puritan-covenant ideology comple-
ments and corrects interpretive frameworks that root in other social-political
theories so that legal analysis is grounded in a more complete understanding of
the historical and intellectual milieu which produced American law.

This article argues that the implications of Puritan covenant ideology encourage the legal recognition of marriage between gays or lesbians. It is meant
to complement—and certainly not to contradict—trenchant legal arguments
for the recognition of gay/lesbian marriage. It begins with a brief sketch of the
history and theology of the Puritan movement in America, to demonstrate the
authority of Puritanism for American law and to set forth Puritanism's basic
themes. The article goes on to infer basic jurisprudential principles, or values,
from that Puritan thought. It then analyzes how those principles encourage the
legal recognition of same-sex marriage.

THE PURITAN UNDERSTANDING OF LIFE AND SOCIETY

Historical Importance of the Puritans

The Puritans and their ideology were essential elements in the development of
American self-understanding and of American law. Puritan influence was felt
early in American history, since Puritans were among the earliest white settlers

in America. The Pilgrims who landed at Plymouth in 1620 were Puritans. The members of the Massachusetts Bay Colony, who arrived in 1629, were Puritans. Rhode Island, Connecticut, New Jersey, Maryland, and Pennsylvania also began as Puritan enclaves.

Once established, Puritan colonies thrived and grew, and all sections of the "new world"—not just "New England"—eventually felt the Puritan influence. In the original thirteen colonies, for example, an estimated 85 percent of the churches were Puritan congregations. That religious dominance greatly influenced the development of American social and political attitudes.

Puritan theology was a major intellectual force behind the development of American "tradition, culture, institutions, and nationality."[7] Puritan thought about the nature of life and of society encouraged and contributed to the formation of American republican polity. Puritan theology inspired political doctrines about human equality, participatory government, and concern for the common good. Puritan influence is apparent from the history of the formulation of the Declaration of Independence and the Constitution of the United States. Even the fundamental image of the United States as a "federation" or a "federal union" roots in Puritan thought. M. Susan Power analyzed the political writings of three early American Puritan leaders and found in them the early expression of essential themes of American constitutional government.[8]

Puritan themes pervaded early American thought and were especially prominent in the struggle to shape the polity of the new nation. Winthrop Hudson summarizes the importance of Puritanism in America:

> [D]emocracy as we understand it in America was derived from the three [Puritan] theological doctrines of the sovereignty of God, human bondage to sin, and a particular understanding of the way in which the implications of revelation are made known and confirmed. From these three doctrines, in turn, were derived an insistence upon fundamental law, limitation of power, and the efficacy of discussion and persuasion.[9]

Hudson understands those three political doctrines—fundamental law, limitation of power, and the freedom of speech—as the core values around which America was "constituted."[10]

The Theological Foundation of Puritan Social Thought

To urge renewed appreciation for the Puritans is not to suggest the adoption of their particular theological or religious stance. Even in the early days the peculiarly religious character of Puritanism was rapidly displaced, even among strict Puritan groups, by the secular concerns of settling the new nation, including government, law, trade, and war. What began as a theological movement was transformed into a more generalized social theory. Nevertheless, Puritanism was religious in its origins, and some sense of Puritan theology is necessary in order to understand secularized Puritan social theory.

Puritans understood themselves to be agents of God on earth, entrusted with responsibility for subjecting all aspects of life to God's rule. They were convinced that they had special duties in the world. All of life was infused with a potential for ministry.

At the heart of Puritan thought about religion and life as Perry Miller has called it, the "marrow of puritan divinity"[11]—was the notion of *covenant*. A covenant is a mutually beneficial relationship formed when two parties pledge absolute faithfulness to each other. A covenant shares some of the features of a contract, in that each party can hold the other accountable for the terms of the arrangement—an arrangement to which both parties freely assent. It is, however, a broader concept than contract, one more akin to romantic notions of marriage: Each party commits, as an integral aspect of the agreement, to remain bound by the agreement even in the event of the other's breach. The Puritans structured their entire theological system around the notions of a covenant between God and humanity and of human covenants that reflected the divine-human covenant. Covenant became the central motif in the exposition of Puritan thought about both religion and society.

For the Puritans, the history of the human race was suffused with covenants. At the creation of the world, God had established a covenant with humanity. In general terms, God promised to care for and protect the human race; humans for their part were to live according to God's will and to care for and protect one another. Eventually, humanity failed to fulfill its covenantal responsibilities, but God did not abandon humanity. Instead, God established a new covenant with humanity through Jesus—who fulfilled the original covenant vicariously for humanity.

Though the second covenant—or "covenant of grace"—was built on faith, it nevertheless incorporated some aspects of the earlier covenant, the so-called "covenant of works." The covenant of grace "repeat[ed] and embellish[ed] for sinful [humans] the terms of the old covenant. . . . Both required that the faithful believer lead his [*sic*] life in devotion, service, and praise of God—not as a condition of salvation, but as an expression of gratitude for God's grace and mercy."[12] Within this scheme, every believer had a contribution to make. Each person was created with a unique combination of traits and talents which she was expected to employ in the service of God.

The Puritans understood both covenants to require service to one's neighbor. The covenant between God and humankind had its correlate in the believer's covenant with her neighbors and with the physical universe. The Puritans understood life to be a vital and exuberant—if sober and responsible—embrace of the world as the place where one expressed her devotion and service to God. Care for and service to one's neighbor were a part of worship, on a par with singing psalms and preaching sermons.

Covenant theology impressed on Puritans that human life is essentially communal. Human being is defined in terms of relationships with others. Every human event and relationship (covenant) is a reflection of the covenant between God and the human race, and each is invested with divine significance.

Puritan notions of covenantal relationship are clearly manifested in the Puritan doctrine of marriage, which Puritans understood to be a covenant between a man and a woman.[13] Puritans played down the Anglican view of marriage as "an expression of the natural requirements of procreation."[14] Instead, Puritans emphasized the partnership of marriage: Puritan sermons on marriage emphasized mutual help, affection, and respect. Puritans married with an open-eyed understanding that in marriage they undertook serious obligations toward their spouses. For that reason, there was an emphasis on a person's freedom to choose whether or not and whom to marry. In addition, marriage served an iconic function, exemplifying in microcosm the love and cooperation, service and care that the city, state, and nation were to practice. . . .

But the Puritan doctrine of covenant embraced realms wider than the family: The emphasis on covenantal service led Puritans to emphasize the believer's duty to contribute to the "common good." "Living in covenant [meant] regarding persons and events with an unselfish eye, with a view to the whole rather than to a partial [individual] interest."[15] The Puritans were by no means communitarians. But they were conscious that those well-off should help those less-well-off. By employing its God-given intelligence, humanity would address human problems in such a way that everyone was better off.

The "common good" encompassed community and nation as well as personal relationships. Puritans understood their individual destinies to be wrapped up with the political subdivisions in which they lived. For example, before landing in Massachusetts, John Winthrop exhorted his fellow travelers to form the kind of closely knit and care-filled society that would fulfill God's covenantal requirements and assure the Puritan community's success in the New World:

> [W]ee must be knit together in this worke as one man [sic], wee must entertaine each other in brotherly [sic] Affeccion, wee must be willing to abridge ourselves of our superfluities, for the supply of others necessities . . . wee must . . . make others Condicions our owne, rejoyce together, mourne together, labor and suffer together. . . .[16]

Winthrop's sermon indicates the interrelatedness of all spheres of life in Puritan ideology. Community and nation were religious concerns as much as church and home.

Whether at the level of the community or at the level of the nation, political covenants, like personal covenants, were "triparty agreement[s among] God, the civil ruler, and the people."[17] Civil rulers were to be accorded great respect because they represented God's authority to the society and guided the society in living according to God's will. Such respect did not require absolute obedience, however. If the ruler violated God's will, it was the people's responsibility to replace the unsatisfactory ruler with one faithful to the ways of God.

Puritans' concern for their righteousness before God led them to profound concern for the orders of society. Since all aspects of life were integrated under the rule of God, politics and law were as much dimensions of religion as was worship. Even after Puritan theological zeal waned, the religious-like dedication to political and legal matters had been planted too firmly in American soil to be dislodged

Puritans and Same-Sex Marriage

There is no suggestion that the Puritans would have sanctioned same-sex marriage. The historical Puritans were people of their times. Official abhorrence of "sodomy" or "unnatural acts" was a part of their milieu. In their denunciations of homosexuality Puritans were scarcely distinguishable from their counterparts. Puritans did not always follow their ideology to its logical implications. For example, while Puritans were remarkably ahead of their times in affording equality and dignity to women in society, they did not extend the right to vote to women. As another example, slavery was the subject of divisive concern for the Puritans at the founding of this country, but their treatment of the question—while radical in some quarters in their day—is unenlightened by modern standards. It is, therefore, neither surprising nor contradictory to suggest that, while the Puritans themselves would not have advocated legal status for same-sex marriage, Puritan ideology planted the seeds which would blossom into just such a stance.

The Puritans are important to contemporary legal analysis because of their importance to the formation of American law; their importance does not derive from their particular structures of society or from their solutions to social problems. The history-bound forms of their society are less important in modern times than are the values that informed their social structure and what they contributed to the American mix:

> A political Puritan paradigm of covenant adequate to contemporary needs cannot be provided by simple resuscitation of some Puritan commonwealth in old or New England. . . . What we want to recover from the Puritan commonwealth is, not its constitution, but the basic normative guidelines that follow from its covenant structure of freedom and accountability.[18]

The Puritan-Covenant Case for Same-Sex Marriage

There exists no systematic Puritan jurisprudence. The earliest Puritans did not develop one and modern advocates of covenant theory have not yet undertaken the task. Even though law and the ordering of society were of vital concern to Puritans, Puritans did not isolate jurisprudential concerns from the rest of their reflections on how to structure their lives in faithfulness to their covenant with God. Still, it is possible to identify a set of basic jurisprudential principles—or "values"—implicit in Puritan ideology.

After an analysis of the "problem" posed by same-sex marriage, this section of the article articulates major principles of Puritan jurisprudence. It relates those principles to modern expressions of legal philosophy. Finally, it demonstrates that each of those principles contributes to the substantial case for the legal recognition of same-sex marriage. Legal recognition is not only permissible under modern articulations of Puritan jurisprudence; it is compelled.

Costs of the Denial of Legal Status to Same-Sex Marriage

Marriage between partners of the same sex is illegal in every state. Despite legal prohibitions, however, gay men and lesbians continue to form committed relationships, marriage-like in all aspects except legal status.

The denial of legal status to the relationships does not have merely incidental repercussions. The costs to a gay or lesbian couple of being denied legal status for their relationship are enormous. The denial of marriage to couples exposes them to discrimination from employers, landlords, and institutions offering facilities to the public. Unmarried couples face discrimination in housing. Gay and lesbian partners are generally barred from spousal benefits under worker's compensation laws, since they are not legal spouses. Married couples receive benefits from the federal government which are denied to gay and lesbian partners, such as special tax treatment and Social Security benefits.

Not only does denial of legal recognition deprive same-sex couples of entitlements accorded "married" couples, but the lack of legal marital status limits the causes of action available in tort to gay and lesbian partners. For example, a California court held that an unmarried partner could not collect damages for negligent infliction of emotional distress or loss of consortium. Another court held that an intimate homosexual relationship does not fall within the "close relationship" standard for negligent infliction of emotional distress.

Domestic relationship law is a field in which gay and lesbian partners face definite hardship. The legal difficulties associated with child custody and visitation, and with conceiving and adopting children, are manifold. There are no rights of inheritance for a gay or lesbian partner in the event of the death of the other partner. Since the famous *Marvin* v. *Marvin* decision there may be grounds, at least in California, for an unmarried heterosexual partner to get support from the other partner—so-called palimony. In the event that a gay or lesbian relationship breaks up, however, there is no precedent for the award of such support as is available to unmarried heterosexual partners. The experience of one lesbian couple in Minnesota demonstrates that the lack of legal status for their relationship has adverse implications even for one partner's rights to visit her disabled lover.

The denial of legal recognition for same-sex marriage takes a toll beyond the economic and legal costs. Richard Mohr has written passionately of the intertwined legal and emotional burdens that he and his "lover and husband" must bear as a result of the lack of legal sanction for their relationship:

> [I]n the eyes of the law we are necessarily strangers to each other, people who had as well never met. In Illinois, [where Mohr and his lover live] one cannot will one's body. By statute, it goes to next of kin. That which was most one's own—the substrate for personality—which was most one's own for another—that in which and by which one loved and made love—is, for gays, not one's own at all. The lover is barred from the lover's funeral. The compulsory intervention of heterosexuality at death is the final degradation worked by The People on gay people.[19]

Numerous rationales have been offered to justify denial of legal status to gay and lesbian marriage. Friedman identified and evaluated several of the most common of those rationales. In every case, she found the rationale inadequate to justify the practice.

States claim an interest in encouraging procreation, but such an interest cannot withstand scrutiny: Certainly, there is little reason to fear the extinction of the human race from underpopulation. Neither do Supreme Court rulings with respect to birth control and abortion support the assertion that the state has an overriding interest in encouraging procreation.

Concern for the well-being of children conceived within or brought into a marriage is a legitimate state interest. But there is no empirical evidence that the legalization of same-sex marriage represents a threat to children of the marriage. Children are no more likely to be molested by gay or lesbian parents than by heterosexual parents. If the concern is to discourage development of homosexual identity in children, there is no evidence that children develop homosexual identities because of their families' makeup. Children of gay or lesbian partners are no more apt to be stigmatized if the partners are married than if they are merely living together. There is thus little support for the claim that children would be more "at risk" in gay- or lesbian-parent families than they are in heterosexual-parent families.

Another claim advanced by those who oppose same-sex marriage is that the denial of marriage to same-sex couples discourages illegal homosexual activity. They argue that the state has an interest in discouraging illicit sexual activity so as to encourage fidelity, responsible sexual activity, and public health. By legalizing same-sex marriage, however, the state does not give up authority to regulate extramarital sexual activity. (Arguably a state would have to decriminalize intramarital homosexual activity. Still, in *Bowers* v. *Hardwick*, the Supreme Court held that while the right to privacy protects marriage, procreation, and family decisions, it does not necessarily protect all sexual practices in marriage. Thus the legalization of marriage between gays or lesbians would not necessarily prevent a state with a sense of the ironic from prohibiting certain sexual practices—as Georgia's sodomy statute does.)

Another common objection to same-sex marriage is that it represents a challenge to the "traditional" family, but how same-sex marriage would undermine the values associated with family life is vaguely defined. The institution of same-sex marriage would foster the same values as does heterosexual marriage: Same-sex marriage would foster commitment, loyalty, and intimacy, just as does heterosexual marriage. There is no evidence that gay men and lesbian women in committed relationships are any less committed to the permanency of their relationships than are heterosexual partners. If, on the other hand, the fear is that legalization of same-sex marriage would lessen the appeal of opposite-sex marriage, the answer is obvious: People do not choose their sexual orientation; neither, then, for the vast majority of people, is the gender of a potential marriage partner a matter of choice.

Courts have given permission for the majority culture to promote and impose its cultural and moral norms, and some justify legal hostility toward gay and lesbian couples by recourse to a history of disfavor of homosexuality. But under the Constitution there are limits to majority rule:

> Majority rule is simply not the same thing as constitutionalism, as that concept was classically defined. One cannot understand the notion of a constitution, at least prior to twentieth-century thought, without including its role of placing limits on the ability of majorities (or other rulers) to do whatever they wish in regard to minorities who lose out in political struggles.[20]

The issue of the rights of gay and lesbian people—and in particular the right to legal recognition of their committed relationships—will not go away. The issue is of vital concern, not only to gay and lesbian Americans, but also to heterosexual Americans. Puritan covenant analysis reveals that what is at stake is fidelity not just to the letter of American law, but also to its "spirit" or its "heart." Puritan covenant analysis reveals both what is at stake in the argument and how to resolve the problem.

Special Protection for Relationships

As a first principle, covenant theory "both in affirmations of its ideals and [in] lamentations over its failure, reminds us that relations between persons in . . . society carry a special weight."[21] That is, because of their importance in the overall scheme of life, personal relationships are due special attention and protection. The fundamental premise of covenant theory is that human life is communal, interpersonal, social: "[O]ur lives . . . are caught up with each other. They cannot be lived in splendid isolation, each pursuing an independent pathway. . . ."[22] Covenanting with others—individuals and collectivities—is of the essence of human being.

Among covenants, marriage is special. Marriage is a covenant between two independent people and the most basic expression of the communal nature of human being. The marriage bond embodies, in covenant terms, a community of mutual "love and service, cooperation and care." It is the basic level of social involvement. The Puritan view suggests that marriage is due special care and protection. Marriage is fundamentally important to the people involved, of the utmost importance to them. As such, it is also of utmost importance to society. As an institution, marriage contributes to the common good of society.

Such high respect for the covenant between two people is neither unique to the Puritan view nor lost to the past. Time and again, the U.S. Supreme Court has recognized—at least implicitly—that one-to-one relationships are of vital importance to the fulfillment of liberty. Thus, for example, it has severely restricted the power of states to interfere with an individual's decisions about whether and whom to marry, birth control, with whom to live, child care and education, and whether to carry a fetus to term. The Court has had to struggle, however, to articulate a rationale for such protection. Most decisions propound an individualistic, social-contract doctrine of "privacy" or "fundamental" rights. For example, Justice Douglas, writing for the majority in *Griswold*, identified a "penumbra of privacy" among the rights guaranteed by the Bill of Rights. The argument is that the Bill of Rights is not a limited specific list of rights aside from which there are no others guaranteed. Rather, the Bill of Rights describes a field of rights from which it is possible to extrapolate specific applications. The Bill of Rights establishes a zone of individual autonomy which the government may not invade or violate.

Covenant theory reinforces "privacy theory" while also transcending it. It builds on the view that not all of the "rights" of members of society are articulated in specific passages of the Constitution. In the case of marriage, protection does not depend solely on "penumbral" guarantees of individual liberty located within the interstices of constitutional amendments. It is grounded in the "morality" of the Constitution's framers, which morality can be "translate[d] . . . into . . . rule[s] to cover unforeseen circumstances."[24]

Marriage is a fundamental right[25]—whether considered from the standpoint of "privacy" doctrine or from covenant theory. States must have a substantial reason for interfering with or denying marriage to heterosexual couples.[26] There is insufficient reason to deny its benefits to couples who are of the same sex. Covenant ideology asserts that committing to a relationship is a basic expression of being human. Such commitment is no less fundamental for gay men and lesbian women than it is for heterosexual couples. The need to connect with another is felt as keenly by homosexual people as by heterosexual people.

There is no valid reason to distinguish between homosexual and heterosexual couples in matters regarding the right to marry; studies suggest that homosexual couples are virtually indistinguishable from heterosexual couples. In many cases, gays and lesbians already live in de facto marriages. Many have formalized and publicized their commitment through rituals, even though those rituals do not have legal effect.

Richard Mohr suggests the positive consequences of legalizing gay and lesbian marriage: "[I]f current discrimination, which drives gays into hiding and into anonymous relations, was lifted . . . one would see gays forming [families]. Virtually all gays express a desire to have a permanent lover. . . . In general, when afforded the opportunity, gays have shown an amazing tendency to nest."[27] The legal recognition of gay and lesbian marriages would afford all people, regardless of their sexual nature, the opportunity to fulfill this aspect of their human nature. From a covenantal perspective, no less can be demanded of a social order. No one suggests that all gay or lesbian couples would choose to marry. To deny the option to those who would marry, however, is to deny them a basic guarantee of the Constitution as Puritans would understand that document.

Equality for All

The heart of covenant theory is the affirmation of the equality of all people. In Puritan thought, even the covenant between God and humanity involved God's treatment of humanity as an equal. The centrality of personhood and the dignity with which each person was to be treated were and are hallmarks of covenant thought.

Covenant equality is equality of participation in society and in the apparatus by which decisions about that society are made. Covenant affords a dynamic model of relationships in which covenant partners "sustain one another, contribute to one another, and constitute a creative center for the ongoing life of the community."[28] Participation is an end in itself; it is not simply a means to some other end, such as peace in society.

Participation is more than equality "before law"—that is, equality in some procedural sense. The concept of equality of participation includes equality of opportunity and of access to the "benefits" of society. Through their participation, people share in the benefits of the whole society, and they learn to gear their individual and group contributions to the "common good" of the society. It is incumbent on a legal system to remove any and all barriers to full and equal participation by all people.

The dual qualities of equality and participation categorically forbid the suppression of or discrimination against minorities. It is a radical denial of covenant for a majority of the members of society to draw lines of participation in the society in such a way as to exclude others. To do so is to deny the humanity of those excluded, effectively denying them both a voice in their own destiny and an opportunity to contribute to the common good.

The society which is faithful to covenant, therefore, must be an open society. A society cannot be accounted free if it closes the door on members—any members. If it does so, it is not a covenant community, for it has thereby institutionalized inequality and barred certain would-be members from the society. Society, if it is to be faithful to the covenant model, must be amenable to change. It must be willing to allow participation by all the members of society to bring about change. An open society is one equally respectful of tradition, contemporary communication, and creativity. Neither the stability of the past nor the innovations of the future can be easily ignored. Both must be tested, however, against the ideal of full participation by all persons in society. The importance of equality in covenant theory "requires a method something like . . . 'strict scrutiny' of any deviation from a standard of equality. . . ."[29] Unless the state can demonstrate a compelling reason for discrimination, discrimination must be abandoned. Any less is the society's breaking faith with those who are the objects of discrimination. Social change to eliminate discrimination has priority over other frequently expressed concerns for cautious development or pragmatic deliberation. "The covenantal idea of equality overrules the usual objections of prudence to tampering with social systems that seem to be working efficiently, if not altogether fairly."[30]

The Constitution already provides for such equality, but without the emphasis of covenant theory the radicality of the Constitution's guarantees is often ignored. The Equal Protection Clause mandates that the government act to end discrimination against disadvantaged groups, regardless of the depth or history of social contempt for the group.[31] Built into the Constitution's structure is a means for "look[ing] forward, serving to invalidate practices that were widespread at the time of [the Constitution's] ratification and that were expected to endure."[32] Where due process guarantees fail to protect substantive rights, the Equal Protection Clause may be invoked to protect "fundamental rights."[33] The Equal Protection Clause allows the Constitution to transcend "common law," "status quo baselines," and "Anglo-American conventions" in favor of a much broader principle of equality.[34]

The Supreme Court has acknowledged that the Constitution requires treating people equally with respect to the right to marry. In *Loving* v. *Virginia*,[35] the Court struck down a Virginia law that prohibited interracial marriages. The law, which classified potential marriage partners on the basis of race, violated the Fourteenth Amendment and was "subversive of the principle of equality at the heart of the Fourteenth Amendment. . . ."[36] Since the freedom to marry is "vital" and "essential to the orderly pursuit of happiness by free men [*sic*],"[37] legal obstacles can only be justified by compelling state interest effectuated by narrowly tailored means.

From a covenant perspective, the equal-protection case for same-sex marriage is even stronger than the due process argument discussed above. The fundamental assumption of covenant ideology is that all members of society are to be treated with fundamental equality. Coupled with the in-place radical Constitutional guarantee of equal protection, that assumption argues vigorously against the denial of marriage to gay and lesbian couples. To deny them the right to marry is to foreclose their enjoying the "benefits" of marriage—benefits which are legal, economic, and emotional. Denial of the right to marry thus excludes them from full participation in the life of the society. It relegates them to the margins of society and isolates them from the processes of government by which they were banished to the periphery.

To deny marriage to same-sex couples violates an essential aspect of government, as Puritan covenant theory understands government. It violates the basic human dignity of gay and lesbian people by treating them as inferiors and excluding them from the society. The fact that no suggested state interest withstands scrutiny compounds the outrage.

The Common Good

A third major strain in covenant thought concerns what is called "the common good." Politics, according to covenant theory, has as its *raison d'être* and its goal the service of society. Its purpose is to serve the public good. That public good, however, is not divorced from the good of the individual; it does not have a significance beyond or transcending the individual:

> [P]ublic good is the good of the public. It is the good of the open society itself. It is the good of the relationships through which the members of the community sustain one another, contribute to one another, and constitute a creative center for the ongoing life of the community. To act in the public good is not to deny the individuality of persons of associations, but it is to reject the indifference to others of individualism.[38]

The function of the legal process is "to pursue ways and means of improving [the] quality [of living together]. It is to create and to sustain those relationships in which the actions of each enhance the life of all."[39] Both individuals and the society itself are duty-bound to work toward the well-being of all individuals.

Covenant theory recognizes that there is no "public life" separate from the individual and collective existences of the individuals. Conversely, the life of each individual is wrapped up with the lives of others. Service to the well-being of the individual and service to society are inextricably linked. If one person is harmed, all people suffer. If one individual harms another, the entire web of social relationships—which is to say, the society—is assaulted. If public action harms an individual, the greater society is also thereby harmed. That harm, furthermore, is not some idealistic imperfection; it is a real and palpable harm. For the stability of a society is in direct proportion to the extent to which it "invites and ultimately requires" citizens to achieve "full citizenship" in the society and "places them in reciprocal relationship to each other."[40] The legitimacy of a social order is integrally related to the well-being of the individuals within society. By assuring the well-being of individuals, a social order serves the good of all. A society is not merely "less good" because it treats some people inhumanely; it is no society at all. A society which breaches the public or common good reverts to lawlessness and threatens to destroy itself.

Society, to the extent that it has an existence independent of those people whom it comprises, benefits when it serves all those who constitute society. Thus, civil liberties do not fulfill a function only for the individual. In principle, they fulfill a critical function for the political association as well, indeed, for the entire community of being. Civil liberties are a means for effective participation in communal decisions. They are a means to press for reform and to introduce novel patterns of relationship. They constitute a structure within which and through which persons and groups may contribute alternative modes of thought and styles of life to the ongoing community.[41]

By drawing persons into the social matrix, the society elicits their loyalty and their effort in behalf of the well-being of the society. It accomplishes the integration of society—i.e., the integrity, unity, and wholeness of the community.

By denying legal recognition to same-sex marriage, American society denies itself the loyalty and integration of a segment of its population. Not only does it disserve those people, but it also disserves itself. By recognizing same-sex marriage, society could channel the personal and political energy of gay and lesbian couples into the society and not away from it. By including them, instead of excluding them, the society establishes its authority with them in such a way as to encourage them to "make an 'internal' commitment to covenant"[42]—commitment to each other and to the society.

A function of covenant society is to assist the members of society to adjust their desires from self-interest toward the good of the larger community. It can only do so if it brings those members into commerce with the wider society. If it blocks the participation in society by some, it fractures the unity of the society and destroys the community by and through which individual desires or interests are socialized. That much should be clear from the African-American civil rights movement.

Richard Mohr implies that the legal recognition of same-sex marriage would be good for America beyond its good to individual Americans:

[I]n extending to gays the rights and benefits it has reserved for its dominant culture and extended selectively to others, America would confirm its deeply held, nearly religious vision of itself as a morally progressing nation, a nation itself advancing and serving as a beacon for others—especially with regard to human rights. . . . Ours is a nation given to a prophetic political rhetoric which acknowledges that morality is not arbitrary and that justice is not merely the expression of the current collective will.[43]

The legal recognition of same-sex marriage would confirm America's commitment to full justice for all people. It would thereby strengthen America's claim to "legitimacy." It would justify society's claim of authority over one segment of the population that currently experiences that authority as repression.

CONCLUSION

Legal analysis of complex and troubling social problems is a sophisticated enterprise. It calls for the contributions of a range of thinkers, not just legal scholars, legislators, and judges. Legal decision making is "contextual"—i.e., it implicates sources of learning outside of case reporters and hornbooks. Values, history, and interpretive frameworks influence how law is made. Legal decisions "must be defended as flowing from a coherent and uncompromised vision of fairness and justice, because that, in the last analysis, is what the rule of law really means."[44]

The treatment of same-sex marriage by the American legal establishment raises profound questions about "the fairness and justice" of that treatment. Gay and lesbian couples are denied the full benefit of their citizenship by laws that refuse legal sanction for same-sex marriages. That legal posture can and should be changed.

Supporting a change in the law is the strain of social thought which this paper calls "Puritan covenant thought." Originating in the sixteenth- and seventeenth-century religious movement, Puritan social thought transcended both its religious origins and its sphere of influence in New England. Puritanism was a dominant intellectual strain which contributed to the development of the new land that became the United States. The importance of that strain of thought should be re-recognized and its themes resuscitated to inform legal and political decisions.

Puritan covenant thought buttresses the arguments which come from many different perspective in favor of the legal recognition of gay and lesbian marriages. The decision to legalize such marriages would afford gays and lesbians the kind of support for their committed relationships which the society rightly offers heterosexual marriages. It would be a step toward the full participation of gays and lesbians in American society, recalling them from the margins of society where they have been forced by legalized discrimination. American society itself would benefit from the decision. It would be able more reasonably to count on the loyalty of those whom it would newly include among its full citizens; it would be truer to its declared ideals; and it would be a more complete incarnation of the just and equitable commonwealth its Founders envisioned.

NOTES

1. There is no single, commonly accepted definition of "Puritan." In general, however, the Puritans were British Calvinists who were zealous in their efforts to reform religion and society. Edmund Morgan has suggested a useful, nontechnical definition of Puritan:

> The Puritans were English Protestants who thought the Church of England as established under Henry VIII and Elizabeth retained too many vestiges of Rom[an Catholi-

cism]. In the 1640's [*sic*] and 1650's [*sic*] they reorganized not only the church but also the government of England and for eleven years ran the country without a king. When the monarchy was restored in 1660, Puritans were disgraced, but their work could not be wholly undone. Moreover, in the 1630's [*sic*] they had carried their ideas to the New World, where the king could not undo them.

Edmund S. Morgan, Introduction, *Puritan Political Ideas 1558–1794,* Edmund S. Morgan, ed. (Indianapolis: Bobbs-Merrill, 1965). See also John Witte, Jr., "Blest Be the Ties That Bind—Covenant and Community in Puritan Thought," *Emory Law Journal* 36 (1987): 579; Goldwin Smith, *The United States: An Outline of a Political History 1492–1871* (1893), p. 4.

Not all scholars define the Puritan movement so inclusively. Margo Todd, for example, stresses that Puritans "were a self-conscious community of [Calvinist] protestant zealots committed to purging the Church of England *from within* of its remaining Romish 'superstitions,' ceremonies, vestments and liturgy, and to establishing a biblical discipline on the larger society, primarily through the preached word." Margo Todd, *Christian Humanism and the Puritan Social Order* (New York: Cambridge University Press, 1987), p. 14 (emphasis added). She thus distinguishes Separatists (such as the Plymouth Pilgrims) from other Puritans, even though the two groups shared common theological and social points of view. Ibid. See also Allan Nevins and Henry Steele Commager, *A Short History of the United States* (5th ed., 1966), pp. 8–16.

The term "Puritan" was, originally, a term of opprobrium, highlighting a kind of "holier-than-thou" attitude within the reformist party. Leon Howard, *Essays on Puritans and Puritanism* (1986), p. 41. By the end of the sixteenth century, however, Puritan persistence "had rescued the term from contempt and given it a definable meaning with reference to church government and morality." Ibid., p. 3. There remains in the modern, colloquial use of the term some of the earlier connotations of excessive strictness and sobriety. Throughout this paper, however, the term is used with no overtones of disfavor. "Puritan" denotes the biologic or ideologic heirs of the British reformers who came to the New World to escape scorn and persecution in England and were instrumental in shaping what became the United States.

2. "Ideology" is used to include both theological and nontheological reflection and is used with no pejorative connotation.

3. Robert Bellah, *The Broken Covenant* (New York: Seabury Press, 1975), p. 27.

4. Perry Miller, "The Puritan Way of Life," in Perry Miller and Thomas H. Johnson, *The Puritans* (New York and Cincinnati: American Book Company, 1938), p. 1.

5. Alexander Bickel, *The Morality of Consent* (New Haven: Yale University Press, 1975), p. 24.

6. Oliver Wendell Holmes, *The Common Law* (Mark DeWolfe Howe, ed., 1963), p. 5.

7. Ralph Barton Perry, *Puritanism and Democracy* (New York: The Vanguard Press, 1944), p. 34.

8. M. Susan Power, *Before the Convention: Religion and the Founders* (Lanham, Md.: University Press of America, 1984).

9. Winthrop Hudson, "Theological Convictions and Democratic Government," in *Puritanism and the American Experience,* Michael McGittert, ed. (Reading, Mass.: Addison Wesley, 1969), p. 227.

10. Ibid., p. 226.

11. Perry Miller, "The Marrow of Puritan Divinity," in Perry Miller, *Errand into the Wilderness* (Cambridge, Mass.: The Belknap Press of Harvard University Press, 1956), p. 48.

12. Witte, "Blest Be the Ties That Bind," p. 583.

13. Puritans held marriage in high regard as a state ordained by God. Nevertheless, they desacralized marriage and made marriage a civil matter. For several years they considered weddings which occurred in church to be illegal. Christopher Durston, *The Family in the English Revolution* (New York: Basil Blackwell, 1989), p. 16.

14. Robin W. Lovin, "Covenantal Relationships and Political Legitimacy," *Journal of Religion* 60 (1980): 5.

15. Ibid., p. 6.

16. Bellah, *The Broken Covenant,* p. 14 (quoting John Winthrop).

17. Witte, "Blest Be the Ties That Bind," p. 592.

18. Lovin, "Covental Relationships and Political Legitimacy," p. 1.

19. Richard Mohr, *Gays/Justice: A Study of Ethics, Society, and Law* (New York: Columbia University Press, 1988), p. 18.

20. Sanford Levinson, *Constitutional Faith* (Princeton, N.J.: Princeton University Press, 1988), p. 70. See also *Bowers* v. *Hardwick,* 478 U.S. at 210 (Justice Brennan dissenting) ("I cannot agree that either the length of time a majority has held its convictions or the passion with which it defends them can withdraw legislation from this Court's scrutiny."). Such a view echoes the Puritan emphasis on personal dignity and has significant implications for the majority's interference with interpersonal relationships. Constitutional rights cannot be abridged by majoritarian moral beliefs. Furthermore, there is little reason for the majority to do so.

21. Lovin, "Covental Relationships and Political Legitimacy," p. 1.

22. Douglas Sturm, *Community and Alienation: Essays on Process Thought and Public Life* (Notre Dame, Ind.: University of Notre Dame Press, 1988), p. 61.

23. Witte, "Blest Be the Ties That Bind," pp. 594–95.

24. Levinson, *Constitutional Faith,* p. 81 (quoting Robert Bork).

25. *Loving* v. *Virginia,* 388 U.S. 1, 12 (1967) ("The freedom to marry has long been recognized as one of the vital personal rights essential to the orderly pursuit of happiness by free men [*sic*]. . . . Marriage is one of the basic civil rights. . . .") Courts have consistently rejected strict scrutiny of marriage laws that distinguish between heterosexual and homosexual orientation. The United States Supreme Court, for example, dismissed the appeal from *Baker* v. *Nelson,* 291 Minn. 310, 191 N.W.2d 185 (1971) "for want of substantial federal question." 409 U.S. 810 (1971). Courts and legislatures need not remain bound, however, to a past that gives short shrift to fundamental rights not heretofore recognized. See *Loving's* rejection of the rationale in *Pace* v. *Alabama,* 106 U.S. 583 (1883), as "represent[ing] a limited view of the Equal Protection Clause which has not withstood analysis in subsequent decisions of this court." *Loving,* 388 U.S. at 10. Both courts and legislatures should be confronted with the covenant case for same-sex marriage and convinced to reverse that part of legal tradition which denies recognition to same-sex marriage.

26. Loving, 388 U.S. at 9.

27. Mohr, *Gays/Justice,* p. 44. Mohr goes on to suggest that the social and legal hostility to homosexuality makes the development of committed relationships difficult: "[A] life of hiding is a tense and pressured existence not easily shared with another." Ibid.

28. Sturm, *Community and Alienation,* p. 85.

29. Lovin, "Covental Relationships and Political Legitimacy," pp. 14–15.

30. Ibid., p. 15.

31. Cass Sunstein, "Sexual Orientation and the Constitution: A Note on the Relationship between Due Process and Equal Protection," *University of Chicago Law Review* 55 (1988): 1161, 1163. Sunstein understands the Due Process Clause to be much less "activist" than the Equal Protection Clause:

> From its inception, the Due Process Clause has been interpreted largely . . . to protect traditional practices against short-run departures. . . . [It] often looks backward; it is highly relevant to the Due Process issue whether an existing or time-honored convention, described at the proper level of generality, is violated by the practice under attack.

The Equal Protection Clause, in marked contrast, has been employed in much more radical ways to eliminate discrimination, "however deeply engrained and longstanding." Ibid.

32. Ibid.

33. Ibid., pp. 1169–70.

34. Ibid., p. 1174.

35. 388 U.S. 1 (1967).

36. Ibid., p. 12 (discussing the denial of due process as a ground additional to equal protection for invalidating Virginia's law).

37. Ibid.

38. Sturm, *Community and Alienation*, p. 85.

39. Ibid., p. 21.

40. Reinhold Niebuhr, "The Idea of Covenant and American Democracy," *Church History* (1954), p. 132.

41. Sturm, *Community and Alienation*, p. 86.

42. Lovin, "Covental Relationships and Political Legitimacy," p. 13.

43. Mohr, *Gays/Justice*, pp. 44–45.

44. Ronald Dworkin, *A Matter of Principle* (Cambridge, Mass.: Harvard University Press, 1985), p. 2.

20.

SINCE WHEN IS MARRIAGE A PATH TO LIBERATION?

Paula L. Ettelbrick

"Marriage is a great institution. If you like living in institutions," according to a bit of T-shirt philosophy I saw recently. Certainly, marriage is an institution. It is one of the most venerable, impenetrable institutions in modern society. Marriage provides the ultimate form of acceptance for personal, intimate relationships in our society, and gives those who marry an insider status of the most powerful kind.

Steeped in a patriarchal system that looks to ownership, property, and dominance of men over women as its basis, the institution of marriage has long been the focus of radical-feminist revulsion. Marriage defines certain relationships as more valid than all others. Lesbian and gay relationships, being neither legally sanctioned nor commingled by blood, are always at the bottom of the heap of social acceptance and importance.

Given the imprimatur of social and personal approval that marriage provides, it is not surprising that some lesbians and and gay men among us would look to legal marriage for self-affirmation. After all, those who marry can be instantaneously transformed from "outsiders" to "insiders," and we have a desperate need to become insiders.

It could make us feel okay about ourselves, perhaps even relieve some of the internalized homophobia that we all know so well. Society will then celebrate the birth of our children and mourn the death of our spouses. It would be easier to get health insurance for our spouses, family memberships to the local museum, and a right to inherit our spouse's cherished collection of lesbian mystery novels even if she failed to draft a will. Never again would we have to go to a family reunion and debate about the correct term for intro-

This is an edited version of an article that originally appeared in *OUT/LOOK National Gay and Lesbian Quarterly,* No. 6 (Fall 1989). Reprinted by permission of the author.

ducing our lover/partner/significant other to Aunt Flora. Everything would be quite easy and very nice.

So why does this unlikely event so deeply disturb me? For two major reasons. First, marriage will not liberate us as lesbians and gay men. In fact, it will constrain us, make us more invisible, force our assimilation into the mainstream, and undermine the goals of gay liberation. Second, attaining the right to marry will not transform our society from one that makes narrow, but dramatic, distinctions between those who are married and those who are not married to one that respects and encourages choice of relationships and family diversity. Marriage runs contrary to two of the primary goals of the lesbian and gay movement: the affirmation of gay identity and culture and the validation of many forms of relationships.

When analyzed from the standpoint of civil rights, certainly lesbians and gay men should have a right to marry. But obtaining a right does not always result in justice. White male firefighters in Birmingham, Alabama, have been fighting for their "rights" to retain their jobs by overturning the city's affirmative-action guidelines. If their "rights" prevail, the courts will have failed in rendering justice. The "right" fought for by the white male firefighters, as well as those who advocate strongly for the "rights" to legal marriage for gay people, will result, at best, in limited or narrowed "justice" for those closest to power at the expense of those who have been historically marginalized.

The fight for justice has as its goal the realignment of power imbalances among individuals and classes of people in society. A pure "rights" analysis often fails to incorporate a broader understanding of the underlying inequities that operate to deny justice to a fuller range of people and groups. In setting our priorities as a community, we must combine the concept of both rights and justice. At this point in time, making legal marriage for lesbian and gay couples a priority would set an agenda of gaining rights for a few, but would do nothing to correct the power imbalances between those who are married (whether gay or straight) and those who are not. Thus, justice would not be gained.

Justice for gay men and lesbians will be achieved only when we are accepted and supported in this society despite our differences from the dominant culture and the choices we make regarding our relationships. Being queer is more than setting up house, sleeping with a person of the same gender, and seeking state approval for doing so. It is an identity, a culture with many variations. It is a way of dealing with the world by diminishing the constraints of gender roles that have for so long kept women and gay people oppressed and invisible. Being queer means pushing the parameters of sex, sexuality, and family, and in the process transforming the very fabric of our society. Gay liberation is inexorably linked to women's liberation. Each is essential to the other.

The moment we argue, as some among us insist on doing, that we should be treated as equals because we are really just like married couples and hold the same values to be true, we undermine the very purpose of our movement and begin the dangerous process of silencing our different voices. As a lesbian,

I am fundamentally different from nonlesbian women. That's the point. Marriage, as it exists today, is antithetical to my liberation as a lesbian and as a woman because it mainstreams my life and voice. I do not want to be known as "Mrs. Attached-To-Somebody-Else." Nor do I want to give the state the power to regulate my primary relationship.

Yet, the concept of equality in our legal system does not support differences. It only supports sameness. The very standard for equal protection is that people who are similarly situated must be treated equally. To make an argument for equal protection, we will be required to claim that gay and lesbian relationships are the same as straight relationships. To gain the right, we must compare ourselves to married couples. The law looks to the insiders as the norm, regardless of how flawed or unjust their institutions, and requires that those seeking the law's equal protection situate themselves in a similar posture to those who are already protected. In arguing for the right to legal marriage, lesbians and gay men would be forced to claim that we are just like heterosexual couples, have the same goals and purposes, and vow to structure our lives similarly. The law provides no room to argue that we are different but are nonetheless entitled to equal protection.

The thought of emphasizing our sameness to married heterosexuals in order to claim this "right" terrifies me. It rips away the very heart and soul of what I believe it is to be a lesbian in this world. It robs me of the opportunity to make a difference. We end up mimicking all that is bad about the institution of marriage in our effort to appear to be the same as straight couples.

By looking to our sameness and deemphasizing our differences, we do not even place ourselves in a position of power that would allow us to transform marriage from an institution that emphasizes property and state regulation of relationships to an institution that recognizes one of many types of valid and respected relationships. Until the Constitution is interpreted to respect and encourage differences, pursuing the legalization of same-sex marriage would be leading our movement into a trap; we would be demanding access to the very institution that, in its current form, would undermine our movement to recognize many different kinds of relationships. We would be perpetuating the elevation of married relationships and of "couples" in general, and further eclipsing other relationships of choice.

Ironically, gay marriage, instead of liberating gay sex and sexuality, would further outlaw all gay and lesbian sex that is not performed in a marital context. Just as sexually active nonmarried women face stigma and double standards around sex and sexual activity, so too would nonmarried gay people. The only legitimate gay sex would be that which is cloaked in and regulated by marriage. Its legitimacy would stem not from an acceptance of gay sexuality but because the Supreme Court and society in general fiercely protect the privacy of marital relationships. Lesbians and gay men who do not seek the state's stamp of approval would clearly face increased sexual oppression.

Undoubtedly, whether we admit it or not, we all need to be accepted by the broader society. That motivation fuels our work to eliminate discrimination in the workplace and elsewhere, fight for custody of our children, create our own families, and so on. The growing discussion about the right to marry may be explained in part by this need for acceptance. Those closer to the norm or to power in this country are most likely to see marriage as a principle of freedom and equality. Those who are acceptable to the mainstream because of race, gender, and economic status are more likely to want the right to marry. It is the final acceptance, the ultimate affirmation of identity.

On the other hand, more marginal members of the lesbian and gay community (women, people of color, working class, and poor) are less likely to see marriage as having relevance to our struggles for survival. After all, what good is the affirmation of our relationships (that is, marital relationships) if we are rejected as women, people of color, or working class?

The path to acceptance is much more complicated for many of us. For instance, if we choose legal marriage, we may enjoy the right to add our spouse to our health insurance policy at work, since most employment policies are defined by one's marital status, not family relationship. However, that choice assumes that we have a job and that our employer provides us with health benefits. For women, particularly women of color who tend to occupy the low-paying jobs that do not provide health-care benefits at all, it will not matter one bit if they are able to marry their woman partners. The opportunity to marry will neither get them the health benefits nor transform them from outsider to insider.

Of course, a white man who marries another white man who has a full-time job with benefits will certainly be able to share in those benefits and overcome the only obstacle left to full societal assimilation—the goal of many in his class. In other words, gay marriage will not topple the system that allows only the privileged few to obtain decent health care. Nor will it close the privilege gap between those who are married and those who are not.

Marriage creates a two-tier system that allows the state to regulate relationships. It has become a facile mechanism for employers to dole out benefits, for businesses to provide special deals and incentives, and for the law to make distinctions in distributing meager public funds. None of these entities bothers to consider the relationship among people; the love, respect, and need to protect that exists among all kinds of family members. Rather, a simple certificate of the state, regardless of whether the spouses love, respect, or even see each other on a regular basis, dominates and is supported. None of this dynamic will change if gay men and lesbians are given the option of marriage.

Gay marriage will not help us address the systemic abuses inherent in a society that does not provide decent health care to all of its citizens, a right that should not depend on whether the individual (1) has sufficient resources to afford health care or health insurance, (2) is working and receives health insurance as part of compensation, or (3) is married to a partner who is working and has health coverage that is extended to spouses. It will not address the underlying unfairness that allows businesses to provide discounted services or goods to families and couples, who are defined to include straight, married people and their children, but not domestic partners.

Nor will it address the pain and anguish of the unmarried lesbian who receives word of her partner's accident, rushes to the hospital, and is prohibited from entering the intensive-care unit or obtaining information about her condition solely because she is not a spouse or family member. Likewise, marriage will not help the gay victim of domestic violence who, because he chose not to marry, finds no protection under the law to keep his violent lover away.

If the laws changed tomorrow and lesbians and gay men were allowed to marry, where would we find the incentive to continue the progressive movement we have started that is pushing for societal and legal recognition of all kinds of family relationships? To create other options and alternatives? To find a place in the law for the elderly couple who, for companionship and economic reasons, live together but do not marry? To recognize the right of a longtime, but unmarried, gay partner to stay in his rent-controlled apartment after the death of his lover, the only named tenant on the lease? To recognize the family relationship of the lesbian couple and the two gay men who are jointly sharing child-raising responsibilities? To get the law to acknowledge that we may have more than one relationship worthy of legal protection?

The lesbian and gay community has laid the groundwork for revolutionizing society's views of family. The domestic-partnership movement has been an important part of this progress insofar as it validates nonmarital relationships. Because it is not limited to sexual or romantic relationships, domestic partnership provides an important opportunity for many who are not related by blood or marriage to claim certain minimal protections.

It is crucial, though, that we avoid the pitfall of framing the push for legal recognition of domestic partners (those who share a primary residence and financial responsibilities for each other) as a stepping-stone to marriage. We must keep our eyes on the goals of providing true alternatives to marriage and of radically reordering society's view of family.

The goals of lesbian and gay liberation must simply be broader than the right to marry. Gay and lesbian marriages may minimally transform the institution of marriage by diluting its traditional patriarchal dynamic, but they will not transform society. They will not demolish the two-tier system of the "haves" and the "have nots." We most not fool ourselves into believing that marriage will make it acceptable to be gay or lesbian. We will be liberated only when we are respected and accepted for our differences and the diversity we provide to this society. Marriage is not a path to that liberation.

21.

GAY MARRIAGE

Christine Pierce

I. INTRODUCTION

"The effort to legalize gay marriage will almost certainly emerge as a major issue in the next decade,"[1] says law professor Nan D. Hunter in the October 1991 *Nation.* Why is this so? In part, what drives this issue is the practice of most United States employers and many institutions (such as the IRS) to give *significant* benefits including health, life, disability and dental insurance, tax relief, bereavement and dependent care leave, tuition, use of recreational facilities, and purchase discounts on everything from memberships at the local Y to airline tickets only to those in conventional heterosexual families. Although employee benefits are sometimes referred to as "fringe" benefits, they, in fact, make up a hefty portion of compensation. As such, married people are paid more than their nonmarried counterparts. Whether or not favoring the institution of marriage is justified, there remains the problem that those in heterosexual relationships at least have the option (indeed, the right) to marry, whereas lesbians and gay men in relationships do not (at least in the United States).[2]

Although I find monetary and benefit arguments convincing, what follows is a discussion of other types of considerations—legal, historical, ethical, and psychological—that are relevant to the issue of gay marriage. Of these, I find the so-called psychological ones most persuasive. Moreover, since some benefits can be gained by domestic partnership plans, the question of the comparative merits of marriage and domestic partnership needs to be addressed.

This article originally appeared in the *Journal of Social Philosophy* 26, no. 2 (Fall 1995). Reprinted by permission of the *Journal of Social Philosophy.*

II. LEGAL ARGUMENTS

Although I will not dwell on the subject of law, a May 1993 Hawaii Supreme Court decision described by the Lambda Legal Defense and Education Fund as "astonishing" and possibly opening the door to gay marriage is worthy of mention. In *Baehr* v. *Lewin,* the first same-sex marriage case to reach a State Supreme Court in twenty years, the Hawaii Supreme Court held that "denying marriage licenses to same-sex couples appears to violate the State constitutional guarantee of equal protection on the basis of sex."[3] Overturning a lower court decision, the Hawaii Supreme Court sent the issue back for a trial at which the state must show compelling reasons for its discriminatory policy. According to Lambda, the Hawaii court refused to be satisfied with the "tortured and conclusory sophistry" of past court hearings on gay marriage and rejected the "tautological and circular nature" of the state's argument that same-sex couples cannot marry because marriage is inherently for opposite-sex couples.[4] Indeed, the argument from definition cited so recently in the Hawaii case has been around for a long time. In 1971, the Minnesota Supreme Court defined marriage as "a union of man and woman . . ."[5] and in 1974, two men were denied a marriage license "because of the nature of marriage itself."[6] As Richard Mohr puts it so nicely, "the courts [have held] that gay access to marriage must be a form of grand theft."[7] The charge, says Mohr, is "theft of essence."[8] ". . . [S]traights wouldn't really be married," he says, "if gays were . . . the meaning of marriage would be revised beyond recognition if gays could marry. . . ."[9] Similar claims about the concept of "family" are commonplace in right-wing rhetoric today; it is said that so-called true families will be undermined if the concept of family is extended to include lesbian and gay couples.

Other possibilities for legal argument include privacy rights[10] and Kenneth Karst's interesting suggestion that the Constitutional freedom of intimate association ". . . extends to homosexual associations. . . ."[11] These ideas I simply mention, concluding my remarks on legal reasoning by noting the importance of a 1967 Supreme Court case, *Loving* v. *Virginia,*[12] which established the right to marry as a fundamental legal right. *Loving* overturned laws against interracial marriage in the United States. Presumably one can make an equal protection argument to the effect that even as the government cannot restrict choice of a marital partner by insisting on a particular race, so the government cannot restrict such a choice on the basis of sex. Of course, such an argument would only work in a state like Hawaii where the category of sex is constitutionally protected from discrimination. In sum, what is new on the legal scene is that gay advocates of gay marriage are making serious arguments that are at long last being taken seriously.

III. QUEER VS. STRAIGHT: HISTORICAL ARGUMENTS

As the title of a recent article conveys, however, "Some Gays Aren't Wedded to the Idea of Same-Sex Marriage."[13] Journalist Anna Quindlen expands on this issue when she says, "Gay marriage is a radical notion for straight people and a conservative notion for gay ones. After years of being sledgehammered by society, some gay men and [lesbians] are deeply suspicious of participating in an institution that seems to have 'straight world' written all over it."[14] Queer things—queer theory, Queer Nation, the protest chant, "we're here, we're queer, we're fabulous, get used to us"—assume that respect for distinctiveness, an opportunity to pursue a life that is "not straight" is what is wanted.[15] While some traditionalists have called same-sex marriage a slap in the face of tradition and some queer theorists have repudiated the institution of marriage as not queer, both may have reason to pause. If Yale historian John Boswell is right, Christian marriage rites between same-sex partners date back to the fourth century, earlier than the widespread performance of heterosexual ceremonies in the eleventh century.[16] Boswell claims to have found gay marriage rites in liturgical manuals and early legal documents that constitute clear evidence that "... gay unions were comparable to heterosexual marriage."[17] "Both men and women were married using these rites, though evidence for lesbian unions is not as geographically widespread nor as ancient," Boswell says.[18] He theorizes that "gay marriage rites ... appear to have started as a religious ceremony and were based principally on love ... includ[ing] an erotic dimension."[19] He contrasts this history with heterosexual marriage which he says started as a civil ceremony with property exchange and later, when appropriated by the church, emphasized progeny and worldly success.[20] So, it appears that queer theorists could claim or reclaim an institution that is part of their history. Indeed, the good history—the part about love and eroticism—is queer.

IV. EQUALITY, JUSTICE, LIBERATION

Whether being able to marry is a desirable political goal is a question pretty much outside of law and history. At the least, it is a question that requires ethical analysis of matters such as equality, justice, oppression, and dignity. Attorney Paula Ettelbrick,[21] who doubts that marriage is the path to liberation for anyone, argues against lesbian and gay marriages on the grounds that they will not alter the elitist character of marriage, that they will at best "minimally transform" the oppressive character of marriage by "diluting its patriarchal dynamic," and that they will not transform society or bring about a just world.

On the subject of a just world, Ettelbrick says,

> Gay marriage will not help us address the systematic abuses inherent in a society that does not provide decent health care to all of its citizens ... nor will it address

the pain of the unmarried lesbian who is prohibited from entering the intensive care unit . . . solely because she is not a spouse or a family member. Likewise, marriage will not help the gay victim of domestic violence who, because he chose not to marry, finds no protection under the law to keep his violent lover away.[22]

Of course, allowing lesbians and gay men to marry will not address the issue of decent health care. Why, one might (indeed, *should*) ask, must one be employed by a company or an institution of a certain size or be married to someone who is in order to get health insurance? Presumably, in a just world, folks could get health care because they are valuable. Ettelbrick is absolutely correct in her view about the notions of "equality" or "rights" or "equal rights" when she says, "A pure 'rights' analysis often fails to incorporate a broader understanding of the underlying inequities that operate to deny justice to a fuller range of people and groups."[23] Despite her claim that rights and justice should be combined, she goes on to argue that gay marriage will gain rights for a few, will make some lesbians and gays "insiders," but will not correct the imbalance of power between the married and the nonmarried. Thus, "justice would not be gained."[24]

One answer to Ettelbrick is that she herself has put her finger on the way equality arguments usually work. They work on a limited scale. They do not do big jobs such as bring about a just society. As Mary Midgley puts it so clearly,

> . . . equality . . . is a rather abstract ideal. . . . Who is to be made equal to whom, and in what respect? Historically the answers given have mostly concerned rather narrow groups. . . . The formula needed is something like, 'let those who are already equal in respect x be, as is fitting, equal also in respect y." . . . Outsiders . . . who are currently not equal in respect x, cannot benefit from this kind of argument. . . . The notion of equality is a tool for rectifying injustices within a given group, not for widening that group or deciding how it ought to treat those outside it.[25]

Ettelbrick least understands the limited and painfully slow way that equality arguments normally work when she suggests that ". . . more marginal members of the lesbian and gay community (women, people of color, working class and poor) are less likely [than those more acceptable to the mainstream] to see marriage as having relevance to our struggles for survival."[26] The fact that achieving the right to marry will not benefit everyone or everyone equally or solve all the world's problems is not an argument against it. What good, asks Ettelbrick, ". . . is the affirmation of our relationships (that is, marital relationships) if we are rejected as women, blacks, or working class?"[27] The answer to the question, "What good is a job in philosophy if I am discredited as a woman?" is "A lot." Moreover, the exclusion of lesbian relationships from legal recognition directly affects survival issues that cut across class and race. As attorney Ruthann Robson notes, ". . . a member of a lesbian couple who becomes incapacitated can be controlled by a person determined in accordance with relationships recognized under the rule of law, such as the father who doeš not believe she is a lesbian, the brother who abused her, or the husband she has not seen for twenty years but never divorced."[28] The recent long and well-publicized estrangement between partners Karen Thompson and Sharon Kowalski (after a car accident which left Kowalski partially paralyzed, her father assumed her guardianship and denied Thompson even any visitation rights) is a textbook example of Robson's point.

Ettelbrick dismisses the importance of equality not only because it is of more use to those "... closer to the norm or to power ...,"[29] but also because "... the concept of equality ... only supports sameness."[30] She continues: "The moment we argue ... that we should be treated as equals because we are really just like married couples and hold the same values to be true, we ... begin the dangerous process of silencing our different voices."[31] I have argued elsewhere against the assumption that equality is similarity. In brief, whether or not differences are relevant depends on what kind of equality one is talking about. If one is talking about equal opportunity, then differences should be ignored, however, if one is talking about equal representation, differences are important.[32] Even if equality did entail similarity, sameness is not always bad. Of course, sometimes sameness *is* bad, and that is part of Ettelbrick's worry. She says, "[Lesbians and gay men] end up mimicking all that is bad about the institution of marriage in our effort to appear to be the same as straight couples."[33]

Others who disagree with Ettelbrick think that the participation of lesbians and gay men in the institution of marriage will alter the institution for the better. For example, Thomas Stoddard says, "... marriage may be unattractive and even oppressive as it is currently structured and practiced, but enlarging [it] to embrace same-sex couples would necessarily transform it into something new."[34] Susan Moller Okin in her recent book *Justice, Gender and the Family*[35] certainly makes a strong case against what she calls *gender-structured* marriage, thereby tempting others to suggest that an alternative, especially an alternative that is not gender-structured, has got to be better. Marriage and the family as currently practiced in our society, Okin says, "... constitute the pivot of a ... system of gender that renders women vulnerable to dependency, exploitation, and abuse."[36] The conventional family, she says, "is the linchpin of gender"[37]; and gendered relationships, private and public, are thoroughly unjust. Martha Nussbaum in her review of Okin's book says, "[Okin] plainly has a strong preference for the nuclear family in something like its modern Western form. . . . But she never tells us what benefits she believes the modern Western family provides, or why, in view of the many alternatives that have been conceived, she still prefers the pattern that has proven, as she herself demonstrates, so resistant to reform in the name of justice."[38]

If same-sex couples could marry, says Nan Hunter,

... the profoundly gendered structure at the heart of marriage would be radically disrupted. Who *would* be the "husband" in a marriage of two men, or the "wife" in a marriage of two women? And either way—if there can be no such thing as a female husband or a male wife, as the right-wing argues with contempt; or indeed in some sense there *can* be, as lesbian and gay couples reconfigure these roles on their own terms—the absolute conflation of gender with role is shattered. What would be the impact on heterosexual marriage?[39]

Unfortunately, Hunter does not answer this question. As we have seen, Thomas Stoddard is hopeful, Paula Ettelbrick is doubtful, and Martha Nussbaum wants to try something new because heterosexual marriage and the nuclear family are unjust institutions. I would not rest a case for the legalization of lesbian and gay marriage on the possibility that lesbians and gay men might improve the institution of marriage, for transformative values may not come about. Nonetheless, I am with Nussbaum here. We ought to pull the pin and see what happens. However, at the least arguments against lesbian and gay marriages based on the oppressive character of marriage should be rejected if the oppressive character referred to is due to the currently accepted gender requirements of marriage. This type of argument, exemplified in the following remarks by Ruthann Robson and S. E. Valentine, is widespread in lesbian writings: "Underlying the lesbian critique of marriage is the gendered perspective of marriage developed by feminists. . . . Marriage has remained interwoven with both the development and the perpetuation of patriarchy and women's status within the patriarchy."[40] Even if the oppressive nature of marriage historically did count as a reason for devaluing marriage per se, and therefore gay marriage, it still could be argued that lesbians and gay men should have the right to marry.[41] It is perfectly coherent to assert that lesbians and gay men should have the option to marry without claiming a necessary value for marriage, even as one can coherently claim that lesbians and gay men should have the option to serve in the military without valuing the military.[42]

Paula Ettelbrick has one last formulation of her anti-equality argument. She says the idea of marriage is inconsistent with the goal of gay liberation which is to recognize the legitimacy of many different kinds of relationships.[43] Interestingly, she favors domestic partnership plans which, she argues, better accomplish this goal. Such plans—on the part of municipalities and employers—almost universally define domestic partners to include lesbian and gay couples as well as unmarried heterosexual partners and extend to them some of the rights accorded to married couples. The qualifications for benefits approximate the qualifications for marriage, although in many instances they are more stringent. For example, domestic partnership requires couples to give evidence of commitment, whereas marriage does not.[44] On Ettelbrick's view, marriage is a "two-tier system of the 'haves' and the 'have-nots,' "[45] and same-sex marriage simply perpetuates "the elevation of married relationships and of 'couples' in general . . . further eclipsing other relationships of choice."[46] Domestic partnership plans, on the other hand, "validate nonmarital relationships,"[47] thereby contributing to the goal mentioned above of recognizing many different kinds of relationships. It does seem that the idea of domestic partnership is more inclusive of diverse relationships than is marriage, although domestic partnership does not abolish the privileging of some relationships. Sisters who are really sisters and not closeted lesbians posing as sisters could get minimal benefits if they set up a household and are financially interdependent.

V. KINSHIP ARGUMENTS

Despite the attractive potential of registered partnerships, I think a separate and compelling argument can be made for lesbian and gay marriages. Although lesbians and gay men have made some progress in the area of individual rights in the United States, until very recently there has been an almost total nonrecognition of gay families. A chapter title of a recent book illustrates the exile of gays from kinship: "Is Straight to Gay as Family Is to No Family?"[48] And Justice White, speaking for the Supreme Court's majority view that homosexual sex between consenting adults in their own bedroom is not protected by the right to privacy, said, in the *Bowers* v. *Hardwick* decision in 1986, "No connection between family, marriage, or procreation on the one hand and homosexual activity on the other has been demonstrated."[49] The right to privacy in *Bowers* protects only marital privacy. Gay people were not seen by Justice White as being in relationships. Lesbians and gay men were not visible to him as couples, partners, families, kin. Had the Court interpreted the right to privacy as a right to sexual autonomy, gay people might have been seen, for all the Court had to be able to see was individuals who desired autonomy and who had some kind of a sexual life. But when the Court said the right to privacy is the right to marital privacy, then they saw no connection between marriage and gay people. A legal system or an ethical system based on principle will not be of any use to lesbians and gay men if they are not seen as the sorts of folks to whom these principles can apply.

Worse yet, think about an ethic based on sentiment. Take, for example, Mary Midgley's view: those nearest to us have special claims—claims which diminish in proportion to distance, either physical or social. Fortunately, Midgley says that those most distant need not always come at the end of the queue. Unfortunately, priority rankings among various kinds of claims are determined by the cultural maps worked out by individual societies, and nearness and kinship are real and important factors in our psychological makeup. The psychology presented here seems right to me. I care more about Morgan, my Maine Coon cat, than I do about the child I don't know who lives six blocks down the street. These feelings I have really matter, however much those folks who believe in universalizing ethical principles say that physical and social distance should not matter. However, appealing to sentiment as a way of justifying behavior as *ethical* can be as dangerous as it is comforting. It is, of course, comforting to hear that those folks one already cares about are just the ones that one ought to care about (or ought to care most about). Such a psychology explains, at least in part, why ethical views based on sentiment have not been applied positively to lesbians and gay men who are perceived as strangers and not as kin in our society.

One would expect lesbians and gay men to get a better deal from ethics based on principle, but arguments based on principle often do not work for gay people—evidenced by the 1986 *Bowers* case. A more recent example is the debate over Colorado Amendment 2 which illustrates how all civil rights of lesbians and gay men can be jeopardized because lesbians and gay men are not perceived as kin or as having important relationships. In July 1993, the state supreme court ruled that the voter initiative to outlaw gay rights laws must prove a compelling state interest in order to meet constitutional standards. The state's attorney general argued that "the State's desire to promote "family values' provide[s] such a compelling interest."[50] Amendment 2 was declared unconstitutional by a district court judge on December 13,1993, on the grounds that it violated equal protection by usurping "the fundamental right of an identifiable group to participate in the political process,"[51] and it may be that the Colorado Supreme Court and the United States Supreme Court will continue in this lead. Nevertheless, the fact that anyone would offer "family values" as a good reason for the denial of equal rights is a measure of just how far lesbians and gay men are from being viewed as kin in our society. As one California court put it, in rejecting a similar initiative in Riverside, California, "All that is lacking is a sack of stones for throwing."[52]

In short, moral arguments based on existing sentiment will not work for gay people; arguments based on principle should work but often do not, in part because sentiment plays a role in even principled ethics and law. Until current sentiments in our society are changed, lesbians and gay men will not be able to expect that ethical (and legal) principles will be applied fairly to them. Thus, it is important for the sake of creating new sentiments to press for gay marriage so that lesbians and gay men can become visible as couples, partners, families, and kin. Pressing for registered partnerships—or what some have called gay near-marriage—may not do the job. Those folks who In 1986 could not even imagine lesbians and gay men in relationships need to know that many lesbians and gay men—to quote the Supreme Court—view their relationships as "noble" and "intimate to the degree of being sacred."[53]

VI. CONCLUSION

In sum, I have raised the following issues: Married people are paid more than their nonmarried counterparts, while the possibility of choice regarding whether or not to marry has not been extended to lesbians and gay men. Marriage has been rejected as an undesirable political goal on the grounds that it is not queer, presumably meaning to a degree that marriage is not part of lesbian and gay history. But John Boswell's new discoveries of historical evidence indicate that marriage is in a very important sense queer. I have argued that the pursuit of equality should not be abandoned simply because it is often compatible with injustice. Nor should equality be discarded because it supposedly means "sameness" and sameness is bad. I have suggested that our assessment of the comparative merits of marriage and domestic partnership is to some extent a reflection of the respective values we place on equality and diversity. Although I have expressed my doubts about the transformative power of same-sex marriage, it seems to me that objections to gay marriage based on the gender structure of heterosexual marriage are misplaced. Lastly, I have argued that Americans have been allowed for too long to view lesbians and gay men only as individuals, i.e., not in relationships and as strangers, i.e., not as kin. I think that gay marriage needs to be on the political agenda for the sake of gaining a certain level of social awareness and acceptance of serious lesbian and gay relationships. I do not worry, as do some queer theorists, that pursuing a goal such as marriage will result in assimilation into invisibility or as Ettelbrick puts it, "[let us] fade into the woodwork."[54] I think it is a far greater worry that the current invisibility as family is threatening to destroy any kind of a decent life at all for lesbians and gay men in the United States.[55]

NOTES

1. Nan D. Hunter, "Sexual Dissent and the Family," *The Nation,* October 1991, p. 441. Nan Hunter was formerly an attorney with the American Civil Liberties Union. The ACLU has endorsed lesbian and gay marriage since 1986.
2. Gay civil marriage is legal in Denmark, Sweden, and Norway.
3. Docket update, *Baehr* v. *Lewin, The Update: The Newsletter of Lambda Legal Defense and Education Fund* 10, no. 2 (Summer 1993): 14.
4. Evan Wolfson, "Hawaii Supreme Court Paves Way for Same-Sex Marriage," *The Lambda Update: The Newsletter of Lambda Legal Defense and Education Fund* 10, no. 2 (Summer 1993): 23.
5. *Baker* v. *Nelson,* 291 Minn. 310 (1971) appeal dismissed, 409 U.S. 810 (1972).
6. *Singer* v. *Hara,* 11 Wash. App. 247 (1974).
7. Richard D. Mohr, *Gay Ideas: Outing and Other Controversies* (Boston: Beacon Press, 1992), p. 90.
8. Ibid.
9. Ibid. Not everyone thinks that gay marriage is a threat to straight marriage. Andrew Sullivan, for example, argues that "[g]ay marriage . . . [u]nlike domestic partnership . . . merely asks that gays be allowed to join in. . . . Gay marriage could only delegitimize straight marriage if it were a real alternative to it." In other words, gay marriage does not challenge the value of ". . . a deeper and harder-to-extract-yourself-from commitment to another human being [which] would foster social cohesion, emotional security, . . . economic prudence" and a nurturing environment for children. (Andrew Sullivan, The Case for Gay Marriage," *The New Republic,* August 28, 1989, p. 22).
10. See, for example, Hannah Schwarzschild, "Same-Sex Marriage and Constitutional Privacy: Moral Threat and Legal Anomaly," *Berkeley Women's Law Journal* 4, no. 94 (1988).

11. Kenneth L. Karst, "Freedom of Intimate Association," *Yale Law Journal* 89, no. 624 (1980): 682.

12. *Loving* v. *Virginia*, 388 U.S. 1 (1967).

13. Peter Freiberg, "Some Gays Aren't Wedded to the Idea of Same-Sex Marriage," *The Advocate* 530, no. 16 (1989).

14. Anna Quindlen, "Evan's Two Moms," *The New York Times*, February 5, 1992, p. A15.

15. There is a variant of this protest chant that does not seek social acceptance of even things queer. "We're here, we're queer, we're fabulous, don't fuck with us."

16. Steve Bryant and Demian, "The Ancient History of Same-Sex Marriage," in *An Indispensable Guide for Gay and Lesbian Couples: What Every Same-Sex Couple Should Know* (Seattle: Sweet Corn Productions, 1993), p. 43. This article consists of notes on a public lecture given by John Boswell; the lecture summarized ideas which are discussed more fully in his recent book on same-sex marriage *Same-Sex Unions in Europe* (New York: Villard Books, 1994).

17. Bryant, Demian, "The Ancient History of Same-Sex Marriage," p. 43.

18. Ibid.

19. Ibid.

20. Ibid.

21. Paula Ettelbrick is Public Policy Director of the National Center for Lesbian Rights, New York City office.

22. Paula Ettelbrick. "Since When Is Marriage a Path to Liberation?" *OUT/LOOK National Gay and Lesbian Quarterly* 6, no. 8 (1990): 17. See chapter 20 in this volume.

23. Ettelbrick, "Since When Is Marriage a Path to Liberation?" p. 14.

24. Ibid.

25. Mary Midgley, *Animals and Why They Matter* (London: Penguin Books, 1983), p. 67.

26. Ettelbrick, "Since When Is Marriage a Path to Liberation?" p. 16.

27. Ibid.

28. Despite her recognition that these practical difficulties arise from the fact that lesbian partners are legal strangers, Robson opposes both gay marriage and domestic partnership, arguing instead that marriage should be abolished. Attorney Thomas Stoddard welcomes abolishing marriage for all couples as an alternative to extending the right to marry to lesbians and gay men but finds the replacement of marriage by a new legal entity unlikely. (Ruthann Robson, *Lesbian (Out)Law: Survival Under the Rule of Law* (Ithaca, N.Y.: Firebrand Books, 1992), pp. 117, 126–27; Thomas Stoddard, "Why Gay People Should Seek the Right to Marry," *Outlook* 6, no. 8 (1990), p. 13.

29. Ettelbrick, "Since When Is Marriage a Path to Liberation?" p. 16.

30. Ibid., p. 15.

31. Ibid., p. 14.

32. Christine Pierce, "Postmodernism and Other Skepticisms," in *Feminist Ethics*, ed. Claudia Card (Lawrence: University Press of Kansas, 1991), p. 66.

33. Ettelbrick, "Since When Is Marriage a Path to Liberation?" p. 15.

34. Stoddard, "Why Gay People Should Seek the Right to Marry," p. 13.

35. Susan Moller Okin, *Justice, and the Family* (New York: Basic Books, 1989).

36. Ibid., pp. 135–36.

37. Ibid., p. 170.

38. Martha Nussbaum, "Justice for Women," *New York Review of Books* 39, no. 16 (October 8, 1992): 46.

39. Hunter, "Sexual Dissent and the Family," p. 411.

40. Ruthann Robson and S. E. Valentine, "Lov(h)ers: Lesbians as Intimate Partners and Lesbian Legal Theory" *Temple Law* 63, no. 511 (1990): 536. For further examples of arguments to the effect that gay marriage should be rejected because marriage is "het" or "patriarchal" or oppressive to women, see Freiberg, "Some Gays Aren't Wedded to the Idea of Same-Sex Marriage," p. 18; Catherine Saalfield, Lesbian Marriage . . . [K]not!" in *Sisters, Sexperts, Queers: Be-*

yond the Nation, ed. Arlene Stein (New York: Penguin Books, 1993), p. 191; Suzanne Sherman, ed. *Lesbian and Gay Marriage: Private Commitments, Public Ceremonies* (Philadelphia: Temple University Press, 1992), pp. 113, 217.

41. Thomas Stoddard takes this position.

42. See Claudia Card, *Lesbian Choices,* chapter 9 (New York. Columbia University Press, 1995).

43. Ettelbrick, "Since When Is Marriage a Path to Liberation?" p. 16.

44. Marrying for the sake of a green card is an exception here.

45. Ettelbrick, "Since When Is Marriage a Path to Liberation?" p. 17.

46. Ibid., p. 16.

47. Ibid., p. 17.

48. See Kath Weston, *Families We Choose: Lesbians, Gays, Kinship* (New York: Columbia University Press, 1991).

49. *Bowers* v. *Hardwick,* 106 S. Ct. 28–41, 2844 (1986).

50. Dirk Johnson, "Colorado Ban on Gay Rights Laws is Ruled Unconstitutional: Violation Found on Rights to Equal Protection," *New York Times,* December 14,1993, p. A11.

51. "Colorado Gay Rights Ban Ruled Unconstitutional," *Washington Post,* December 15, 1993, p. A24.

52. Tamar Lewin, "Colorado Bill on Gay Rights Laws is Ruled Unconstitutional: Gay Rights Groups See Ruling as Curb on Other States," *The New York Times,* December 14, 1993, p. A11.

53. Stoddard, quoting from the Supreme Court's 1965 decision to strike down an anti-contraception statute, p. 12.

54. Freiberg, "Some Gays Aren't Wedded to the Idea of Same-Sex Marriage," p. 18.

55. My thanks to the CHASS (College of Humanities and Social Sciences) Research Fund and Humanities Foundation Travel Grants at North Carolina State University for funds to travel to the Kinsey Institute; to the Kinsey Institute for Research in Sex, Gender, and Reproduction, Bloomington, Indiana, for their staff time and bibliographical assistance; and to the audience of the Midwest Society for Women in Philosophy, University of Cincinnati, October 2,1993, for their comments.

22.

TIME HAS COME TO MAKE A CASE FOR POLYANDRY

William Safire

The institution of marriage has been put into play.

A couple of judges in Hawaii, tossing judicial restraint to the gentle breezes, have declared that marriage need no longer be construed as the legal union between a man and a woman. They have ruled that the denial of marriage licenses to homosexual couples is discrimination on the basis of sex, unconstitutional in that state.

What is upsetting Americans in the other forty-nine states (not to mention the great majority of Hawaiians) is the possible extension of this ruling throughout the nation by virtue of the "full faith and credit" clause of the U.S. Constitution. That says plainly that each state must recognize "public acts, records and judicial proceedings of every other state."

Remember the old days when unhappy spouses traveled to Nevada for a quickie divorce, which had to be recognized as legal at home? Same principle: If the state judges get their way, marriage in Hawaii would enable a gay couple to claim all the legal and insurance protections of marriage anywhere in the United States.

Those of us who run our thumbs along the cutting edge of social change, however, are less interested in the pros and cons of "same-sex marriage" than in the possibility its acceptance would open up for a far larger segment of the population.

With the age-old institution of one-man, one-wife finally in play, the time has come to make the case for polyandry.

For those who have not given the matter much thought, polyandry is the marriage of one woman to two or more men. (Do not confuse it with the discredited, sexist "polygamy," the marriage of one man to more than one woman.) Consider what the adoption of polyandry would do for the social fabric of families in America.

What is the reason for the divorce explosion, wedlock-free children, the loss of our traditional values, galloping anomie and rampant ennui? The root cause is the way some men have their way with women and then run out on them. "Deadbeat dads" are an alliterative blight on our society.

But if just one judge in one state dared to strike a blow for polyandry, think of the positive repercussions:

1. A woman's chance of being left alone would be cut in half overnight. If one man left, there would still be another standing by. Both the wife and the stay-behind spouse would, in their joint rejection, be drawn more closely together. Moreover, the search for a replacement second husband would be easier, conducted by two abandoned spouses, one of whom could work or stay home with the children while the other cruised singles bars or followed up personal ads. Also, because women live longer, a backup husband reduces full widowhood.

2. The likelihood of the presence of a male role model in the home for children would be doubled. The era of the latchkey child would end abruptly, as one of the husbands would be at home at all times for roughhouse and nurturing.

3. Marital fidelity would be enhanced by internalizing the eternal triangle. The costs of living together could be cut sharply by eliminating the need for assignations. Three can live as cheaply as two; remove the adult from adultery.

Who could oppose this modest proposal to extend connubial rights, inheritance-tax advantages and benefits blessings to millions of lonely women and angry extra males?

Oh, we can expect to hear from feminists who fear to go too far, as well as male chauvinists who are not into sharing and caring. Traditionalists may mutter about the risks of fiddling with fundaments, though research will show the origins of polyandry in biblical times.

To the peroration: If you believe marriage to be indispensable to the upbringing of children; if you argue for the stability this institution brings to human relationships: if you sense the values inherent in the mutual love and loyalty of families; and if you believe, with our Federalist Fathers, in the "full faith and credit" clause—then how, in the name of all that virtuous men and women hold sacred, can you object to the expansion of this bulwark of civilization?

Ladies and gentlemen of the Platform Committee, if this polyandry plank is not included intact, I am marching my people right out of this convention.

23.

I HAVE ANGUISHED

Ed Fallon

I have anguished over this [state anti-gay marriage] bill, not because there is any doubt in my mind as to how I should vote, but because I believe strongly that what we are dealing with here is the defining civil rights issue of this decade. Historically, this issue may prove to be the most significant matter we deal with this year, and so I would respectfully ask the body's indulgence and attention during this debate.

My remarks are directed both toward those who sincerely believe that this bill is good and just and to those who know in their hearts and consciences that this bill is wrong, but in fear of public opinion and of how this issue will be used in campaigns next fall, they are inclined to vote in favor of its passage.

Back in the 1950s, many, many Americans were victimized by relentless, fear-driven red-baiting. There was a Bolshevik lurking in every bathroom, and you never knew, but your neighbor or even your uncle might turn out to be a communist.

In the 1990s, red-baiting is out. But pink-baiting is in. Gay-bashing, generally thought of as a Friday night frolic for inebriated thugs, has its parallel expressions in voting booths, city council halls, and legislative chambers across this country. Today we are witnessing one of those expressions in the form of this bill. By singling out gay and lesbian marriages as a union unacceptable in the eyes of the law, we fuel the fires of ignorance, intolerance, and hatred.

And if anyone here thinks that the positions we embrace, the laws we enact do not affect the mood of the public, then you have a very low, and I believe, a very inaccurate view of the powerful influence we here in this body exert over the formation of public opinion. The message we're sending today is that it's okay to discriminate against people of a different sexual orientation, even though for the most part, that's the way they were born and there's

This address was delivered to the Iowa House of Representatives on February 20, 1996.

nothing they can do to change it. And for those who would argue that homosexuality is a choice, I ask you: do you really believe that anyone in their right mind would voluntarily choose to be in a class of people who are constantly made fun of, despised, beaten up and even killed, discriminated against, fired from their jobs, denied housing, and prevented from marrying?

For gay and lesbian people, this array of abuse is par for the course. If you believe that homosexuality is a personal choice, then you have not tried very hard to see this issue from a gay or lesbian person's point of view.

Well, I suppose this is as good a time as any for me to come out of the closet. I can't help the way I was born. It's just who I am. I've never announced this to a group publicly, but I guess it's about time. I am heterosexual. I am absolutely certain in my entire being that I could never be homosexual, no matter how hard I might try. I've never been attracted to another man in my life, and the idea of engaging in a homosexual act is foreign and distasteful to me. But just as I would hope that homosexual men and women could accept me for who I am, I promise to try to accept them for who they are. Why can't you do the same? Why can't we all do the same?

Hatred grows out of fear, and fear grows out of ignorance. Though I've never hated homosexuals, I used to fear them. When I was a kid growing up, the worst name you could call someone was a gay loser. And the stereotype that still pervades the minds of many in this chamber—that of the highly aggressive, promiscuous gay man seeking countless, anonymous relationships—is the stereotype that I grew up with, and the stereotype that contributes to volumes of ignorance and volumes of fear.

Over time, I've come to learn that this stereotype, like most stereotypes, is based on hearsay, not fact. The rogues who may fit the previous description are the exception to the rule, just as there are male heterosexual rogues who are aggressive, promiscuous, and constantly hitting on and harassing women.

In my evolving experience with homosexuals, familiarity has displaced ignorance and dispelled fear. I now count as friends and constituents many same-sex couples. Some have children. Most are in longterm, stable relationships. All are very decent, kind, and normal people. I make no effort to judge the integrity of what they do in their bedroom, and, to their credit, they've never judged the integrity of what I do in mine.

One lesbian couple I count as friends have two children the same age as my son and daughter. They attend the same elementary school as my children. They play together. They go to the same birthday parties. They swap overnights. These two children are healthy, bright, and courteous, and their parents probably do a better job of parenting than I do.

Though you may have personal, religious reasons why this arrangement seems distasteful to you, there is absolutely no way you could rationally argue that this is not a stable happy, healthy family. In a pluralistic society that allegedly values the separation of church and state, why can we not simply live and let live? Accept the reality that this couple's religious beliefs on homosexuality are different than yours. Just leave religion out of it, as our founding fathers and mothers saw fit. If the fruit which falls from the tree is good, the tree must also be good.

Indeed, there are many religious groups that openly and lovingly celebrate unions between same-sex couples. For example, Methodists, the United Church of Christ, Congregationalists, Reform Jews, the Metropolitan Community Church, Unitarian Universalists and Quakers.[1]

There is no shortage of gay or lesbian couples that value and revere marriage. In fact, just last fall I attended the wedding of two women. Their son was present. The wedding was held in a local church. It was conducted by two ministers. And there were 150 family members and friends of the happy couple there to celebrate with them.

Yet, we're told by the bill's supporters that we need legislation to protect ourselves from this kind of marriage? No, ladies and gentlemen, this is not a marriage-protection bill. It is emphatically an anti-marriage bill.

This rhetoric used by supporters of HF 2183 may be slick but it is grossly inaccurate. What are you trying to protect heterosexual marriages from? There isn't a limited amount of love in Iowa. It isn't a nonrenewable resource. If Amy and Barbara or Mike or Steve love each other, it doesn't mean that John and Mary can't.

Marriage licenses aren't distributed on a first-come, first-served basis here in Iowa. Heterosexual couples don't have to rush out and claim marriage licenses now, before they are all snatched up by gay and lesbian couples.

Heterosexual unions are and will continue to be predominant, regardless of what gay and lesbian couples do. To suggest that homosexual couples in any way, shape, or form threaten to undermine the stability of heterosexual unions is patently absurd.

And I know, you'll say: "What about the gay agenda?" Well, just as there turned out to be no Bolsheviks in the bathroom back in the 1950s, there is no gay agenda in the 1990s. There is, however, a strong, well-funded anti-gay agenda, and we have an example of its efforts here before us today.

All that gay and lesbian people are asking for is, if not understanding, then at least tolerance. All they are asking for is the same basic civil equality that all Americans yearn for and should be entitled to.

To those in this body who know in their hearts and consciences that this bill is wrong, yet are afraid to vote against it, I ask you to consider the powerful message this bill sends to the people of Iowa. It sends the message that discrimination against gays and lesbians is acceptable and officially sanctioned. It sends the message that it's okay to deny civil and equal rights to some minority groups in our society. It sends the message that the gift of marriage is good for some yet forbidden to others. And for those in my own party who plan to vote for this bill, it sends the message that Democrats, who have traditionally stood up for and protected everyone's civil rights, aren't willing to do so in the case of homosexuals.

If you are weighing the political consequences of opposing this bill and find they are too heavy, I'd like you to think about the great moral changes that have occurred in this country over the past two hundred years. Ask yourself when you would have felt safe to speak in favor of the separation of the colonies from Great Britain? When would you have taken a public stand for the abolition of slavery? When would you have spoken in favor of women's suffrage? In the 1960s, when would you have joined Martin Luther King and others in calling for equal rights for African Americans? When would you have spoken out against restrictive marriage laws banning interracial marriages?

While the choice before us today—between a green button or a red one—is a difficult one to make, it is nowhere near as difficult or dangerous as the choices faced by the many freedom fighters who came before us.

We're elected not to follow but to lead. We're elected to cast what might sometimes be a difficult, challenging, and politically inexpedient vote. We're elected to represent our constituents when they're right, and to vote our consciences regardless of whether our constituents are right. And our conscience should be telling us to stand up for civil rights regardless of how unpopular it may appear.[2]

The Reverend Dr. Martin Luther King, Jr., once said, "A time comes when silence is betrayal." Such a time is now. With your "no" vote on this bill, you can help break the silence and stand with those who have no one to stand with them.

NOTES

1. See *Where to Get a Religious Blessing.*
2. See *Poll of New Hampshire Republican Voters on Marriage Issues.*

24.

RELATIONS BETWEEN CONSENTING ADULTS: SODOMY LAWS AND HOMOSEXUAL MARRIAGE

Richard A. Posner

Analysis . . . seems to me decisive in favor of repealing laws punishing homosexual acts between consenting adults. Not that repeal will do many homosexuals much good. The enforcement of these laws has become exceedingly rare. It is better not to have laws on the books that reflect ignorance and prejudice; but if they are not enforced, they do little harm, despite much lore to the contrary.

A well-known book by Herbert Packer on the criminal sanction lists the reasons for not punishing homosexual behavior between consenting adults:

1. Rarity of enforcement creates a problem of arbitrary police and prosecutorial discretion.

2. The extreme difficulty of detecting such conduct leads to undesirable police practices.

3. The existence of the proscription tends to create a deviant subculture.

4. Widespread knowledge that the law is violated with impunity by thousands every day creates disrespect for law generally.

5. No secular harm can be shown to result from such conduct.

6. The theoretical availability of criminal sanctions creates a situation in which extortion and, on occasion, police corruption may take place.

7. There is substantial evidence that the moral sense of the community no longer exerts strong pressure for the use of criminal sanctions.

8. No utilitarian goal of criminal punishment is substantially advanced by proscribing private adult consensual sexual conduct.[1]

The list is less impressive than it looks. Points 1, 2, and 6 are the same. A rarely enforced law creates opportunities for law enforcement abuses, including extortion and the invidious exercise of police and prosecutorial discretion. These used to be serious problems in the administration of the sodomy laws,[2] but that was when the laws were being enforced. The level of enforcement has fallen so low that police abuses have become rare, although the facts of *Bowers* v. *Hardwick* . . . may illustrate such abuse. Point 3 seems wrong . . . ; the distinctive homosexual subculture is not an artifact of law, let alone of unenforced law. Points 5 and 8 are again one point, not two: the sodomy laws, unenforced as they are, are not preventing any conduct that we have a good reason to prevent. They almost certainly do not deter much homosexual behavior. Whether they make a "statement" about social attitudes toward homosexuality that might influence people depends in the first place on whether one thinks the presence of laws on the books is more important than the fact that they are not enforced—whether, that is, words speak louder than actions. Even if they do in some cases, it is exceedingly unlikely that they do in this case: that they influence either the formation or retention of homosexual preference, or the amount of homosexual behavior.

Point 7 is of course true; it is no doubt one reason (along with cost, civil liberties concerns, and competing demands on law enforcers) why these laws are not being enforced. But nonenforcement may be an adequate, if parsimonious, response to the moral sense of the community. Point 4 (knowledge that the law is violated creates disrespect for law generally) is the kind of point that lawyers love to make but that lacks either theoretical or empirical support. . . . It is true that many people in our society disobey many laws; and this is another way of saying that there is widespread disrespect for law in this society, at least if "respect' is more than notional. But whether, as Packer implies, this disrespect feeds on itself is unknown.

A reason he does not mention for repealing the sodomy laws is to give homosexuals more entrée to professions from which they are now largely excluded. There is, for example, a natural reluctance, given the strong (possibly much exaggerated) belief in the effect of "role models" on behavior, to appoint to judicial positions people who have committed hundreds or even thousands of criminal acts simply because they are homosexuals living in states in which sodomy is a crime. The criminal status of homosexuals' characteristic manner of sexual expression provides at least a talking point for all sorts of other exclusions as well. This is not to say that none of these exclusions is justified; that is a question still to be addressed. But repealing the sodomy laws would clear away one bad reason for the exclusions and enable valid concerns to be addressed more cleanly.

If the sodomy laws ought to be repealed, the logical next question is whether homosexual marriage ought to be permitted. The connection between the two questions lies in the fact that both involve homosexual relations between consenting adults. This makes them different from whether homosexuals should be excluded from military or other occupations and whether laws forbidding discrimination should protect homosexuals. The latter are questions about relations between homosexuals and others, primarily employers.

The libertarian places the burden of proof on those who would limit the right to marry, and adds that there are arguments as well as dogma in favor of including homosexuals within this permission. The existence of a right to marry would raise homosexuals' self-esteem. It would contribute, although perhaps only marginally, to the stability of homosexual relationships, and by doing so would not only make homosexuals happier but also reduce the spread of venereal disease in general and of the justly dreaded AIDS in particular. These are the benefits of permitting homosexual marriage; and the costs seem slight, if I am correct that the removal of the legal disabilities of homosexuality is unlikely to increase the amount of homosexual preference. Homosexual acts, as distinct from preference, would actually be reduced if homosexual marriage reduced homosexual promiscuity.

But there are three differences between punishing sodomy and confining the right to marry to heterosexuals. The first is that permitting homosexual marriage would be widely interpreted as placing a stamp of approval on homosexuality, while decriminalizing sodomy would not, at least not to anywhere near the same extent. To say that an act is not a crime is not to commend it; a great deal of behavior that is disgusting or immoral or both is nevertheless not criminal. But marriage, even though considered sacramental only by Catholics, is believed by most people in our society to be not merely a license to reproduce but also a desirable, even a noble, condition in which to live. To permit persons of the same sex to marry is to declare, or more precisely to be understood by many people to be declaring, that homosexual marriage is a desirable, even a noble, condition in which to live. This is not what most people in this society believe; . . . it would be misleading to suggest that homosexual marriages are likely to be as stable or rewarding as heterosexual marriages, even granting as one must that a sizable fraction of heterosexual marriages in our society are not stable and are not rewarding. I do not suggest that government's pronouncing homosexual marriage a beatific state would cause heterosexuals to rethink their sexual preference. My concern lies elsewhere. It is that permitting homosexual marriage would place government in the dishonest position of propagating a false picture of the reality of homosexuals' lives.

Against this it can be argued that as heterosexual marriage becomes ever more unstable, temporary, and childless, the suggestion that it differs fundamentally from what homosexual marriages could be expected to be like becomes ever more implausible. And this is true. But it is a point in favor not of homosexual marriage but of chucking the whole institution of marriage in favor of an explicitly contractual approach that would make the current realities of marriage transparent.

The second difference between the sodomy and marriage issues will strike many readers as a trivial addendum to the first. It is that the more broadly *marriage* is defined, the less information it and related terms convey. When we read that Mr. X is married or that Ms. Y is married, we know immediately that X's spouse is a woman and Y's a man. If we invite people to a party and ask them to bring their spouses, we know that each man will either come alone or bring a woman and that each woman will either come alone or bring a man. So a homosexual man will come alone and likewise a homosexual woman. If we do not care to limit the additional guests to spouses, we ask the invitees to bring not their spouses but their "guests." If our son or daughter tells us that he or she is getting married, we know the sex of the prospective spouse. All these understandings would be upset by permitting homosexual marriage. This of course is one reason homosexual rights advocates want homosexual marriage to be permitted. All I wish to emphasize is that there is an information cost to the proposal.

But there is also an information benefit. The denial of marriage to homosexuals prevents a homosexual couple from signaling the extent of their commitment. If marriage were abolished, heterosexual cohabitation would denote indifferently the briefest and the most permanent of relationships. If the "freedom to marry" of which the Supreme Court spoke in *Loving* v. *Virginia*[3] were taken seriously, the deprivation to the homosexual couple denied the right to marry would carry a heavy weight; but of course the Court was thinking of heterosexual marriage.

The third difference between the sodomy and marriage issues is the most important. Abolishing the sodomy laws would have few collateral effects, though I have suggested that it would have one: it would make it easier for homosexuals to obtain jobs in fields at present closed to them. Authorizing homosexual marriage would have many collateral effects, simply because marriage is a status rich in entitlements. It would have effects on inheritance, social security, income tax, welfare payments, adoption, the division of property upon termination of the relationship, medical benefits, life insurance, immigration, and even testimonial privilege. (The *Commercial-News* of Danville, Ohio, carried an article under the intriguing banner, "Homosexual Loses Court Battle over Use of Mate's Testimony." The mate in question was another man.) These incidents of marriage were designed with heterosexual marriage in mind, more specifically heterosexual marriages resulting in children. They may or may not fit the case of homosexual marriage; they are unlikely to fit it perfectly. Do we want homosexual couples to have the same rights of adoption and custody as heterosexual couples? Should we worry that a homosexual might marry a succession of dying AIDS patients in order to entitle them to spouse's medical benefits? These questions ought to be faced one by one rather than elided by conferring all the rights of marriage in a lump on homosexuals willing to undergo a wedding ceremony.

None of these points is decisive against permitting homosexual marriage.

All together may not be. The benefits of such marriage may outweigh the costs. Nonetheless, since the public hostility to homosexuals in this country is too widespread to make homosexual marriage a feasible proposal even if it is on balance cost-justified, maybe the focus should be shifted to an intermediate solution that would give homosexuals most of what they want but at the same time meet the three objections I have advanced.

Denmark and Sweden, not surprisingly, provide the model. What in Denmark is called registered partnership and in Sweden homosexual cohabitation is in effect a form contract that homosexuals can use to create a simulacrum of marriage. The Danish law goes further than the Swedish: it places the registered partners under all the provisions of the marriage code except those relating to children, although a question has arisen whether the registered partner has the same beneficial rights in his (or her) partner's private pension that a spouse would have.[4] Sweden, which already has defined a quasi-marital status for cohabiting heterosexuals, allows cohabiting homosexuals to elect that status, the main feature of which is an even division, upon the dissolution of the relationship, of what in this country would be called community property.[5] The Danish approach is mechanical in assuming that the presence of children is the only thing that distinguishes heterosexual from homosexual marriage. The Swedish approach assumes, realistically I think, that a homosexual relationship, even when meant to last, is more like heterosexual cohabitation than like heterosexual marriage, so the forms that the Swedes have worked out to regularize what is after all an extremely common relationship in their country provide the appropriate model for homosexuals who want to live together in ours. It may indeed offer an increasingly attractive model for heterosexuals as well.

NOTES

1. Herbert L. Packer, *The Limits of the Criminal Sanction* 304 (1968). See also American Law Institute, *Model Penal Code and Commentaries* (Official Draft and Revised Comments) (Stanford, Calif.: Stanford University Press, 1980), pt. 2, 365–73.

2. Project, "The Consenting Adult Homosexual and the Law: An Empirical Study of Enforcement and Administration in Los Angeles County," 13 *UCLA Law Review* 643 (1966): 690–720, 763–92.

3. 388 U.S. 1, 12 (1967). The decision invalidated a state law forbidding miscegenation. In subsequent decisions the Supreme Court has continued to describe the right to marry as a "fundamental right." See, for example, *Zablocki* v. *Redhail,* 434 U.S. 374, 383–86 (1978); *Turner* v. *Safley,* 482 U.S. 78, 94–99 (1987).

4. Michael Elmer and Marianne Lund Larsen, "Explanatory Article on the Consequences Etc., of the Danish Law on Registered Partnership." This article, the English translation of an article that appeared in the Danish law journal *Juristen* in 1990, is available from Landsforeningen for Bosser og Lesbiske (National [Danish] Organization for Gays and Lesbians) in Copenhagen. Incidentally, in the first nine months in which the law on registered partnerships was in effect, 553 couples were registered, of which 119 were lesbian couples. Letter from Dorthe Jacobsen to John A. Shope, November 14, 1990. This is further evidence that lesbianism is indeed less common than male homosexuality.

5. Ake Saldeen, "Sweden: More Rights for Children and Homosexuals," *Journal of Family Law* 27 (1988–89): 295, 296–97; Mary Ann Glendon, *The Transformation of Family Law: State, Law, and Family in the United States and Western Europe* (Chicago: University of Chicago Press, 1989), p. 276.

25.

MAKING THE FAMILY FUNCTIONAL: THE CASE FOR SAME-SEX MARRIAGE

Larry A. Hickman

Several years ago, when I was a regular columnist for the *Bryan-College Station* (Texas) *Eagle,*[1] I wrote a piece in which I suggested that Americans need to rethink their notion of the family. I argued that we would all benefit from thinking of the family as a functional unit rather than as something with a fixed and finished essence. I urged my readers to entertain the idea that if a particular social arrangement *functions* like a family then we should count it as a functioning family. The philosophical idea behind my column was this: hardline essentialism often bars the way to the solution of pressing social problems. We need to pay more attention to how things work than to their purported "essences."

Few if any of us would admit to being anti-family, so there should be widespread agreement that our society needs more functioning families. But most of us know of nontraditional social units that perform precisely the same functions that traditional families perform. So why should we not count them as families? Why should we not afford them the same kind of legal protection that is given to traditional families?

A consequence of this way of thinking, I argued, is that we as a society should begin to offer legal recognition to marriages between gay men, between lesbians, among certain polygamous and polyandrous groups, and even among small associations of elderly men and women insofar as those small associations perform certain functions.

Here is a quotation from one of the angry letters printed in response to my suggestion: "The *American Heritage Dictionary* definition of a family is 'the most instinctive, fundamental social or mating group in man and animal, especially the union of man and woman through marriage and their offspring; parents and their children; persons related by blood . . .' You tell me: What does homosexuality have to do with a family?"

My respondent continued: "Can you imagine the havoc the legal system and the insurance system would suffer if, as [Hickman] suggests, America began to recognize and accept his nontraditional family units? Shame on you . . . for allowing this man to continue to publicly promote a homosexual lifestyle."[2]

There you have it in a nutshell: a traditional definition of the family, as enshrined in the *American Heritage Dictionary,* relying on hard-line essentialist criteria. There is in nature a biological union in which a male and a female come together in order to procreate and to nurture their offspring.[3] What makes this view hard-line essentialist is that it says that there is a fixed and finished essence of "family" which we must recognize and honor if we are to know, to act appropriately, and to flourish in the world. Put a bit differently, the claim is that if we do not recognize and acquiesce to this fixed and finished essence, then we can expect havoc.

For those who suspect that I have constructed a straw argument, let me assure you that this is a quotation from an actual letter. I am confident that most of us would not have to leave our own towns or cities in order to find people who hold a similar point of view.[4]

Now the author of the response to my column did not elaborate on or justify her claim that she had articulated the essence of the family. Except for her vague warning about the havoc that would result from following my suggestion she did not appeal to anything beyond the *American Heritage Dictionary.* So let's consider how she might have justified her claim.

She might have appealed to a supernatural ordering of things, such as one finds in certain theological treatises on the family. Or she might have appealed to certain naturalist criteria, thus extrapolating from the larger biological order of which human beings are a part. Finally, she might have appealed to a somewhat weaker form of essentialism, namely, that human societies have worked out over several centuries a satisfactory set of rules for establishing the essence of what it means to be a family, and that the time has now come to stop inquiry into the matter because all the work of defining the family has been done.

In fact all three of these responses, which I will call the *supernaturalist,* the *naturalist,* and the *historical-cultural* strategies, would be an appeal to work already done, either by a god, nature, or culture, and therefore not in need of any further revision.

I suggest that this is one of the main problems of hard-line essentialist views in general: they are static or backward-looking and thus do not take into sufficient account the fact that we live forward in time, that we must take changing circumstances into account if we are to act intelligently, and that foresight and experimental problem solving are required wherever human beings expect to continue to flourish.

But what, more specifically, are the problems with the hard-line essentialist notion of the family? In the remainder of this essay I will point out and discuss several of those problems. Then I will indicate some of the ways in which a pragmatic or functional understanding of the family can be more productive of both proximate and longterm good. In order to do this I will have to explain what goods I hope to gain by such a functional understanding of the family, that is, what is to be gained by making the family functional.

‖

The first problem with essentialist views as I have described them is that they suffer from a type of historical dislocation that we might call antiquation: they do not begin where we *are* but where we have *been*. Like the notorious generals who send their troops into battle to fight the previous war, essentialists busily prescribe goals and plans of action for societies and cultures that have ceased to exist.

I will pass rather briefly over the types of antiquation involved in the supernaturalist and naturalist claims advanced by the essentialist in order to get to what I take to be the more important cultural claim.

Regarding the supernaturalist claim, it is clear that theological doctrines and organized religions, like other types of institutions, either change and develop as their environing conditions alter or else they become at best irrelevant and at worst extinct. Some progressive mainstream religious groups in the United States are beginning to recognize this fact and are now moving—some slowly, others more rapidly—toward acceptance of the idea that homosexuals should not be discriminated against on the basis of their homosexuality alone.

On the other hand, religionists of the literalist-fundamentalist stripe tend to claim (even against the testimony of their own sacred texts) that their theology involves a fixed essence and that changing conditions must therefore measure up to their theology. It is on such grounds that they oppose the legalization of homosexual marriage. It is they who have mounted most of the anti-gay initiatives in cities and states across our nation.

But their position is historically dislocated in a double sense. First, it fails to take into account the historical facts that militancy with respect to theological views has a history of failure, that the source of most of the major conflicts in the world today are due to such religious intransigency, and that much of the success of contemporary social and political arrangements has been built upon compromise and understanding, not on the basis of drawing lines in the sand.

Second, their position fails to take into account the historical fact that American society is increasingly secular and to an even greater extent increasingly multicultural, with all that this entails. In character and outlook, American society is no longer predominantly Christian, or for that matter even predominantly Judeo-Christian. What is called for at the present time is therefore not narrow secularism, but what John Dewey termed "a common faith," which can resolve rather than engender strife, and can unite individuals and groups in their quest for shared goals and social amelioration.

\

In addition to their supernaturalist strategy, hard-line essentialists sometimes employ naturalist strategies. These also suffer from antiquation. By arguing from "nature" that families must by definition be heterosexual and reproductive, the hard-line essentialist is arguing that what has in fact occurred in terms of the developmental history of nonhuman and human biology ought to be the pattern for what should be held as valuable, now and in the future, as components of human cultural practice.

Ironically, the same type of argument is sometimes advanced by proponents of legalized homosexual behavior. This is the claim that such behavior is acceptable because it occurs among nonhuman animals: "lesbian" gulls and "gay" dolphins were at one time favorite cases. But the argument from "nature," whether marshaled by pro- or anti-homosexual partisans, is flawed. It suffers not only from a missing premise, but one which probably cannot be supplied, namely that the behavior of nonhuman animals constitutes grounds for the justification of human behavior.

Regarding the third, and to my mind the most important strategy open to the essentialist in this regard, namely, the historical-cultural strategy, the functionalist is compelled to make the following admission. There are good indications that there have been times in the history of humankind during which infant mortality rates were high, disease and famine were rampant, and the population of tribal groups was regularly decimated by warfare. These factors made it highly desirable that high levels of reproduction should have been maintained. The various prohibitions in the Hebrew Bible, especially in the book of Leviticus, against same-sex copulation and masturbation have their roots in a culture that suffered all of these adversities. It is probable that when these proscriptions were articulated they had a high level of pragmatic value.

But the world of the ancient Hebrews is not the world in which we in industrialized countries now live. If we have a problem associated with our population, it is certainly not that it is too small. Further, the means of eradicating disease and hunger are now within our grasp, even if the expenditure of funds to combat these problems is not always a high priority among our elected representatives. A moment's reflection indicates, too, that tribal warfare in industrialized countries—with the possible exception of Northern Ireland—is now minimal.

It is telling, than, that one of the most frequently utilized arguments against the acceptance of homosexual family units is that such units do not allow for procreation. A heterosexual couple can procreate, or so the argument goes, and so they are a family. A homosexual couple cannot procreate, so they are not a family.

This argument is unacceptable on at least three counts of empirical error. As I have already indicated, it is historically antiquated: it does not take into account the current need within industrialized societies—and other societies as well—to manage population growth. Second, not all heterosexual couples can procreate. Should they thereby be denied the legal protection afforded to other families? Third, this argument fails to recognize that homosexuals as a group are as capable of procreation as are heterosexuals as a group. Many homosexuals do in fact have children: some are the products of former heterosexual marriages, and others are the result of various methods such as sperm donorship. I mention in this regard the famous technique known among lesbian couples as the "turkey baster" method of insemination.

From the functionalist's point of view, then, the essentialist is at fault because she has divided up the world in the wrong place. On one side, the side on which she places things and practices that are acceptable to her, she puts the kinds of things that are ordained by a god or gods, by nonhuman nature, or by cultures historically prior to our own. On the other side she places everything else as either neutral or unacceptable.

The functionalist, on the other hand, divides up the world in a quite different manner. He attempts to determine what problems are currently being experienced, and he attempts by experimental means to find ways of solving those problems. He understands, for example, that there now exist enormous pressures on the family as a result of increased geographic mobility, the technological pull toward ever more complex and rapid-paced lifestyles, the increased use of debilitating and life-threatening drugs, unemployment, and so on. He also understands that the family, creatively understood and restructured, can function as a bulwark against these pressures.

Because of this, he thinks it appropriate to divide up matters differently. On one side of the dividing line he places what works or what might work out in the sense that it promises solutions to these problems and should therefore be tried out. On the other side he places what he knows does not work because it has been tried out and it has failed.

With respect to the question at hand, then, what we ought to count as a family, his different method leads the functionalist to place on one side of his dividing line *small associations of mutual support, usually involving individuals living together under one roof, and who exhibit unconditional love, financial cooperation, and longterm commitment.* Again with respect to the question at hand, he places on the other side of the dividing line groups that do not function in this way.

To put matters succinctly, the functionalist's sorting criterion is pragmatic. He divides not on the basis of heterosexuality and the capacity for reproduction on one side and everything else an the other, but rather on the basis of what well-functioning families do, on the one side, and what groups that do not function as families do, on the other. Further, the functionalist is not afraid to try out nontraditional, experimental solutions to problematic situations. He takes into account empirical data that indicate that under the proper circumstances homosexual domestic partnerships not only function well but also tend to stabilize their environing social institutions. And this is ground enough for him to count a homosexual domestic partnership as a family.[5]

The first problem with the hard-line essentialist's definition of the family, then, is that it tends to be historically antiquated: it does not take into account where we are, speaking historically, but where we have been.

A second problem, and one that is intertwined with the essentialist's tendency to appeal to antiquated ideas and practices, is that her view is reductionistic. By this I mean that the hard-line essentialist isolates a small number of the functions of well-functioning families at the expense of other functions, some of which are at least as important as the ones that she isolates and holds as valued. It is certainly true that one of the functions of a family may be reproduction and nurturing of offspring. This may take place in a variety of ways; it may occur "naturally," which is to say without the intervention of much technological apparatus (although this is now less and less the case), or by highly artificial means, such as *in vitro* fertilization. When we look at the possibilities now impinging just on the "reproduction" part of the hard-line essentialist's definition, however, we can say that her desire to reduce the many diverse functions of the family to one or two simple ones is thwarted.

The "reproductive" component of the essentialist's definition of the family turns out to be much more complex than she has been willing to admit. This complexity has the effect of pushing her central concern back step after step until it becomes a different issue entirely, that is, one that concerns the ethics of reproductive technology.

The functionalist, on the other hand, is quite willing both to work out an experimental functional account of the family, and he is also willing to address the complex issues surrounding the technology of human reproduction. But he insists that these issues be kept separate wherever there is no good reason for mingling them. He insists even more emphatically that one issue should not be reduced to the other. (And of course he challenges the hard-line essentialist to give good reasons if she insists on such a reduction.)

What I as pragmatist and functionalist am suggesting, then, is that we ought to characterize families in terms of what families do when they function well. Now, my hard-line essentialist opponent may reply that I am begging the question. Since an essentialist of the type who responded to my newspaper column would be loath to admit that a family unit comprising two lesbians could function well as a family under any set of conditions, and therefore that she and I would be at loggerheads from the outset. She would say that it is now just a matter of my values against hers, and that she at least has cultural tradition, perhaps "the Judeo-Christian tradition," on her side.

In an attempt to break the logjam, I would then offer her my working characterization of a family, the one that I have already sketched: *a small association of mutual support, usually involving individuals living together under one roof and who exhibit unconditional love, financial cooperation, and long-term commitment.* My consequent claim would be that when you encounter such a situation, you have found a more or less well-functioning family and that there is no reason to deny a group its proper status, even though the group may incidentally be an association of partners of the same sex or perhaps a polygamous or polyandrous association. In order to make my point, all I have to do is to present one case in each category of association that functions well as a family. And such cases are not hard to find.

Once I have put my argument in this way, my opponent is faced with a choice. She may respond either that such a group is not functioning well, or that it is in fact functioning well but as something other than a family. If she takes the latter tack, than she must retreat into a reductionistic position which accepts heterosexual associations and rejects other types on that basis alone, and so her argument becomes circular. A family would be defined only as a heterosexual couple and their offspring, and nothing else would count as a family. A homosexual union could not, by that very fact, be counted as a family. Her reductionistic argument would then miss the point of what families in our society do, as opposed to how they are defined in her view or as a part of some other dogmatic position.

If she were to take to former tack, however, and tell me that a loving, monogamous relationship of two decades between two gay men which meets the functional definition I have advanced does not in fact function as a family, then she would be obligated to tell me why this is so. She might choose one of several strategies, including the argument that such a unit cannot procreate, and is therefore not a family. This would have the unfortunate consequence of committing her to the view that heterosexual unions in which one or more of the partners is sterile or else past the age of child bearing, are not families by her own definition.

Of course the hard-line essentialist might shift the argument somewhat at this point and say that she is not talking about actual reproductive capacities, but "natural sexual attraction," or perhaps more strongly, "natural sexual attraction that could, under normal circumstances, product offspring." But a functionalist would have a series of ready replies to this argument.

First, neither the strong nor the weak version of her argument would disallow heterosexual associations that are polygamous or polyandrous. Second, the weak form of her argument does not take into account the well-documented innate, which is to say "natural," attraction between gay men and between lesbians. Third, the strong form of her argument relies on the very reductionistic move that she sought to avoid by shifting her argument in the first place. Under at least one interpretation of this argument, marriage between heterosexuals where one or both is sterile or past the age of reproduction would be disallowed. Her argument therefore remains faulty because she has too closely identified sexual attraction with reproductive capacities. In short, her strong argument is so strong that it becomes circular, excluding from its premise any but heterosexual unions. It could even be read as excluding some of those unions as well.

Alternatively, she might argue that acceptance of legalized marriage between two gay men would lead children in our society to conclude, erroneously, that such an arrangement was acceptable. But of course this merely pushes the argument back one step, because she would then be required to provide reasons why the homosexual family *should not* be presented to children as acceptable. She might appeal to one or more of the standard arguments against accepting homosexual sexual behavior as moral behavior, such as are found in fundamentalist-literalist or other traditionalist accounts. But then the functionalist might ask: "What reasons can you give us for accepting your theology or your tradition over others?" This question would have the effect of pushing the debate into another territory—perhaps into the study of anthropology or comparative religion—where the essentialist's footing is even less secure.

As a part of the essentialist's move to reduce the function of the family to sexual behavior, or at the very least to make sexual behavior central to its definition, she might argue that the sex act is a uniquely apt symbol of the marriage union, and that it is a medium of communication without which a marriage is "defective." But there are several difficulties which vitiate this line of argumentation. First, in the absence of some additional premise, sex between gay males or lesbians might also be considered a uniquely apt symbol of the marriage union, and as a medium of communication without which a marriage is defective. If the hard-line essentialist wishes to deny this parity between heterosexual and homosexual sex, then she must either provide a missing premise or risk begging the question. A second difficulty with this line of argumentation is that it is reductionistic. As I have already argued, given the complex and multifarious ways in which families do in fact function in our society, to isolate sex as a defining characteristic would constitute a form of reductionism that is both empirically false and tactically absurd.

Here is a third point: the hard-line essentialist's position with respect to the family is overly exclusive. Its exclusivity follows from its reductionism. It first reduces the notion of the many and varied functions of the family to a few representative ones, a kind of synecdochial move in which sexual behavior is taken as standing for a whole complex of functions. It then utilizes the reductionist thesis to warrant exclusion of well-functioning social units that do the same type of work that heterosexual families do when they function at their best, and it does so only on those reductionistic grounds.

The fact is that recent (1993) census bureau figures indicate that there are some 3.5 million households or unmarried couples in the United States.[6] Using even a conservative estimate of 3 percent, over 100,000 of these households probably comprise gay men or lesbians. My hard-line essentialist opponent thus seems to want to deny that there are among this sizable contingent of our population any well-functioning families. She does so without the slightest empirical inquiry into whether there are among this population any viable and ongoing relationships of the sort I have described; she does so on the basis of an essentialist definition which I have claimed is indefensible.

Finally, the hard-line essentialist position is wasteful. In a time of the notorious "breakdown" of the family, including the instability that is consequent to divorce, the rise in the number of single parents who live below the poverty line, and the technological pressures on family units (such as job loss and geographic mobility), the hard-line essentialist's insistence on her reductionistic and exclusive position regarding what counts as a family is to a certain extent self-fulfilling. As long as her position is held as the social norm, it serves to create stresses on alternative family associations that tend to render them more fragile than they would otherwise be. This is wasteful because family associations that would otherwise function so as to strengthen the social fabric are weakened as a result of the enforcement of the norms she is defending.

Her argument that the acceptance of gay marriages would wreak havoc on the legal system is absurd to the point of undermining her general claim. I know of no one who has advanced the position that there should be fewer heterosexual marriages because of their burden on the legal system, although it is certainly possible to argue that current levels of divorce among heterosexual unions do place a burden on the court system. What we generally say in this regard is that this is a price we as a society are willing to pay in order to sanction associations which benefit society. If the essentialist is willing to admit, as I expect that she is, that heterosexual marriages benefit society, then she is obligated to explain (in a noncircular manner) why homosexual marriages do not and cannot provide the same or similar benefits.

Her concern about burdening the insurance system is likewise a red herring. If we hold the view that it strengthens our society to extend rights of inheritance, rights of next of kin in medical emergencies, survivor's benefits, and other such rights to heterosexual couples, then one is just left wondering at her claim that society would be harmed if those same rights were extended to homosexual couples. Would homosexuals carry more, or less, insurance as a result of participating in legalized marriage? And whatever they did, is it clear that insurance companies would suffer as a result? It is at least conceivable that homosexuals who were accepted as members of legal, functional families would experience less stress, and therefore be less prone to physical and psychological disorders than they are under the current arrangement. In the absence of evidence to the contrary, then, it is reasonable to expect that legalized homosexual marriages would have very little impact on the insurance industry. Even if there were some modest impact an that industry, it is perhaps more reasonable to conclude that it would be beneficial than to conclude that it would be detrimental.

III

At this point I want to recall a suggestion made over a hundred years ago by the American pragmatist William James. He wrote that "*the only meaning of essence is teleological and . . . classification and conception are purely teleological weapons of the mind.* The essence of a thing is that one of its properties which is so *important for my interests* that in comparison with it I may neglect the rest."[7]

I believe that James has here given us a key to effecting social amelioration with respect to the problem at hand. Notice that the pragmatic functionalist does not give up essences entirely, but merely functionalizes them by making them contextual, that is, by choosing them in a way that renders them appropriate to a specific process of deliberation.

Perhaps the reason that the hard-line essentialist and the pragmatic functionalist remain at an impasse is that they are in fact asking different sorts of questions, that is, that they have different ends in view. Perhaps the problem that the hard-line essentialist is working on is this one: "How can I maintain a world in which I am not threatened by what is foreign to me and unknown in its consequences?" Or put another way, perhaps the hard-line essentialist holds that her prescription has worked in the past and would work again if only we returned to those conditions. On the other hand, the problem that the pragmatic functionalist is working on is this one: "How can I find a solution to a serious social problem by means of active and controlled experimentation?" Or put another way, the functionalist holds that what the hard-line essentialist prescribes either never really worked or has ceased to function, so that something needs to be done to fix an unsatisfactory situation.

If this is true, perhaps no amount of discussion will serve to bring the two sides to a common ground. It may be that the hard-line essentialist will change her mind only when she begins to achieve some level of familiarity with the types of alternative family associations I have described, and as they consequently become less threatening to her.

It may even be that the solution to the problem here under consideration does not ultimately lie with the type of activity I am undertaking in this essay, namely, the articulation and analysis of the arguments on both sides of the issue. It may be that the solution lies rather in members of alternative family units working through social and political means to establish themselves as nonthreatening, credible—in a word, as functional. But, to add a word in defense of the exercise I have just undertaken, it may also be that the kind of analysis I have just done will be of some help to members of alternative family units as they seek to establish themselves through judicial and legislative action.

NOTES

1. "American Family Must Be Nurtured," *Bryan-College Station Eagle*, October 22, 1991, p. 6A.

2. "Gays Cannot Be a Family," *Bryan-College Station Eagle*, November 7,1991, p. 4A.

3. I should note that the person who responded to my column cited the second edition of the *American Heritage Dictionary*. The third edition, published since I wrote my column, contains a definition that is similar to the one to which my critic objected. The "b" definition is now: "Two or more people who share goals and values, have longterm commitments to one another, and reside usually in the same dwelling place."

4. This paper was first presented in Colorado. Voters in that state have registered just such an opinion.

5. Here is an example of the counterproductive effects of accepting the hard-line essentialist's position as reported in the *New York Times*, January 1, 1994. It involves a woman, Megan Lucas, who gave up parental rights to her child in 1992. "But she says she was twenty-one years old then and at a low point in her life, abusing drugs and alcohol. She had a history of trouble with the law and had abandoned the boy when he was five months old." Her son was "moved around, spending time in at least six foster homes until, in September, he was placed with a new couple, Ross and Louis Lopton, two gay men. This time Mrs. Lucas, who says she is now devoutly Christian, objected. Since learning of the Loptons' homosexuality, Mrs. Lucas has been fighting in court to get her son back. First she contended that she had been coerced by social workers into giving up permanent parental rights to the state. But a Whatcom County Superior Court judge rejected that argument." Her husband, Mr. Lucas, who is thirty, "has had his own run-ins with the law. On February 24 he was given a suspended one-year jail sentence and ordered to perform 240 hours of community service for stealing a vacuum cleaner from his employer."

The *Times* reported in the same article that "two conservatives in the Washington Legislature, Val Stevens, a Republican, and Thomas Campbell, a Democrat, plan to introduce a bill that would prohibit adoptions in the state except by married, heterosexual couples."

The argument put forward by Mrs. Lucas, her attorney, and the anti-gay Rutherford Institute, a conservative think tank in Charlottesville, Virginia, which has helped sponsor her case, is remarkable. Its explicit claim is that a married heterosexual couple, at least one of whom has a recent felony conviction and one of whom has a history of drug abuse and child abandonment, would make better parents than a homosexual couple, neither of whom has been shown to possess a criminal record and neither of whom has had questions raised concerning his character, except for his admitted homosexuality. In other words, the Rutherford Institute is claiming that the felonious Mr. Lucas and the child-abandoning Mrs. Lucas are a functioning family because they are heterosexual and married, whereas the law-abiding Loptons, because they are homosexual, are not a functioning family.

This is only one of many such cases. On February 3, 1996 (p. 4A) the *Southern Illinoisan* reported that "A killer who won custody of his eleven-year-old daughter because his former wife is a lesbian said Friday he can give the girl a better home. John A. Ward, who murdered his first wife, won custody of his daughter in August from a judge who wanted to give the girl a chance to live in 'a nonlesbian world.' " In this case, the judge seems to have concluded that it was worse to be a lesbian than to be a convicted wife murderer!

6. *Statistical Abstract of the United States 1994* (Washington, D.C.: U.S. Department of Commerce, 1994), p. 56.

7. William James, *The Principles of Psychology* (New York: Holt, 1890; Cambridge, Mass.: Harvard University Press, 1981), p. 961.

Part Four

THE HAWAII CASE

26.

BAEHR V. LEWIN:
AN EDITED VERSION OF THE 1993
HAWAII SUPREME COURT DECISION

Ninia BAEHR, Genora Dancel, Tammy Rodrigues, Antoinette Pregil, Pat Lagon, Joseph Melilio, Plaintiffs-Appellants,

v.

John C. LEWIN, in his official capacity as Director of the Department of Health, State of Hawaii, Defendant-Appellee.

No. 15689.

Supreme Court of Hawaii.

May 5, 1993.

Opinion Granting in Part and Denying in Part
Clarification and Reconsideration May 27, 1993. . . .

I. BACKGROUND

On May 1, 1991, the plaintiffs filed a complaint for injunctive and declaratory relief in the Circuit Court of the First Circuit, State of Hawaii, seeking, inter alia: (1) a declaration that Hawaii Revised Statutes (HRS) § 572-1 (1985) [FN1]—the section of the Hawaii Marriage Law enumerating the [r]equisites of [a] valid marriage contract"—is unconstitutional insofar as it is construed and applied by the DOH to justify refusing to issue a marriage license on the sole basis that the applicant couple is of the same sex; and (2) preliminary and permanent injunctions prohibiting the future withholding of marriage licenses on that sole basis. . . .

The plaintiffs' complaint avers that: (1) the DOH's interpretation and application of HRS § 572–1 to deny same-sex couples access to marriage licenses violates the plaintiffs' right to privacy, as guaranteed by article I, section 6 of the Hawaii Constitution, as well as to the equal protection of the laws and due process of law, as guaranteed by article I, section 5 of the Hawaii Constitution; (2) the plaintiffs have no plain, adequate, or complete remedy at law to redress their alleged injuries; and (3) the plaintiffs are presently suffering and will continue to suffer irreparable injury from the DOH's acts, policies, and practices in the absence of declaratory and injunctive relief.

On June 7, 1991, Lewin filed an amended answer to the plaintiffs' complaint. . . .

On July 9, 1991, Lewin filed his motion for judgment on the pleadings, pursuant to Hawaii Rules of Civil Procedure and to dismiss the plaintiffs' complaint. . . .

In his memorandum, Lewin urged that the plaintiffs' complaint failed to state a claim upon which relief could be granted for the following reasons: (1) the state's marriage laws "contemplate marriage as a union between a man and a woman"; (2) because the only legally recognized right to marry "is the right to enter a heterosexual marriage, [the] plaintiffs do not have a cognizable right, fundamental or otherwise, to enter into state-licensed homosexual marriages"; (3) the state's marriage laws do not "burden, penalize, infringe, or interfere in any way with the [plaintiffs'] private relationships"; (4) the state is under no obligation "to take affirmative steps to provide homosexual unions with its official approval"; (5) the state's marriage laws "protect and foster and may help to perpetuate the basic family unit, regarded as vital to society, that provides status and a nurturing environment to children born to married persons" and, in addition, "constitute a statement of the moral values of the community in a manner that is not burdensome to [the] plaintiffs"; (6) assuming the plaintiffs are homosexuals (a fact not pleaded in the plaintiffs' complaint), they "are neither a suspect nor a quasi-suspect class and do not require heightened judicial solicitude"; and (7) even if heightened judicial solicitude is warranted, the state's marriage laws "are so removed from penalizing, burdening, harming, or otherwise interfering with [the] plaintiffs and their relationships and perform such a critical function in society that they must be sustained." . . .

The circuit court heard Lewin's motion on September 3, 1991, and, on October 1, 1991, filed its order granting Lewin's motion for judgment on the pleadings on the basis that Lewin was "entitled to judgment in his favor as a matter of law" and dismissing the plaintiffs' complaint with prejudice. The plaintiffs' timely appeal followed.

II. JUDGMENT ON THE PLEADINGS WAS ERRONEOUSLY GRANTED. . . .

We conclude that the circuit court's order runs aground on the shoals of the Hawaii Constitution's equal protection clause and that, on the record before us, unresolved factual questions preclude entry of judgment, as a matter of law, in favor of Lewin and against the plaintiffs. Before we address the plaintiffs' equal protection claim, however, it is necessary as a threshold matter to consider their allegations regarding the right to privacy. . . . *The right to privacy does not include a fundamental right to same-sex marriage.*

It is now well established that " 'a right to personal privacy, or a guarantee of certain areas or zones of privacy,' is implicit in the United States Constitution." And article I, section 6 of the Hawaii Constitution expressly states that "[t]he right of the people to privacy is recognized and shall not be infringed without the showing of a compelling state interest." . . .

Accordingly, there is no doubt that, at a minimum, article I, section 6 of the Hawaii Constitution encompasses all of the fundamental rights expressly recognized as being subsumed within the privacy protections of the United States Constitution. In this connection, the United States Supreme Court has declared that "the right to marry is part of the fundamental 'right of privacy' implicit in the Fourteenth Amendment's Due Process Clause." *Zablocki* v. *Redhail* (1978).

The issue in the present case is, therefore, whether the "right to marry" protected by article I, section 6 of the Hawaii Constitution extends to same-sex couples. Because article I, section 6 was expressly derived from the general right to privacy under the United States Constitution and because there are no Hawaii cases that have delineated the fundamental right to marry, this court . . . looks to federal cases for guidance.

The United States Supreme Court first characterized the right of marriage as fundamental in *Skinner* v. *Oklahoma* ex rel. Williamson (1942). In *Skinner,* the right to marry was inextricably linked to the right of procreation. . . . Whether the Court viewed marriage and procreation as a single indivisible right, the least that can be said is that it was obviously contemplating unions between men and women when it ruled that the right to marry was fundamental. This is hardly surprising inasmuch as none of the United States sanctioned any other marriage configuration at the time.

The United States Supreme Court has set forth its most detailed discussion of the fundamental right to marry in *Zablocki,* supra, which involved a Wisconsin statute that prohibited any resident of the state with minor children "not in his custody and which he is under obligation to support" from obtaining a marriage license until the resident demonstrated to a court that he was in compliance with his child support obligations. . . . In so doing, the *Zablocki* court delineated its view of the evolution of the federally recognized fundamental right of marriage. . . .

Implicit in the *Zablocki* court's link between the right to marry, on the one hand, and the fundamental rights of procreation, childbirth, abortion, and child rearing, on the other, is the assumption that the one is simply the logical predicate of the others.

The foregoing case law demonstrates that the federal construct of the fundamental right to marry—subsumed within the right to privacy implicitly protected by the United States Constitution—presently contemplates unions between men and women. (Once again, this is hardly surprising inasmuch as such unions are the only state-sanctioned marriages currently acknowledged in this country.)

Therefore, the precise question facing this court is whether we will extend the present boundaries of the fundamental right of marriage to include same-sex couples, or, put another way, whether we will hold that same-sex couples possess a fundamental right to marry. In effect, as the applicant couples frankly admit, we are being asked to recognize a new fundamental right. . . . However, we have also held that the privacy right found in article I, section 6 is similar to the federal right and that no "purpose to lend talismanic effect" to abstract phrases such as "intimate decision" or to "personal autonomy" can "be inferred from [article I, section 6], any more than . . . from the federal decisions." . . .

Applying the foregoing standards to the present case, we do not believe that a right to same-sex marriage is so rooted in the traditions and collective conscience of our people that failure to recognize it would violate the fundamental principles of liberty and justice that lie at the base of all our civil and political institutions. Neither do we believe that a right to same-sex marriage is implicit in the concept of ordered liberty, such that neither liberty nor justice would exist if it were sacrificed. Accordingly, we hold that the applicant couples do not have a fundamental constitutional right to same-sex marriage arising out of the right to privacy or otherwise.

Our holding, however, does not leave the applicant couples without a potential remedy in this case. As we will discuss below, the applicant couples are free to press their equal protection claim. If they are successful, the State of Hawaii will no longer be permitted to refuse marriage licenses to couples merely on the basis that they are of the same sex. But there is no fundamental right to marriage for same-sex couples under article 1, section 6 of the Hawaii Constitution.

Inasmuch as the applicant couples claim that the express terms of HRS § 572–1, which discriminates against same-sex marriages, violate their rights under the equal protection clause of the Hawaii Constitution, the applicant couples are entitled to an evidentiary hearing to determine whether Lewin can demonstrate that HRS § 572–1 furthers compelling state interests and is narrowly drawn to avoid unnecessary abridgments of constitutional rights.

In addition to the alleged violation of their constitutional rights to privacy and due process of law, the applicant couples contend that they have been denied the equal protection of the laws as guaranteed by article I, section 5 of the Hawaii Constitution. On appeal, the plaintiffs urge and, on the state of the bare record before us, we agree that the circuit court erred when it concluded, as a matter of law, that: (1) homosexuals do not constitute a "suspect class" for purposes of equal protection analysis under article I, section 5 of the Hawaii Constitution; (2) the classification created by HRS § 572–1 is not subject to "strict scrutiny," but must satisfy only the "rational relationship" test; and (3) HRS § 572–1 satisfies the rational relationship test because the legislature "obviously designed [it] to promote the general welfare interests of the community by sanctioning traditional man-woman family units and procreation." . . .

The applicant couples correctly contend that the DOH's refusal to allow them to marry on the basis that they are members of the same sex deprives them of access to a multiplicity of rights and benefits that are contingent upon that status. Although it is unnecessary in this opinion to engage in an encyclopedic recitation of all of them, a number of the most salient marital rights and benefits are worthy of note. They include: (1) a variety of state income tax advantages, including deductions, credits, rates, exemptions, and estimates; (2) public assistance from and exemptions relating to the Department of Human Services; (3) control, division, acquisition, and disposition of community property; (4) rights relating to dower, curtesy, and inheritance; (5) rights to notice, protection, benefits, and inheritance; (6) award of child custody and support payments in divorce proceedings; (7) the right to spousal support; (8) the right to enter into premarital agreements; (9) the right to change of name; (10) the right to file a nonsupport action; (11) post-divorce rights relating to support and property division; (12) the benefit of the spousal privilege and confidential marital communications; (13) the benefit of the exemption of real property from attachment or execution; and (14) the right to bring a wrongful death action. For present purposes, it is not disputed that the applicant couples would be entitled to all of these marital rights and benefits, but for the fact that they are denied access to the state-conferred legal status of marriage.

Notwithstanding the state's acknowledged stewardship over the institution of marriage, the extent of permissible state regulation of the right of access to the marital relationship is subject to constitutional limitations or constraints.

The equal protection clauses of the United States and Hawaii Constitutions are not mirror images of one another. The Fourteenth Amendment to the United States Constitution somewhat concisely provides, in relevant part, that a state may not "deny to any person within its jurisdiction the equal protection of the laws." Hawaii's counterpart is more elaborate. Article I, section 5 of the Hawaii Constitution provides in relevant part that "[n]o person shall . . . be denied the equal protection of the laws, nor be denied the enjoyment of the person's civil rights or be discriminated against in the exercise thereof because of *race, religion, sex, or ancestry*" (emphasis added). Thus, by its plain language, the Hawaii Constitution prohibits state-sanctioned discrimination against any person in the exercise of his or her civil rights on the basis of sex. . . .

In a landmark decision, the United States Supreme Court, through Chief Justice Warren, struck down the Virginia miscegenation laws on both equal protection and due process grounds. The Court's holding as to the former is pertinent for present purposes:

[T]he Equal Protection Clause requires the consideration of whether the classifications drawn by any statute constitute an arbitrary and invidious discrimination. . . .

There can be no question but that Virginia's miscegenation statutes rest
solely upon distinctions drawn according to race. The statutes proscribe generally accepted conduct if engaged in by members of different races. . . . At the very
least, the Equal Protection Clause demands that racial classifications . . . be subjected to the "most rigid scrutiny," . . . and, if they are ever to be upheld, they
must be shown to be necessary to the accomplishment of some permissible state
objective, independent of the racial discrimination which it was the object of the
Fourteenth Amendment to eliminate. . . .

There is patently no legitimate overriding purpose independent of invidious
discrimination which justifies this classification. . . . We have consistently denied
the constitutionality of measures which restrict the rights of citizens on account
of race. There can be no doubt that restricting the freedom to marry solely because of racial classifications violates the central meaning of the Equal Protection Clause.

We hold that sex is a "suspect category" for purposes of equal protection
analysis under article I, section 5 of the Hawaii Constitution and that HRS §
572–1 is subject to the "strict scrutiny" test. It therefore follows, and we so
hold, that (1) HRS § 572–1 is presumed to be unconstitutional (2) unless
Lewin, as an agent of the State of Hawaii, can show that (a) the statute's sex-
based classification is justified by compelling state interests and (b) the statute
is narrowly drawn to avoid unnecessary abridgements of the applicant couples'
constitutional rights. . . .

III. CONCLUSION

Because, for the reasons stated in this opinion, the circuit court erroneously
granted Lewin's motion for judgment on the pleadings and dismissed the
plaintiffs' complaint, we vacate the circuit court's order and judgment and remand this matter for further proceedings consistent with this opinion. On remand, in accordance with the "strict scrutiny" standard, the burden will rest on
Lewin to overcome the presumption that HRS § 572–1 is unconstitutional by
demonstrating that it furthers compelling state interests and is narrowly drawn
to avoid unnecessary abridgements of constitutional rights.

Vacated and remanded.

27.

REPORT OF THE HAWAII COMMISSION ON SEXUAL ORIENTATION AND THE LAW*

Thomas P. Gill, Chair
Morgan Britt
L. Ku'umeaaloha Gomes
Lloyd James Hochberg, Jr.
Nanci Kreidman
Marie A. "Toni" Sheldon
Bob Stauffer

December 8, 1995

PREFACE

This report is submitted by the Commission on Sexual Orientation and the Law to the Eighteenth Legislature as requested by Act 5, Session Laws of Hawaii 1995.

I. BACKGROUND AND AUTHORITY

The Commission on Sexual Orientation and the Law was convened by the Legislature to address some of the issues that have arisen in the case of *Baehr* v. *Lewin,* 74 Haw.530, (1993).

---

*This edited version includes the minority report and the majority response.

A. *BAEHR V. LEWIN:* AN OVERVIEW

A lawsuit filed in May 1991 by three same-gender couples against the State of Hawaii, specifically against John Lewin, in his capacity as the Director of Health, complained of an unconstitutional marriage law that prohibited same-gender couples from obtaining marriage licenses. The complaint alleged a violation of the couples' right to privacy and equal protection under the Constitution of the State of Hawaii. The trial court dismissed the case on the pleadings and the couples appealed to the Supreme Court of Hawaii.

In May 1993 the Supreme Court reversed the trial court and remanded the case back for trial. Although the Supreme Court found that there is no fundamental right to same-sex marriage under the right to privacy, the court did conclude that the marriage law does deny the same-gender couples equal protection rights in violation of article 1, Section 5 of the Hawaii Constitution. The Hawaii Supreme Court held that the discrimination is based on the "gender" of an individual and is a "suspect category." Therefore, for purposes of the equal protection analysis, the marriage law is subject to a "strict scrutiny" test. This places the burden on the State to show that the statute's gender-based classification is justified by compelling state interests and the statute is narrowly drawn to avoid unnecessary abridgments of the applicant couples' constitutional rights.

B. LEGISLATIVE ACTION

The legislature reacted to the Supreme Court's decision in *Baehr* v. *Lewin* by holding public hearings throughout the State in September and October of 1993. At the next legislative session the legislature proceeded to pass Act 217, Session Laws of Hawaii 1994. Act 217 accomplished several things. First, Act 217 provided a venue in its purpose section for the Legislature to express its position. The purpose section of Act 217 has been interpreted to create legislative history after the fact while at the same time telling the Supreme Court not to interpret the law in a different fashion. Second, Act 217 also amended the marriage law to specifically require a man and a woman to be eligible for a marriage license, but it did not prohibit the private solemnization of any ceremony. Third, Act 217 created the prior Commission on Sexual Orientation and the Law. . . .

SEXUAL ORIENTATION AND THE LAW COMMITTEE REPORT

FINDINGS AND RECOMMENDATIONS

I. Findings

1. The commission finds that the conferring of a marriage certificate can bestow benefits in other jurisdictions. While those may be beyond the scope of this commission, the ability of the state to extend those benefits by providing a marriage certificate to individuals is significant.

2. The commission finds that major legal and economic benefits conferred by the marriage certificate through the Hawaii Revised Statutes include intangible, substantial-quantifiable, and general benefits.

3. The commission finds there are substantial public policy reasons to extend those benefits in total to same-sex couples. Those public policy reasons include:

   a. Article 1, sections 2, 3, and 5 of the Constitution of the State of Hawaii clearly states that all persons in Hawaii are entitled to equal protection under the law, including the right to enjoy their inherent and inalienable rights to life, liberty and pursuit of happiness, and be free from illegal discrimination or the denial of basic rights on the basis of gender.

      The commission finds that the denial of the benefits of marriage to same-gender couples, purely on the basis of their gender, is a violation of those basic constitutional rights.

   b. In the case which gave rise to the establishment of this commission, *Baehr* v. *Lewin,* 74 Haw. 530 (1993), the Supreme Court of Hawaii recognized the relevance of the United States Supreme Court's 1967 decision to strike down a Virginia statute which prohibited miscegenation, or interracial marriage, *Loving* v. *Virginia,* 388 U.S. 1 (1967). The Hawaii Supreme Court has found that denial of same-gender marriage was presumed to be a violation of equal protection of the law unless the state could show a "compelling state interest" for such denial. The commission finds that the various reasons advanced for denying same-gender marriages, including religious, moral and public health and safety, are similar to the *Loving* case and do not constitute a "compelling state interest" and, as a matter of public policy, should not be used to deny equal rights under the law to same-gender couples.

   c. The argument that same-sex marriage should be barred because it cannot lead to procreation is invalid, inconsistent, and discriminatory. Public policy should not deny same-sex couples the right to marriage and the right to raise a family if they wish to do so, on the excuse that they, between themselves, cannot procreate, when this reason is not applied to opposite-gender couples. State law does not require that opposite-sex couples prove that they are capable of procreation before they can be married, and many are obviously not, because of age, medical, or other reasons. Individuals in a same-gender marriage may have children from a prior opposite-gender marriage, or can adopt children if they desire a family.

d. Under our constitutional government the fact that some religions or churches condemn same-gender marriages does not mean that those religious beliefs can be imposed on others. Our separation of church and state prevents religious enforcement through state institutions, such as the Department of Health. Furthermore, the Constitution prohibits any religious group from having to perform the marriage of a couple that is not recognized by that religion.

4. The commission finds that, based on the major legal and economic benefits and the substantial public policy, the only logical conclusion is to recommend that same-gender couples be allowed to marry under chapter 572, Hawaii Revised Statutes. The commission also acknowledges that the extension of marriage to same-gender couples may not be a legislative alternative at this time.

5. In the event that same-gender marriage under chapter 572, Hawaii Revised Statutes, is not a legislative alternative, the commission recommends a universal comprehensive domestic partnership act that confers all the possible benefits and obligations of marriage for two people regardless of gender.

II. Recommendations

Based on the findings stated above, the commission first recommends the legislature amend chapter 572 to allow two people to marry, regardless of their gender. The commission also recommends the legislature adopt a universal comprehensive domestic partnership act that confers all the possible benefits and obligations of marriage for two people, regardless of gender.

MINORITY OPINION

The irony of this "minority" opinion is that its conclusions actually reflect the view of a majority of Hawaii's residents. According to the most recent poll taken by SMS Research, the *Honolulu Advertiser,* and KHON, July 19–29, 1994, more than two-thirds of the respondents stated that Hawaii should not allow people of the same sex to marry. The public response to the Draft Final Report of this commission confirms this as well. Of 1,033 written comments received, 455 were in favor and 578 were opposed to homosexual marriage. At the December 6, 1995, meeting, where public comment was received, of 103 who testified, 22 were in favor and 81 were opposed to homosexual marriage. . . .

Opposition to changing the definition of marriage is also consistent with the policy in Hawaii prohibiting "common law marriage." The State of Hawaii has protected traditional marriage and has narrowly circumscribed marriage rights since 1920.

So zealously has this court guarded the state's role as the exclusive progenitor of the marital partnership that it declared, over seventy years ago, that 'common law marriages'—i.e., 'marital' unions existing in the absence of a state-issued license and not performed by a person or society possessing governmental authority to solemnize marriages—would no longer be recognized in the Territory of Hawaii. . . .

I. INTRODUCTION

A. Reason for Minority Opinion

Due to the five-member majority of commission members who vigorously support homosexual rights, the debate needed for serious analysis did not occur. The Governor's Commission on Sexual Orientation and the Law failed in its effort to seriously analyze the issues presented. . . .

This opinion of a minority of the Governor's Commission on Sexual Orientation and the Law is written because the two-member minority disagreed with the substance of the majority's analysis and because the process employed by the majority to reach their conclusions is faulty. Instead of looking to Act 5, 1995 Session Laws, for guidance, the majority of the commission saw its role as validating favorable portions of the court opinion in *Baehr* v. *Lewin* even though in Act 217, 1994 Session Laws, the legislature roundly criticized the court opinion in *Baehr.* As a result, during the actual commission meetings, the majority of commissioners refused to examine the major legal and economic benefits reserved for married couples, but instead simply reached their conclusions. In addition, the majority refused to examine substantial public policy reasons not to extend these benefits in part or in whole to homosexual couples. The overwhelming credible evidence available to the commission requires that the State of Hawaii not recognize homosexual unions as equivalent to traditional, heterosexual marriage.

B. Recommendations

The minority of the commission recommends that no action be taken to extend any legal or economic marital benefits to homosexual couples that they do not already enjoy. . . . The minority also strongly recommends that the legislature undertake to amend the Constitution of the State of Hawaii to reserve marriage and marital rights to unions between one man and one woman. If any marital rights are granted to homosexual couples, the minority vigorously recommends that the legislation contain a sweeping religious exemption. Finally, the minority recommends that the legislature consider reviewing Hawaii laws to determine whether it should enlarge the definition of "family" in some statutes in order to protect legitimate "family" needs for unmarried people. In evaluating which, if any, statutes should be changed in this regard, the minority also strongly recommends that the legislature evaluate the cost to the state from such change.

C. Summary

This report presents information received from persons who testified before the commission as well as material included in the commission's bibliography. This modern literature concerns legal, economic, and social policy analysis of marriage and marital rights, family and child rearing, the attributes of homosexuality and the effects of homosexuality on the community. Many people testified that they were opposed to homosexual marital rights on economic, religious, historical, medical, and psychological grounds. Of critical importance to many people who testified was the protection of children. The majority report simply rejects all these bases of opposition to homosexual marital rights. The majority's argument relies on the tenuous assumption that the present legal status of gay marriages parallels the laws against interracial marriages in the 1960s. The minority opinion addresses some of the reasons why this is a false assumption. Race and gender are immutable characteristics. Clearly, sexual orientation is not in the same category—sexual orientation is known to change and is, to a large extent, behavioral. The argument that homosexuality is genetically determined and so in the same category as race or gender has no valid scientific support. There are many elements of behavior, such as the propensity to violence for which a genetic determinant has been found. This does not mean that such a behavior should be elevated to the status of the most favored in the state. Homosexual marital rights are simply not civil rights. . . . Homosexuality is not immutable but is caused by disturbed family environment and interaction between the parents and their children.

Regardless of any person's philosophy that homosexuality is either deviant or an acceptable alternative lifestyle, the issue of homosexual marital rights must be resolved on the basis of what is good for society. While the majority were not interested in discussion of reasons not to extend the benefits of marriage to homosexual couples, this minority opinion identifies the following major reasons why there should not be a drastic revision of the marriage law. The minority refutes the assumption that legalizing same-sex marriage will be of any benefit at all to Hawaii's economy. On the contrary, it is more likely that Hawaii's major industry, tourism, will be negatively affected, as the image of

Hawaii deteriorates from the aloha state to the gay honeymoon and wedding destination of the world.

The minority is seriously concerned about the adverse effect legalizing homosexual marriage will have on the social, sexual and psychological development of children. The majority did manage to find some "expert" to testify that being raised in a homosexual household had no detrimental effects on children, but the vast body of work done on the issue suggests the opposite.

The minority believes that the ramifications on the education system would be far-reaching, touching all elements of the curriculum. Parents are protective and concerned about their children's education. . . . The rights of parents must be favored over the rights of the homosexual community.

Every person's review of this report should focus on resolving the issue of homosexual marital rights in such a manner as to protect and preserve society, both in Hawaii and the United States. Clearly, this issue will affect everyone in the state. It will affect the entire country, since other states will be forced to deal with whether their states must accept any homosexual marital rights granted on a statewide basis in Hawaii. There is even a home page on the Internet where homosexual activists freely discuss this issue across the country.

The majority supports its position by arguing that withholding marital rights constitutes discrimination against homosexuals. However, even the Hawaii Supreme Court in *Baehr* held that there is no fundamental right to homosexual marriage:

> Applying the foregoing standards to the present case, we do not believe that a right to same-sex marriage is so rooted in the traditions and collective conscience of our people that failure to recognize it would violate the fundamental principles of liberty and justice that lie at the base of all our civil and political institutions. Neither do we believe that a right to same-sex marriage is implicit in the concept of ordered liberty, such that neither liberty nor justice would exist if it were sacrificed. Accordingly, we hold that the applicant couples do not have a fundamental constitutional right to same-sex marriage arising out of the right to privacy or otherwise.

Therefore, the resolution of this issue cannot be analyzed solely on the basis of the value of autonomous freedom for homosexuals, or an assumption of improper discrimination. Permissible discrimination occurs in many ways on a daily basis.

Not all forms of discrimination are inappropriate, and one should not jump to the conclusion that opposition to endorsing homosexuality constitutes inappropriate discrimination. Discrimination (approval or disapproval of a person or group) based on judgments in the absence of evidence is inappropriate. However, certain distinctions can reflect prudent judgment based on evidence. Therefore, the commission should have first examined the evidence of the attributes of homosexuality and the effects those attributes have on children, family, and society. Although the majority of the commission did not even consider such information important, only with that information can one take a rational position regarding the extent to which the State of Hawaii should endorse—and by its endorsement encourage—homosexual practices. The majority's recommendations actually constitute prejudiced discrimination against those whose prudent judgment, based on the evidence, does not equate homosexuality and heterosexuality. . . .

The majority of the commission failed to consider whether homosexuality and heterosexuality are so distinctly different that the two cannot be equivalents. However, significant evidence of that fact was available to the commission, but ignored. The interests of society in marriage and family have justified substantial regulation of marriage throughout history. Aristotle taught that it was the first duty of legislators to establish rules regulating entrance into marriage. Throughout history societies have given unique and special preference to heterosexual marriage because of the benefits that those relationships provide for society in general, and for individual women, men, and children.

To justify giving similar preferred legal protection to same-sex couples, it is necessary to consider the social purposes of marriage, and to compare heterosexual unions with same-sex unions in terms how each relationship furthers those purposes.

It is important to not oversimplify and distort the heterosexual-marriage position. We acknowledge that two men or two women may share a deep, meaningful personal relationship with each other (usually called "friendship"), support each other, develop and pursue mutually fulfilling, socially beneficial common interests, make strong commitments to each other, and in many ways be as good citizens as persons in heterosexual marriages. However, we believe that same-sex unions simply do not equate with heterosexual union of husband and wife in terms of the purposes of marriage.

We believe that the majority's Commission Report denies and devalues the unique strengths and social contributions of heterosexual marriage, and that legalization of same-sex marriage or domestic partnership would put the state in the position of presenting a false image of both marriage and of same-sex unions. We agree with Governor Pete Wilson of California who said, when he vetoed a much narrower, much more modest domestic partnership proposal last year: "Government policy ought not to discourage marriage by offering a substitute relationship that demands much less—and provides much less than is needed by the children . . . and ultimately much less than is needed by society."

He also stated that government has an obligation to "encourage and reward marriage and the formation of strong families." He added: "A society that devalues marriages, and which accepts illegitimacy as commonplace, encourages the explosion of teenage out-of-wedlock births that California has in fact experienced."

There are numerous social purposes of marriage as to which heterosexual marriages provide tremendous benefits to society that are unequaled by homosexual unions. They are: (1) protecting safe sexual relations, (2) social concerns regarding procreation and child-rearing, (3) protecting the status of women, (4) fostering marital stability, (5) promoting economic security for parents and children, (6) providing for recognition of Hawaii marriages in other jurisdictions, and (7) protecting the foundations of self-government. Clearly, the marriage statute itself regulates who may marry in order to prevent incest (HRS 572-1[1]), to protect children (HRS 572-1[2] and 572-2), to prevent the spread of venereal disease on public health grounds (HRS 572-1[5]), and to prevent bigamy (HRS 572-1[3]).

First, sexual behavior is a central concern in marriage and marriage regulation. Same-sex marriage is, by definition, homosexual marriage because sexual relations between the spouses is an integral part of marriage. Thus, it is disingenuous (and simply erroneous) to suggest, as a plurality of the Hawaii Supreme Court did in *Baehr* v. *Lewin,* that not all same-sex marriages will be homosexual marriages. If, however, homosexual marital rights are extended to all unmarried people, then marriage would be stripped of all of its value to society and simply reduced to a vehicle for obtaining benefits from government without contributing to society those benefits which were historically given by marriage to society. Moreover, in these days of sex-saturated entertainment, when the exploitation of children in pornography is such a severe problem that Congress has had to pass laws to try to restrain it, when incidents of forcible rape and "date rape" are skyrocketing, when American servicemen incite an international incident bringing dishonor on the nation they serve because of their callous rape of a pre-teen girl in another nation in which they were guests, when children are receiving less sex-education in the home and more on the street; when rates of adolescent sexuality, pregnancy, and even abortion are at near-disaster levels, it would be an act of unforgivable irresponsibility to brush aside the tremendous social interest in regulating sexual behavior.

Moreover, it is the very nature and acts of homosexual behavior that are the core and identifying feature of homosexual relations. It is not friendship between persons of the same gender, or mere cohabitation of persons of the same gender that creates social concern, but the acts of homosexual sexual relations that is at the core of the moral concern. Thus, to try to evade that issue, to refuse (as the majority) to investigate it or even to listen to witnesses discuss it, is to evade a critical dimension of the marriage issue.

Second, marriage has long been favored because it is the most favorable setting in which to bring children into the world and to raise them. If anything is clear in social science, it is that conventional male-female marriage provides the best environment for the nurture, care, training, education and responsible socialization of children. It is equally clear that children suffer most from the creative "alternative" relationships that adults sometimes pursue for their own adult self-interest. Children are the most numerous (and most innocent) victims of the disintegration of marriage. The impoverishment of children has been shown repeatedly and irrefutably to be a direct result of the change in family structure in the past three decades. Yet, incredibly, the majority of the commission blithely ignores the suffering of children and proposes yet another radical destructuring of marriage. Why must Hawaii's children pay and suffer for the faddish social experimentation of same-sex marriage or domestic partnership?

The concern for our children is not limited to specific children living with specific parents. Undoubtedly, one can find conscientious and devoted adults caring for children under any kind of family structure. Rather, the greater concern is that children generally will suffer from the message that homosexual marital rights send to all prospective parents the message that a mother and a father are not both optimally necessary for the raising of children. In a time when fathers are abandoning their children's lives in record numbers, it would be irresponsible to adopt a marriage or domestic partnership reform that sent the false message that same-sex marriage and domestic partnership clearly convey about the disposability of two-gender parenting. A state and society that cares for its children and its future will not be so reckless when the interests, futures, and lives of its children are at risk. The law should emphatically model, support, and encourage two-parent, mother-father parenting rather than create yet another ill-considered alternative to that institution that will impose untold misery on yet another generation of Hawaii's children.

Third, studies repeatedly have shown that wives and mothers make the greatest investment in marriage and children, and suffer the greater economic disadvantage when marriage is undermined. Marriage is the one institution which historically has recognized the indispensable equality of women because a man could not have a marriage without a woman. It is the oldest equal rights relationship in law and society. Since male homosexuals outnumber female homosexuals, even this new domestic institution will become just another male-dominated institution. How many mothers in Hawaii will lose custody to their "gay" former husband and his same-sex partner if same-sex marriage or domestic partnership is legalized? The message of same-sex marriage and domestic partnership trivializes the contributions of tens of thousands of Hawaii wives and mothers and says to them, "your contributions to your children, your family, and our society are no different, no better than those of a homosexual partner."

Fourth, fostering marital stability is a great concern of the state. Given the indisputable evidence (summarized elsewhere in the Minority Opinion) of the unavoidably promiscuous, fleeting nature of most same-sex relationships, it is facetious to compare the stability of same-sex marriage with conventional male-female marriage—even in these days of high divorce rates marriages are as solid as the Rock of Gibraltar compared to same-sex liaisons. While one might shrug and say it is up to the adults to choose for themselves whether they want one stable relationship or many temporary relationships, that is simply irresponsible when one is talking about marriage, the basic unit of society. Male-female relations are complementary in ways that same-sex relations are not. The law should not pretend otherwise and send false messages about reality simply because that happens to be the popular political fashion of the day. And, again, the people who suffer the most from unstable families are children. Their interest must not be sacrificed to the instability of same-sex relationships.

Fifth, marriage has been repeatedly shown to promote economic security for parents and children. Marital instability is associated with poverty for women and children. Again, the concern is not so much for particular couples because undoubtedly exceptional cases can be found in any family form. The greater concern is for the impact on society and the children of society generally if the law presents unstable unions as the equivalent of and as socially as valuable as real heterosexual marriage. The law should not engage in false advertising. Equating same-sex unions with conventional male-female marriage would clearly send a false message which would hurt untold thousands of individuals and their families when the bitter realities of the instability of same-sex unions set in. Not only are unstable marriages impoverishing for the individuals involved, but they impose heavy costs on society, ranging from the costs to the state (for the agencies typically involved in dealing with family instability—courts, social work agencies, domestic violence, welfare, etc.) but also many great indirect costs resulting from lowered productivity of the individuals involved in the unstable relationship, stress, emotional problems, etc.

Sixth, Hawaii, like all states, has an important interest in providing for recognition of Hawaii marriages in other jurisdictions. Hawaii has an interest in not creating a form of marriage that will not be recognized elsewhere. Indeed, if Hawaii legalizes same-sex marriage or domestic partnership and that new institution is not recognized, persons who rely on the legality of the marriage in Hawaii may find that their rights in other jurisdictions are severely curtailed or rejected. Again, this would do a great disservice to many people. Rights derived from lawful marriages (including inheritance rights, insurance rights, pension rights, property rights, etc.) may be denied in other states and other nations. Spouses and children of a person who once entered into a same-sex marriage and later entered into a conventional marriage could find their marriage-derivative rights were challenged or not recognized in other jurisdictions.

Seventh, the state has a profound interest in preserving society from disintegration. Dr. Socarides opined in 1994:

> As regards the creation of a new psychosexual institution (i.e., homosexual "marriage") alongside that of heterosexual marriage, I submit the following. The institutions of heterosexuality and heterosexual marriage are created for family structure. To introduce homosexuality as a valid psychosexual institution is to destroy the function of heterosexuality as the last place in our society where affectivity can still be cultivated. Homosexuals cannot make a society, nor keep ours going for very long. It operates against the cohesive elements of society in the name of a fictitious freedom. It drives the opposite sex in a similar direction and no society can long endure when the child is neglected or when the sexes war upon each other.
>
> The adoption of children by homosexual couples is a serious issue. A child

should be brought up with a mother and a father, in order to develop appropriate gender-defined self identity. If he does not do so, severe individual problems will occur. The matter should be approached with great caution for the child has no voice in this matter and he may be unfortunately consigned to a pathological family setting from which he can not escape without serious psychological damage. . . . The negative effect on children who are adopted into homosexual "family" structure can be profound. I believe that:

1. a normal environment provides a child with the opportunity to utilize his capacities in order to further the promotion of a sense of autonomy and identity, to enhance and affirm ego-boundaries between himself and other family members, and to promote a healthy self-esteem as a member of his own sex;

2. the parents' function is to promote the child's separation from the mother into an independent entity, all the while supplying physical and emotional security needs;

3. both mother and father are models for identification toward the assumption of appropriate sexual identity and sexual role in accordance with anatomy;

4. the alleviation of conflicts, especially those involving distortion of roles during the earliest years, help the child to channel his drives, energy, and role-learning in the proper direction . . .

The families of homosexual patients I have treated are markedly deficient in carrying out many of the functions necessary for the development of an integrated heterosexual child. Distorting influences are very profound in families in which the child is not helped to develop the appropriate gender-identity. . . . The disturbance in gender-defined self-identity sets the stage for the development of all sexual deviations and many of the neurotic conditions.

Not all marriages and families "work," but it is unwise to let pathology and failure, rather than a vision of what is normative and ideal, guide us in the development of social policy. . . .

The majority of commissioners refused to discuss the necessity for a very broad religious freedom exemption covering religious institutions and individuals who have religiously motivated objections to accepting homosexual couples as marriage-equivalent.

Many of the people who testified before the commission expressed opposition to homosexual marital rights on the basis of their religious beliefs. The majority dismisses all of these arguments based on an extreme view of the doctrine of separation of church and state. This view has, as recently as 1986, been rejected by the U.S. Supreme Court. In upholding criminal punishment for sodomy in Georgia, the Supreme Court relied on "the millennia of moral teaching" in opposition to homosexuality. Clearly, in Hawaii, our common law restricting same-sex couples from marrying reflects that same moral teaching. In addition, looking to the sometimes-cited ancient Hawaiian cultural view of homosexuality in reference to the Alkane and the Mahu, cannot support same-sex marriage in light of the fact that before going to war, the Hawaiians would purge all the Mahus, including in many instances, killing them. Abandoning such Hawaiian traditions was a great improvement in Hawaiian society.

The majority also find that no one should "impose" his religious or moral views on others. Yet, that is precisely what the majority seeks to do with ho-mosexual marital rights to more than two-thirds of the Hawaii population for the benefit of some portion of 2 percent of the population. The majority goes so far as to report . . . that the religious groups opposed to homosexual marriage will be able to refuse to solemnize homosexual marriages, but that the pressure which will be exerted on these traditional religious people and their churches will force them to abandon their religious objections to homosexuality. It is for exactly these reasons that the religious exemption must be as broad and sweeping as possible.

Richard Duncan, Esq., Constitutional Law Professor, University of Nebraska, College of Law, desired to discuss the critical need for a religious exemption via telephone with the commission. He was not permitted; however, he did send written suggestions to adopt a very broad religious exemption. Even Dan Foley, Esq., the lawyer for the plaintiffs in *Baehr,* supports a religious exemption.

If homosexual marital rights are recognized in Hawaii, either in the form of domestic partnership, homosexual marriage, or otherwise, a very broad religious exemption is necessary for many reasons. Parents of public school students, teachers in the public schools, people who are licensed to solemnize marriages, owners of rental housing, and employers who object to homosexual marriage rights on religious grounds should be protected from government-forced acknowledgment of homosexual marriage rights.

One of the serious consequences of including homosexual coupling in the marital partnership will occur in the public school setting. If homosexual coupling is acknowledged on the same level with heterosexual marriage, the public schools will be forced to teach children that homosexual coupling is equivalent to marriage. Since as many as two-thirds of the people polled in Hawaii do not support homosexual marriage rights, it is safe to assume that a great majority of parents and teachers also do not agree with homosexual marriage rights.

Public anxiety about homosexuality is preeminently a concern about the vulnerabilities of the young. This, we are persuaded, is a legitimate and urgent public concern.

Indeed, we do not think it a bad thing that people should experience a reflexive recoil from what is wrong. To achieve such a recoil is precisely the point of moral education of the young.

Those parents who on religious grounds object to the school teaching their children that homosexual coupling is equivalent to heterosexual marriage, must be given the express statutory right to remove their children from such school lessons. However, the difficulty in enforcing such a right counsels the legislature to prohibit such teaching in any public school by teachers or invited speakers. . . .

Teachers who, for religious reasons, do not desire to teach that homosexual coupling is on par with heterosexual marriage must be protected by express statutory provisions as well. Their religious freedom must be protected by specifically creating in the homosexual marriage rights legislation their freedom to oppose the teaching of homosexual marriage rights as equivalent to heterosexual marriage. At least one of the commissioners, Morgan Britt, desires to ensure that schools are forced to teach, and children forced to learn, that homosexuality and heterosexuality are equivalent.

Any legislation creating homosexual marriage rights must expressly state that no person shall be subject to fine, loss of license, liability for damages, or other punishment or penalty for rejecting homosexual marriage rights on religious grounds.

In addition, religious people who are authorized to solemnize marriages based upon licensing from the State Health Department must not be required to solemnize homosexual couples, and must not be in any manner punished for refusing to do so. The legislation creating homosexual marriage rights must expressly state that no person licensed to solemnize marriages in Hawaii shall be subject to fine, loss of license, liability for damages, or other punishment or penalty for rejecting homosexual marriage rights on religious grounds.

Furthermore, people who on grounds of religious belief oppose homosexual coupling must not in any manner be forced to acknowledge homosexual coupling, either as a landlord renting a house or apartment, as an employer extending spousal benefits, or otherwise. The legislation creating homosexual marriage rights must expressly state that no person shall be subject to fine, liability for damages, or other punishment or penalty for rejecting homosexual marriage rights on religious grounds.

The religious freedom of the U.S. Constitution and the Constitution of the State of Hawaii must be fully protected in the event homosexual couples are extended any marriage benefits. . . .

MAJORITY RESPONSE TO MINORITY OPINION

Many minority witnesses, and their testimony made it clear, consider homosexual marriage immoral and completely unacceptable under their religious doctrines or beliefs.

However, testimony and written statements from various Christian churches and Buddhist groups made it clear that the minority position was by no means universal in the religious community.

The basic position of the minority then becomes that their religious-based position should determine the marriage law of the State of Hawaii, regardless of other religious beliefs or the civil rights of the individuals involved.

This is, of course, unacceptable to the majority, which seeks to protect the right of every church or religious group to believe and preach as they wish. But such groups have no right under our constitution to impose their beliefs on others through state law.

The "moral" position of the minority is based on the presumption that homosexuality is completely voluntary on the part of the individuals involved and therefore they are intentionally committing an "immoral" act and should be sanctioned. . . .

At the very least the jury is still out on the question of the causes of homosexual behavior. . . .

Whether the behavior is voluntary or not, the individual concerned is entitled to equal rights under the law.

The protection of family values is another reason claimed by the minority and their witnesses for the banning of same-gender marriages. When you consider the high proportion of divorces, teenage pregnancies, single parent families, and the not uncommon practice of couples living together without marriage, it would seem a bit ironic that the minority and their supporters would seek to prevent one group that wishes to promote marriage from doing so. Is it possible that there are many more troublesome areas where the minority and its supporters could productively promote family values than the one they have chosen here?

Other minority positions which seem questionable are the rejection of the relevance of the *Loving* v. *Virginia* case and the claim that homosexuals are not a suspect class and therefore—like criminals—can be subject to legal discrimination.

The United States Supreme Court some thirty years ago struck down a statute of the State of Virginia that prohibited interracial marriage (*Loving* v. *Virginia,* 388 U.S. 1 [1967]). This case, which was cited by the Hawaii Supreme Court in its *Baehr* decision, raises the question of equal protection of the law. The opposition to interracial marriage (called miscegenation) was as emotional and passionate in the 1960s as the opposition to same-gender marriage now. Many of the same reasons, including destruction of existing society, were given then as they are now. The *Loving* case did not cause the collapse of society in Virginia or elsewhere, and the arguments now seem ridiculous, particularly in Hawaii. The minority apparently thinks our Supreme Court was misguided when it cited *Loving.* The majority agrees with the Supreme Court.

The minority attempt to reduce the status of homosexuals to that of a group that is somehow not entitled to certain constitutional rights deserves notice but not credence. . . .

Conclusions

The majority of the commission—while not all agree on every point—believe that they have prepared a reasonable report and suggested appropriate action to be taken by the legislature. The majority also is aware that its first recommendation—to allow same-gender couples to marry under state law—is vehemently opposed by many people of certain religious persuasions. The majority has also recommended the adoption of a comprehensive Domestic Partnership law. This would apply to all couples, regardless of gender, and apply most of the benefits and burdens of marriage to many in the community who not only live together, but also raise children without being married. We propose either of these solutions, or both.

28.

BAEHR V. LEWIN: A STEP IN THE RIGHT DIRECTION FOR GAY RIGHTS

Anthony C. Infanti

Courts have done backflips in order to uphold cases of the legal existence of marriages even when the formal requirements (like age) and procedural requirements (like solemnization) for entry into marriage have been wholly or blatantly violated. They have done so to an extent as to draw into doubt the rule of law in this area. The one area where they have balked at allowing access to marriage, however, is access for gays. The courts have used every legal contrivance to block the recognition of gay marriages.[1]

I. INTRODUCTION

Baehr v. *Lewin*,[2] a recent plurality decision of the Supreme Court of the State of Hawaii, represents the first victory for gay rights activists seeking to secure the legal right of marriage. In its decision, the plurality held that strict scrutiny must be applied to the state's denial of a marriage license to a same-sex couple. The application of strict scrutiny resulted from the gender-based classification embodied in the state's interpretation of its marriage law. The court distanced itself from any notion that the decision may be based on the sexual orientation of the plaintiffs. *Baehr* is presently on remand to the trial court for a decision on the question whether the state of Hawaii can show a "compelling interest" in its marriage law's discrimination against same-sex couples.

The Hawaii Supreme Court goes far in *Baehr* toward debunking many of the standard anti-gay arguments employed in the earlier case law. The plurality also takes great strides in applying the law, rather than the prejudices and biases of the individual judge, to the facts. Nevertheless, *Baehr* v. *Lewin* is not

This article first appeared in *Law & Sexuality: A Review of Lesbian and Gay Legal Issues* 4 (1994). Reprinted by permission of the author.

an unfettered victory for gay rights. In fact, it may be somewhat of a failure. The plurality took every opportunity to distance itself from gay marriage and explicitly based its decision on the farcical construct of a "same-sex marriage": a marriage touted to be not just for gays, but for any two persons of the same sex who wish to marry. While this decision is a de facto victory for gays and lesbians in that it may actually permit them to marry, de jure it gains no specific rights for gays or lesbians. At bottom, the reasoning of the court serves only to relegate gays and lesbians to the status of second-class citizens once again. . . .

The court's holding that the sex-based classification in § 572–1 is subject to strict scrutiny has far-reaching implications. Section 572–1 is now presumed to be unconstitutional.[3] On remand, it will be the Defendant Director of the DOH's burden to show that "(a) the statute's sex-based classification is justified by compelling state interests and (b) the statute is narrowly drawn to avoid unnecessary abridgments of the applicant couples' constitutional rights."[4] The burden imposed on the government by the strict scrutiny test is great, and it will be a difficult burden to shoulder. For now, we must simply await the trial court's decision as to whether the state of Hawaii has carried its burden and proved the constitutionality of its marriage statute as applied to same-sex couples. Nevertheless, of greater importance in the struggle for equal rights for gays and lesbians than the possibility of gay marriage in Hawaii is the plurality's rationale behind applying strict scrutiny to the state's marriage statute. The plurality's reasoning has the potential of being either a great service or a great disservice to future battles over gay rights in other areas of the law.

The plurality's decision in *Baehr* represents a radical departure from the case law on gay marriage discussed above. Most obviously, *Baehr* is the first case to apply strict scrutiny to a state's denial of a marriage license to a same-sex couple. In doing so, the Hawaii Supreme Court not only rejected many of the arguments employed to uphold the constitutionality of marriage statutes in other states, but also riddled those arguments with quite a few holes.

Loving v. Virginia

Most importantly, the Hawaii Supreme Court was the first court to find the U.S. Supreme Court's rationale in *Loving* to be applicable to the same-sex marriage context. In all previous same-sex marriage cases, the courts either avoided analyzing *Loving* or attempted to distinguish it. In *Singer,* the Washington Court of Appeals avoided analyzing *Loving* by refusing to find any sex-based classification at all.[5] In *Baker,* the Minnesota Supreme Court acknowledged the existence of a sex-based classification, but distinguished a race-based restriction on marriage from "one based upon the fundamental difference in sex."[6]

Once the facts and rationale of *Loving* are explored, it would seem somewhat disingenuous for a court to reject application of this case to the context of same-sex marriage. In *Loving,* an interracial couple married under the laws of the District of Columbia took up residence in the state of Virginia.[7] Shortly thereafter, the couple was prosecuted by the state of Virginia under its ban on interracial marriages.[8] The Lovings were sentenced to one year in jail; however, the trial judge suspended their sentence on the condition that the couple leave the state of Virginia and not return for twenty-five years.[9]

On appeal from the Virginia Supreme Court of Appeals, the U.S. Supreme Court struck down the anti-miscegenation statute as violating the Equal Protection Clause of the U.S. Constitution.[10] The court first noted that the state's powers to regulate marriage are limited by the Fourteenth Amendment.[11] The Supreme Court then rejected the "equal application" argument put forth by the state of Virginia to the effect that the statutes satisfy the Equal Protection Clause because both the white member of the couple and the African-American member of the couple are punished equally.[12] The court found that mere equal application of the statutes does not "remove the classifications from the Fourteenth Amendment's proscription of all invidious racial discriminations. . . ."[13] Consequently, the Supreme Court applied the strict scrutiny test to the statutes; a standard that they could not meet.[14]

After considering the Supreme Court's rationale in *Loving,* the plurality stated that "[s]ubstitution of 'sex' for 'race' and article 1, section 5 for the Fourteenth Amendment yields the precise case before us together with the conclusion that we have reached."[15] To reject application of *Loving* either because (1) a race-based classification is not the same as a sex-based classification, or (2) no sex-based classification exists at all, ignores the facts.

The *Singer* court's argument that no sex-based classification exists is circular at best. The court held that no sex-based classification exists since the applicants were not denied a marriage license because of their sex but because what they proposed did not fit the "recognized definition" of a marriage.[16] Such a statement ignores the entire premise of the Supreme Court's rationale in *Loving.* As noted above, the starting point of the Supreme Court's analysis was the notion that the state's power to regulate marriage is not unlimited, but is subject to constitutional constraints.[17] The premise of the *Singer* court's analysis was just the contrary: the institution of marriage is mired in the history of this country and statutes embodying the definition of this institution will be presumed constitutional.[18]

The *Singer* court distinguished *Loving* because the Supreme Court did not change "the basic definition of marriage as the legal union of one man and one woman; rather, they merely held that the race of the man or woman desiring to enter that relationship could not be considered by the state in granting a marriage license."[19] Thus, following the Washington court's reasoning, *Loving* is inapposite simply because it did not hold same-sex marriage to be included in the definition of marriage. This narrow view of precedent can only be explained by the court's predisposition to reject the legality of gay marriage absent express direction from a higher authority, whereby any responsibility for making the decision can be abdicated.

While acknowledging that the statute contained a marital restriction based on sex, the *Baker* court refused to analogize *Loving* on the ground that "in commonsense and in a constitutional sense, there is a clear distinction between a marital restriction based merely upon race and one based upon the fundamental difference in sex."[20] This statement evidences either the personal prejudices of the judges deciding *Baker* or a complete ignorance of the changes this country was undergoing in the 1970s.

The 1970s was the time period of the national and state movements for the Equal Rights Amendment. In addition, just one month after *Baker* was decided, the United States Supreme Court came down with its decision in *Reed v. Reed*,[21] the first case to take seriously an equal protection challenge to a sex-based classification. Although the views of the Minnesota Supreme Court judges that heard and decided *Baker* may be explained as vestiges of the attitudes of a time gone by, such views should not be tolerated today. Given the great strides that have been made in the equal protection case law concerning sex-based classifications, a classification based on sex should no longer be dismissed as not meriting any serious scrutiny.

Procreation Argument

The plurality also rejected the dissent's argument that the purpose of Hawaii's marriage statute is to promote and protect propagation.[22] The basis of the plurality's finding that procreation is not the aim of marriage under Hawaii law was the state legislature's amendment of § 572–1 in 1984 to delete the "prerequisite that '[n]either of the parties is impotent or physically incapable of entering into the marriage state.' "[23] At the same time, the state legislature also deleted impotence or physical incapability as a ground for the annulment of marriage. . . .[24]

The New York Supreme Court in *Anonymous* found a New York case diametrically opposed to the court's rationale in *Baehr*.[25] Nevertheless, it simply defies logic how a court can find that the legislature's removal of impotence and physical incapacity as grounds for annulment is an expression of "the public policy that such relationship (marriage) shall exist with the result and for the purpose of begetting offspring."[26] If anything, the deletion of impotence and physical incapacity from the statutory grounds for annulment indicates that the public policy of the state no longer grounds the marital relationship in procreation.

Judicial Legislation

The Hawaii Supreme Court was also the first court to deny that the application of heightened scrutiny to a marriage statute construed to prohibit same-sex marriage is a form of judicial legislation. . . .[27] The plurality in *Baehr* rejected any suggestion that what the court had done by applying strict scrutiny was judicial legislation.[28] Instead, the court construed what it had done as maintaining state legislation within the constraints of the constitution: "The result we reach today is in complete harmony with the *Loving* court's observation that any state's powers to regulate marriage are subject to the constraints imposed by the constitutional right to the equal protection of the laws."[29]

Baehr v. *Lewin* represents a long stride toward the recognition of homosexuality not as a social disease but as a legitimate expression of love and affection between two individuals; however, this decision does not completely vindicate gay rights. The plurality correctly applied strict scrutiny to 572-1, but did not reach this end via the preferred path. The path chosen by the plurality was sex, not sexual orientation. The plurality took every opportunity to note that this was not a decision about "homosexual" marriage, but one concerning "same-sex" marriage.[30] In making this distinction, the court posited the union of two heterosexual women or two heterosexual men.[31] Consequently, the court held that "it is irrelevant, for purposes of the constitutional analysis germane to this case, whether homosexuality constitutes 'an immutable trait' because it is immaterial whether the plaintiffs, or any of them, are homosexuals."[32] Nevertheless, the court's attempt to distance itself from the issue of homosexuality does not change the nature of the decision, and only serves to diminish the victory by relegating homosexuality to the closet once again.

The member of the plurality who took a more enlightened view of the question was Judge Burns, who is the Chief Judge of the Hawaii Intermediate Court of Appeals. Judge Burns wrote a separate concurring opinion in which he stated that the defendant's motion for judgment on the pleadings was erroneously granted because a question of fact remained to be addressed by the trial court.[33] The question that Judge Burns felt needed to be answered before the issue presented by the case could be addressed is "whether heterosexuality, homosexuality, bisexuality, and asexuality are 'biologically fated.' "[34] Judge Burns defined "sex" as including "all aspects of each person's 'sex' that are biologically fated."[35]

Judge Burns went on to cite news articles that had appeared in the *Honolulu Advertiser* concerning the nature versus nurture controversy. The concurrence cited an article discussing the results of research performed at the Salk Institute in San Diego that found "anatomical differences between homosexual and heterosexual men in parts of the brain noted for differences between men and women."[36] The opinion also quoted an article reporting that "genes appear to play an important role in determining whether women are lesbians. . . ."[37] This controversy has received increasing publicity since the decision in *Baehr* was issued, as researchers published a study in July 1993 concluding "that a region on the X chromosome 'contributes to homosexual orientation in males.' "[38]

Judge Burns indicated in his concurrence that if it were found that sexual orientation is biologically fated, "the Hawaii Constitution probably bars the State from discriminating against the sexual orientation difference by permitting opposite-sex Hawaii Civil Law Marriages and not permitting same-sex Hawaii Civil Law Marriage."[39] In other words, Judge Burns indicated that if sexual orientation was found to be biologically determined, which is becoming increasingly obvious by virtue of the continuing scientific research quoted above, he would find sexual orientation to be part and parcel of sex-based classifications. In turn, sexual orientation-based classifications would become immediately suspect and subject to heightened judicial scrutiny.

The analytical starting point advocated by Judge Burns is the one that bears the most promise for the gay rights movement. Following Judge Burns's lead, the plurality could have arrived at the same conclusion by taking the politically unpopular position that sexual orientation-based classifications should be subjected to heightened judicial scrutiny as are sex-based classifications. The court could have based this decision on an examination of the scientific literature on the source of sexual orientation, including that referenced by Judge Burns, along with the extensive history of discrimination that gays and lesbians suffered, the most recent example of which is the government's own policy of excluding gays and lesbians from the military.[40] Such a decision would have been precedent-setting not only in the sense that it would allow gays and lesbians the opportunity to marry, but it would also have given gays and lesbians a solid ground on which they might have constructed arguments for equality in other areas.

Notwithstanding the existence of a more preferable manner in which *Baehr* might have been decided, the gay community must work with the decision that has actually been rendered by the Hawaii Supreme Court. The next question that needs to be addressed concerns the practical effect of this decision. What does *Baehr* v. *Lewin* promise?

What *Baehr* does promise is an opportunity for activists to challenge indirectly the marriage statutes of the remaining forty-nine states. The indirect challenges will occur when same-sex citizens of other states go to Hawaii, properly contract a marriage under its laws, and return to their states of origin. At that time, these newlyweds can challenge their state governments to grant them the same rights and benefits as are granted to heterosexual married couples.

The United States Constitution states that "Full Faith and Credit shall be given in each State to the public Acts, Records, and judicial Proceedings of every other State."[41] This clause is the legal basis for recognizing marriages from one state to another. For example, the Full Faith and Credit Clause has been used to recognize common law marriages in states where they have been outlawed.[42] Nevertheless, the "Full Faith and Credit Clause does not require a state to apply another state's law in violation of its own legitimate public policy."[43] This exception of the mandate of the Full Faith and Credit Clause has been utilized in the context of recognizing an out-of-state marriage.[44] In *Metropolitan Life Insurance Company* v. *Spearman,* the United States District

Court for the Middle District of Alabama held that the Full Faith and Credit Clause did not compel the recognition of a bigamous marriage entered into in California when a valid Alabama marriage existed first and the public policy of Alabama against bigamous marriages was well settled.[45]

This public policy exception to the Full Faith and Credit Clause presents a rather high hurdle to overcome. The states that are least likely to recognize same-sex marriages consecrated in Hawaii will be those that have specifically prohibited same-sex marriages and those that retain sodomy laws.[46] While the remaining states do not have quite as firm a ground on which to deny recognition of a Hawaii same-sex marriage, they are probably not less likely to do so. Much will depend on the political bent of the individual judges, as it is easy to imagine the revisitation of the earlier gay marriage case law with its quotation of dictionaries and references to the long history of the institution of marriage. Consequently, *Baehr* may not be the boon to Hawaii's tourism industry that some expect[47]; In fact, this case, which has been much lauded in the gay community, may prove to be of benefit only to gay and lesbian Hawaiians.

CONCLUSION

The Hawaii Supreme Court provided a ray of light to many in the gay community when it issued its somewhat surprising decision in *Baehr* v. *Lewin* in May 1993. If the state of Hawaii cannot show a compelling interest in the discriminatory application of its marriage laws, gay and lesbian couples will be legally permitted to marry in that state. For proponents of gay marriage, this decision may be the one victory they need to change the tide of a twenty-year war. Armed with *Baehr,* a series of legal gay marriages, and the Full Faith and Credit Clause, proponents may be able to effect de facto changes in state marriage laws throughout the country.

Despite this gain in the struggle for equal rights for gays, *Baehr* does carry negative aspects as well. First, opposition exists to the idea of gay marriage in the gay community itself, and for good reason. Marriage forces gays and lesbians into a heterosexual mold that does not seem to fit heterosexuals very well. In addition, marriage, as an institution, is fraught with many of its own difficulties and problems. Moreover, securing the right to marriage for that portion of the gay community that wishes to marry ignores the needs of the remainder of the community and the goal to achieve acceptance despite our differences from the heterosexual community.

Second, the plurality in *Baehr* took every possible opportunity to establish that this was a sex-based and not a sexual orientation-based decision. This distinction ignores the reality of the situation, and demeans gays and lesbians by relegating them to a second-class status. In fact, this distinction goes far toward assuring gays and lesbians a continued second-class status in this country, as it prevents this decision from being used in future legal battles for gay rights.

Third, the public policy exception to the Full Faith and Credit Clause will prevent Hawaii same-sex marriages from being recognized in other states. Many states have laws and judicial decisions that clearly establish that gay unions, whether sexual or contractual, are contrary to their public policy. The states in which this question has not been addressed may choose to follow the overwhelming majority in rejecting same-sex marriage rather than following the anomalous position taken by the Hawaii Supreme Court. Thus, when the dust has finally settled, *Baehr* v. *Lewin* may have secured the right to marry for gays and lesbians in Hawaii, but that may be all that it will have secured.

NOTES

1. Richard D. Mohr, *Gays/Justice: A Study of Ethics, Society, and Law* (New York: Columbia University Press, 1988), p. 252.

2. 852 P.2d 44 (Haw. 1993).

3. *Baehr* v. *Lewin*, 852 P.2d 44, 67 (Haw. 1993).

4. Ibid., pp. 67–68.

5. *Singer* v. *Hara*, 522 P.2d 1177 (Wash. Ct. App. 1974).

6. Ibid., p. 187.

7. *Loving* v. *Virginia*, 388 U.S. 1, 2 (1967).

8. Ibid., pp. 2–3.

9. Ibid., p. 3.

10. Ibid., p. 12.

11. Ibid., p. 7.

12. Ibid., pp. 7–8.

13. Ibid., p. 8.

14. Ibid., pp. 11–12.

15. *Baehr* v. *Lewin*, 852 P.2d 44 (Haw. 1993).

16. Ibid.

17. *Loving* v. *Virginia*, 388 U.S. 1, 7 (1967).

18. *Singer* v. *Hara*, 522 P.2d 1177, 1195–97 (Wash. Ct. App, 1974).

19. Ibid., p. 1192 n. 8.

20. *Baker* v. *Nelson*, 191 N.W.2d 185 (Minn. 1971).

21. 404 U.S. 71 (1971).

22. *Baehr* v. *Lewin*, 852 P.2d 44, 73 n. 8 (Haw. 1993).

23. Ibid., p. 49 (quoting Act 119, § 1, 1984 Haw. Sess. Laws 238–39) (Court's emphasis deleted).

24. Ibid.

25. See *Mirizio* v. *Mirizio*, 242 N.Y. 74, 81 (N.Y. 1926).

26. Ibid.

27. *Baehr* v. *Lewin*, 852 P.2d 44 (Haw. 1993).

28. *Baehr*, 852 P.2d at 68.

29. Ibid.

30. See, e.g., ibid., pp. 51 n. 11 and 53 n.14.

31. Ibid., p. 51 n. 11.

32. Ibid., p. 53, n. 14.

33. Ibid., pp. 68–69 (Burns, J., concurring).

34. Ibid., p. 70 (Burns, J., concurring).

35. Ibid., p. 69 (Burns, J., concurring).

36. Ibid. (Burns, J., concurring) (quoting the *Honolulu Advertiser,* Mar. 9, 1993, at A8.).

37. Ibid.

38. Sharon Begley and Mary Hager, "Does DNA Make Some Men Gay?" *Newsweek,* July 26, 1993, at 59. See also William A. Henry, III, "Born Gay?" *Time,* July 26, 1993, p. 36.

39. *Baehr* v. *Lewin,* 852 P.2d 44, 70 (Haw. 1993) (Burns, J., concurring),

40. Ibid.

41. U.S. Const. art. IV, § 1.

42. See *Ram* v. *Ramharack,* 571 N.Y.S.2d 190, 191 (N.Y. 1991); *Wyble* v. *Minvielle,* 217 So. 2d 684, 688 (La. Ct. App. 1969).

43. *Nevada* v. *Hall,* 440 U.S. 422 (1979), *reh'g denied,* 441 U.S. 917 (1979).

44. *Metropolitan Life Ins. Co.* v. *Spearman,* 344 F. Supp. 665 (M.D. Ala. 1972).

45. Ibid., p. 668.

46. Note that approximately twenty-nine states still have sodomy laws. See Donald E. Batterson, Comment, "A Trend Ephemeral? Eternal? Neither?: A Durational Look at the New Judicial Federalism," *Emory Law Journal* 42 (1993): 209, 246.

47. Michelangelo Signorile, "Bridal Wave," *Out,* December/January 1994, p. 68.

29.

HAWAIIAN AYE:
NEARING THE ALTAR ON GAY MARRIAGE

Andrew Sullivan

Whatever your view of same-sex marriage, the December 3[, 1996,] lower court ruling in Hawaii was undoubtedly a watershed. It means one remarkable thing: in all likelihood, within a year, some same-sex couples will be legally married in America. The legal precedent is a critical one—and to understand why, it's worth reviewing a little history. Although marriage has essentially been a heterosexual institution, of course, there have been scattered instances in which societies have recognized some forms of same-sex marriage. Same-sex union ceremonies—of contested significance—date from the first millennium in some parts of Christian Europe; formal same-sex marriages were instituted in places as diverse as nineteenth-century Africa (between women) and seventeenth-century China (between men). They were known among Native Americans, as historians and anthropologists have long documented. But in broader, Western culture, although they have existed underground for centuries, they have a relatively recent history as a political issue. Early gay rights campaigners raised the issue in the 1950s, and legal suits in pursuit of equal marriage rights for homosexuals date from the 1970s. But it was not until 1993 that an American court agreed that the denial of a marriage license to a lesbian or gay couple constituted discrimination.

That was the case behind our current drama. The Hawaii Supreme Court ruled in *Baehr* v. *Lewin* (now renamed *Baehr* v. *Miike*) that a lesbian woman, Nina Baehr, had been denied the right to marry her female partner because she was a woman and not a man. Under Hawaii's Constitution, the court held, that was sex discrimination. The court sent the case back to a lower court to see if the state government of Hawaii could prove it had a "compelling interest" to sustain such discrimination. It couldn't. Its attempt to do so was refuted point

From *The New Republic,* December 30, 1996. Reprinted by permission of *The New Republic,* 1996, The New Republic, Inc.

by point by the lower court's Judge Kevin Chang in last week's ruling. The case is now referred back to the state Supreme Court for a final ruling. But, since that court found in Baehr's favor the first time and since in the intervening years its composition has, if anything, become more favorable to Baehr's position, the die seems essentially cast.

But didn't the Defense of Marriage Act preempt the entire issue? As it turns out, no. For all of last summer's hullabaloo, the act cannot affect what happens in Hawaii. The act essentially said two things: the federal government defines marriage as between a man and a woman, and no state is obliged by the U.S. Constitution to recognize Hawaii's same-sex marriages. The first part is an explicit statement of what was already implicit in federal regulations (it could, however, have the bizarre side-effect of ensuring that a married couple in Hawaii is married according to state law, but unmarried according to federal law). The second part was premised on the notion that the Full Faith and Credit Clause of the U.S. Constitution would mandate same-sex marriage across the nation as soon as it became legal in Hawaii. But that scenario was always extremely unlikely. The Full Faith and Credit Clause has almost invariably taken a backseat to states' rights in the area of marriage. In almost all legal precedents, states have successfully invoked what's called the "public policy exception" to Full Faith and Credit. This means a state can refuse to recognize an out-of-state marriage if such a marriage offends the public policy of its own jurisdiction. The historical precedents here mainly involve miscegenation, where states with bans on interracial marriage regularly refused to recognize such marriages entered into legally in other states.

So where does that leave us now? The most likely turn of events is that in the next few months more and more states will deal with the issue of recognizing—or not recognizing—Hawaii's imminent same-sex marriages. So far, thirty-seven states have considered such legislation, and sixteen have passed bills that would deny recognition to any out-of-state same-sex marriages. In twenty states, however, such bills failed to make it into law. (In one state, New Jersey, the issue is pending.) In the wake of the recent ruling, the fundamentalist right is likely to make an extraordinary push to pass more of these laws, leading to dramatic and divisive battles in many states. The critical one to watch is California. Historically, California has had an extremely liberal record of recognizing out-of-state marriages. As the state closest to Hawaii, and with a large gay and lesbian population, it's likely also to see the largest number of married couples suing for recognition. Last year, a bill designed to ban recognition failed to make it into law. Fundamentalist groups are organizing to push it again. If they succeed, it will be much harder for Hawaiian marriages to find broad national recognition. If they fail, California could prove pivotal to equal marriage rights across the country.

Another possibility is that a couple of states may proactively decide to recognize such marriages, de facto nationalizing equal marriage rights; or, alternatively, that another state court, interpreting equal gender rights protections in its own state constitution, will reach the same conclusion as Judge Chang. Fourteen other states have explicit E.R.A.-style protections similar to Hawaii's. Massachusetts Governor Bill Weld has already said he is in favor of Massachusetts honoring Hawaii's marriages. What are the odds that, in ten years' time, Hawaii will be the sole state with equal marriage rights? Close to zero.

Still, assume every other state bans same-sex marriage and refuses to recognize Hawaii's. Even under those conditions, as law professors Andrew Koppelman, Seth Kreimer and Larry Kramer (no, not *that* Larry Kramer) have pointed out such marriages may still find niches in the rest of the country. When the couples travel, for example, they are likely to be accorded some constitutional recognition in transit. The right to travel is deeply embedded in the Constitution. Consider a Hawaiian couple traveling in Utah on vacation (ignore, for a moment, the unlikelihood of that occurring). Say they're involved in a car accident with a Utahan drunk driver and one spouse is killed. Imagine, further, that the other spouse files a wrongful death suit against the drunk driver. It is highly likely, according to experts in this area of law, that Utah would be obliged to recognize the Hawaiian marriage for the purposes of that suit. The same goes for the right of the offspring of Hawaiian same-sex marriages to some secure claim to legitimacy across the country. How fair is it to children, after all, to have them declared illegitimate when their parents move across the country for a new job or a new start? In fact, this is one area of the law that looks set for rapid expansion: same-sex marriage and child custody.

Of course, some wild cards remain. One is that fundamentalists could amend the Hawaii state Constitution to bar same-sex marriages, and so trump the state Supreme Court. The timetable for such an effort, however, is unlikely to beat the timetable for legal same-sex marriage in Hawaii, which could be instituted as early as the beginning of 1998. Such marriages, in other words, could be constitutionally mandated and then constitutionally outlawed, creating an extremely messy legal tangle. It's also possible that were such an amendment to pass it would be vulnerable under the U.S. Supreme Court's ruling against the Colorado amendment, *Romer* v. *Evans*. For such an amendment would also be designating a group of citizens for discrimination by the state in perpetuity, rendering homosexuals "a stranger to laws" of Hawaii. Just as possible is that such an amendment could fail to pass; Hawaii is a remarkably tolerant, predominantly Democratic state. If national right-wing groups invade the island to amend its Constitution, there could well be a backlash.

Another wild card—with the opposite effect—is that the U.S. Supreme Court could rule that a bar on same-sex marriage is as unconstitutional as bars on interracial marriage once were, under the Fourteenth Amendment, and so mandate same-sex marriage rights across the country. Although this now looks highly unlikely, it's not inconceivable. The difference between *Bowers* v. *Hardwick* (the 1986 Supreme Court ruling that enforced Georgia's discriminatory sodomy law) and *Romer* v. *Evans* last year is great enough that a gay version of *Loving* v. *Virginia* (the interracial marriage case) is not unthinkable early in the new millennium. Such a ruling would, of course, end all the uncertainty, just as *Loving* superseded the morass of state miscegenation laws thirty years ago.

We are, in other words, at the beginning of a protracted and elaborate struggle. Good. This is surely how the system is supposed to work. A civil rights movement moves in fits and starts—in cases, legislation, speeches, debates and votes. We have in Hawaii a perfect example of federalism: in one state we can see what will happen if same-sex marriage is legalized. It should be allowed to go ahead and for the ramifications to sink in. We will then have a chance to debate the issue in every state of the country, for years and maybe decades to come. A deep breath is in order. This week may have been a watershed, but it is the beginning—and not the end—of the attempt to bring homosexuals into the center of American life.

LIST OF CONTRIBUTORS

Douglas Carl is deceased.

Barbara J. Cox is a professor at the California Western School of Law.

Paula L. Ettelbrick is Legislative Counsel for the Empire State Pride Agenda and Adjunct Lecturer in Law at the University of Michigan Law School.

Ed Fallon is a member of the Iowa House of Representatives.

Jeffrey Hart is a contributing columnist to the *Conservative Chronicle*.

Larry A. Hickman is Associate Professor of Philosophy, Southern Illinois University at Carbondale.

Anthony C. Infanti is an attorney with the New York firm Rosenman and Colin.

Jeff Jordan is Assistant Professor of Philosophy, University of Delaware.

Elizabeth Kristol is a writer contributing to such publications as *Commentary* and the *Washington Post*.

Robert H. Knight is Director of Cultural Studies at the Family Research Council.

Daniel Maguire is Professor of Moral Theology at Marquette University.

Richard D. Mohr is Professor of Philosophy, University of Illinois at Urbana.

Dwight J. Penas is a practicing attorney in Minneapolis.

Christine Pierce is Associate Professor of Philosophy, North Carolina State University.

Richard Posner is a judge, United States Court of Appeals for the Seventh Circuit.

William Safire is a syndicated columnist.

Andrew Sullivan is the former editor of *The New Republic*.

Cal Thomas is a syndicated columnist.

Lindsy Van Gelder is a contributing editor to *Ms.* magazine.

James Wilson is Collins Professor of Management and Public Policy at UCLA.

Homeopathy
& Your Child

Homeopathy & Your Child

A Parent's Guide to Homeopathic Treatment
From Infancy Through Adolescence

Lyle W. Morgan II, HMD, PhD

Healing Arts Press
Rochester, Vermont

Healing Arts Press
One Park Street
Rochester, Vermont 05767

Note to the reader: This book is intended as an informational guide. The remedies, approaches, and techniques described herein are meant to supplement, and not to be a substitute for, professional medical care or treatment. They should not be used to treat a serious ailment without prior consultation with a qualified health care professional.

LIBRARY OF CONGRESS CATALOGING-IN-PUBLICATION DATA
Morgan, Lyle W.
    Homeopathy and your child : a parent's guide to homeopathic
treatment from infancy through adolescence / Lyle W. Morgan II.
      p. cm.
    Includes bibliographical references and index.
    ISBN 0-89281-330-X
    1. Children—Diseases—Homeopathic treatment. I. Title.
    [DNLM: 1. Drug Therapy—in infancy & childhood—handbooks.
    2. Drug Therapy—in infancy & childhood—popular works.
    3. Homeopathy—in infancy & childhood—handbooks. 4. Homeopathy—in
infancy & childhood—popular works. WS 39 M848h]
    RX501.M67 1991
    615.5'32'083—dc20
    DNLM/DLC
    for Library of Congress   91-20894
                                             CIP

Text design by Randi Jinkins

Printed and bound in the United States

10 9 8 7 6 5 4 3 2

Healing Arts Press is a division of Inner Traditions International, Ltd.

Distributed to the book trade in the United States by American International Distribution Corporation (AIDC)

Distributed to the book trade in Canada by Book Center, Inc., Montreal, Quebec

Distributed to the health food trade in Canada by Alive Books, Toronto and Vancouver

Dedication

This book is dedicated, first and foremost, to those parents—mothers and fathers—who strive for the optimum health and well-being of their children and who believe that there is an effective, safe, rapid, and natural nondrugging, nonsuppressing health care system that promotes health and well-being.

This book is also dedicated to all those people, my best friends, who have encouraged me throughout my years of study in homeopathic health care: H. Neal Sievers, MD, FAAFP, the most humane and brightest physician I have ever known; William H. McEachen, MD, pediatrician *par excellence;* James F. Bellman, PhD; Kathryn A. Bellman, J.D., PhD; Michael J. Heffernan, PhD, and Kathy; Aubrey "Sarge" and Carol Anglen; Kevin Sean Anglen; Lewis Charles McArthur; and Dana Ullman, MPH, among the world's greatest "seed planters" of homeopathy, for his many kind thoughts over the past five years. Certainly not least of all to my father, Lyle W. Morgan, and my late mother, Ione E. Morgan, who believed that I could achieve anything to which I set my mind. To Anna Marie Kluthie, a fine friend, a "second mother," and a cheerful Christian spirit.

May God bless you all, in every way, throughout Eternity.

About the Author

Dr. Lyle W. Morgan has been a practicing homeopath and homeopathic educator for 17 years. He holds the Doctor of Homeopathic Medicine degree from the Universitie Internationale, the PhD from the University of Nebraska-Lincoln, the Doctor of Nutrimedicine (honorary), and is a Fellow of the American Nutrimedical Association of the International Alliance of Nutrimedical Associations. He is a professor and academic program director at Pittsburg State University, Pittsburg, Kansas, and the author of several books on homeopathic medicine and natural health care.

Contents

Foreword   ix

A Reader's Advisory   xi

INTRODUCTION
The Advantages of
Homeopathic Treatment in Children   1

PART I
The Homeopathic Treatment of Childhood Diseases   13

CHAPTER 1
The Childhood Immunization Controversy
and a Safe, Successful Homeopathic Alternative   15

CHAPTER 2
Common Contagious Diseases   29

CHAPTER 3
Infant Colic   37

CHAPTER 4
Diarrhea   41

CHAPTER 5
Vomiting and Nausea   46

Chapter 6
Fever   52

Chapter 7
Ear Infections   57

Chapter 8
Tonsillitis and Sore Throat   71

Chapter 9
Diaper Rash, Teething, and Thrush   76

Part II
Child hood Injuries, Their Prevention,
and Homeopathic Treatment   83

Chapter 10
Prevention of Injuries   85

Chapter 11
Shock   88

Chapter 12
Injuries to Bones and Joints   90

Chapter 13
Injuries to the Soft Tissues   96

Appendixes

Appendix One
Sources of General Information   110

Appendix Two
Homeopathic Medicine
Suppliers, Manufacturers, and Pharmacies   111

Appendix Three
Homeopathic Organizations in North America   112

Index   114

Foreword

Dr. Lyle W. Morgan is an experienced homeopathic physician and a sensible writer. In his latest book he provides the reader with sufficient examples from common, everyday life to provide a valuable reference book on health care for infants and adolescents. Being a parent is the toughest job in the world, and this is a valuable resource.

The homeopathic medications Dr. Morgan recommends are generally as safe and effective as the medications prescribed by orthodox physicians, and sometimes more so.

Why don't more physicians use homeopathic medications?

I think a major reason is that there are no drug salespersons ("drug company representatives") making calls on physicians and extolling the virtues of the homeopathic medicines. It is a well-known fact in medicine, but perhaps not as commonly known to the general public, that physicians following their training are introduced to drugs and learn about their effectiveness primarily through pharmaceutical representatives—and many drug representatives constantly visit physicians about the newest antibiotic or other pharmaceutical (with a current patent that quite fairly allows a company to charge a goodly amount of money to cover research, development, and profits). Because most homeopathic medications are not covered by patents, any drug company can manufacture these remedies as long as they adhere to the

Homeopathic Pharmacopoeia of the United States. But at the same time, since most homeopathic medicines are not patented, profits for the manufacturer are not high.

Homeopathic medicines do work as described, whether they are nonprescription remedies available over the counter or those available by prescription only.

I feel that reputable homeopathic medication manufacturers should do more to "educate" physicians. *Then* perhaps we would see physicians start to use these medicines, and pharmacies begin to carry them. But until this happens I see no easy way to get homeopathy into general medical practice.

But for you, the parent, the choice of a qualified homeopathic practitioner might provide a very attractive alternative.

H. Neal Sievers, MD, FAAFP
The Blair Medical Group

A Reader's Advisory

The use of this book does not replace the services of a physician or other licensed, certified, or registered health care professional. The reader should not hesitate to consult a professional health care provider for any illness or injury that requires professional care.

Homeopathic medicines have been used by physicians, licensed or certified health care practitioners, and lay people for nearly 200 years. Scientific research together with clinical practice is now proving that homeopathic medicines have remarkable healing properties. The United States Food and Drug Administration has recognized the legal status of the homeopathic medicines listed in the *Homeopathic Pharmacopoeia of the United States* as approved medicines, so long as their formulations have not been altered or inaccurate claims made concerning their effectiveness. Most homeopathic remedies are available as nonprescription, over-the-counter drugs, except for some tinctures and special combinations that can be used only by licensed physicians.

The medication indications in this book have been taken from authoritative sources: the homeopathic *Materia Medica* and the writings of physicians, clinicians, and researchers as published in scientific laboratory reports, medical documents and journals, and other related sources. The reader should not attempt self-treatment using any of this information for any serious illness or injury that requires the care of a professional health care provider.

PRINCIPAL SOURCES OF INFORMATION
USED FOR THIS BOOK

Boericke, William, MD. *Pocket Manual of Homoeopathic Materia Medica,* 9th ed. Calcutta, India: Sett Dey & Company, 1976.

Chavanon, Paul, MD, and Rene Levannier, MD. *Emergency Homeopathic First-Aid.* Wellingborough, England: Thorsons Publishers, Ltd., 1977.

Clarke, John Henry, MD. *The Prescriber,* 9th ed. North Devon, England: Health Science Press, 1972.

Clarke, John Henry, MD. *A Clinical Repertory to the Dictionary of Materia Medica.* North Devon, England: Health Science Press, 1979.

Dewey, W. A., MD. *Practical Homoeopathic Therapeutics,* 3rd ed. New Delhi, India: Jain Publishing Company, 1981.

Morgan, Lyle W., HMD, PhD. *Homeopathic Medicine: First-Aid and Emergency Care.* Rochester, Vermont: Healing Arts Press, 1990.

Nash, E. B., MD. *Leaders in Homeopathic Therapeutics.* Calcutta, India: Sett Dey & Company, 1959.

Smith, Trevor, MD. *Homoeopathic Medicine.* Rochester, Vermont: Healing Arts Press, 1984.

Tyler, M. L., MD (Brux.). *Homoeopathic Drug Pictures.* North Devon, England: Health Science Press, 1952.

Wheeler, Charles E., MD. *An Introduction to the Principles and Practice of Homoeopathy,* 3rd ed. North Devon, England: Health Science Press, 1948.

The Advantages of Homeopathic Treatment in Children

The following introduction to homeopathic medicine and its use and effectiveness in treating the common health problems of children appeared in American Homeopathy *and is reprinted here by permission.*

"To intelligently understand the fully developed man in health and disease, it seems self-evident that the anatomy and physiology not only of the final stage of growth should be studied, but also that the various stages of development, from embryo to infant to child and child to adult, should successfully be dealt with. This in the past, however, has been but little done. On the contrary, the very opposite method has been adopted; the most careful attention being paid to adult anatomy and physiology, and then deductions made backward from adult to child—a retrograde means of acquiring knowledge, which has proved eminently unsuccessful."

We have come a long way in understanding the anatomy and physiology of infants and children, as well as the ailments specific to them, since Dr. Thomas M. Rotch, first incumbent of the chair of pediatrics established by the Harvard Medical School in 1888, made the above statement. Modern allopathic medicine has made great strides, usually through the use of antibiotics, in alleviating the pain associated with many childhood ailments. Many doctors, however, and parents as well, are becoming increasingly concerned with the amount of antibiotics sometimes given to children, especially for sore throats, fevers, tonsillitis, recurring chest infections, etc.

Antibiotics, which are supposed to destroy microbes, do not promote our body's own defense powers. With many acute diseases, especially those of childhood, we find that at first the disease is quickly cured by antibiotics, but that relapses occur frequently. Some children also develop side effects from antibiotics that include chronic catarrh, secretory otitis media, deafness or discharging ears, enlarged adenoids, tonsils and glands, and even, irreversible neurological disorders. That is one of the reasons why, as Adolf Voegeli, MD, points out in his book *Remedies for Home and Surgery—Homeopathic Prescribing,* "The time when nearly everybody enjoyed the best of health is past; today the majority of our population suffers continually from some disease or other. Even children are very often under medical treatment."

What then can doctors and parents do in the many cases where antibiotics should not be administered? Learning about and treating with homeopathic remedies is a big comfort for those of us intent on restoring our children to good health. Not only are homeopathic medicines safe and effective, they are inexpensive and virtually free from side effects. . . .[1]

Many children are generally healthy and seldom need medical care. But when kids are sick, they can disrupt an entire household, causing misery for all within. H. Fergie-Woods, MD, author of *Essentials of Homoeopathic Prescribing* believes that anyone wanting to test the value of homeopathic medicine should study its results on children. "That children respond even better to Homeopathy than do adults, is probably due to the fact of their systems being comparatively unspoilt by wrong methods of living, unsuitable food, the strain of life, etc. Apart from this, nature seems to try to make a fresh start with the child in its early years. . . . Homoeopathy can aid . . . not only in childhood, but throughout life, by the raising of the vital forces resulting from its natural and scientific remedies."

Dr. Fergie-Woods goes on to suggest additional reasons why homeopathy is "the ideal method of treatment" for children and infants:

1. *Pleasant to take*—children seldom need to be *forced* to take their medicine since homeopathic remedies have either no taste or a sweet milk sugar taste.

2. *Harmless*—even if a child gets hold of a bottle of homeopathic medicine, he or she will not suffer ill effects. Because of the homeopathic law of the minimum dose, there are also virtually no side effects. (The safety of homeopathic medicines is also a benefit to patients who may not choose the correct remedy at first.)[2]

Writing in the Preface to her book *Homoeopathic Remedies for Children,* Phyllis Speight, one of the most respected homeopathic practitioners in England, writes:

No mother likes to see her child unwell or suffering. Children change from being well and rushing around one minute to being off-colour and exhibiting symptoms the next; and then medicines like aspirin or antibiotics are frequently administered to give relief.

More and more people are becoming concerned about the effects of drugs, particularly in relation to children. Many mothers telephone me to ask for help and advice because they do not wish to give their children drugs which have been prescribed.

There is an alternative in homoeopathy. Our medicines are safe. . . . When the correct remedy is chosen, spectacular things happen in many cases of acute diseases and there is no reason why parents cannot use homoeopathic remedies effectively if they will give a little time to understand and study.[3]

When homeopathic physicians or well-trained licensed, registered, or certified homeopathic practitioners are available for consultation, it is not unusual, as Phyllis Speight has stated, for them to be called by the parents of infants, children, and adolescents to render a second opinion on the proposed health care treatment by a nonhomeopathic (allopathic) physician. Homeopaths are usually the first, and last, to be consulted by parents who are knowledgeable about homeopathy.

Homeopathy is a viable, reliable, and extraordinarily effective alternative therapy for the common and acute illnesses and accidental injures of children.

WHAT IS HOMEOPATHY?

Homeopathy (often spelled *homoeopathy* in British English) is a complete, highly effective, and comprehensive system of health care treatment. In the decades of the eighties and into the nineties, the homeopathic method of medicine is being called by various names: homeotherapeutic medicine, ultramolecular medicine, probiotic medicine. By whatever name, homeopathy is the comprehensive system of health care first developed by a German physician and chemist, Samuel C. F. Hahnemann, MD (1755–1843), at the end of the eighteenth century. Homeopathy has truly undergone the test of time: for nearly 200 years, it has proved itself an effective alternative in health care delivery.

In textbooks on the history of medicine, Sir William Osler is often referred to as the father of modern medicine. In his famous farewell address to the American Medical Association in 1905, Dr. Osler said, "It is not as if our homeopathic brothers are asleep; far from it, they are awake . . . to the importance of the scientific study of disease."[4]

Dr. Samuel Hahnemann, a brilliant and insightful man, proposed what has become a basic guiding principle of homeopathy—the Law of Similars—"let like be cured by like." According to George Vithoulkas, widely considered to be the greatest living homeopathic theorist, "Many [scientists] would simply have ignored [Hahnemann's] observation . . . Hahnemann, however, was a true empirical scientist. To him, the observation itself was what counted . . . He accepted the observation and went on to make further experiments which further proved this 'chance' observation of a fact of Nature: *A substance which produces symptoms in a healthy person cures those symptoms in a sick person.*"[5]

The "chance observation" Vithoulkas mentions here is Hahnemann's discovery that as a man in perfect health himself at the time, by drinking approximately one-half ounce of decoction of Peruvian bark (a source of the malaria-fighting drug quinine) he produced within himself symptoms similar to those of malaria without actually having the disease, which is caused by the bite of the malarial mosquito. Vithoulkas, in his book *Homeopathy: Medicine of the New Man,* goes on to say, "Imagine the astounding revelation that struck Hahnemann as a result of this experiment! The standard medical assumption had always been [as it is today] that if the body produces a symptom, a medicine must be given to relieve that symptom. This was so deeply ingrained that it had almost become an automatic reflex in the mind of doctor and patient. But here, in his own personal experience, Hahnemann found that a drug which was known to be curative in malaria actually produces those very symptoms when given to a healthy person!"[6]

TRADITIONAL MEDICINE VERSUS HOMEOPATHIC MEDICINE

Simply stated, homeopathy uses medicines that are natural substances—found in nature rather than synthesized in the laboratory—plants, herbs, minerals, and animal products, that if given to a healthy person would produce symptoms of disease. This is the homeopathic application of the Law of Similars. Unlike the practice in standard medicine (often called by homeopaths *allopathy,* meaning "other disease"), homeopathic medicines are always tested in healthy human beings rather than on laboratory animals. Hahnemann believed, as do modern homeopaths, that medicines to be used *in* people must be tested and proved *on* people. Animals, because of the qualities of their nonhuman body chemistries and physiologies, cannot be expected to react to medicine in exactly the same way human beings react. All homeopathic medicines are therefore thoroughly tested on provers—men and women in clinically certifiable good health. The physical reactions of these provers are then meticulously studied. From these careful observations, symptom pictures, "the identical symptomatologies of many illnesses,"[7] are created.

Homeopaths employ these symptom pictures to match the totality of symptoms of disease, illness, or injuries. Once the symptom picture of a person in ill health is matched to a similar set of symptoms that a drug in its raw state would produce in a healthy individual, the homeopath can then select a single medicine (remedy) or a combination medicine (polypharmacy remedy) that will eliminate the condition according to the time-tested and well-proved Law of Similars.

It should be here noted that *homeopathic remedies never mask—never cover up—diseases*. They do not merely relieve outward symptoms while allowing the disease to progress while the person merely "feels better."

In homeopathic literature, homeopathic medicines are usually referred to as *remedies*. Although United States federal law requires all medicines to be labeled with the advisory warning *Keep this and all medicines out of the reach of children,* the homeopathic remedies are not dangerous pharmaceuticals. In fact, they are far safer than the over-the-counter nonprescription drugs found on the shelves of supermarkets, neighborhood convenience stores, and discount centers. Were a child to swallow half a bottle of Tylenol or other acetaminophen pain reliever, irreversible liver damage could result. Were a child to accidentally take an overdose of almost any over-the-counter drug (not to mention prescription drugs, which are far more potent), the consequences could be serious or even fatal. In the United States hundreds of thousands of children are accidentally poisoned by over-the-counter and prescription drugs every year. This is not possible with homeopathic remedies, which are available without prescription. But, of course, *all* medicines must always be treated with respect. Homeopathic remedies are manufactured in a completely different manner than are standard pharmaceuticals and work in the body on an entirely different level.

How Homeopathic Remedies Are Manufactured

When the science of homeopathy began, Dr. Samuel Hahnemann discovered that when a drug in its raw or crude form was diluted and then potentized, that drug both became more highly reactive in the body (more effective in its action) and lost any poisonous qualities it might possess. These facts give homeopathy a major advantage over standard drug therapy, and most certainly reduce the risk of accidental poisoning of infants and children.

To manufacture a homeopathic remedy, one first begins with the raw, full-potency substance. It is then prepared for homeopathic purposes by one of several systems of manufacture. The two most common methods are based on the *decimal* or the *centesimal* scale. Plant, mineral, or animal substances that are soluble in water and alcohol are made first into *dilutions.* Substances insoluble in alcohol or water are made into *triturations.* In the decimal system, 1 part of the basic substance is added to 9 parts of a diluting medium: alcohol and water for soluble substances, lactose (milk sugar) for insoluble substances such as some minerals. This produces the first, or 1x, potency. The 1x potency is one-tenth the strength of the basic substance. This first decimal dilution is called the *mother tincture.* Successive potencies of homeopathic remedies are made by adding 1 part of the first (1x) potency to 9 parts of the diluting medium, and so forth along the scale of dilution as shown here:

POTENTIZATION

The first potency (∅ = 1x) equals the mother tincture, designated by the Greek theta (∅).
The second potency (2x) is manufactured from:
    1 part mother tincture and
    9 parts alcohol
The third potency (3x) is manufactured from:
    1 part of the second potency (2x) and
    9 parts alcohol

At each stage in the complex manufacturing process of homeopathic medicines, the resulting potencies are vigorously shaken in a process called *succussion.* It is succussion that creates the special "magnetic blueprint" of the homeopathic pharmaceutical.

The other most common system of homeopathic manufacture, called the centesimal, adds 1 part of the basic substance to 99 parts of the appropriate diluting medium. This creates the 1c potency.

In some parts of the world, a decimal potency may be designated as 1D, 3D, 6D, etc., rather than the more common 1x, 3x, 6x, etc. In this designation, D = x; the "D," of course, means *decimal*. This "D" system of notation is uncommon and becoming rare. The centesimal system may be designated as c or cH (centesimal Hahnemann) or even more commonly by just a number. For example, these designations are co-equal in homeopathic potency: 3, 3c, 3cH. The following table demonstrates the actual dilution ratio of the decimal and centesimal systems.

Dilution Ratio	Decimal Scale	Centesimal Scale
$1/10$ or 10^{-1}	1x	—
$1/100$ or 10^{-2}	2x	1c
$1/1,000$ or 10^{-3}	3x	—
$1/10,000$ or 10^{-4}	4x	2c
10^{-6}	6x	3c
10^{-12}	12x	6c
10^{-24}	24x	12c
10^{-30}	30x	15c
10^{-60}	60x	30c
$10^{-2,000}$	—	M (1,000c)
$10^{-20,000}$	—	10M (10,000c)
$10^{-200,000}$	—	CM (100,000c)

The decimal scale of potentization stops at the 200x potency.

Homeopathic remedies work *with* the body's own natural defense mechanism—the immune system—by stimulating the body's defenses against the disease process. This is the reason that homeopathy is fast becoming known as probiotic (in favor of life) medicine. Standard medical drugs work *against* the disease process. Only in the last few years have scientists themselves been able to explain the nature of homeopathic medicines and how they work within the body.

"Until recently, [homeopathic] physicians have been unable to explain the mechanism involved in the healing effect of their particular practice. Today's physicist can explain the mechanism of action of both acupuncture and homeopathy. Medicines in homeopathy are often diluted beyond the existence of a single atom of the original substance. The unique energy field of a substance, the magnetic blueprint, maintains its identity in the absence of that substance in a material sense. Indeed, the less of a material substance present, the greater the intensity of the magnetic field and the greater or more profound is the effect upon the body."[8]

The most current presentation on the scientific research conducted on the homeopathic principle of the potentization of remedies, of how and why they work, is contained in an excellent book by Dana Ullman, MPH: *Homeopathy: Medicine for the 21st Century*.[9] This book is highly recommended to everyone who seriously wishes to learn about homeopathic health care.

SOME ADVANTAGES OF HOMEOPATHY

Garth W. Boericke, MD, a noted American homeopathic physician, has presented ten brief reasons why the homeopathic treatment of disease, illness, and injury is an effective collaborative (alternative) form of health care treatment for children as well as for adults. Dr. Boericke's remarks are paraphrased or quoted here by permission of the Society of Ultramolecular Medicine.

1. *Individualization of treatment:* Treatment is directed to the individual patient through Keynote symptoms rather than at a disease as a diagnostic name. (The patient may not have the disease that is at first suspected.)

2. *Extensive human experimentation:* Homeopathy employs tests on human beings clinically certified as healthy rather than on animals that might not react exactly the same as human beings in all cases.

3. *The homeopathic method:* Homeopathy uses symptoms (the "totality," which is a major principle of homeopathy). Symptoms, called the symptom picture, are used as a guide for the elimination of disease rather than merely treated palliatively. Drugs such as aspirin for a headache, the narcotic codeine for a cough, or milk of magnesia or bicarbonate of soda for an upset stomach merely cover up symptoms but do nothing to treat the underlying cause of illness.

4. *Time-tested:* Homeopathic remedies have been employed successfully for nearly 200 years worldwide. No other system of health care has lasted so long without the necessity of adjustments in treatment regimens and changes in theory. As Dr. Boericke has stated so well: "Medical fads, fakes, and delusions always run a course and are forgotten—not so with homeopathy. It is ethically practiced today by physicians who have studied it and many more who have taken postgraduate courses."

5. *No drugging effect:* There are so few, if any, side effects in homeopathic remedies that when they are used as directed, there is virtually no possibility of harming a patient. The first rule of medicine is "First do no harm," and this is exactly what homeopathy exemplifies best.

6. *Low cost:* Homeopathic medicines are generally very inexpensive, lowering the overall cost of health care.

7. *Noninvasive:* The majority of homeopathic remedies are taken orally. Although some practices in homeopathy employ injections, remedies for in-home health care are used in tablet, pellet, or liquid drop form.

8. *Freshness of remedy ingredients:* Homeopathic manufacturing pharmacists use fresh plant tinctures and preparations rather than dried. Homeopathy maintains that the true medicinal value of plants and herbs used in homeopathic remedies resides in the freshest sources.

9. *Long-lasting:* Unlike nearly every nonhomeopathic medicine, both over-the-counter and prescribed, remedies do not deteriorate over time when used as directed. They are clinically active indefinitely.

10. *No risk:* Unlike any other system of health care that uses medicines, homeopathy is the *only* health care delivery system that "can be put in the hands of intelligent laymen [women] without risk and with reasonable assurance of success."[10]

---

1. *Author's note:* Using Traumeel, a homeopathic combination medicine developed over 30 years ago in West Germany and used primarily in injuries to muscle and connective tissues as a representative example, Wilfried Stock, MD, has stated that effective therapy for illness and injury should demonstrate a minimum of side effects; that homeopathic medicine "fulfills . . . [this] expectation, as [physicians and researchers] have had confirmed from countless examples of administration and from reports from medical practice. The side-effect rate, for example, is less than three ten-thousandths of one percent. This means about three cases of side effects in one million applications. The very few side-effects which [do] occur [are] basically the results of minor allergic reactions in the form of extreme sensitivity to [a] component [of a homeopathic medicine]." "Latest Clinical Results with Traumeel Ointment in Sports Injuries," *Biological Therapy: Journal of Natural Medicine* VI (October 1988): 76.

2. "Keeping Kids Healthy—Start with Homeopathy," *American Homeopathy* 2 (March 1985): 1–13.

3. Phyllis Speight, *Homoeopathic Remedies for Children* (Essex, England: Health Science Press, 1983), vi.

4. Sir William Osler, "Unity, Peace, and Concord—A Farewell Address to the American Medical Profession in 1905" contained in *The Collected Writings of Sir William Osler* (Birmingham, AL: *Classics of Medicine Library*, 1985), Vol. 1.

5. George Vithoulkas, *Homeopathy: Medicine of the New Man* (New York: Arco Publishing, Inc., 1979), 15.

6. Vithoulkas, 15.

7. Vithoulkas, 16.

8. F. Fuller Royal, MD, HMD, "Accupath 10000: Combining Acupuncture Diagnosis with Homeopathic Treatment," *Journal of Ultramolecular Medicine* 1 (1983): 42.

9. Dana Ullman, MPH, *Homeopathy: Medicine for the 21st Century* (Berkeley, CA: North Atlantic Books, 1989).

10. Garth W. Boericke, MD, "Some Advantages of Homeopathy," *American Homeopathy*, 1 (September 1984): 17.

PART I

The Homeopathic Treatment of Childhood Diseases

The Childhood Immunization Controversy and a Safe, Successful Homeopathic Alternative

The following article, which constitutes this entire chapter, is reprinted in its entirety by permission of the Society of Ultramolecular Medicine.[1]

IMMUNIZATIONS: DO THEY PROTECT OUR CHILDREN?

The subject of vaccinations is difficult to approach in an objective way. An increasing number of practitioners and consumers, especially parents, are voicing serious doubts about immunizations. The rigid immunization requirements for school entry have been relaxed, and 22 states now have personal choice exemptions to compulsory immunization laws. The arguments for immunization are nonetheless convincing.

DO VACCINES WORK?

Historically, immunization was designed for serious, life-threatening diseases (smallpox, diphtheria, etc.). The risk of getting the disease, as well as the mortality rate, was great. Since the time when the common vaccines were introduced, a remarkable decline has been seen in the incidence and severity of the corresponding natural infections. According to Richard Moskowitz, MD, however, in his article, "The Case Against Immunization" (first printed in the *Journal of the American Institute of Homeopathy*), "the customary assumption that the decline is attributable to the vaccines remains unproven, and continues to be seriously questioned by eminent authorities in the field." The incidence and severity of whooping cough had already begun to decline long before the pertussis vaccine was introduced, and improvements in public health and sanitation contributed to the disappearance of TB, cholera, typhoid, and other diseases. However, there can be little doubt that conditions like smallpox, poliomyelitis, and measles were dramatically influenced by vaccination.

According to the World Health Organization, reporting on health statistics for 1973–1976, there has been a steady decline in most developing countries regardless of the percentage of immunizations administered in those countries. It appears that generally improved sanitary conditions are largely responsible for preventing infectious diseases.

If vaccines were not responsible for the reduction in death or permanent harm from childhood diseases, perhaps it has been responsible for a reduction in the overall incidence of those diseases. There has been a general reduction in the incidence of diseases for which there are vaccines, but the protection afforded by vaccines may not be as complete as is widely assumed. The records of epidemics that occurred after the introduction of mass immunizations are too numerous to be ignored. In the recent measles epidemic in Dade County, Florida, most of the cases were children who had been vaccinated. There was no difference in protection between the vaccinated and the unvaccinated.

In some instances, the reduction in the number of epidemics may be due to a redefinition of terms. For example, prior to the introduction of the Salk vaccine, 20 cases of polio per year per 100,000 population constituted an epidemic. This number was raised to 35 cases *after* the Salk vaccine was introduced.

Conversely, the outbreak of pertussis, or whooping cough, in Great Britain in 1983 and early 1984 was thought to be due to a large unprotected, and therefore susceptible, population. Parents had stopped having their children immunized when the disease became rare. Interestingly, the British press was filled with information about the use of homeopathy [as] an alternative to immunization. British statistics show that in 1981 one in 300,000 children suffered serious neurological illness within seven days of receiving the whooping cough vaccine. The figures rose to one in 100,000 for the full course of three injections. During the height of the epidemic an estimated 1,000 parents in one city alone chose homeopathy as an alternative because of fears about the side effects of the free government-sponsored vaccine.

Recently, Wyeth Laboratories, one of two major US manufacturers of the pertussis vaccine, stopped production of the vaccine citing rising liability problems from rare complications linked to the shots. And the vaccine compensation legislation currently before Congress was stimulated largely by public concern about pertussis complications and by lawsuits.

WHAT IS IMMUNIZATION?

Immunization is one of the few areas in which allopathic and homeopathic medicine operate from the same basic premise—like cures like. Allopathic and homeopathic vaccines are both developed from tissues infected with the active agent, but the similarity ends there. Active immunization is based on the theory that the injection of an antigen (disease product) into the body will stimulate antibody formation against that disease. These antibodies will then work to fight off pathogenic bacteria in the future, just as they do in a person who has previously had the disease. The immunizing agent is prepared either from a live weakened strain of the disease agent, or from processed, inactivated components of the agent.

The mechanism of the allopathic preparations is heroic. The vaccine is seen as confirming immunity based on the production of virus-specific immunoglobulin. From the homeopathic viewpoint the use of artificially attenuated virus to produce an artificial suppression of susceptibility to infectious disease may result in a shift of the center of gravity of illness of the immunized population to another, perhaps deeper, area.

Robert Mendelsohn, MD, states that "most of the degenerative diseases of today are going to be shown to be due to x-rays, drugs, polluted food, additives, preservatives, and immunizations." In 1976 Dr. Robert Simpson of Rutgers University pointed out that "immunization programs against flu, measles, mumps, polio, etc., actually may be seeding humans with RNA to form pro-viruses, which will then become latent cells throughout the body. Some of these latent pro-viruses could be molecules in search of disease, which under proper conditions, become activated and cause a variety of diseases, including rheumatoid arthritis, multiple sclerosis, lupus erythematosus, Parkinson's disease, and perhaps cancer." Nicholas J. Nossaman, MD, suggests that the shift in the center of gravity of illness as a result of the artificial suppression of susceptibility is extremely difficult to prove, but the emergence of newer illnesses, such as Legionnaire's disease, Reye's syndrome, toxic shock syndrome, and AIDS (acquired immune deficiency syndrome), are evidence of such a shift. And Dr. Moskowitz draws attention to the already existing models for predicting and explaining what sorts of chronic illnesses are likely to result from the long-term persistence of viruses and other foreign proteins found in allopathic vaccine preparations.

OTHER ARGUMENTS AGAINST IMMUNIZATION

The notion of inflicting disease on healthy children so that they will be immune to that disease in the future has seemed paradoxical to many critics. Homeopathic critics maintain that constitutional treatment to raise resistance, immunization with homeopathic preparations during an epidemic, and homeopathic treatment during an outbreak will guarantee safety from any of these dangerous diseases.

Another criticism involves the manipulative influence of the drug industry on the governmental institutions that make recommendations on immunization procedures. Commercial pressure sustains the use of vaccines.

A third argument against blind immunization, as postulated by Simon Mills, a British medical herbalist, is that even if it is safe as well as effective, its arbitrary use distracts patients and practitioners alike from the task of tackling the root causes of diseases, and the much more important concerns of improving nutritional and social conditions. Mills says, "We presumably all try to subscribe to the dictum that every person is a unique individual, demanding unique treatment, and most of us would wish to correct individual failures of vital resistance as we encountered them, rather than relying on an arbitrary intervention."

A final argument against immunization, especially compulsory vaccination, is the increase in vaccine-related illness—immunizations have been known to cause disease and occasionally death. Deaths from smallpox inoculations have been widespread. Polio has occurred following diphtheria and pertussis immunizations, as well as after administration of the polio vaccine itself. Fevers, convulsions, death, and general lowering of resistance have all followed various immunizations and brain damage has been caused by DPT shots.

Although immunizations cause a very mild, usually unnoticeable case of the disease, if for some reason an individual's resistance is lowered or the reaction is overstimulated, then serious symptoms may develop. This rarely happens, but it has been theorized that resistance can be lowered for years following immunization and that chronic disease can stem from an initial dose of a vaccine, toxoid, or serum.

LATENT VIRUSES

It has long been known that live viruses are capable of remaining latent for many years. Herpes, shingles, and warts are examples of episodic or recurrent acute latent viruses, while subacute or chronic, progressive, often fatal latent viruses include Kuru, Creutzfeldt-Jacob disease, and possibly Guillain-Barre syndrome. Some tumors have also been associated with latent viruses.

The latent virus becomes permanently incorporated within the genetic material itself, but it is still recognized as a "foreign" element. Logic decrees that the antigenic response will of necessity be auto-immune based because the destruction of "self" cells containing the latent virus is the only way that the chronic antigenic insult can be removed. Since circulating antibodies cannot normally cross the cell membrane, however, a stalemate develops. It does not strain credibility to envision that, under certain circumstances, a breakdown of this balance might occur triggering a full-blown auto-immune reaction leading to necrosis and tissue destruction. If auto-immune disease represents the destruction of chronically infected cells, then the increase in auto-immune illnesses over the past several decades makes sense in light of large scale immunization programs.

TODAY'S STORY

Most parents still believe it is their duty to have their children vaccinated against certain diseases, and they are willing to accept whatever immunization program happens to be currently popular. Yet there are few people today who are still unaware of the dangers of the smallpox vaccine, and it is now realized by most authorities that mass vaccination of children was ineffective in preventing smallpox and that its dangers were only masked from view when the disease was epidemic.

One answer to the present day dilemma facing parents regarding immunization of their children is to learn other ways of prevention. Homeopathy, which acts by stimulating the body's own defense, is perhaps the best alternative. The homeopathic alternatives are safe, even in those children who are not robust, or have had some pre-existing illness, all are given orally, and they are easy to administer.

Henry N. Williams, MD, in a paper titled, "Immunizations," writes, "Homeopathic physicians also recognize with educators, parents, and others that an illness, especially in a child, may have a freeing or stimulating effect if the patient is allowed to go through the illness with a minimum of medication. This leads to the realization that the body in which the child is born is a *loaned body*, loaned by the mother, built out of her substance by the incarnating being of the child. In the first six or seven years the child builds his or her own body from the food it digests. It throws off that of the first body which it cannot use through the kidneys, liver, and/or skin. The latter may appear as one of the childhood diseases with a rash.

"In light of these considerations the homeopathic physician is reluctant to inject into the body of the child foreign protein material which may cause an immediate severe reaction, even death, or a more subtle response that reduces the patient's future health. It must be borne in mind that the same diseases may cause serious chronic conditions such as mental retardation or even death. Thus each case must be judged on its own merits."

WHOOPING COUGH

Whooping cough (pertussis) is a fairly common infectious disease of childhood which is usually characterized by a period of cold symptoms followed by an extended period (four to six weeks) of violent coughing. It occurs primarily in infants and young children. Since whooping cough is most serious in very young babies who are too young to be vaccinated, the routine administration of whooping cough vaccine to older babies does not seem to have much justification.

Whooping cough is caused by bacterial infection of the respiratory organs. Epidemics are said to occur every four years and it can also follow on after an attack of measles.

VACCINE

The whooping cough vaccine has an effectiveness of only about 50 percent. It also may cause high fevers and convulsions as well as a form of encephalopathy (brain damage). The attack rate of whooping cough has been so high in vaccinated children that at times the vaccine appears to give no protection at all. Reasons for this have been given, and they include the antigenic change of the organism *Bordetella pertussis* and the fact that whooping cough–like disease is often associated with other bacteria, or even viruses, which remain totally unaffected by the vaccine.

According to Dr. Nossaman, "Pertussis is one of the most controversial immunizations with relatively frequent adverse reactions and relatively low effectiveness for an illness which was already on the wane before the vaccine's widespread use."

REMEDY

The homeopathic remedy for whooping cough is *Pertussin 30*. A dose consists of three tablets of the remedy given in one day approximately four hourly intervals [every 4 hours], preferably before food. According to Dr. R. A. F. Jack, MRCGP, FFHom., of the British Homoeopathic Association, subsequent "doses" should be given at intervals between doses of six weeks, three months, six months, and twelve months, and thereafter every 12 months until the child is six. An extra "dose" should be given with new exposure to whooping cough.

The homeopathic preparation is actually made from the sputum of whooping cough sufferers. It's absolutely safe and there has not been a recorded case of harmful side effects in over 50 years of use.

MEASLES

Measles (rubeola) is a highly contagious and common disease of childhood transmitted by a virus. Its usual characteristics are cold symptoms, cough, irritated eyes, and high fever with the appearance of a rash on the fourth day of illness. The symptoms, including the rash, reach a climax on about the sixth day and then subside within a few days.

Measles can on occasion cause complications, including ear infections, pneumonia, lymph node infection, encephalitis, and brain damage.

VACCINE

The measles vaccine is designed primarily to prevent measles encephalitis which is said to occur in one out of every thousand cases of measles. Measles was also on the decline before immunizations were developed. The vaccine contains live virus which bypass usual defense barriers in its administration. Immunization has shifted the incidence back to older age groups who historically are less able to tolerate the illness.

Dr. Mendelsohn points out that the vaccine is associated with ataxia (inability to coordinate muscle movement), retardation, learning disability or hyperactivity, and seizure disorders. Says Mendelsohn, "I wonder whether the current epidemic of hyperactivity in children may have its origin, at least in part, in the measles vaccine."

REMEDY

Homeopathy offers consistently successful treatment for measles. The disease is usually limited to its mild forms with the use of homeopathic medicines and, reportedly, complications can be prevented. Treatment of complications or severe symptoms is also possible.

Morbillinum 30x is the recommended remedy for measles. Dr. Andrew Lockie of Great Britain suggests one dose every 12 hours for three doses, followed by one dose every three weeks from autumn to spring. As with Pertussin, if there is an epidemic, dose more frequently, especially if incubating the illness.

MUMPS

Mumps, another common childhood illness, goes unnoticed in 30–40 percent of cases. It begins with fever, headache, and tiredness. Within 24 hours the child usually complains of earache near the lobe of the ear. The next day the salivary gland in front of the ear becomes swollen. The illness runs its course within one to six days.

VACCINE

An attack of mumps confers permanent immunity. Immunization with live mumps virus gives immunity to almost 95 percent of those inoculated. No reactions to the immunization have been observed. The vaccine has now become incorporated into the trio of measles-mumps-rubella vaccine, and is usually administered before a child is two years of age.

The main concern about the illness, and the reason for the immunization, is the fear of sterility due to bilateral orchitis (inflammation of the testes) in boys. The fear is extremely overrated as most of the few cases of acute orchitis are unilateral, leaving one functioning and adequate testicle. Of concern is the fact that the vaccine may not confer lifelong immunity as does the natural disease. Therefore, it places male children, especially, at risk of contracting the illness after puberty when symptoms are more severe and more likely to result in sterility.

REMEDY

Parotidinum is the homeopathic remedy and it is administered exactly like the measles remedy, Morbillinum.

RUBELLA (GERMAN MEASLES)

German Measles is a trivial childhood ailment entailing a three-day rash with fever and aching joints. The reason for concern, however, is the ability of the virus to produce congenital abnormalities in a large percentage of infants born to mothers who contract the illness during the first third of their pregnancy. Such defects include congenital heart disease, cataracts, nerve deafness, and mental retardation.

VACCINE

The vaccine is made from attenuated live virus and is injected. Side effects include rash and swollen lymph nodes, but pain in the joints is more common. Joint pain and arthritis occur in up to 35 percent of adult females vaccinated.

Following the 1964 rubella epidemic in the US, a mass immunization program was begun in 1969 in an effort to head off the expected epidemic which had occurred every six to nine years previously. Small children were immunized with the dual objectives of (1) decreasing transmission of rubella virus among children and, subsequently, to pregnant women; and (2) expecting the immunity of the vaccinated female children to extend into their childbearing years.

Interestingly enough, the incidence of rubella in the US in individuals over 15 years of age is exactly the same as it was before the introduction of the vaccine. Presumably, however, the immunization of small children since 1969 has prevented an epidemic in women of childbearing age. There is, though, still great controversy about the effectiveness of the vaccine for the long term.

REMEDY

Rubella 30x, one dose taken immediately after the first sign of symptoms, is what homeopathic practitioners suggest for German Measles. The remedy is safe to take while pregnant, a distinct advantage since pregnant women cannot be vaccinated. . . .

DIPHTHERIA

Diphtheria is a rare but serious, rapidly progressing, infectious disease. Caused by a bacteria and characterized by a sore throat and the development of a membrane covering the throat, it is primarily a disease of the temperate zones. In 1900 diphtheria was the tenth leading cause of death of all children in the United States but in 1920 (before widespread immunization) the mortality rate had already been halved.

VACCINE

Immunization for diphtheria is by means of a toxoid: the diphtheria toxoid is chemically inactivated with formaldehyde and then concentrated. Immunization confers partial immunity with adults more likely to have adverse reactions than children. The vaccine has been the direct cause of diphtheria in some cases.

REMEDY

An oral homeopathic immunization can be given. It is theorized that immunity from a high potency of *Diphtherinum* gives two and a half years' protection. In one of the only studies done on homeopathic immunizations, *Diphtherinum 200* and *Alum Precipitated Toxoid 30* were given in repeated doses to children who proved to be susceptible to diphtheria. This extended study using the homeopathic preparations was carefully conducted and it was determined that immunity to diphtheria (of the degree indicated by a negative Schick skin test) can be produced, following an original positive test, in a statistically significant number of cases. It did not determine whether this immunity is long-lasting.

TETANUS

Tetanus is special in that it is not communicable between humans, but results from trauma. Having the illness does not confer immunity. The bacterium which "causes" tetanus is pervasive in the environment, especially in the soil, and in the gastrointestinal tracts of humans, horses, and other animals. The tetanus bacillus can gain access through open wounds, although in 10–30 percent of cases, the entry point cannot be found. It does damage to the central nervous system and peripheral nerves by means of a toxin it secretes, rather than by invasion.

VACCINE

Immunization for tetanus, also known as "lockjaw," is by means of a toxoid, like diphtheria, prepared similarly, and injected. Usually tetanus immunization is combined with diphtheria and pertussis vaccine in infants and young children. Immunizations should not be given to persons with acute illness accompanied by fever. Immunization confers nearly 100 percent protection if booster vaccinations are given every ten years. It is a relatively safe immunization process which does not involve a live or killed microorganism.

REMEDY

Hypericum 30x is the most commonly used homeopathic remedy for tetanus.[2]

POLIOMYELITIS

During the period 1900–1930, 80 to 90 percent of those afflicted with polio were under five years of age, and the disease received its name of "infantile paralysis." New epidemics are now beginning to appear in tropical and subtropical areas, but since 1954 and the introduction of polio immunization in children on a mass scale, major epidemics in the US have ceased.

VACCINE

There are two vaccines available for polio. Jonas Salk developed a vaccine using killed virus. In 1977 Salk and others testified before Congress that most of the few cases of polio occurring in the US since the early 1970's were the byproduct of the attenuated live virus vaccine developed by Sabin, which is the vaccine of choice in the US.

Severe reaction to polio vaccines have occurred. There have been many cases of poliomyelitis in fully vaccinated persons and instances of the vaccine actually leading to the disease. Predisposing factors to polio include recent tonsillectomy, recent immunization, and tooth extractions. Epidemics seem to be more common in summer months.

REMEDY

Homeopathic medicine is the most effective treatment of polio. Homeopathic immunizations have been used during epidemics. In one test of 82 people exposed to polio (including 53 children), given *Lathyrus sativa 30,* repeated in 16 days, no polio developed. In a group of 34 children with polio symptoms who were given three doses of Lathyrus 30 at half-hour intervals, only four required hospitalization. Dr. Grimmer of Chicago recommended Lathyrus 30 or 200 to be given once every three weeks during an epidemic.

It's important to remember that the risk of acquiring paralytic polio from live-virus vaccine is now greater than the risk of contracting polio from contacts.

It's also important to remember that no vaccine, whether allopathic or homeopathic, carries a guarantee of 100 percent immunity. But the homeopathic remedies are safe, cheap, and effective.

The decision of whether or not to immunize children lies with parents. But parents should consider the risks of the disease and of immunizations and the availability of homeopathic medicines when making their decisions.

1. "Immunizations: Do They Protect Our Children?" *American Homeopathy* 1 (September 1984): 1, 5, 8, 9, 16.

2. The author knows of nothing in the current literature of homeopathy, or the recommendation of any homeopathic physician or nonmedically trained legally licensed or registered practitioner, that recommends against tetanus inoculation or the update of booster vaccination every ten years.)

CHAPTER 2

Common Contagious Diseases

TOPICS COVERED

Measles
Rubella
Mumps
Chicken Pox

Prevention of common contagious childhood diseases using safe, effective oral immunization has already been presented. Prevention is of course much more desirable than cure. However, homeopathy offers an effective, curative treatment of these illnesses.

MEASLES (RUBEOLA)

An acute, infectious, highly contagious disease, measles is characterized by a generalized body rash and an eruption of the lining of the mouth (buccal mucosa) or the lips (labial mucosa). This eruption, known as Koplik's spots, resembles tiny grains of white sand surrounded by an area of redness and appears 2–4 days after the onset of other symptoms. The rash first begins on the face and then spreads over the body, and follows by 3–5 days the initial onset of symptoms and by 1–2 days the appearance of the oral eruption. General symptoms include fever of 101°F or higher; runny nose; a barking, hacking cough;

irritation of the eyes (conjunctivitis); and overall tiredness. At the peak of measles the fever may reach or surpass 104°F. The incubation of the illness following exposure is 7–14 days, and isolation is recommended until five days after the rash.

As has been earlier noted, measles is usually a nonthreatening illness unless complications develop. Complications can include (in infants) pneumonia, middle ear infection (otitis media), and secondary bacterial infections, especially streptococcal. In measles with complications, encephalitis (sleeping sickness) can occur in perhaps one in 600–1,000 cases and is denoted by a high fever, convulsions, and coma.

HOMEOPATHIC TREATMENT

Aconite
Apis mellifica
Belladonna
Bryonia album
Gelsemium
Pulsatilla

Aconite is especially useful at the earliest onset of symptoms, when catarrhal symptoms of chest congestion with a dry hacking or barking cough and runny nose are present, with fever and accompanying chills. The child is *restless* and the skin is *dry*. In Aconite the eyes are inflamed and often sensitive to light.

Potency & Dosage: Unless otherwise directed by a homeopathic health care specialist, employ Aconite in the 6x or 30x standard emergency care potencies and as directed on the labeling for acute conditions, reducing the frequency of dosage as symptoms improve.

Apis mellifica (*Apis mel.*) has Keynote symptoms of high temperature, in which the child is extremely uncomfortable under covers or in a warm room. The eyes are red, sore, and tearful. All pains experienced by the child will be stinging in nature. In Apis, the child will have little thirst and is always *better* from cool or cold and *worse* from heat of any sort.

Potency & Dosage: Unless otherwise directed by a homeopathic health care professional, give Apis in the 6x or 30x potency as directed by product labeling for acute symptoms, reducing the dosage repetition as symptoms improve.

Belladonna is among the first homeopathic remedies to consider in measles. The Keynote symptoms for Belladonna are high fever, considerable restlessness, headache, and red face and eyes. If sore throat is present, characterized by sticking pains and pain on swallowing, Belladonna is indicated. Concurrently with those symptoms, the child will often have a dry, hacking or barking cough, especially toward midnight.

Potency & Dosage: Give Belladonna in either the 6x or 30x potency as directed by product labeling or from a homeopathic health care professional. Repeat the remedy every 30 minutes to 1 hour at the earliest stage of illness, reducing dosage as symptoms lessen.

Bryonia album (*Bryonia*) is most useful when chest symptoms predominate. There will be a dry, painful cough with considerable pain in the chest. The child will prefer to lie as motionless as possible, as symptoms are *worse* from movement. Thirst, another important Keynote symptom, is intense for large amounts of *cold* water.

Potency & Dosage: Give Bryonia in the standard emergency care potencies of 6x or 30x as directed by product labeling or by a health care professional. In the beginning stages of acute illness, repeat the remedy every 30 minutes to 1 hour, reducing the frequency of dosage as symptoms improve.

Gelsemium shows as a Keynote symptom a high temperature accompanied by chilliness. The child is always tired and sluggish, with a couldn't-care-less attitude. There will be a runny discharge from the nose with considerable irritation of the nostrils and upper lip; another Keynote symptom. In a Gelsemium measles the skin will be red and very itchy. In this case the remedy should be continued after the rash has developed.

Potency & Dosage: Unless otherwise directed by a health care professional, give Gelsemium in the 6x or 30x potency, repeating every 30 minutes to 1 hour and reducing the frequency of dosage as symptoms begin to subside.

Pulsatilla is always used in measles in the *last* stages of the illness. In Pulsatilla the temperature will have fallen or even returned to normal, and chest and catarrhal symptoms are dominant. A Keynote symptom will be a dry *nighttime* cough that *loosens* in the daytime. The child will always want to sit up to cough.

Potency & Dosage: Pulsatilla should be employed in the 6x or 30x potency, or as otherwise directed by a health care provider. As in all administrations of homeopathic remedies, give Pulsatilla more frequently when symptoms are acute and reduce the dosage as they improve.

RUBELLA (GERMAN MEASLES)

Rubella, as it is best called, is a contagious disease of children and of teenagers and adults as well. Unlike common measles (rubeola), it is usually a mild disease. Shorter- lasting than measles, it is often called the three-day measles. The rash of rubella is less prominent than in common measles, the skin is more flushed, and the rash is more rose-colored and mild-appearing.

Following an incubation period of 14–21 days, symptoms will usually consist of malaise, swelling of the lymph nodes of the head and neck, and the typical rash, which lasts about three days. The Koplik's spots of common measles will not be present in rubella.

The homeopathic treatment of rubella is conducted on the basis of the Keynote symptoms.

HOMEOPATHIC TREATMENT

Rubella
ABC

If *Rubella 30x* is available, it should be given at the *first* symptoms of the illness. This nosode (a product of the disease itself) will often stop any progress of the disease. Unfortunately, this remedy is not included in the household emergency care kit. The best standard treatment of rubella is the homeopathic combination *ABC* in the 6x or 30x potency. ABC is, of course, *Aconite, Belladonna,* and *Chamomilla.* If this combination remedy is unavailable, the best-selected single remedy may be used on the basis of its Keynote symptoms.

Potency & Dosage: The best-indicated remedy of 6x or 30x potency should be employed, as indicated earlier under measles (rubeola).

MUMPS

Mumps is an acute, contagious, virus-caused disease. It is spread from child to child by contact with materials contaminated by infected saliva. After an incubation period of 14–21 days, onset of the disease is characterized by chills, a low to moderate fever, headache, lack of appetite, and a generalized tiredness. Following the fever (if fever is present), the parotid glands may swell. The salivary glands are the *parotid,* located below and in front of the ear, the *submaxillary,* under the jaw, and the *sublingual,* under the tongue. In mumps, the parotid glands are affected, hence the other name for mumps—parotitis. As the disease progresses the other salivary glands are sometimes affected. The parotid swelling may be one-sided (unilateral) or double-sided (bilateral), giving the person a definite "puff-cheeked" appearance.

HOMEOPATHIC TREATMENT

> *Mercurius*
> *Belladonna*
> *Pulsatilla*
> *Rhus toxicodendron*

Mercurius is generally considered to be the principal remedy in mumps because of its special affinity for the salivary glands. Clinical experience has shown that Mercurius, given at the onset of salivary symptoms for a few doses, is often sufficient to stop further progress of the disease. The Keynote symptoms of Mercurius are swelling and tenderness of the glands, and copious salivation with an accompanying offensive breath.

Potency & Dosage: Employ Mercurius in the standard 6x or 30x potency, giving a dose every 3 hours until there is noticeable improvement.

Belladonna is frequently used in treating mumps whenever its most prominent Keynote symptoms are present: swollen glands, skin red and hot and *very sensitive* to any pressure, symptoms *worse* on the right side, and pains extending into the ear.

Potency & Dosage: The best-indicated potencies are 6x or 30x, given according to labeling instructions or as prescribed by a health care professional. At the acute onset of symptoms, give one dose every 30 minutes to 1 hour, reducing the frequency of dosage as symptoms subside.

Pulsatilla as the indicated homeopathic remedy comes into play whenever there are pains in and behind the ear(s) and a sensation as if the ears were closed or stopped up. The patient will generally be weeping and tearful, demanding constant attention. If a fever is present there will be no thirst for liquids, even if the mouth is dry. Pulsatilla is also well indicated whenever the testicles are involved.

Potency & Dosage: The standard 6x or 30x potency is given, as indicated under the other remedies above.

Rhus toxicodendron (*Rhus tox.*) shows Keynote symptoms of severe restlessness and a continual desire to change positions in the bed. The jaw will be very sensitive to pressure and touch. The glands under the ears are swollen, dark red, and always *worse* on the left side.

Potency & Dosage: Give Rhus tox. in the same way as indicated for the other remedies listed above.

Chicken Pox (Varicella)

Chicken pox is an acute, infectious disease of viral origin. After an initial incubation period averaging 14 days but having a range of 12–21 days, onset of the disease is denoted by a mild headache, a moderate fever, and general tiredness, which develops a day to a day and a half before the characteristic skin rash appears. The rash (or "pox") appears as an itching, "tear-drop" eruption filled with fluid and surrounded by a red circle, or *areola*. This eruption appears first on the trunk of the body and spreads to the arms, legs, and face. The rash may spread as well to the soles of the feet, the palms of the hands, and the mucous membranes of the mouth. Chicken pox is generally a noncomplicated childhood illness. However, in children with leukemia, and children being treated with corticosteroids, it can be especially severe or even fatal.

HOMEOPATHIC TREATMENT

> *Rhus toxicodendron*
> *Aconite*
> *Belladonna*
> *Pulsatilla*

Rhus toxicodendron (*Rhus tox.*) is the *first* homeopathic remedy to consider in chicken pox. It must be given in the earliest stages, as clinical practice over decades has shown that it prevents further development of the disease. Keynote symptoms of Rhus tox. are great restlessness, both mental and physical.

Potency & Dosage: Use the standard 6x or 30x potency, as directed by the product label or on the advice of a homeopathic health care professional. As in all acute stages of illness, repeat the dosage frequently (every 30 minutes to 1 hour), reducing the frequency to every 3–4 hours as symptoms subside.

Aconite is very useful when employed at the early feverish stage of chicken pox. Homeopaths consider Aconite to be "required" whenever fever is present. There will be symptoms of anxiety, fear, and thirst. The fever will be "dry"—without perspiration—and the pulse rapid, hard, and full.

Potency & Dosage: Use the standard 6x or 30x potency as directed under Rhus tox., above.

Belladonna is the indicated remedy in chicken pox whenever the child experiences a severe headache. Other leading Keynote symptoms include fever, sore throat, and flushing of the skin with a telltale paleness of the skin surrounding the mouth.

Potency & Dosage: Employ the 6x or 30x potencies in the same dosages as given above for Rhus tox.

Pulsatilla is indicated in chicken pox whenever the child is tearful and mild-mannered. These symptoms and another Keynote symptom, *freedom from all thirst,* are indicative of Pulsatilla. Many homeopaths, relying on decades of clinical experience, have found that Pulsatilla both prevents the disease whenever an epidemic breaks out and also has the ability to shorten the disease process. As a preventive measure, Pulsatilla should be used in the 30x potency, given once every 3 days.

Potency & Dosage: Give the 6x or 30x potency during the acute stages of illness every 30 minutes to 1 hour initially, reducing the frequency to every 3–4 hours as symptoms subside.

CHAPTER 3

Infant Colic

Colic is a complex of symptoms in early infancy characterized by outbursts of crying, periods of cranky irritability, and apparent sharp abdominal discomfort.

Usually, babies around 2 to 4 weeks of age and shortly out of the hospital will develop this symptom complex. Colic might last until the child is 3 or 4 months old, by which time the symptoms usually disappear. The exact cause or causes of colic are not known, but it occurs far more often in bottle-fed babies than in those fed naturally from the breast. It seems most probable that colic derives from one of two causes: negligent bottle feeding, which permits air to enter the nipple so that the sucking baby swallows air and experiences abdominal distention, and unnatural fermentation of carbohydrates or starches that have passed incompletely digested from the small intestine and are then subjected to breakdown by the flora—the natural bacteria in the lower bowel. Flatulence ("gas") builds, and the abdomen becomes hard and distended, creating the typical colic symptoms of abdominal pain, irritability, and incessant crying.

Incessant crying and irritability are symptomatic not only of colic; other causes need to be ruled out. For example, an infant with an ear infection will often scream out and cry nonstop.

DIAGNOSIS OF COLIC

Fever is seldom present; the infant will have a normal temperature; vomiting may occur.

A guiding symptom of colic is the relief of pain when gentle but firm pressure is applied to the child's abdomen. In colic, when the child is gently lifted by its arms, it will bend the thighs upward to the abdomen.

TREATMENT

Standard medicine offers little in the way of effective management of infant colic; little more help is generally given than the physician's reassurance to the parent(s) that the condition is self-limiting and will pass without harm in 3 or 4 months. To limit the amount of air swallowed during feeding, the physician might suggest obtaining nipples with smaller holes, thus permitting the feeding to take at least 20 minutes. In rare cases, a liquid sedative, such as phenobarbital, will be prescribed prior to feeding. Generally, however, the physician offers parental reassurance that there is nothing seriously wrong with the baby's health.

HOMEOPATHIC MANAGEMENT

Homeopaths will, of course, offer the same assurance to the parent(s) of a colicky infant—there is nothing seriously wrong with the child. However, homeopathy can go a productive step further and offer both *safe* and highly *effective* medicines to relieve the condition, quiet the baby, and greatly relieve the parent(s) frazzled nerves.

Nearly every homeopathic pharmaceutical manufacturer markets a totally safe, all-natural combination remedy for colic. These products contain at least two of the most often called for remedies: *Chamomilla* and *Colocynth*. In the United States the most well-known and widely available combination is Standard Homeopathic Company's "Hyland's Colic Tablets," which contain the above-mentioned single remedies as well as *Dioscorea* (wild yam). These products are easily administered by dissolving 2 tablets in a teaspoonful of water. Older children with intestinal carbohydrate dyspepsia may be given the rapidly dissolving tablets directly on the tongue.

SINGLE REMEDY SELECTION

If a combination remedy is not readily available and the parent has a homeopathic home remedy kit or children's kit, he or she should select from the following single remedies based upon the Keynote symptoms:

Colocynth, perhaps the foremost remedy in infant colic, is made from the herb bitter apple. The Keynote symptoms of a Colocynth colic are as follows: the infant doubles up from pain, the thighs spasmodically flex toward the abdomen, and pain is *relieved* or *improved* by gentle, firm pressure on the abdomen.

Potency & Dosage: Give Colocynth in the 3x or 6x potency, whichever is available, 2 tablets every 30 minutes during an acute attack. As colic symptoms are relieved, discontinue the medicine. In infants, the tablets should be dissolved in a teaspoonful of water and given by mouth. In older children, the tablets can be placed directly on the tongue or against the inside of the cheek and permitted to dissolve.

Note: Some homeopaths find that a favorable complimentary or synergistic action occurs when *Nux vomica* in the same potency is added to Colocynth. Two highly regarded homeopathic physicians, Dr. Bishambardas and Dr. M. T. Santwani, both of the Homeopathic Medical Association of India, consider this treatment specific to infant colic. The Keynote symptoms of Nux vomica are these: flatulent distention of the abdomen, soreness of the abdomen on pressure, upward pressure from flatulence ("gas") and resultant shortness of breath, sour belching, and possibly vomiting.

Chamomilla, derived from the chamomile flower, is often noted for its ability to nearly instantly relieve the total symptom picture of infantile colic: pain, irritability, and crying. In Chamomilla the Keynote symptoms are as follows: pains are unbearable; pains develop at night, are *worse* at night and *worse* from the applications of hot cloths to the stomach and abdomen; the child is extremely restless and irritable and cannot be easily quieted; the child's cries are pitiable, extended, and *loud*.

Potency & Dosage: Give Chamomilla in the 3x or 6x potency in the same manner as indicated under Colocynth.

A final remedy that should never be overlooked in colic is ***Magnesium phosphate*** (Mag. phos.), which is a homeopathic cell or tissue salt. The action of Mag. phos. is antispasmodic. The Keynote symptoms of Mag. phos. include pain of colic because of flatulence ("gas"); abdomen is full and bloated with gas; passing gas provides great relief of pain; pain is *better* from pressure and *better* from warm applications.

Potency & Dosage: Mag. phos. is used differently than almost all other homeopathic remedies. It works best when 15–20 1-grain tablets are dissolved in hot water. Give 1 teaspoonful every 15–30 minutes until relief is obtained.

Note: An interesting Keynote symptom of Mag. phos. is colic-like pain in toddlers *accompanied by hiccup* and gas.

Chapter 4

Diarrhea

Diarrhea is usually not serious or long-lasting in infants or children and is serious only in young infants when dehydration—serious loss of vital fluids from the body—occurs. Dehydration resulting from diarrhea produces great loss of life among infants and young children in the underdeveloped Third World nations.

> ADVISORY WARNING: If diarrhea is especially severe and lasts longer than 24 hours, despite homeopathic treatment most appropriate to a close match of Keynote symptoms with the symptom picture, the infant or child *must* be taken for qualified medical care *immediately*. The child will probably be dehydrated, and will require both rehydration and medical treatment of the cause of the diarrhea.

Diarrhea is uncommon in breast-fed babies. Mother's milk is the most natural of all foods for infants. Immediately before childbirth and for the first few days afterwards, before milk production begins, the mammary glands secrete a substance called *colostrum,* which is a watery fluid containing a high concentration of the mother's own antibodies against disease. Colostrum is Nature's way of providing protection to an infant during its earliest days of life. It has a strong inhibitory effect on harmful bacteria in the lower bowel, especially on

Escherichia coli, the bacteria usually most responsible for diarrhea in infants and young children. It is unfortunate that relatively few mothers in Western countries choose to breast-feed even when able to do so. Bottle feeding, while convenient and thoroughly "modern," is often the indirect cause of infant diarrhea. Improperly sterilized bottles, poorly or improperly stored formula, and dirty nipples all provide routes for possible infection. All mothers who bottle-feed their infants should carefully read and follow the label directions on formula preparations, especially those concerning proper storage of any unused formula. Generally, leftover formula must be immediately refrigerated and used within 48 hours. All formula remaining in the nursing bottle must be rinsed out, and the nipple and coupling cap of the bottle sterilized and sealed to protect from any contamination.

For the inexperienced nursing mother, it should be noted here that *breast-fed* babies normally pass five or six soft, semisolid stools daily. This is natural and does not constitute diarrhea.

CAUSES OF DIARRHEA

The possible causes of diarrhea in babies and children are as varied as they are numerous. In *infants* the autonomic nervous system, while developed, is not always fully functional. This permits a very rapid transit of food through the intestinal tract and frequent bowel movements. Some babies are lactose intolerant; that is, they do not possess they enzyme necessary for the proper digestion of milk sugar (lactose). Some bottle-fed infants are allergic to one or more of the commercial formulas. The ingestion of contaminants and bacteria from the environment is yet another factor. In *children* the diarrhea can often be traced to overeating of fruits and vegetables, and the ingestion of unripe fruits ("green apple diarrhea"). Laxatives used to treat childhood constipation may cause overreaction of the bowel and rapid transit. Children are especially prone to diarrhea in the hot summer months, and diarrhea is not uncommon in children who live in tropical and subtropical climates. Finally, in children who are cutting teeth, diarrhea is often a problem, not because of the erupting teeth but because of the ingestion of environmental contaminants when the child puts objects in his or her mouth to chew upon.

HOMEOPATHIC TREATMENT

> *Arsenicum album*
> *Chamomilla*
> *China*
> *Podophyllum*
> *Pulsatilla*

Arsenicum album (*Arsenicum alb.*) diarrhea shows the following Keynote symptoms: severe diarrhea that is foul-smelling (many people compare the odor of an Arsenicum diarrhea to that of decaying flesh); stools are very loose, watery, pale brown or greenish, and frequent; the infant or child is completely prostrated from the diarrhea; burning pains from the diarrhea are most often noted as is an excoriation (inflammation) of the anus; diarrhea is almost always accompanied by vomiting; the child wants water but drinks very little.

Potency & Dosage: Use Arsenicum alb. in the standard emergency care 6x or 30x potencies. In acute conditions, give one dose of 2–3 tablets, dissolved in a teaspoonful of water or placed directly on the tongue or inside the cheek depending upon the age of the child, every 30 minutes until symptoms subside. As the symptoms become less severe, reduce the dosage to 2–3 tablets every 3–4 hours, as needed, stopping all administration of medication as symptoms lessen.

Chamomilla is most often called for in diarrhea that is related to cutting teeth. The Keynote symptoms will be extreme irritability, the child is restless and whiny; oversensitivity to everything even when the child is normally even-tempered; stools are watery, foul-smelling, and slimy; stool color is often greenish or will change color from greenish to yellowish-green. It must also be noted the Chamomilla presents an odd symptom of "one cheek red and hot, the other cheek pale and cold" if the child is cutting teeth.

Potency & Dosage: Use Chamomilla in the standard emergency care 6x or 30x potencies. In acute conditions follow the standard administration and dosage as given under Arsenicum album, above.

China diarrhea is always *worse* at night; *worse* from eating fruit; stools are pale and sometimes appear white, are slimy and may appear to have clumps of mucus that looks like white popcorn.

Potency & Dosage: Follow the standard administration and dosage as under Arsenicum alb. above.

Podophyllum is often the remedy of choice in severe and chronic diarrhea. Dr. M. T. Santwani, in his book *Common Ailments of Children and Their Homoeopathic Management,* writes: "Besides *Chamomilla,* no other remedy is as effective against diarrhea in infants and children as this remedy and is very frequently found indicated for almost any type of diarrhea, as it covers bilious, bloody, changeable, light-colored, coffee-ground-like, flatulent, fermented, spluttering, gelatinous, green, gushing, involuntary when passing flatus [gas], offensive, papescent, profuse, sour, undigested or lienteric, watery, white and yellow stools."[1] The diarrhea of Podophyllum shows a Keynote symptom, a modality, of *worse* in the early morning.

Potency & Dosage: Follow the standard administration and dosage as under Arsenicum alb., above.

Pulsatilla is most often indicated in those children who are known to be intolerant to *fat* and/or *starch.* Fatty, greasy, or starchy foods disagree with a Pulsatilla child. Keynote symptoms of Pulsatilla diarrhea include the following: changeable and variable stools—at one bowel movement watery, at another soft and semisolid. *Changeability* of the stool is the leading Keynote symptom. Diarrhea is *worse* in the evening; associated pains *shift* in the lower abdomen; child wants to pass "gas" but is often unable to do so; the child has a "weepy" disposition and is highly sensitive. The Pulsatilla child desires to be coddled and consoled, and is of a mild temperament.

Potency & Dosage: Follow the standard administration and dosage as under Arsenicum alb., above.

---

1. M. T. Santwani, MD, *Common Ailments of Children and Their Homoeopathic Management* (New Delhi, India: Jain Publishing Co., 1983), 56.

Chapter 5

Vomiting and Nausea

In the *Materia Medica,* the "encyclopedia" of homeopathic remedies listed according to Keynote symptoms, there are dozens of useful candidates for the treatment of vomiting and nausea. This section will present only ten—those that are most often called upon in general practice and that cover the most usual symptoms in infants and children.

Infants "spit up" and there is nothing unusual or alarming in this phenomenon. This is often seen in bottle-fed babies when air is trapped inside the nipple. Keeping the bottle tilted properly prevents this problem. As the child grows older spitting up becomes less and less troublesome and eventually stops altogether. Spitting up is not to be considered vomiting.

> ADVISORY WARNING: Vomiting and nausea in infants and children is usually a symptom of a nonserious problem. Vomiting and/or nausea are not illnesses themselves but are symptomatic of some underlying cause.
>
> However, in some circumstances the cause may be serious. Meningitis, certain serious diseases, Meniere's disease, and even tumors can cause vomiting. *Should the best-selected homeopathic remedy fail to alleviate vomiting and/or nausea within 24 hours, stop the remedy and seek qualified medical attention.*

Of course, continued vomiting, like serious diarrhea, can lead to dehydration in an infant or child. In all such cases, seek and follow qualified professional advice.

HOMEOPATHIC TREATMENT

Aconite
Aethusa cynapium
Antimonium crudum
Arsenicum album
Cocculus
Ipecacuanha
Nux vomica
Pulsatilla
Tabaccum
Veratrum album

Aconite is not often considered in vomiting. Instead it is usually thought of as a paramount remedy for fever when Keynote symptoms agree. However, Aconite is an important remedy in vomiting when the Keynote symptoms are these: vomiting is brought on by *fright* or *fear*; child is full of fear and anxiety and may express fear of dying; vomiting is accompanied by nausea; everything taken by mouth is *bitter* except water; child has intense thirst for *cold* water, drinks, and vomits; child feels a burning sensation from stomach to throat. In Aconite there is also the possibility of increased urination and profuse perspiration.

Potency & Dosage: Use the standard emergency care potencies of 6x or 30x. In acute cases administer a dose of 2–3 tablets every 30 minutes, decreasing the dosage as improvement occurs. In infants, the tablets should be dissolved in a teaspoonful of water. In older children, the tablets may be placed in the mouth or inside the cheek and allowed to dissolve. If a liquid dilution is used, 4 drops in a teaspoonful of water is the standard method of administration. Follow labeling instructions, or use as directed by a health care professional. As symptoms subside, reduce the frequency, then stop the medication.

Aethusa cynapium is not normally available in either the home first-aid kit or the children's kit. However, it is one of the homeopathic medicines most often called upon. The following are Keynote symptoms of Aethusa cyn.: in *infants* who are intolerant to milk, vomiting occurs as soon as milk is drunk, and the vomitus may appear as large curds; vomiting occurs within 30 minutes of eating; violent vomiting is accompanied by a white, frothy material; the child is distressed and experiences great weakness, prostration, and sleepiness; pains are severe and extend from the stomach to the throat, and children who can express how they feel may describe a "bubbling" sensation in the area of the navel; vertigo (dizziness) is felt, and the head is hot to the touch.

Potency & Dosage: Use the 6x or 30x potency, 2–3 tablets, as indicated under Aconite, above.

Antimonium crudum as a diarrhea remedy is determined by mental and gastric symptoms. Its Keynote symptoms include an irritable, peevish, and contradictive disposition, and desire not to be touched; a thick coating of whitish matter on the tongue (considered together, these symptoms are nearly "key" to the selection of Antimonium crud.); constant belching; in the nursing infant, vomiting after nursing and refusal to nurse afterward despite obvious hunger; in the older child, a craving for sour and acid foods.

Potency & Dosage: Employ the 6x or 30x potency, 2–3 tablets, as indicated under Aconite above.

Arsenicum album, well known for diarrhea, is equally valuable in the treatment of vomiting, as its Keynote symptoms present a clear picture of its use. Arsenicum's symptoms are these: distaste for the slightest smell or sight of food, extreme thirst for cold drinks. The child can drink only a little and almost always vomits fluids immediately; heartburn with reflux of acid into the throat; profuse vomiting with great exhaustion. Arsenicum alb. is of special value in the so-called *ptomaine* food poisoning, when spoiled food has been eaten.

Potency & Dosage: Use the 6x or 30x potency, 2–3 tablets. In acute cases give one dose every 30 minutes until symptoms improve. As symptoms greatly lessen, reduce the dosage to 2–3 tablets every 3–4 hours. If liquid dilution is used, the standard dosage is 4 drops in a teaspoonful of water, or as directed by product labeling or on the advice of a health care professional.

Cocculus, derived from the Indian cockle, is exceedingly valuable in the treatment of nausea and/or vomiting whenever symptoms of vertigo (dizziness) are associated. It is a remedy of great usefulness in *motion sickness* from riding (car sickness) or travel on the water (seasickness). Any sort of movement, such as sitting up or turning over in bed, will establish symptoms. Other Keynote symptoms include great dislike of food or drink; nausea with a metallic taste in the mouth; often, abdominal bloating with gas and relief being obtained by lying on one or the other side.

Potency & Dosage: Use the 6x or 30x potency, 2–3 tablets, as indicated under Arsenicum alb. above.

Note: The author has witnessed great success in the symptomatic treatment of Meniere's disease using Cocculus 30x, the excessive and debilitating symptoms of vertigo and dizziness totally clearing after as few as 3 days.

Ipecacuanha (always called simply *Ipecac*), plays an outstanding role in the treatment of vomiting and nausea in children. Its major action is on the pneumogastric nerve. The chief Keynote symptom of Ipecac is *persistent, unrelenting nausea and vomiting.* Other Keynote symptoms include great salivation; vomiting of bitter bile as well as food; a cutting pain around the navel; loss of all appetite; green tar-like stool.

Note: Ipecac is a perfect example of the homeopathic Law of Similars, "let like be cured by like," in its philosophy of treatment. Ipecac is the standard treatment for many forms of poisoning in children, sold in its raw form as syrup of Ipecac. When syrup of Ipecac is given to a child, he or she experiences extreme nausea and persistent, violent vomiting. In its homeopathic potency, Ipecac reverses those same symptoms.

Potency & Dosage: Use in the 6x or 30x potency, 2–3 tablets, as directed under Arsenicum alb. above.

Nux vomica is indicated in nausea and vomiting in children when the Keynote symptoms are considerable retching and continuous desire, but possible inability, to vomit; symptoms *worse* in the morning and after eating, *better* in the evening and while resting.

Potency & Dosage: Use in the 6x or 30x potency, 2–3 tablets, as directed under Arsenicum alb. above.

Note: Homeopaths have found after decades of observation that Nux vomica works best when given in the evening.

Pulsatilla, made from the wind flower, is a remedy of *changeability*. It is best indicated for children whose personalities are mild and gentle. In a Pulsatilla illness, the child will become *changeable,* sad, weepy, crying easily, and exhibiting a contradictory disposition. Other Keynote gastric symptoms include belching, leaving a bitter and long-lasting taste in the mouth; dislike of fatty food, warm food, and warm drinks; *no desire for drinks* (a marked major symptom).

Potency & Dosage: Employ the 6x or 30x potency, 2–3 tablets as a dosage. In acute stages of illness, repeat the dosage every 30 minutes, reducing the dosage to every 3–4 hours as symptoms lessen.

Tabaccum is a homeopathic remedy made from raw tobacco. Anyone who remembers a first experience with tobacco bears an indelible recall of the effects it produces. The symptoms of Tabaccum resemble those of sea-sickness with its giddiness, skin pallor, coldness, icy sweat, and the attendant nausea. Other Keynote symptoms include constant nausea; vomiting from *movement;* giddiness (dizziness and vertigo) caused by motion, producing nausea and vomiting; a sinking feeling at the pit of the stomach.

Potency & Dosage: Use the 6x or 30x potency, 2–3 tablets, as directed under Pulsatilla above.

Veratrum album rounds out the discussion of homeopathic remedies of nausea and vomiting in this chapter. Veratrum alb. is derived from the white hellebore plant and has exceptionally distinctive Keynote symptoms: "a perfect picture of *collapse*" (as described by William Boericke, MD); extreme coldness throughout the body; great weakness; great vomiting with violent retching; desire for *cold* drinks but vomiting as soon as they are swallowed; aggravation of the symptoms from *motion.*

Potency & Dosage: Employ the 6x or 30x potency, 2–3 tablets, as directed under Pulsatilla above.

To close this section on the homeopathic management of vomiting and nausea in children, it should be stated that homeopathic medicines do not mask or merely cover up symptoms. They will not simply treat the outward appearance of a condition. It must be remembered that while vomiting is normally not serious, if the *best-selected* remedy chosen by its Keynote guiding symptoms fails to resolve the condition within 24 hours, or if the symptoms worsen or increase within that time, the child should be examined by a qualified health care professional.

CHAPTER 6

Fever

"Fever is our strongest weapon in the fight of nature against all bacteria; through its influence all healing reactions are accelerated, the heart beats faster in order to carry the blood, containing all healing matters, quicker to all the organs, respiration is speeded up, thus increasing the intake of the all-important oxygen."[1]

Fever has been so highly played up in pseudomedical notions and folklore, as well as in old wives' tales, that parents—especially new and inexperienced parents—have too little understanding, and a great deal of misunderstanding, concerning it. Fever, together with diarrhea and vomiting, sends more parents rushing to the emergency room than almost any other childhood situation outside of injury.

In general considerations, fever is to be favored, not feared. Fever is one of the body's natural defenses against illness of all sorts, and it is important to the healing process. Of itself, fever is not an illness but the outward symptomatic sign that the body is under assault and attempting to defend itself. If the natural immunological defenses of the body are in top working order, the body is well able to defend itself. Homeopathy can assist here better than any other system of health care by stimulating the immune defense system.

"NORMAL" TEMPERATURE IN CHILDREN

The human body's natural temperature is 98.6°F. In children, however, "normal" temperature can vary from that figure slightly, up or down, at various times throughout the day. Because of the uniqueness of each child, "normal" body temperature can vary from child to child. The "normal" temperature range in children is anywhere from 97.1°F to 100°F. Fever might therefore be defined as any rise above "normal" as a result of the body's battling off a bacterial infection or a virus. Most fevers of children are of viral origin. A child's temperature of 100–101°F should be of only mild concern.

> ADVISORY WARNING: Whenever the child's temperature reaches 102°F or higher and remains there for *more than 24 hours,* or if it stays below 101°F but above normal for more than 3 days, the child should receive medical evaluation. A newborn infant with a fever should *always* receive medical attention.

SOME CAUSES OF FEVER IN CHILDREN

Fevers usually result from some kind of infection—bacterial or viral—in a child. They can be caused by many factors such as upper respiratory infections, cold, the "flu," tonsillitis, and middle ear infections. Other causes include childhood immunizations, childhood diseases such as the measles, dehydration due to high activity levels in play, and, in infants, even by overdressing or an overheated room.

SOME COMMONSENSE
MEASURES IN THE MANAGEMENT OF FEVER

Keep the child cool. The child should always be dressed lightly, however. There is no need to pile the child's bed high with heavy blankets; a lightweight sheet will do. Do not turn up the thermostat in the child's room; maintain an even 70°F. In fever there will be some loss of body fluids through dehydration. Keep the child hydrated by giving him or her cool liquids. Drinking water from a safe, approved supply is most recommended. Cool fruit juices are also recommended but *should not replace* plain water.

Years ago the medical profession recommended alcohol sponge baths to bring down fever. *Do not use alcohol* unless specifically ordered to do so by a licensed physician. Alcohol cools the body through its rapid evaporation from the skin's surface and will lower body temperature. However, it produces fumes that the infant or child can inhale, possibly causing serious harm. An ordinary sponge bath with lukewarm water for 15–30 minutes is an acceptable way to deal with fever.

All of the above information is standard medical advice. At this point, traditional allopathic medicine would recommend some brand of chemical antifever medication such as a child's dosage of acetaminophen (e.g., Tylenol) or aspirin. However, some children have adverse reactions to aspirin, such as gastrointestinal bleeding, and in fever following any *viral* infection such as a cold or "flu," giving aspirin can lead to a life-threatening condition of as yet unknown cause called Reye's syndrome.

HOMEOPATHIC MANAGEMENT OF FEVER

Homeopathic medicines do not treat fever—they treat the *whole child* who has a fever. This is a major difference between homeopathic medicine and traditional allopathic medicine. Homeopathy never suppresses a fever as acetaminophen and aspirin do. Why, homeopathy asks, should something that is beneficial to the biology be suppressed?

HOMEOPATHIC TREATMENT

Aconite
Belladonna
Bryonia album
Ferrum phosphoricum

The above list of homeopathic medicines is not exhaustive. A dozen or more remedies listed in the *Materia Medica* have fever as a Keynote symptom. However, the remedies offered here are those most often used to treat a child who has a fever—as always, as the Keynote symptoms of that remedy agree with the symptom picture of the child.

Aconite fever exhibits itself in the following Keynote symptoms: symptoms come on *suddenly;* skin is hot and dry; thirst with restlessness is always present; the child's pulse is easily felt and described as "bounding"; the child is restless, uneasy, very nervous, and full of fear (*great fear* and *fear of death* are often expressed in Aconite).

Note: A "cold stage" of fever also demonstrates itself in an Aconite fever. The Keynote symptoms of this stage are icy coldness of the face; cold sweat; alternating cold and heat; evening chills.

Potency & Dosage: Give Aconite in the standard emergency care potencies of 6x or 30x, 2–3 tablets allowed to dissolve inside the mouth. In infants, Aconite can be administered by dissolving the tablets in a teaspoonful of water. In acute symptoms, one dose every 15–30 minutes until a noticeable reduction in symptoms occurs. As symptoms considerably abate, 1–3 doses may be given, one dose every 3–4 hours, as needed, and stopped.

Belladonna is often called upon in fever and is a homeopathic wonder worker. This remedy's Keynote symptoms are these: fever symptoms come on *suddenly;* the child is thirstless and asks for little or no water or liquids; red flushed face; high temperature; perspiration over the body except the head, which is dry. An odd symptom of Belladonna is that while most of the body is hot, the feet are icy cold.

Potency & Dosage: Give Belladonna as directed under Aconite, above.

Bryonia album (*Bryonia*) in fever is indicated whenever these Keynote symptoms are present: excessive thirst for large amounts of water or other liquids; the child is usually quiet and pale; the child is *worse* from any movement, preferring to lie completely still; full, quick pulse; *worse* from warmth; *better* from cool/cold.

Potency & Dosage: Give Bryonia as directed under Aconite, above.

Ferrum phosphoricum (Ferr. phos.) is a homeopathically prepared mineral compound, *iron phosphate*. The *Materia Medica with Repertory* of William Boericke, MD, states that "In the early stages of febrile [feverish] conditions [Ferrum phosphoricum] stands midway between . . . Aconite and Belladonna . . . The typical *Ferr. phos.* subject is not full blooded and robust, but nervous, sensitive . . ."[2]. The Keynote symptoms of Ferr. phos. are these: fever comes on *gradually;* child's face is red and flushed (but not as violently as in Belladonna); symptoms are *better* from cold applications, such as a cool damp cloth on the forehead.

Potency & Dosage: Give Ferr. phos. in the 3x, 6x, or 30x potency, 2–3 tablets, following the general guiding directions given under Aconite, above.

For feverish conditions, many experienced "homeopathic parents" swear by the combination remedy *ABC* (Aconite nap., Belladonna, Chamomilla). ABC is often referred to as the "ABC's of childhood homeopathy." Its effectiveness is well known. The Chamomilla component of ABC is always indicated in children who are sensitive, irritable, thirsty, and hot, and in those who are restless and peevish whereas they are normally calm and of a mild disposition. The face of a child with Chamomilla symptoms will show *one cheek red and hot; the other cheek cool or cold and pale.*

Homeopathic management of childhood fevers is exceedingly successful because homeopathic remedies are natural and safe to use. They work *with* the body's own natural defense system and never against it. Homeopathy never suppresses symptoms; neither does it mask potentially serious, underlying causes of illness or disease.

---

1. William Gutman, MD, *The Little Homeopathic Physician* (Philadelphia: Boericke & Tafel, Inc., 1961).

2. William Boericke, MD, *Pocket Manual of Homoeopathic Materia Medica,* 9th ed. (Calcutta, India: Sett Day & Co., 1976), 286.

Chapter 7

Ear Infections

Topics Covered

The Structure of the Ear
The Reason Underlying Children's Ear Infections
The Homeopathic Management of Ear Infections
Middle Ear Infection
Simple Earache
External Ear Inflammations
Swimmer's Ear

Ear infections in children from 3 months to 3 years of age provide a large population of patients for pediatricians and family practitioners. Dr. Stephen A. Messer, a family practice naturopathic physician with a specialty in homeopathic medicine, states that "ear infections are a serious health problem for America's children. It has been estimated that over two billion dollars are spent on medical and surgical treatment of otitis media (ear infections) each year."[1]

THE STRUCTURE OF THE EAR

The *external ear,* or *auricle,* the *middle ear,* and the *inner ear* compose the three distinct parts of the complex mechanism that enables us to perceive sounds.

The external ear can be compared to a funnel that catches sound waves and channels them along the narrow canal called the *external auditory meatus*, or ear canal, to the eardrum. This passageway is quite short and is lined with skin called *epithelium*, which secretes wax (cerumen) that both lubricates the ear canal and assists it to trap and then expel any foreign material that may enter the canal. The "eardrum," or *tympanic membrane*, separates the external ear from the middle ear.

Just beyond the eardrum lies the middle ear. Three extremely small bones called the *auditory ossicles* sit adjacent to the eardrum and transfer sound waves into the middle ear as the eardrum vibrates. The chamber of the middle ear is connected to the rear of the throat by the *eustachian tube*. This tube, which is very short in infants and young children, allows an equilibrium of air pressure between both sides of the eardrum.

The inner ear contains a bony labyrinth and a membranous labyrinth that encloses three semicircular canals and a bony *cochlea*. The cochlea appears similar to a snail shell, is divided into chambers, is filled with a fluid required to maintain normal balance, and is lined with fine hairs that transmit sound vibrations along the eighth cranial nerve to the brain, where sounds are perceived and understood. Overall, the ear is an extremely complex and very delicate mechanism.

THE REASON UNDERLYING CHILDREN'S EAR INFECTIONS

Whenever we speak of "ear infection" we actually refer to an inflammation of the middle ear called *otitis media*. There are also inflammations of the external ear, which will be discussed later in this section.

Ear infections afflict hundreds of thousands of children annually. Under standard (allopathic) medical treatment, these infections require antibiotics and sometimes a surgical procedure called *tympanostomy*, in which a small plastic tube is inserted through the eardrum to create a passageway for fluid that forms behind the eardrum to escape into the external ear canal.

A major reason for middle ear infections in children appears to be infectious bacteria that pass from the nose and/or throat through the eustachian tube that leads into the middle ear. Another cause is perforation of the eardrum, which permits bacteria to enter the middle ear.

THE HOMEOPATHIC MANAGEMENT OF EAR INFECTIONS

Dozens of carefully conducted medical studies have been done in the United States, Great Britain, and Europe which show that traditional treatment of otitis media using antibiotics and/or tympanostomy is less effective than would be thought. Children frequently reappear with middle ear infection following such therapy. Homeopathy offers a safe, natural, and effective therapy in the majority of ear infections when the most specific medicine, based upon its guiding Keynote symptoms, is selected. The following approach is indicated for *acute otitis media* at its onset *before* a condition called "otitis media with effusion" develops. *Effusion* refers to the formation of pus behind the eardrum.

MIDDLE EAR INFECTION

If there is any doubt concerning the diagnosis of this condition, the parent(s) should always consult a health care professional for a medical diagnosis and should observe the Advisory Warnings that follow.

The symptoms of acute otitis media frequently occur rapidly and usually include a sudden, severe earache; a possible loss of hearing sensitivity (hearing may be impaired); sleeplessness; nausea, vomiting, diarrhea may be present; fever of 102–103°F or higher.

An additional diagnostic indication of an acute middle ear infection is shown by *painlessness* when the earlobe is gently pulled downward, or inward pressure is applied to the *pinna* (the small cartilaginous projection lying at the middle of the external ear, nearest the face). If the child feels pain from this simple procedure, the problem is most likely an inflammation of the *external* ear. The parent who has been trained in the use of an otoscope or orotoscope[2] to examine the ear will see that the eardrum in acute otitis media appears bright red and opaque and may bulge outward.

HOMEOPATHIC TREATMENT

Aconite
Belladonna
Chamomilla
Ferrum phosphoricum
ABC

Aconite should be considered whenever there is a sudden and very rapid onset of symptoms that are accompanied by *fever*. Additional Keynote symptoms include anxiety, restlessness, tossing about, fear, bright red face.

Belladonna, which is often nearly specific to acute middle ear infection, produces symptoms similar to Aconite through the *sudden* onset of symptoms, but with the notable exception that the child is *not* especially restless. The additional Keynote symptoms of Belladonna include considerable pain in the affected ear; beating, throbbing, or tearing pains deep inside the ear as described by an older child; bright red eardrum upon examination.

Chamomilla, a preeminent children's remedy, is generally keynoted by red face (often with the telltale symptom that one cheek is red and hot and the other cheek pale and cold); violent ear pain, an older child complaining of stitching pain; restlessness and fretfulness; all pain is worse from warmth.

Ferrum phosphoricum (*Ferr. phos.*) is a homeopathic tissue or cell salt—the mineral compound iron phosphate. In acute otitis media its Keynote symptoms are fever of 102–103°F or higher; bright red face; restlessness; *gradual* onset of symptoms (this is the opposite of Aconite and Belladonna); sensitivity to sound in the affected ear; throbbing pain in the ear, or sharp, stitching pains that come and go, as described by an older child.

Note: Ferr. phos., in the author's experience, works best in the lower 3x–6x potency, repeated frequently (every 15–30 minutes) for several hours. Some homeopathic pharmaceutical manufacturers make a mixed potency, 3x–200x, which appears to work especially well in children.

ABC, often available from homeopathic pharmacies in the 6x or 30x potency, is a combination remedy composed of *Aconite, Belladonna,* and *Chamomilla* and covers the broadest symptoms of acute otitis media. This outstanding polypharmacy remedy is seldom available in a commercial first-aid/emergency-care kit or in a children's kit. A parent may easily substitute individual doses of the three remedies using this method: 1 tablet each of Aconite, Belladonna, and Chamomilla following the Potency & Dosage recommendation below.

Potency & Dosage of Remedies Listed: Give the standard emergency care potencies of 6x or 30x. These are the potencies most commonly available in household homeopathic first-aid kits. The standard dosage is 2–3 tablets dissolved on or under the tongue. For infants and small children the tablets may be dissolved in a teaspoonful of water. In acute cases repeat the dosage every 30 minutes for several doses, then as symptoms improve, reduce the frequency of the dose to every 2–3 hours as required until symptoms subside.

> ADVISORY WARNING: If the *best* indicated homeopathic medicine based upon the totality of its Keynote symptoms fails to improve the child's condition greatly within 24 hours, or if the fever remains high or increases, discontinue the medicine and consult a health care practitioner. In *all* cases where fever is accompanied by a headache and stiff neck or whenever the pain extends into the neck, and/or redness and swelling in the neck are observed, seek professional advice at once.

SIMPLE EARACHE

Children often complain of earaches. The simple earache of childhood is *not* accompanied by a fever and is most often caused by environmental factors such as exposure to cold, damp drafts. It may also be brought on by a viral cold extending to the ear, or even by a dental cavity.

HOMEOPATHIC TREATMENT

Chamomilla
Ferrum phosphoricum
Plantago majus tincture
Pulsatilla

Chamomilla is the homeopathic medicine made from the German chamomile flower. It is predominately a children's remedy and is especially useful in the simple earaches of young children. Chamomilla's Keynote symptoms include earache with localized soreness; a feeling that the ear is plugged up; ringing noises in the ear; possible swelling of the external ear with a sensation of heat.

Potency & Dosage: Chamomilla in the 3x, 6x, or 30x potency in dosages of 2–3 tablets. Repeat the lower 3x or 6x potency frequently until symptoms subside.

Ferrum phosphoricum (*Ferr. phos.*), the homeopathic tissue or cell salt, is an oxygen carrier from the blood to areas of inflammation. It is best given in the *early* stages of earache and in frequent doses.

Potency & Dosage: Ferr. phos. in 3x or 6x potency should be given, 2–3 tablets being repeated every 15–30 minutes until symptoms subside. Because of its ability to carry oxygen to the tissues, this remedy is often used as a supplemental treatment no matter what other best indicated medicine might be given.

Plantago majus tincture, an extract of the common plantain herb, is not common in household first-aid kits or children's kits. It is often effective in simple earache, especially if the earache is caused by or accompanies a toothache. In this situation Plantago pulls double duty.

The Keynote symptoms of Plantago are these: earache often accompanies toothache; pain moves between tooth and ear(s); pain passes from one ear to the other; noises are painful.

Potency & Dosage: The tincture, warmed to at least room temperature or body temperature, is instilled into the affected ear, 3–4 drops. If a cavity is present, the tincture can be applied to the painful tooth and will temporarily stop the pain until a dentist can be consulted.

Pulsatilla is a widely used homeopathic remedy and one of the most versatile in children's earaches. Pulsatilla is marked by an interesting characteristic, called a *modality* in homeopathy, which is meaningless in orthodox allopathic medicine. The children who most often benefit from Pulsatilla are sensitive, timid, and gentle and are often characterized as being of a "weepy" disposition. Whenever these mild and highly sensitive children develop an earache, they react by becoming highly emotional, change from their normal personality, and may even become delirious when ill. Keynote symptoms of Pulsatilla are pains characterized by nearly every description: aching, boring, stitching, jerking, a feeling of pressure as if something were pressing from inside the ear outward (aching and outward pressing are two predominate symptoms); pain from the ear traveling through the face on the affected side; pain *worse* from heat and local warm applications (such as warmed ear drops or a warm wash cloth placed over the ear), *worse* toward evening and at night, *better* from cold and cool or cold applications; sometimes, a local discharge from the affected ear, heavy, thick, and yellowish-green.

Potency & Dosage: Use Pulsatilla in the 6x or 30x standard emergency care or children's kit potencies. Give 2–3 tablets dissolved on or under the tongue. In especially acute cases, the dosage may be repeated every 15–30 minutes for several doses. As pain lessens, reduce the repetition of the dosage to 2–3 tablets every 2–3 hours as needed. For infants and small children the tablets may be dissolved in a teaspoonful of water.

External Ear Inflammations

External ear inflammations are characterized by conditions that localize in the ear canal and not behind the eardrum. These conditions are called *otitis externa*—an inflammation of the *external auditory meatus*. There are various causes, which range from too much wax in the ear to a foreign object in the ear such as a dry bean or a small button. A foreign object stuck in the ear must first be removed.

> ADVISORY WARNING: Never dig into the ear canal in an attempt to remove an object. No health care professional would recommend this. Often when a parent or well-meaning adult inserts tweezers or another pointed implement into the ear in an attempt to get the object out, it is only pushed in farther. The adult may attempt to rinse the ear canal out, using an oral medicine syringe or an eye dropper and water, or 3% hydrogen peroxide solution because of its foaming action, to flush out the small object. If the object is a dry bean or pea, this should *not* be done, as the pea or bean will swell and make its removal even more difficult.

Parents should also teach their children, as soon as they are old enough to understand, that the ear is very delicate and easily damaged. Putting anything into the ear (as most health care professionals state, "smaller than an elbow") may lead to trouble. This includes pencils, pens, nails, pins, and toothpicks—any small sharp object.

If no object is detectable in the ear canal, the parent(s) can proceed with the indicated homeopathic treatment.

HOMEOPATHIC TREATMENT

Aconite
Belladonna
Chamomilla
Echinacea tincture
Ferrum phosphoricum
Pulsatilla
ABC

As most of the above remedies have already been presented in considerable detail in the discussion of middle ear infections, they will be given only a passing review here.

A simple diagnostic procedure can be used to determine whether the condition is in the *external* ear. Press gently but firmly on the pinna—the small projection lying midway on the ear near the face. Pull downward gently on the ear lobe. If there is pain the problem is most likely an external ear infection.

Note: Painlessness resulting from this test is suggestive of a middle ear infection.

Let's review the homeopathic remedies quickly for external ear inflammations.

Aconite is characterized by these Keynote symptoms: external ear is hot, red, painful, swollen; ear is painful, with the sensation as if a drop of water were in the ear (especially the left); ear(s) sensitive to sound.

Belladonna produces the Keynote symptoms of a tearing pain in the external ear; considerable sensitivity to loud noises; complaint of noises (humming) in the ear. Belladonna is one of the outstanding remedies for use whenever there is a boil in the ear canal.

Chamomilla is characterized by these Keynote symptoms: ear feels stopped up; pain is *worse* from heat or warmth; pain is violent and stitching; the child is fretful and restless.

Echinacea tincture, an extract of the purple coneflower, is valuable in the external treatment of a boil in the external ear canal or of any local inflammation caused by an insect bite or sting. A diluted solution, 9 parts purified or distilled water to 1 part Echinacea tincture, can be placed into the ear canal and left for several minutes before being allowed to run out. If there is no break in the skin of the ear canal, the undiluted tincture can be applied with a cotton-tipped applicator. *Do not insert the cotton swab any farther than your unaided eye can see.*

Ferrum phosphoricum (Ferr. phos.), the oxygenating tissue remedy in homeopathy, may be used alone as its Keynote symptoms agree, or concurrently with any other best-selected remedy as a valuable adjunct medicine. In an external ear inflammation, its Keynote symptoms are these: throbbing and beating or intermittent, sharp, and stitching pain; sensitivity to sound.

Pulsatilla exerts a strong effect on many external ear inflammations. Its Keynote symptoms are these: pain is *worse* in the evening and/or at night; pain is throbbing, tearing, or darting; ear is hot, red, and swollen.

ABC, the famous combination remedy of many childhood complaints, combines the powers of Aconite, Belladonna, and Chamomilla in a homeopathic polypharmacal medicine of great value. Many parents who rely on the simplicity of prepared combination homeopathic medicines find ABC of exceptional value.

Potency & Dosage of remedies listed: The standard emergency and children's kit potencies of 6x or 30x are normally used. Dosage is 2–3 tablets on or under the tongue and allowed to dissolve. In infants and small children the tablets may be dissolved in a teaspoonful of water. Repeat the dosage as required. In especially acute cases the remedy can be given every 15–30 minutes for several doses and then reduced to one dose every 2–3 hours, stopping as symptoms greatly subside.

SWIMMER'S EAR

This condition, a form of otitis externa, most often occurs as youngsters or teenagers engage in water activities in swimming pools, ponds, or lakes. Usually swimmer's ear is caused by a bacteria or, rarely, by a fungus infection. It most often occurs during the warm summer months. The ears are normally self-cleaning. However, sometimes water becomes trapped by wax accumulated in the ear canal. The result is a breeding ground for bacteria, which produce an acute infection.

The symptoms of swimmer's ear are as follows: The condition often begins with itching in the ear followed by pain. As the ear canal becomes inflamed, the lining of the canal can begin to swell and a loss of hearing sensitivity occurs. Later an oozing discharge may be noticed as the condition becomes advanced.

Prevention of any condition is preferable to cure. Several over-the-counter medicines are available for swimmer's ear that are used for both prevention and treatment. However, a simple home remedy works well as a preventive. Take distilled white vinegar, available in any supermarket, and dilute it to 1 part vinegar to 3 parts water (distilled water or water produced by reverse osmosis is preferred). After swimming, place several drops of the dilution into the ear and allow it to remain for a minute or two. This preventive treatment changes the acid-alkaline (pH) balance of the ear canal and prevents the growth of harmful bacteria. Doctors use a similar treatment, a 0.5 percent acetic acid solution, several drops three times daily for a week, to treat otitis externa.

The homeopathic approach to well-advanced otitis externa is, of course, based upon the totality of the Keynote symptoms. Swimmer's ear is easily and rapidly cured by homeopathic treatment.

HOMEOPATHIC TREATMENT

> *Aconite*
> *Belladonna*
> *Chamomilla*
> *Echinacea tincture*
> *Pulsatilla*
> *ABC*

Because in the symptoms of swimmer's ear the first three homeopathic medicines listed above often overlap, many parents use the combination remedy *ABC,* which is available from most homeopathic pharmacies and in the 6x or 30x potencies. The author has used ABC 30x for several years and has achieved 100 percent success in eliminating swimmer's ear within 24 to 36 hours. As all the remedies listed here have already been discussed in great detail, the reader is asked to refer to the Keynote symptoms under each in the earlier part of this chapter.

CASE HISTORIES

An active swim team competitor and summertime camp staff member of the aquatics program, 16-year-old Jason was constantly developing swimmer's ear. The symptoms were always the same as the condition developed. First Jason's ear canal would itch, and then pain would develop, which he described as "like sharp fingernails tearing at my ear inside." The homeopath gave Belladonna 30x, 2–3 tablets, four times a day, and the condition, caught in the early stages of inflammation, almost always vanished within 24 hours. A few drops of Echinacea tincture were usually placed into the ear as Belladonna was administered internally. Belladonna often works exceedingly well in swimmer's ear, but, as always in homeopathy, treatment must be based on the patient's overall symptoms. Sometimes Pulsatilla is the best-indicated remedy, or the combination remedy ABC, all producing the same excellent results within 24 to 36 hours.

Homeopathy, when it is applied based upon the whole picture of illness that a child exhibits, works and works time and time again. However, some cases can be complicated, as the following case history shows.

Some years ago I was called by a friend to attend her 4-year-old daughter, Jennifer. The girl had become fretful. Her temperature, taken under her arm, was 102°F and rising; she complained of a sore throat and earache.

The little girl's throat was a shiny bright red and her right ear was painful. The sound of the TV at its normal volume bothered her ear. Swallowing was painful. Belladonna was the best-indicated medicine on the basis of these Keynote symptoms: throat bright red and shiny; pain *worse* on the right side and from swallowing fruit juice; hearing sensitive to noise. Twenty-four hours after a few doses of Belladonna 30x had been given, Jennifer was feeling much better. There was no more pain from swallowing juice, milk, or water, and the earache was gone too. A homeopathic success? Not quite. Sometimes the best-indicated remedy will work but fail to "hold." When this happens, homeopaths can judge that either the remedy given did not match the totality of Keynote symptoms, or the remedy was definitely the appropriate one to give but was not "deep acting" enough. Sometimes, if a low potency (3x or 6x) has been given, and the totality of the medicine's Keynote symptoms definitely match the condition, the potency is increased to the next highest available potency (3x to 6x; 6x to 12x or 30x, etc.). But in Jennifer's particular case that would not have worked. Her Keynote symptoms had changed to produce a different symptom picture. One day following the "success" of the Belladonna treatment, she was sick again. Her sore throat returned, but this time on the *left* side, whereas it had first appeared on the right. The throat was dry and red but not shiny red. Unlike before, she was able to drink liquids, but not if they were cold. Her mother was giving her hot tea, which appeared to soothe the child's throat. To make matters more complicated, the earache returned too, but this time on the *left* side, whereas it had been, like the sore throat, on the right only a day before.

If a parent wants to be an in-home homeopath, he or she should not only study the basic remedies thoroughly, but be prepared to repertorize[3] the case. A good homeopathic repertory combined with a *Materia Medica* is an invaluable guide to have, together with an emergency care or children's homeopathic kit. As Jennifer's mother was only slightly acquainted with homeopathy, I showed her Boericke's *Pocket Materia Medica with Repertory.* The little girl's symptoms that had before been Belladonna were now ***Lycopodium.*** Lycopodium is prepared from the finely ground seed spores of the club moss plant. The Keynote symptoms of Lycopodium are these: sore, dry throat is *better* from warm or hot drinks; and—the most useful Keynote symptoms—symptoms begin on the right side and move to the left. This right-to-left movement would mean little or nothing to orthodox health care, but in homeopathy "sidedness," as this phenomenon is called, is all-important. Jennifer received four doses of Lycopodium 30x, and her symptoms disappeared in little more than a day and did not recur.

1. Stephen A. Messer, ND, "Homeopathic Treatment for Ear Infections in Children," *Homeopathic Miscellany* 7 (1987): 3.

2. Some degree of specialized training is needed for use of a physician's otoscope. Another instrument—a home medical device called an orotoscope—is available for parents' use in examining the external ear canal and eardrum of a child. Far less expensive than an otoscope and simple to use, the orotoscope is a penlight flashlight with a curved fiberoptic "tongue blade" attachment that enables examination of the mouth and throat. The device is available from the Piper Brace Sales Corporation, 811 Wyandotte, PO Box 807, Kansas City, MO 64141. Detailed instructions for its use are included.

3. A sick person often exhibits several Keynote Symptoms. We repertorize the patient by selecting several prominent symptoms and the remedies listed under each symptom. The remedies that recur under the *majority* of these symptoms are then carefully studied. The remedy that recurs most often under the totality of symptoms is the one that most closely matches the "symptom picture" of the illness, and is therefore the remedy of choice in that particular illness.

CHAPTER 8

Tonsillitis and Sore Throat

In the world over, sore throats in children cause more lost school days than are caused by the flu.

As this section discusses both sore throats and tonsillitis, parents should be aware that there is a difference between the two conditions. The common sore throat, or *pharyngitis,* is most often brought on by exposure to a virus rather than to bacteria. Viral sore throats are self-limiting conditions that usually disappear in a few days as rapidly as they came on. While 80–85 percent of children's sore throats are viral, the remainder are caused by a bacterial overgrowth due to a weakening of the immune system—the body's natural defense against illness. *Streptococcus* and, less commonly, *Staphylococcus* bacteria are the usual infective agents.

Tonsillitis is differentiated from the common sore throat in that its most common cause is a bacterial infection, usually by *Streptococcus.* In tonsillitis the tonsils become inflamed, creating severe pain on swallowing. The pain often shoots into the ears, and the child experiences a fever of 102–103°F or higher, accompanied by weakness, tiredness, and often headache and vomiting.

Note: Most children vomit when they have tonsillitis; vomiting is common in children. But not all children with tonsillitis vomit, and not all have a headahe. Each child is different.

In treating the common viral sore throat, the medical community is still divided as to whether an appropriate antibiotic should be given. Antibiotics, it should be remembered, have no effect on viruses. Many pediatricians and family practitioners recommend a simple home treatment of rest, a nonaspirin pain reliever such as Tylenol, and salt water or hydrogen peroxide gargles.

> ADVISORY WARNING: Because of an increase in the incidence of a life-threatening disease called Reye's syndrome in children between 5 and 18 years of age, parents are advised *not to give aspirin* to children who have or have just recovered from any illness caused by a virus such as a viral sore throat, the flu, or chicken pox.
>
> The cause of Reye's syndrome is unknown, but there appears to be a link between the disease, a recent viral illness, and the use of aspirin. If your child begins to vomit frequently during a viral infection or shortly thereafter, consult a physician immediately. Suspect Reye's syndrome, the first symptom of which is always persistent, unrelenting vomiting. In the later stages of the disease, the child becomes listless, shows little energy, has no desire to play, and may begin to show definite personality changes. These changes may include combativeness, disorientation, and even seizures, and can occur very rapidly, in 6 to 36 hours.
>
> For more detailed information on Reye's syndrome, the parent is encouraged to call the National Reye's Syndrome Foundation, Bryan, Ohio: (419) 636-2679.

It is often in the common sore throat and tonsillitis that homeopathic medicine best shows its great healing power. Homeopathy can successfully treat both the bacterial and the viral sore throat. The parent must watch the child carefully, closely noting all symptoms. If the child is old enough, ask questions, and from the response select the medicine that *most closely matches* the totality of the Keynote symptoms. Marked improvement or complete remission of symptoms can usually be expected in as little as 24 to 36 hours.

HOMEOPATHIC TREATMENT

> *Aconite*
> *Apis mellifica*
> *Belladonna*
> *Hepar sulphuris calcareum*
> *Lachesis*
> *Lycopodium*
> *Phytolacca*

Aconite, made from the monkshood plant, is most effective in the *earliest* acute symptoms of sore throat and tonsillitis. It tends to be less effective or ineffective as the condition becomes advanced. The Keynote symptoms of Aconite are these: throat is red and dry; throat feels constricted (closed up); child complains of pain and difficulty in swallowing or talking; throat is redder than normal but *not* deep-red or glossy-shiny; child may complain of burning pain or "pin-pricking" sensations; child has a marked dislike of *either* cold or hot drinks.

Apis mellifica (*Apis mel.*) is made from the common honey bee and is a major homeopathic medicine for children's sore throats. The Keynote symptoms of Apis are swelling of the throat, both inside and outside; stinging pains (like a bee sting on swallowing); a feeling as if the throat is constricted (closed up); fire-red, puffy tonsils and often a swollen, fire-red *uvula* (the small bag-shaped projection at the back of the throat); a feeling as if a pin, sharp object, or fishbone were stuck in the throat; all symptoms made *worse* by heat, swallowing warm or hot liquids, pressure applied against the throat, and touch, and made *better* by cold drinks.

Belladonna, another often-considered, major medicine for sore throat and tonsillitis, has these Keynote symptoms: throat is dry, bright red, and shiny; throat feels constricted (closed up); child shows extreme difficulty in swallowing and may complain of feeling a lump in the throat; throat is *worse* on the right side and is made worse by all swallowing, touch, or pressure.

Hepar sulphuris calcareum (*Hepar sulph.*), the great mineral compound developed by the founder of homeopathy, Samuel Hahnemann, MD, is characterized by these Keynote symptoms: stitching pains in the throat that move into the ear on swallowing; a feeling as if something were stuck in the throat; painful attempts to get up a thick, clinging mucus from the throat and to clear the throat (often called "hawking"); abscessed or ulcerated appearance of the tonsils; throat *worse* from cold and from touch and *better* from warmth (such as warm drinks and warm applications) and after eating.

Lachesis is a masterful homeopathic medicine made from the venom of the Surucucu snake. In its homeopathic potency of 6x or higher it is perfectly harmless but extremely effective in conditions that agree with its Keynote symptoms. Lachesis produces, and therefore cures, the sore throat that has these symptoms: very dry; greatly swollen both inside and outside; there is pain from the slightest touch and pressure; the throat appears a purple-red, dusky color and the tonsils appear dark colored and purplish; pain runs from the throat into the ear; *severe* sore throat; child tries to clear the throat but clinging mucus cannot be brought up; condition is *worse* on the left side, on swallowing liquids; *worse* by hot drinks, but *better* from warm applications to the outside of the neck.

Lycopodium, made from the club moss, is a very powerful homeopathic medicine in children's sore throats. Lycopodium shows an odd characteristic of both "sidedness" and "periodicity." The symptoms of an illness that Lycopodium will treat *always* begin on the right side and either remain on the right side or move from right to left. Symptoms of the illness generally begin from 4:00 to 8:00 PM. If those special conditions are present and the other Keynote symptoms agree, Lycopodium is the medicine of choice.

Keynote symptoms also include these: throat is *dry*; child is thirsty; throat is inflamed and there are stitching pains on swallowing; anything the child eats or drinks is often forced upwards into and through the nose; symptoms are made *worse* by cold drinks and *better* by warm drinks.

Phytolacca, the homeopathic medicine prepared from the poke root, is another commonly used remedy in sore throats. The Keynote symptoms of Phytolacca are these: throat is dark red to blue in color; soft palate (the soft fleshy part of the throat just behind the roof of the mouth) is sore, and tonsils are swollen and dark red or blue; base of the tongue is sore and painful; pains from swallowing shoot into the ears; throat feels burning hot, and it is hard to swallow any drinks; as the inflammation advances, the throat and the tonsils become ulcerated and show gray-white spots, and a thick yellow mucus clings to the throat and tonsils; swallowing is *worse* from hot drinks and on the right side; in tonsillitis only the right tonsil is usually affected.

Potency & Dosage of Remedies Listed: The above-named homeopathic medicines are available in the standard emergency homeopathic kit in either the 6x or 30x potencies. The standard dosage is 2–3 tablets taken in the mouth, dissolved on or under the tongue and not swallowed. For infants and very young children, the tablets may be dissolved in a teaspoonful of water. In the early acute stages of the illness, a dose may be given every 15–30 minutes, the dosage frequency then being reduced to once every 2–3 hours until a noticeable lessening of the symptoms occurs. If the best-selected homeopathic medicine fails to produce improvement in the child's condition within 24 hours, reread the remedies' Keynote symptoms for the next closest remedy.

CHAPTER 9

Diaper Rash, Teething, and Thrush

DIAPER RASH

This skin problem is perhaps the most common cause of annoyance and irritation to parents and their infant children.

How often mothers and fathers feud over this condition! As well, how frequently families are hotly divided in the cause, and cure, of irritation to children's bottoms. Over the years, the author has been caught in the middle of spirited debates between mothers and their adult-parent children: "When *you* were a baby, I never allowed *you* to get diaper rash." And, "If you listened to *my* advice, Jennifer (or Johnny) wouldn't have this problem!"

Some babies never get diaper rash. Others suffer from this irritating condition almost constantly, to the consternation of the best of caring parents. In part, the debate focuses on "old-fashioned" cloth versus modern plastic disposable diapers. It is a debate that about 40 percent of American hospital nurseries are currently involved in, experimenting to determine which is better—cloth or disposable.

The family feuds over diaper rash tend to ignore a basic and vital fact that homeopathy has never ignored: *all children are unique; each is an individual.*

The author's observation is that in a majority of cases, when cloth diapers are properly washed in a hypoallergenic soap or detergent and

76

properly rinsed to remove as much soap or detergent residue as possible, and when babies are changed as soon as they soil their diaper, they are less likely to suffer diaper rash. However, this is not always true.

A new young mother recently visited with me. Her 7-month-old son was continually plagued by the most serious diaper rash. His skin was red and raw, at times even blistered and bleeding. The mother was beside herself. Her husband had accused her of neglect, and both her own mother and her mother-in-law were outraged. She had been to a family physician who advised her to change the diaper the instant it was soiled, thoroughly clean the baby's skin, make certain the skin was absolutely dry, and apply an ointment that prevented moisture from reaching the surface of the baby's delicate skin. Nothing had worked. She experimented with advanced-design disposable diapers with "moisture barriers" and impregnated with a gel that instantly absorbed wetness, pulling it away from the baby's skin. The diaper rash continued. She had switched to cloth diapers and hypoallergenic laundry products and closely followed washing directions. The diaper rash still continued.

CANDIDA ALBICANS:
A CONTRIBUTING FACTOR IN CHRONIC DIAPER RASH

At fault in some serious rashes, when the best treatment advice has failed, is a "yeast" infection called *Candida albicans*. Actually not a yeast but a fungus, *Candida* is an opportunistic organism that requires both moisture and warmth to flourish. In ideal conditions, human skin has a natural acid/alkaline balance called pH that maintains skin health. In the case of newborns and children not yet toilet trained, whenever the skin comes into contact with urine and the moisture of fresh feces, the natural pH balance is disrupted, and the *Candida* fungus takes advantage rapidly. The skin becomes red and raw; it may even blister and bleed. By the way, this fungus is the selfsame one that causes the common thrush (trench mouth) infection common in many infants and is, in fact, the same fungus that causes vaginal "yeast" infections experienced by so many women. Therefore, if your child has a chronic diaper rash despite your best efforts, *Candida albicans* fungus may be a causative factor.

HOMEOPATHIC TREATMENT

Calendula ointment
Hypericum

Chief among the homeopathic remedies available for diaper rash is **Calendula**. The healing properties of this medicine made from the African marigold are legendary. Available in lotion, ointment, and gel forms, as well as in non–alcohol-containing liquid preparations, Calendula offers the best homeopathic approach to diaper rash. Following commonsense practices in the cleaning and changing of infants and then applying Calendula, parents frequently find that the rash heals rapidly. Used at changings, a small amount of Calendula smoothed over the skin and gotten well into the folds most often prevents diaper rash from recurring.

Another remedy parents might consider if their child's rash is especially severe is **Hypericum**. Like Calendula, Hypericum is available in lotion and ointment forms and is most useful whenever the skin is angry-red and raw. In fact, combining the two remedies (since the author knows of no combination of Hypericum and Calendula currently available as an ointment or lotion) may resolve the most serious diaper rash, to the relief of baby and parent.

A word of caution here. If Calendula or Hypericum is available to you only in tincture form, which contains alcohol, it will "burn" the skin. The tincture must be diluted in a ratio of 1 part remedy and 3 parts water before use.

ADDITIONAL ADVICE

In their excellent book *Everybody's Guide to Homeopathic Medicines,* Stephen Cummings, F.N.P., and Dana Ullman, M.P.H., recommend treating the skin of infants experiencing *Candida* as a contributing factor in diaper rash with "[distilled white] vinegar diluted half- or quarter-strength."[1] The diluted vinegar, which is 5 percent acetic acid, slows the growth of the *Candida* fungus and helps to restore the skin's ideal pH balance. Parents should allow the diluted vinegar solution to dry and also apply Calendula as directed above, two or three times a day.

Earlier in this section, I mentioned the new young mother who was in such despair over her son's severe diaper rash. She has gone back to disposable diapers, but used both a quarter-strength dilution of distilled white vinegar and Calendula gel. The rash began to heal immediately, whereas everything she attempted prior to homeopathic treatment had disappointed her. At last report, her son's skin has returned to normal and remained so. I had also recommended to her that as the child was taking 2 percent milk occasionally, as well as formula and solid foods as approved by her own family physician, she should substitute a fresh acidophilus milk. *Lactobacillus acidophilus* is an active bacteria contained in high-quality yogurts. Also available in fresh acidophilus milk, it promotes the growth of beneficial "friendly" intestinal flora and appears to have an inhibiting effect on the growth of *Candida albicans*.

TEETHING

Another troublesome problem of infants occurs at teething time. The baby becomes difficult, whines and cries, and chews on everything available—sometimes even on mother. Of course, all this ruckus occurs from the deciduous teeth forcing their path through the child's tender gums.

HOMEOPATHIC TREATMENT

> *Chamomilla*
> *Belladonna*
> *ABC*

Few homeopathic medicines are used more often for teething infants than ***Chamomilla***. It presents the most often experienced Keynote symptoms, chief among which are the Mentalities—whining restlessness, when nothing wanted by the child that is given pleases; and snappish, irritable behavior. The child needing Chamomilla will normally show a calm and even-tempered disposition (barring those "moments" all children experience). Suddenly, as dentition (cutting of teeth) sets in, the child turns into a "little monster." The Chamomilla child can be quieted for a time, but only by being carried, caressed, and cooed over. Other Keynote symptoms indicating Chamomilla include these: one cheek red and hot, the other cheek pale and cool; slightly feverish; the forehead warm; diarrhea during teething.

Potency & Dosage: Chamomilla works well in a broad range of available potencies, the most favored being 3x, 6x, or 6c. Experience shows that the mid-range 30x potency, that found in many homeopathic home first-aid kits, works well too. In small children, 3–5 tablets are dissolved in a teaspoonful of water and the dosage given every 2–3 hours as needed. The tablets may also be held against the lower gums or inside the cheek and allowed to dissolve. Homeopathic tablets are soft and dissolve in seconds, allowing the medicine to be absorbed directly through the mucous membranes of the mouth.

Belladonna is another remedy to consider in teething. Its Keynote symptoms are quite opposite to those of Chamomilla: child is irritable but not as difficult or ill-tempered as the child described under Chamomilla; skin is red and flushed; child is feverish; child may strike out at anyone around, or bite.

Potency & Dosage: Belladonna should not be used below the 6x potency, and that potency to the 30x works well. Administer as under Chamomilla, above.

ABC, mentioned elsewhere in this book, is a combination remedy composed of Aconite, Belladonna, and Chamomilla. The Aconite in ABC contributes in the treatment of teething problems where its Keynote symptoms are present: early onset of fever; skin is hot and dry, and face is flushed; child is sensitive to noise; child shows signs of considerable anxiety and is noisy, restless, and obviously distressed.

Potency & Dosage: ABC is most often offered as a proprietary remedy specialty by homeopathic pharmaceutical manufacturers in the 6x or 3c potencies. The remedy may be given every 2–3 hours as needed until symptoms subside. Dissolve 3–5 tablets in a teaspoonful of water, or hold tablets against the cheek or gums until they have dissolved.

THRUSH

Thrush, whose common name is trench mouth, is a common disorder in newborns and infants. As has been earlier mentioned, the cause of thrush is a fungus, *Candida albicans.*

The symptoms of thrush are unmistakable—white patches that are slightly raised above the surface, resemble small-curd cottage cheese, and appear usually first on the tongue and the mucous membrane lining of the mouth. As thrush spreads it does so to the roof of the mouth and gums, and sometimes to the throat. The mouth often appears to be dry.

In newborns and infants, the body's natural biological defense mechanism—the immune system—is just beginning to develop. The causative factor of thrush, *Candida albicans,* opportunistically takes advantage of this weakness, and thrives. As has been earlier stated, severe and chronic diaper rash is often abetted by a thrush infection.

Another causative factor in thrush is the use or overuse of antibiotic therapy. Antibiotics are the most commonly prescribed (and some physicians say the most overprescribed) drugs in modern medicine. Antibiotic therapy is designed to directly destroy or otherwise impair the growth of susceptible bacteria. The intestinal tract is the home of many beneficial "friendly" bacteria, called "intestinal flora," that are a normal part of the human biological machine. These friendly bacteria are required for the proper and full absorption of nutrients taken in through food. Antibiotics not only destroy or interfere with disease-causing bacteria but diminish or destroy these beneficial bacteria as well. Parents often observe that their child develops thrush during or shortly following a course of antibiotic therapy.

HOMEOPATHIC TREATMENT

Borax

This homeopathic medicine is made from the mineral borax and is considered nearly specific to thrush infections regardless of the cause. The Keynote symptoms of ***Borax*** are dryness of the mouth and raised white patches on the tongue, roof of mouth, or gums.

Potency & Dosage: The 3x, 6x, or 30x potencies of Borax work well. Give Borax, 3–5 tablets dissolved in a teaspoonful of water, or hold tablets against the inside of the cheek or on the gums until they have dissolved. Repeat this treatment three times daily until symptoms subside.

---

1. Stephen Cummings and Dana Ullman, *Everybody's Guide to Homeopathic Medicines* (Berkeley, CA: North Atlantic Books, 1984), 213.

Part II

Childhood Injuries, Their Prevention, and Homeopathic Treatment

CHAPTER 10

Prevention of Injuries

In their order of frequency, the most common causes of personal injury to children from birth through the early teenage years are *burns, drowning, suffocation* and *strangulation, falls, poisoning, outdoor injuries,* and *injuries from toys.*[1]

Children seem prone to accidental injury, and more children are injured in and around the home than anywhere else. Statistics show that boys are more likely to be injured than girls, and those who are injured are more likely to be hyperactive, impulsive, and daring. In recent years, children, their parents, their teachers, and other supervisors of childhood activities have been trained and counseled in injury prevention, safety procedures, and health. Yet children continue to suffer from the accidents of childhood, even when and where they are properly supervised.

"An ounce of prevention is worth a pound of cure" is of course the best advice, and most parents and supervisors of children follow this ancient saying. Burns can be mild to extremely severe, disfiguring, and even lethal. Yet many household burns can easily be prevented when parents follow simple common sense. Small children should never be permitted in the kitchen during meal preparation. The handles of cooking pots, pans, and skillets should always be turned away from the stovetop edge and out of reach of small inquisitive hands. The temperature of the household water heater should be set, according to standard medical advice, at a maximum of 125°F, and the temperature of the bath or shower water always checked first by an adult before a youngster is permitted to enter. When vaporizers are used around children, cool-water models are preferred over the traditional hot-vapor models. Many burns could easily be prevented if parents would always think **Hot Hurts!** *Anything* hot should be kept away from infants and small children. Too often overlooked by parents are adult hot drinks—cups of coffee, tea, and hot cocoa placed within easy reach of a young child's hands.

Strangulation and suffocation are easily prevented. Safety requirements for infant cribs and young children's beds are now well established; yet, in the United States hundreds of accidents occur when children stick their heads through rails placed too widely apart. Most often this occurs because a hand-me-down crib or baby bed has been used, built before strict construction standards applied. A rail may be loose or broken. Some parents and well-meaning family friends purchase over-the-crib toys for infants that attach to the top siderails, either clamped on or tied down. After about 4 months of age, most infants are able to coordinate their growing muscles enough to raise themselves up, often to fall neck-downward against the bar or chord that suspends these toys. Too often, unable to wriggle free, they strangle. Obviously, plastic bags of all kinds must never be left lying around the house whenever infants and small children are around.

In a multistoried house or apartment, low windows must be made secure against falls. Parents must never depend on only a screen to prevent a child from falling through a window. Tables, chairs, bookcases, and other furniture must always be moved away from beneath the windows. Stairways leading to the basement, the attic steps, and steps leading from a back or front porch must be covered with an approved childproof cover gate.

All household cleaning chemicals must be kept either *high* up in the kitchen or pantry, or in *locked* cabinets. All medicines, both over-the-counter and prescribed, must be kept away from inquisitive youngsters. Parents and babysitters often believe, falsely, that cleaning chemicals, because they smell bad or "must certainly have a bad taste" pose no really serious problem. This is wrong-headed thinking! Many household cleaners smell good, and a young child whose taste is still developing may not notice any bitterness until the chemical is inside the mouth or already swallowed. Too many adults forget that children will get into a basement or garage where chemicals—gasoline, paints, and garden insecticides—are stored. Whenever young children are around, all these must be placed *high* and made impossible to reach, or better, locked away. Never place any chemicals inside other kinds of containers. This author himself experienced a childhood poisoning when his own extremely conscientious mother placed cleaning fluid in a cough syrup bottle, forgetting to remove the label and relabel the bottle with its current contents.

Children cannot protect themselves. As long as children are inquisitive, fascinated by the indoor and outdoor world around them, and unable to capably think for themselves, all adults must do so for them.

---

1. Robert A. Dershewitz, MD, ScM, "Safety Procedures That Prevent Childhood Injuries in the Home," *Medical Aspects of Human Sexuality: A Journal for Physicians Covering the Physical, Psychologic, and Cultural Components of Family Life* 18 (October 1984).

CHAPTER 11

Shock

Many decades of experience of people the world over show that homeopathic treatment, given as soon as possible after an injury, speeds healing, prevents prolonged suffering, and reduces the possibility of complications. In children, homeopathy invariably enables a rapid recovery.

Shock should be suspected in *every* case of accidental injury to a child. As every human being is unique, some children will react more strongly to shock than others. Unfortunately, many people—parents included—believe that shock occurs only in the most serious accidents. This is demonstrably untrue.

Homeopathic medicine recognizes two forms of shock: *physiological* and *psychic* or *emotional*. The symptoms of physiological shock are pale, light-gray, or white skin tone; profuse perspiration (sweating); pupils of the eyes fixed (unmoving) and dilated (wide open); and lethargy or even unconsciousness.

HOMEOPATHIC TREATMENT

Arnica montana
Aconite

Arnica montana (*Arnica*) is the first homeopathic remedy to consider in both physiological and psychic shock. It is both preventive (prophylactic) of shock and curative when given immediately following an injury. No harm and only benefit, real or potential, can come from administering a dose or two of Arnica.

Note: Arnica has similar symptoms to those of Aconite in psychic shock, but not the same symptoms, and every parent should memorize them. The Keynote symptoms of Arnica are these: fear of being touched; unconsciousness; indifference, nervousness, delirium, extreme oversensitiveness throughout the body; and possibly, the statement that there is nothing wrong.

Potency & Dosage: Give Arnica in the 6x, 30x, or 200x (or c) potency as soon as possible after an injury. In the 200x potency, it should be given sparingly: 1 or 2 doses some 30 minutes apart. Homeopathic "high" potencies (above 30x) are highly reactive, especially in children. In the lower 30x or 6x potency, Arnica can be given, 2–3 tablets every 15–30 minutes until symptoms subside, placed directly on the tongue or inside the cheek and permitted to dissolve.

ADVISORY WARNING: No liquids should ever be given to an unconscious person, regardless of age. Unconscious persons may choke and inhale liquids into the lungs.

In tablet or pellet form, Arnica can be given with total confidence even to an unconscious person.

Aconite is a homeopathic remedy for psychic (emotional) shock that results from fear or extreme fright. The Keynote symptoms of Aconite are as follows: great fear and anxiety from any injury or illness regardless of how minor; restlessness; fear of death; difficult breathing, shortness of breath on the least movement brought on from fright or fear.

Potency & Dosage: Aconite is used in the same way as Arnica, above.

CHAPTER 12

Injuries to Bones and Joints

TOPICS COVERED

Fractures
Sprains
Bone Bruises

FRACTURES

Children are usually highly active. Hard, sometimes rough, play and sports activities of every kind all contribute to the possibility of broken bones. Homeopathic medicines cannot, of course, set a fracture. That must be done by an experienced and skilled physician. However, following the medical reduction of a fracture, homeopathy can greatly speed the healing time required for the bone(s) to reknit and reduce pain and discomfort.

Suspect a fracture whenever there is swelling at the site of injury, localized pain at the slightest touch or movement, or any deformity of the injured body part. Sometimes it is difficult to differentiate a fracture from a sprain. Generally, a sprain will distribute pain over a larger area; in a fracture, the pain tends to localize at the site of injury. Often only an x-ray can determine positively whether an injury is a fracture or a sprain.

ADVISORY WARNING: Never place pressure on a suspected fracture or needlessly move any body part—arm, leg, neck—as this may cause additional injury and can send the victim into deep shock. In *all* cases of suspected fracture, search out medical attention as soon as possible.

HOMEOPATHIC TREATMENT

Arnica montana
Symphytum

Arnica montana (*Arnica*) should be the first remedy to consider if a fracture is suspected. Remember that Arnica is of great value in possibly preventing shock and certainly in treating it. Shock will certainly be present to some extent in a fracture injury. To refresh the reader's memory, the major symptoms of shock are as follows: pale, grayish, or white skin tone; profuse perspiration (sweat); fixed (unmoving) or dilated (wide open) pupils of the eyes; lethargic, "shocky," or even unconscious condition.

Potency & Dosage: Arnica in the 30x or 200 (x or c) potency, 2–3 tablets for one or two doses, is often sufficient to prevent shock from setting in an will also greatly assist in the recovery from shock if the condition is present. If the 30x or 200 potency is unavailable, Arnica in whatever lower potency is available (6x, 12x) may be substituted. For the lower potencies, repeat the 2–3 tablet dosage every 15 minutes for several doses. The symptoms of shock should begin to clear quite rapidly.

Symphytum is the homeopathic remedy of choice in postfracture treatment after the bone has been medically set. Two or three 2–3 tablet doses of Symphytum 6 times daily for several weeks will promote bone healing. Homeopathic clinical studies have shown that this treatment can reduce healing time by 50–75 percent.[1]

SPRAINS

Sprains are the results of injuries to the tough connective tissues called *ligaments* surrounding the joints. In children the most common joints to be sprained are the ankles, wrists, and thumbs. Sprains can be mild, moderate, or severe, and in some instances a sprain can be far more painful and debilitating than a fracture.

Recall the general symptoms of a sprain; *pain,* over a broader and more general area at the site of injury; swelling, often with bruised discoloration of the tissues; and tenderness to touch.

General first-aid treatment is required in all sprains. First, remember H.R.I.C.E.H., and in all cases of physical injury, give a dose of **Arnica montana,** 30x or 200 (x or c) or 6x, which will relieve the pain quite rapidly.

H.R.I.C.E.H. stands for *Homeopathic Remedy* (given at once to speed healing and pain relief), *Rest* (keep the injured body part motionless), *Ice* (place an ice pack or chemical cold pack directly over the injury site for 10 minutes every hour), *Compression* (apply an elastic bandage over and above the injury site; this will help reduce swelling and also immobilize the joint to prevent any further injury), *Elevation* (raise the site of injury above heart level to reduce inflammation and allow body fluids to drain), and *Heat* (after initial cold treatment, usually in 24 hours, apply heat to the injury). Heat, like elevation, helps the body eliminate excess fluids and reduce inflammation.

HOMEOPATHIC TREATMENT

> *Rhus toxicodendron*
> *Bryonia*

Rhus toxicodendron (*Rhus tox.*) is made from the poison ivy plant. Again we see the homeopathic principle "Let like be cured by like" in the use of Rhus tox. in the treatment of most sprains when the Keynote symptoms agree. In its pure form, poison ivy extract produces, in a healthy person, painful tenderness and stiffness in the joints, tendons, and ligaments. If a sprained joint produces similar symptoms, Rhus tox. is the homeopathic remedy of choice, as it is in most cases. The Keynote symptoms of Rhus tox. are these: hot, painful swelling of joints; tearing pains in joints, tendons, ligaments; pains made *worse* by cold and by rest; pain made *better* by warmth, warm applications, and movement.

Potency & Dosage: Give Rhus tox. in the standard emergency care potency of 6x or 30x, 2–3 tablets. In cases of acute injury a dose may be given every 15–30 minutes for several doses. As pain lessens, reduce the dosage to 2–3 tablets every 3–4 hours, discontinuing treatment when a noticeable improvement occurs.

Bryonia album (*Bryonia*) is made from wild hops, and in sprains shows these Keynote symptoms: hot swelling of joints; red area surrounding the joint; pain made *worse* by all movement and *worse* by warmth and warm applications.

Potency & Dosage: Give Bryonia in the 6x or 30x potency, 2–3 tablets, as described under Rhus tox. above.

CASE HISTORY OF THE HOMEOPATHIC TREATMENT OF A SPRAIN

Kent was a 16-year-old boy at a summer camp. During a good-natured swimming competition with friends, he forcefully rammed his hand into the pool wall, severely injuring his thumb. The thumb was extremely tender and began to swell immediately. He could not move the thumb without a good deal of pain. An ice pack applied at the pool should have relieved some of the pain but did not. The arm was elevated to assist in reducing swelling, and Arnica 30x was given, one dose. Because the swelling was so severe it was not possible to tell whether a Keynote symptom —better or worse from movement—was present. It was decided to take the boy to the local clinic for evaluation of the injury. X-ray showed the injury to be a third-degree sprain with probable damage to the joint capsule. Kent was told by the attending physician that the thumb would be painful and useless for at least 2 weeks. After 24 hours, the swelling around the joint of the thumb remained as severe as the day before, and all attempted movement was impossible and extremely painful. On the basis of this symptom,

Bryonia 30x was given. One day later the boy was seen again. He had taken off the elastic bandage. Swelling had nearly disappeared, and he had almost free and painless movement of this thumb. How rapidly the correctly prescribed homeopathic remedy had worked!

In the above-mentioned case history, Bryonia was the *most similar* remedy to the injury. Had Rhus tox. been given instead, there would probably have been some overall improvement but not as rapid a healing as when the correct remedy was administered.

Parents should remember the difference between these two outstanding sprain remedies:

Rhus toxicodendron: *better* from movement, *worse* from cold.

Bryonia: *worse* from movement, *better* from warmth.

And, of course, if it is available, always give at least one dose of Arnica montana for pain and to prevent the possibility of even mild shock.

BONE BRUISES

A bone bruise is a common minor injury in children, especially those who participate in soccer or hockey, where a good kick to the shin is common as the players tussle for the ball or jostle for the puck. It occurs in children during friendly backyard games.

A bone bruise is an injury to the thin covering of bone called the *periosteum*. It differs only from a soft-tissue bruise in that it occurs to the skeletal system instead of the soft tissues. As with a bruise, however, pain, local tenderness, some swelling, and discoloration of the skin are symptomatic.

HOMEOPATHIC TREATMENT

Arnica montana
Ruta graveolens
Symphytum

Arnica montana (*Arnica*) is always called for in bruising injuries, especially to help speed relief of pain and to assist in the repair of underlying damage to the soft-tissue structures. A dose of Arnica in 30x or 6x potency is always helpful. More specific to a bone bruise, however, is *Ruta graveolens (Ruta grav.)*, made from the common garden rue. A deep-acting homeopathic remedy, Ruta will greatly assist in bringing about a rapid healing of this injury. The Keynote symptoms of Ruta are these: pain and stiffness in the hands and wrists; soreness in tendons; pain in the thighs when stretching the legs; pain in the bones; aching pain in the Achilles tendon.

Potency & Dosage: Give Ruta in the standard emergency care potency of 6x or 30x, 2–3 tablets allowed to dissolve in the mouth every 2–3 hours, repeating a dose whenever there is a recurrence of pain. Ruta ointment is also useful when applied directly to the skin's surface, as an adjunctive treatment for internal medication.

Symphytum is a homeopathic remedy derived from the comfrey herb. Its common name is boneset. While Ruta grav. is most often called upon in the treatment of a bone bruise, sometimes it will fail to "hold," and should this occur, Symphytum, a deeper-acting remedy than Ruta, may be substituted. Its Keynote symptoms include the following: injuries to the periosteum and tendons; pricking pain and soreness in the periosteum. Symphytum also acts on the body's joints in general.

Potency & Dosage: Symphytum 6x is often a preferred potency in periosteal injury, although its work is remarkable in the lower 3x and in the higher 30x potencies. As is usual in homeopathy, the lower (3x, 6x) potencies bear repetition of dosage longer than the higher potencies. Follow the dosage instructions given for Ruta. Symphytum is also available in an ointment, which can be applied locally to the site of injury for considerable relief from painful soreness.

---

1. "Homeopathy and Sports Medicine," *American Homeopathy,* Professional Edition 1 (1984): 5.

CHAPTER 13

Injuries to the Soft Tissues

TOPICS COVERED
Bruises
Burns
Abrasions
Other Open Wounds

BRUISES

As all parents know, bruises are common in childhood. A bruise, called medically a *contusion,* is an injury to the soft tissues of the body caused by any hard impact. In a bruise, the tissue structures beneath the skin's surface are damaged. Blood and body fluids leak from the damaged network of small blood vessels called *capillaries.* This leakage results in the black or black-and-blue appearance of a bruise. As the bruise ripens, the skin often turns yellowish or multicolored. The pain may be mild, moderate, or severe, and there is usually some attendant localized swelling.

> ADVISORY WARNING: The vast majority of bruises are not serious and do not required the attention of a health care professional. If a bruise is the result of a severe blow, *especially around the eye,* or if the area of the bruising injury is extensive, the parent should seek qualified health care advice.

HOMEOPATHIC TREATMENT

Arnica montana
Bellis perennis
Ledum palustre

Homeopathy offers considerable assistance for healing and a subsequent rapid recovery from all bruising injuries, including the most severe.

Arnica montana (*Arnica*) is the first homeopathic medicine to consider for bruising. Not only does Arnica benefit the initial shock that might attend the injury, it is a great healer of damaged tissues. On its own, Arnica has no pain-relieving action, but Arnica stimulates healing so rapidly that pain is naturally relieved, usually in minutes. Arnica is indicated in any injury in which the Keynote symptom of a *bruised feeling* is present. Arnica also benefits the soreness, muscle stiffness, and overall lame feeling resulting from injuries.

Potency & Dosage: Give the standard emergency care potency of Arnica 6x or 30x, in the preferred dosage of 2–3 tablets. In acute conditions, Arnica can be given every 15–30 minutes as needed until pain and discomfort subside. Lessen the dosage to 2–3 tablets every 3–4 hours, as needed, and discontinue dosage when strong improvement is established.

Bellis perennis (*Bellis*) is a remedy made from the common daisy. Its remarkable healing action occurs on the deeper tissues, muscle fibers, and blood vessels. "Deep" bruises respond well to Bellis in its homeopathic potency.

Potency & Dosage: Bellis is best given "low"—in the 3x or 6x potency; 2–3 tablets under the tongue or dissolved in the mouth and repeated every 2–3 hours will prove its benefits.

Ledum palustre, usually referred to simply as Ledum pal. or Ledum, is another wonder homeopathic remedy for bruises. Its special action lies in its ability to remove the black-and-blue discoloration from the skin while the other remedies, Arnica (for pain, stiffness, and soreness) and Bellis (for healing of deeper tissues and ruptured blood vessels) have a more direct action on the trauma of the bruise itself.

Potency & Dosage: Give Ledum in the 6x or 30x potency, 2–3 tablets permitted to dissolve slowly in the mouth every 3–4 hours for a few doses.

BURNS

Burns are the most common injury in children. They range from the mildest *first-degree* to the most severe and permanently scarring *third-degree* burns.

All parents and caretakers of children and youth should recognize the three classifications of burns.

First-Degree
1. Redness of the surface of the skin.
2. Mild swelling of the skin.
3. Pain.

Second-Degree
1. Redness or a mottled discoloration of the skin.
2. Blisters appear on the skin's surface.
3. Pain—moderate to severe.

Third-Degree
1. White or charred brown, deep-brown, or black skin.
2. Skin literally burned away.

Surprisingly, perhaps, a third-degree burn is usually less painful than a second-degree or first-degree burn. This is because the damage to the skin's structures, including the nerves, is so extensive that pain messages cannot be transmitted to the brain where pain is perceived.

A first-degree burn is akin to a sunburn. The extent of damage to the skin is limited to the immediate surface, with attendant redness, burning discomfort, and heat, followed later during the end of the healing stage by a flaking off of the damaged surface skin as it is replace by healthy tissue.

A second-degree burn occurs when the child touches a very hot object such as a heated skillet on the stove, splashes hot grease or cooking oil on some part of the body, or undergoes long overexposure to the sun. In second-degree burns, the skin not only is red, burning, and hot but forms small or sometimes large fluid-filled blisters, which can break open and become infected. A second-degree burn is a blistering burn.

Finally—and God forbid that any parent or any child should experience it—is the third-degree burn, in which the skin is severely damaged to include all the layers of the skin and its subsurface structures—connective tissues, blood vessels, and muscle tissues. The skin is literally burned away, leaving charred remains, which will require surgical skin grafting for repair, and will leave lifelong disfiguring scars.

> ADVISORY WARNING: Burns in children that cover a portion of the body larger than the surface of a hand require expert medical attention. Most simple first-degree burns and many second-degree burns can be easily and successfully treated using homeopathic emergency care. If, however, the burn is large, and *always* in every case of third-degree burn, qualified medical attention must be sought.

EXPECT SHOCK IN BURNS

As has been expressed throughout this book, parents should suspect shock even in what appear to be minor injuries. All children are unique. No two children will react in the same way; some children are more constitutionally susceptible to shock than others, even in the same family. As soon after beginning the homeopathic treatment of a burn, give one dose of *Arnica* in the 30x or 200 (x or c) potency, or, if the child is particularly restless, anxious, and frightened, substitute a dose of *Aconite* in the same potency. The parent will recall that Arnica successfully treats physical shock, whereas Aconite is the best-indicated remedy for emotional shock.

The Standard Treatment of Burns

First, *cool* the burn. Immerse the burned area in cold water, or allow cold water to run over the burned area to cool the skin. An ice pack or chemical cold pack also can be placed against the burned area. Cold relieves pain and prevents any further damage to the injured area.

Added to the above first-aid treatment is the homeopathic treatment of burns.

Homeopathic External Burn Treatments

Homeopathy offers several successful medicines that have proved to be useful, safe, and effective in burn management. While there exist many over-the-counter nonhomeopathic burn ointments, they should not be used. Such medicines have a thick, sticky, greasy base that actually retards healing. Their only usefulness comes from sealing off the surface of the skin from air, which irritates damaged nerve endings, thereby helping to relieve pain. They do not, however, help the body to heal the burn. Homeopathic medicines, on the other hand, *do* help the body to heal the burn injury quickly. The ointments listed here are *nongreasy* and do not merely sit on the surface of the skin.

HOMEOPATHIC TREATMENT

> *Hypericum ointment or tincture*
> *Calendula officinalis ointment or tincture*
> *Urtica urens ointment or tincture*

Hypericum, derived from the St. John's wort plant, works remarkably well on burns. Hypericum is a specific homeopathic remedy wherever there is damage to the *nerves,* and in first-degree and second-degree burns, the pain-perceiving nerve endings in the skin are damaged and transmit pain signals to the brain. Hypericum is available in several external forms: Hypericum tincture (an alcoholic extract of the plant juice), and Hypericum 10 percent lotion (10 percent of the tincture in a nongreasy, water-soluble base). Either form of Hypericum may be used with the fullest confidence in the treatment of first-degree and minor second-degree burns.

Because of the alcohol content of the tincture, it is best to dilute the tincture in a ratio of 1 teaspoonful of tincture to 1/4 cup of water. Dampen a gauze pad and place this pad directly onto the burned area. As the pad dries, remoisten it regularly with additional diluted tincture.

Calendula tincture or ointment is another extremely effective homeopathic treatment for mild first-degree and second-degree burns. Follow the directions as given above. Calendula has a stimulating effect on the skin's natural healing ability. It is also bacteriostatic—it will not permit bacteria to flourish—and thereby is an excellent preventive measure against infection.

An excellent new product appeared on the American market in 1988. Califlora Calendula Gel, composed of a 10 percent tincture of Calendula in a water-soluble nongreasy cooling gel base, is marketed nationwide by Boericke & Tafel, Inc., of Philadelphia. This author's experience with Califlora Gel in common burns, especially in first-degree sunburn and windburn in both youngsters and adults, has been highly satisfying.

Urtica urens in tincture or ointment form is made from the dwarf stinging nettle plant. Urtica can be used in mild first-degree and second-degree burns as one would Hypericum or Calendula, with equal effectiveness. Here again, with Urtica urens, we see the homeopathic principle "Let like be cured by like" in its fullest effect. If one were to drop the raw extract of the dwarf stinging nettle directly onto the skin, it would produce a stinging sensation, redness, burning, and blisters. In its safe homeopathic form, Urtica urens is especially effective in treating mild second-degree burns wherever blisters have formed.

CASE HISTORY USING URTICA URENS

While I was serving as the health officer at a summer camp in 1979, a 14-year-old boy entered the health lodge. He was obviously in pain, considering his stiff-legged walk and the way he carried himself, much as if a board had been strapped to his back, almost as if he was afraid to move—and he was.

All across the boy's chest and upper back, the skin was fiery red and covered by water-filled blisters. From long overexposure, shirtless, to the sun, the boy had received a combination of first-degree and second-degree burns. It was most unfortunate that someone else in the camp had seen him first, because a thick layer of drugstore burn ointment had been applied, which first had to be removed with green soap and water. The boy was in agony; this is a major reason that greasy ointments ought never to be used on a burn—especially a blistering burn. Next I poured out one capful of Urtica urens tincture into about 2 ounces of water and applied it liberally to the burn. The boy's father was given a bottle of Urtica urens tincture and told to dilute and apply it with a cotton ball every hour for the next several hours.

The next day, scarcely 24 hours later, the boy and his father returned to the health lodge. The skin, once red, was now merely light pink, and the large crop of blisters had nearly vanished. The boy's father reported that his son had slept peacefully throughout the night.

HOMEOPATHIC TREATMENT

Cantharis
Causticum

Homeopathy offers two outstanding internal remedies in the management of burn injuries.

Cantharis is made homeopathically from an extract of the blister beetle and has a truly remarkable ability to alleviate the pain of a burn as well as speed natural healing. Cantharis 30x, given in a 2–3 tablet dose, will quickly act to relieve the pain of a first-degree or second-degree burn and stimulate the body to begin a rapid healing process. In acute cases Cantharis may be given every 15 minutes, or as pain returns.

CASE HISTORY USING CANTHARIS

Pete, a fair-skinned, blond-haired 14-year-old, spending a weekend in a sunny and hot southwest Missouri Scout camp, was acting as a chief for a group of Webelo Scouts. During a long afternoon on the waterfront with supervised swimming and rowboating, Pete sunburned his face and upper body. In addition, later that evening his lips began to swell and became painfully tender and disfigured by crops of fluid-filled blisters, some as small as pinheads and others as large as a little fingernail. Cantharis 30x, one 3-tablet dose, was given at intervals of 2 hours for three total doses. At the conclusion of the weekend encampment some 48 hours later, Pete's lips had fully returned to normal. It is noteworthy that about 15 minutes following the first dose of Cantharis, the boy experienced a complete resolution of pain from the burn.

Causticum is a homeopathically prepared mineral compound composed of sublimated lime and bisulfate of potash. Its reputation as a powerful pain-reliever in burns is equal to that of Cantharis. The potency and dosage of Causticum and its administration is the same as for Cantharis.

CASE HISTORY USING CAUSTICUM

This case occurred in late 1982. A mother, a long-time friend of the author, called to say that her 2-year-old daughter Rachael had toasted the palm of her hand and the forepart of her arm on a fully heated waffle iron. The mother had immediately run cold water over the child's burn, and that relieved the pain, but as soon as the burn was removed from the water, the pain returned with great intensity. Rachael had both first-degree and second-degree burns. She screamed and screamed; tears rolled down her cheeks, and there appeared to be nothing that would either calm her or stop the searing discomfort.

I rushed over and quickly gave the little girl Causticum 30x for the pain and applied Urtica urens 10 percent lotion to the burn. Within 3 minutes Rachael stopped crying. Her mother was instructed to apply the Urtica urens lotion every 2–3 hours to remoisten the skin and to give one dose of Causticum 30x whenever the pain returned. Two days later, the burn that only 48 hours earlier had been bright red and blistered had nearly returned to normal. Her mother found it "amazing!" that Rachael had gone to sleep following the second dose of Causticum and slept peacefully with no apparent discomfort.

It still amazes me, after some 17 years in the study and practice of homeopathy, just how rapidly homeopathic medicines work. They are all-natural products, completely safe, rapidly effective, and pleasant to use and to take.

ABRASIONS

An abrasion is a scraping injury to the surface of the skin. This is very common in active children—the so-called "skinned knee" that happens whenever a child falls and the skin is scraped away. Usually, little serious damage is done. The only real danger in an abrasion occurs when gravel, dirt, or small particles of paving asphalt become embedded in the wound. There is always the possibility of infection.

HOMEOPATHIC TREATMENT

> *Calendula officinalis*
> *Hypericum*
> *Pyrogen*

The potential for infection from an abrasion improperly treated is perhaps greater than from a simple but deeper cut because a much larger area of the skin's protective surface has been scraped away, exposing the underlying structures to bacteria.

The parent should inspect the abrasion carefully to make sure that no dirt, sand, or other foreign material is embedded in the wound. The abrasion should be well irrigated with water. Flushing out the wound will help remove bacteria-bearing dirt. It may be necessary in some cases to clean the wound out with soap and water. Use a bland soap—calendula or castile soap or Ivory soap if available—rather than a chemical detergent bar. Wash from the center outward past the edges of the abrasion. Once the wound has been cleaned, apply a homeopathic preparation of **Calendula.** Calendula is available in many forms: the tincture, which contains a large amount of alcohol; the succus, which is the pure plant extract preserved with only a small concentration of alcohol; a nonalcoholic preparation of Calendula extract in glycerine and water; and various ointment and gel preparations. Any of these are effective.

Calendula is made from the African marigold. In the author's experience it is the best treatment for the majority of open wounds. Calendula is not *antiseptic*—it does not destroy bacteria. Rather it is *aseptic*—bacteria cannot grow in the presence of Calendula, and it actually promotes healing. Many of the common antiseptic products available on the market actually inhibit healing by damaging the skin cells. This has been noted in several medical research studies of iodine-based antiseptics.

If Calendula tincture is used, it should be diluted, one to two capsful to a quarter-cup of water. The nonalcoholic and succus forms, as well as the ointment and gel preparations, may be applied directly to the wound. Dress an abrasion with a sterile gauze pad or adhesive bandage. Without removing the sterile dressing, simply remoisten it with Calendula during the first 24 hours as it dries out.

The power of Calendula in all wound treatment has been extensively proven over time. The late Dorothy Shepherd, M.D., an English homeopath, noted its effectiveness as a treatment for abrasions and lacerations during World War II when she worked in children's health clinics. She states: "We scrapped the antiseptics; deciding for a time to use nothing but herbal [Calendula and Hypericum] tinctures, lotions and ointments and to give homoeopathic remedies a thorough trial. If the herbal lotions did not work better than orthodox methods, we could always go back to the old ways; but we never had to. In four-and-a-half years we [had] proved to our satisfaction that the homoeopathic methods work more rapidly, are cleaner, less painful and, in short, more satisfactory than the recognized orthodox ones. I have proved by a vast number of cases that this is so."[1]

Hypericum, the tincture or lotion made from the great healing herb St. John's wort, may be substituted for Calendula if Calendula is not available. Hypericum is especially satisfactory in treating wounds that have already become septic. It is applied in the same way as Calendula. A combination of Hypericum and Calendula is available. Called *Hypercal,* it combines the tremendous healing properties of both herbal extracts.

Pyrogen is an internal homeopathic medicine that is exceptionally valuable in treating any wound that becomes, or threatens to become, infected. If an abrasion or any wound shows signs of heat, redness, and swelling, Pyrogen should eliminate the infection.

Potency & Dosage: Give Pyrogen in the 6x or 30x potency, 2–3 tablets dissolved under the tongue every 2 to 3 hours for half a dozen doses.

OTHER OPEN WOUNDS

Open wounds other than burns and abrasions can be classified into three general types: *incisions, lacerations,* and *punctures.*

An *incision* is a cut. This kind of wound can be very minor, as in the simple cut common to children that involves only the skin's surface, or it can be severe, involving the deep and deepest structures of the skin.

A *laceration* is a jagged wound. The skin appears to have been torn or ripped. The edges of the wound are irregular, and the damage to the skin and its underlying structures of blood vessels, connecting tissues, and nerves is generally greater than in an incised wound. Contamination from dirt or embedded foreign matter is usually greater.

Puncture wounds are common in children, especially if they are allowed to run about barefoot outdoors. A puncture wound is a penetrating wound made by a sharp object, like a nail, driving deep into the skin. There is usually very little bleeding from a puncture wound, since it often closes over itself. The danger from a puncture is in contamination from bacteria and certainly from the tetanus microorganism, which lurks naturally in the soil, especially in farming areas.

HOMEOPATHY IS SUPERIOR IN WOUND HEALING

We recall the experience of Dr. Dorothy Shepherd as she treated children's cuts, scrapes, and most severe wounds during the Battle of Britain in World War II. Unfortunately, in the 1990s, many parents think that the antiseptics, highly advertised and widely sold, are somehow "better." This is false thinking. Double-blind, fully scientific research studies conducted in the 1980s at the University of Florida and the University of Virginia concluded that the antiseptics commonly used by both parents and doctors actually retard rapid healing. Why is this true? The body has a remarkable ability to heal itself, if given the opportunity and if the immune response is not overwhelmed. Research has shown that the skin is covered with both potentially dangerous bacteria (*Staphylococcus*) and "friendly" bacteria that actually assist the body to fight off any overgrowth of disease-causing bacteria. The commonly used antiseptics and the highly touted antibiotic ointments destroy both the "bad" and "good" bacteria. Homeopathic herbal preparations such as Calendula and Hypericum act *with* the body's natural defense system. Neither medicine destroys bacteria; but the potentially dangerous bacteria cannot flourish when these preparations are used.

> ADVISORY WARNING: Certain kinds of skin wounds require medical attention. If a cut is especially large; if the edges of the wound are jagged, torn, and do not fit nicely together, if yellowish or whitish tissue bulges from the wound, or if bleeding is severe, it is time for the parent to seek skilled professional attention. In all cases of deep puncture wounds, the parent must check the child's medical record to make certain that the tetanus immunization is up to date (within ten years).

CASE HISTORY TO ILLUSTRATE THE IMPORTANCE OF PROPER WOUND TREATMENT

In the summer of 1987, 12-year-old Charlie was playing barefoot in his yard, stepped on an old roofing nail, and drove it deep into the arch of his foot. His mother washed the neat little hole that bled but a drop or two and put an adhesive bandage over it. One week later, Charlie's foot began to hurt, and shortly afterward he was walking with a serious limp. The homeopath was consulted. By that time, the "minor" puncture wound had become seriously infected. The point of the old roofing nail had not only driven into the skin but punctured the *periosteum*—the thin membrane covering of the bone. Charlie had developed osteomyelitis, a serious infection of the bone. He required 2 weeks of hospitalization with IV antibiotics and an additional 12 weeks of in-home antibiotic therapy.

Could homeopathic treatment have prevented this serious complication? Quite possibly.

Let's review what Charlie's mother *didn't* do. First, because the wound didn't bleed more than a drop or two, she wasn't very concerned. Most parents think of tetanus in puncture wounds, and Charlie's immunization record was up to date. In treating the puncture wound, Charlie's mother washed the wound with soap and water. But instead of carefully washing *away from the puncture,* she simply scrubbed it, thereby probably moving the *Staphylococcus* bacteria that are always present on the skin's surface into the wound rather than away from it. In cleaning a puncture wound, always work away from it—*from the edge of the wound outward.* She did not apply Calendula or Hypericum or Hypercal to the wound, and she gave nothing that might have prevented infection. A dose or two of Hypericum 30x or Pyrogen 30x will usually work to prevent infection. Frankly, there is no way of knowing with 100 percent certainty that the correct homeopathic treatment would have prevented the boy's osteomyelitis. But from my personal experience in treating puncture wounds in children for nearly 17 years, all without complications of any kind, I would be inclined to say that yes, homeopathy would have prevented a serious complication.

If a child steps on a sharp object, treat the wound with careful concern. Always watch for signs of infection—redness at the site of injury, swelling of the surrounding tissue, any increase in pain, fever after a day or two. These are all signs of an infection of some sort: an abscess, or worse.

Ledum palustre (*Ledum pal.*), another homeopathic herbal medicine, has proved itself over many decades in the treatment of puncture wounds. Because a puncture tends to close immediately after the penetrating object (nail, wood splinter, piece of glass) is removed, the wound is best soaked for 10–15 minutes in a 1:5 dilution of the tincture. If Ledum pal. is not available, Calendula, Hypericum, or Hypercal is a worthy substitute.

Ledum is often thought of in puncture wounds when the Keynote symptom *wounded part is cold* occurs. If that symptom is dominant, Ledum pal. in 6x or 30x potency should be given orally, 2–3 tablets, the dosage being repeated until symptoms subside. If there is excessive pain and pain seems to "shoot upward" from the site of injury, the most appropriate remedy is Hypericum in 6x or 30x potency given as directed above.

In conclusion, wounds treated by homeopathy rarely become infected and generally heal up to 50 percent more rapidly than under any other form of treatment.

---

1. Dorothy Shepherd, MD, *The Magic of the Minimum Dose: Experiences and Cases,* 3d. ed. (Devon, England: Health Science Press, 1973), 150.

Sources of General Information

Homeopathic Educational Services
2124 Kittredge Street
Berkeley, CA 94704

In the United States, Homeopathic Educational Services is the largest source of information and materials on homeopathy. It provides books, homeopathic educational programs on tape, medicines, kits, and various computer software for laypersons and professionals. A catalog is available on request. Send a large, stamped business envelope.

Homeopathic Medicine Suppliers, Manufacturers, and Pharmacies

Biological Homeopathic Industries, Inc.
P.O. Box 11280
Albuquerque, NM 87192

Boericke & Tafel
1011 Arch Street
Philadelphia, PA 19107

Boiron
1208 Amosland Road
Norwood, PA 19074
West Coast Branch:
98 C West Cochran Street
Simi Valley, CA 93065

Dolisos
6125 West Tropicana Ave
Las Vegas, NV 89103

Ehrhart & Karl
33 North Wabash Ave
Chicago, IL 60602

Longevity
9595 Wilshire Blvd No. 502
Beverly Hills, CA 90212

Luyties Pharmacal Company
4200 Laclede Street
St. Louis, MO 63108

Standard Homeopathic Company
P.O. Box 61067
Los Angeles, CA 90061
Walk-In Pharmacy:
204 West 131st Street
Los Angeles, CA 90061

Homeopathic Organizations in North America

American Institute of Homeopathy
1500 Massachusetts Ave NW
Washington, DC 20005

This is a professional organization for physicians and dentists.

Foundation for Homeopathic Education and Research
5916 Chabot Crest
Oakland, CA 94618

Sponsoring research in homeopathy worldwide, the foundation also provides education for health care professionals and interested laypersons.

International Foundation for Homeopathy
2366 Eastlake Ave E, No. 301
Seattle, WA 98102

Publishes a newsletter on classical homeopathy and offers training programs for health care professionals.

National Center for Homeopathy
1500 Massachusetts Ave NW
Washington, DC 20005

The National Center for Homeopathy is the primary organization in the United States promoting homeopathy. Training programs for laypersons and health care professionals are available, as well as information, a newsletter, and publications.

Index

ABC, 32, 56, 60, 61, 64, 66, 67–68, 79, 80–81
Abrasions, 104–6
Aconite, 30, 35–36, 54, 55, 60, 64, 65, 67, 73, 88, 89
Aethusa cynapium, 47, 48
AIDS, 18
Alum Precipitated Toxoid, 26
Antimonium crudum, 47, 48
American Homeopathy, 1–3
Apis mellifica, 30–31, 73
Arnica montana, 88–89, 91, 92, 94–95, 97
Arsenicum album, 43, 47, 48-49

Belladonna, 30, 31, 33, 34, 35, 36, 54, 55, 60, 64, 65, 67, 68–69, 73, 79, 80
Bellis perennis, 97
Boericke, Garth W., 9
Bones
  bruises, 94–95
  fractures, 90–91
Borax, 82
Bruises, 96–98
  bone, 94–95
Burns, 85–86, 98–104

Bryonia album, 30, 54, 55–56, 92, 93

Calendula, 78, 100, 101, 104, 105
Cancer, 18
Candida albicans, 77–78
Cantharis, 102–103
Capillaries,96
"Case Against Immunization" (Moskowitz), 16
Case histories
  burns, 101–4
  earache, 68–70
  sprain, 93–94
  swimmer's ear, 68
  wounds, 107–8
Causticum, 102, 103–104
Chamomilla, 38–40, 43–44, 60, 62, 64, 65, 67, 79
Chemicals, 86–87
Chicken pox, 35–36
China, 43, 44
Cholera, 16
Cocculus, 47, 49
Colic, 37–40
Colocynth, 38, 39
Colostrum, 41–42
Contusion, 96

Creutzfeldt-Jacob disease, 19
Cummings, Stephen, 78

Diaper rash, 76–79
Diarrhea, 41–45
Diphtheria, 25–26
Diphtherinum, 25–26

Ear
  infections, 58–70
  inflammations, 64–66
  structure, 57–58
  swimmer's, 66–68
Earache, 61–63
Eardrum, 58
Echinacea tincture, 64, 65, 67
Emotional shock, 88–89
*Essentials of Homeopathic
  Prescribing* (Fergie-Woods), 2–3
*Everybody's Guide to Homeopathic
  Medicines* (Cummings and
  Ullman), 78
External ear inflammations, 64–66

Falls, 86
Fergie-Woods, H., 2
Ferrum phosphoricum, 54, 56, 60–61,
  62, 64, 66
Fever, 52–56
Fractures, 90–91

Gelsemium, 30, 31–32
German measles, 24–25, 32–33
Grimmer, Dr., 27
Guillain-Barre syndrome, 19

Hahnemann, Samuel C. F., 4, 6–7, 74
Hepar sulphuris calcareum, 73, 74
Homeopathic remedies
  manufacture of, 6–9
Homeopathic Remedies for Children
  (Speight), 3
Homeopathy
  advantages, 9–11
  defined, 4–5

*Homeopathy: Medicine for the 21st
  Century* (Ullman), 9
*Homeopathy: Medicine of the New
  Man* (Vithoulkas), 5
Homeopathic Educational Services, 110
Hypericum, 26, 78, 100–101, 104, 106

Illness, vaccine-related, 19
Immunizations, 15–21
"Immunizations" (Williams), 20–21
Incisions, 106
Infection, middle ear, 59–61
Ipecacuanha (Ipecac), 47, 49–50

Jack, R. A. F., 22
Joints
  fractures, 90–91
  sprains, 92–94

Kuru, 19

Lacerations, 106
Lachesis, 73, 74
Latent viruses, 19–20
Lathyrus sativa, 27
Law of similars, 4–5
Ledum palustre 97–98, 108–109
Legionnaire's disease, 18
Lockie, Andrew, 23
Lockjaw, 26
Lupus erythematosus, 18
Lycopodium, 69, 73, 74–75

Magnesium phosphate (Mag. phos.),
  40
Manufacture of homeopathic
  remedies, 6–9
Manufacturers of homeopathic
  medicine, 111
Measles, 16, 22–23, 29–32
  German, 24–25, 32–33
Medicine, traditional vs. homeopathic,
  5–6
Mendelsohn, Robert, 18, 23
Mercurius, 33–34

Messer, Stephen A., 57
Middle ear infection, 59–61
Mills, Simon, 19
Morbillinum, 23
Moskowitz, Richard, 16
Multiple sclerosis, 18
Mumps, 23–24, 33–34

Nausea and vomiting, 46–51
Nossaman, Nicholas J., 18
Nux vomica, 47, 49

Organizations, 112
Osler, Sir William, 4
Otitis externa, 64
Otitis media, 58

Parkinson's disease, 18
Parotidinum, 24
Periosteum, 94
Pertussis, 16, 17
Pharmacies, 111
Physiological shock, 88–89
Phytolacca, 73, 75
Plantago majus tincture, 62–63
Podophyllum, 44
Poliomyelitis, 16, 27–28
Psychic shock, 88–89
Pulsatilla, 30, 32, 33, 34, 35, 36,
    44–45, 50, 62, 63, 64, 66, 67
Punctures, 106
Pyrogen, 104, 106

Rash, diaper, 76–79
Remedies for Home and Surgery—
    Homeopathic Prescribing, 2
Reye's syndrome, 18, 72
Rheumatoid arthritis, 18
Rhus toxicodendron, 33, 34, 35, 92–
    93
Rotch, Thomas M., 1
Rubella, 24–25, 32–33
Rubeola, 29–32
Ruta graveolens, 94, 95

Salk, Jonas, 27

Shepherd, Dorothy, 107
Shock, 88–89
    and burns, 99
Similars, law of, 4–5
Simple earache, 61–63
Simpson, Robert, 18
Smallpox, 16
Society of Ultramolecular Medicine,
    9, 15
Sore throat, 71–75
Speight, Phyllis, 3
Sprains, 92–94
Suffocation, 86
Suppliers of homeopathic medicine,
    111
Swimmer's ear, 66–68
Symphytum, 91, 94, 95

Tabaccum, 47, 50–51
Teething, 79–81
Tetanus, 26
Throat, sore, 71–75
Thrush, 77–78, 81–82
Tonsillitis, 71–75
Toxic shock syndrome, 18
Tuberculosis, 16
Tympanostomy, 58
Typhoid, 16

Ullman, Dana, 9, 78
Urtica urens, 100, 101

Vaccines, 15–17
Varicella, 35–36
Veratrum album, 47, 51
Viruses, latent, 19–20
Vithoulkas, George, 4–5
Voegeli, Adolf, 2
Vomiting and nausea, 46–51

Whooping cough, 16, 17, 21–22
Williams, Henry N., 20
Wounds, open, 104–9
Wyeth Laboratories, 17

Yeast infection, 77–78